In loving memory of my sister, Betsy Schechter Hofmann, and in honor of the women who became like sisters and founded the shelter movement.

Contents

Acknowledgments

I owe a great debt to the seventy people I interviewed and whose names appear at the end of this book. They and many others labored with me so that this book might accurately represent their experiences. The staff and residents of Women Against Abuse in Philadelphia and the Domestic Violence Service Center in Wilkes Barre generously allowed me into their shelters and homes throughout several weeks in 1980. The staff and members of the Pennsylvania Coalition Against Domestic Violence also opened their lives and work to an outsider's scrutiny. Later the residents of Women's Survival Space in Brooklyn contributed to my understanding as we explored the importance of shelters in their lives.

The published work of R. Emerson Dobash and Russell Dobash enriched my thinking. Many friends and co-workers critically read sections of the book and I would like to thank Deb Friedman, Freada Klein, Laurie McLaughlin, Valle Jones, Wendy Chavkin, Nick Freudenberg, Ros Everdell, Holly Sklar, Michelle Fine, Mary Morrison, Catlin Fullwood, Susan Kelly-Dreiss, Sharon Vaughan, Isidore Penn, Andrew McCormack, Kathryn Conroy, Nancy Andrews, Gail Sullivan, Lucy Gilbert, Laurie Woods, Michael Merrill, and Ruthann Evanoff. Rita Elardo was a skilled typist and perceptive reader.

The generosity of Ann Beaver and Margaret Hess allowed me

the time to turn my dreams into reality. Research grants and the donated labor of many women gave me the resources to make phone calls, travel, and stop working long enough to write a first draft of the manuscript. The Women Employed Institute in Chicago helped with the bookkeeping and with general support. Years ago, organizations like the Chicago Women's Liberation Union and the Chicago Abused Women's Coalition and women such as Marcia Alpert, Day Piercy, Miriam Socoloff, and Stacia Super taught me my first lessons in sisterhood.

Barbara Hart, Lisa Leghorn, Mary Haviland, and Allen Steinberg read large sections of the manuscript, sometimes twice, and made detailed criticisms and suggestions that improved the final draft considerably. Their encouragement kept me going through many a rough moment.

I want to especially acknowledge Liz Phillips whose gifted editing, insight, and clarity turned a sometimes chaotic manuscript into a book.

The South End Press collective believed in the importance of this book when it was just an idea and Ellen Herman helped mold its development through many stages.

Finally, I acknowledge Allen Steinberg and the women in the shelter movement for their continued ability to tug at me, politically and emotionally.

Introduction

Between 1974 and 1980, projects to help battered women suddenly appeared in hundreds of towns and rural areas. With the forceful declaration, "We will not be beaten," women organized across the country. By 1982, the words "battered women's movement" had come to symbolize the conglomeration of organizations serving abused women and their children. Embodied in over 300 shelters, 48 state coalitions of service providers, a national grassroots organization, and a multitude of social and legal reforms, the battered women's movement grew astronomically, transforming public consciousness and women's lives. Its zeal, dedication, achievements, and political dilemmas are the subject of this book.

I have spent six years as an activist and service provider in the movement whose efforts I am chronicling. As an early member of the Chicago Abused Women's Coalition in the days when there was still nowhere for most battered women to go and later as coordinator of the Park Slope Safe Homes Project in Brooklyn, I found my life and political views enriched, challenged, and deepened by the experiences I shared with battered women and other activists. Although by 1980 I was exhausted from helping too many people in too hostile an environment, I was eager to continue participating in the movement by writing about it.

Trained as a social worker but identifying as an activist, I first dreamed of this book as a way to refute the sociological and psychological theories that were proliferating about battered women in the early and mid-1970s. Radical feminists and grassroots activists were deeply worried by these theories and the likelihood of professional encroachment into the movement. As I set out to topple theories of psychopathology and the intergenerational transmission of "family violence," refute the view that professionals knew more about battered women than grassroots activists, and develop a feminist analysis of wife beating, I soon realized that it was impossible to write about battered women separately from the movement that emerged to help them.

The shelter movement caused us all to see abused women in a new light. Before the growth of shelters, many people viewed battered women as passive, dependent, or aberrant. Shelters offered the supportive framework through which thousands of women turned "personal" problems into political ones, relieved themselves of self-blame, and called attention to the sexism that left millions of women violently victimized. Temporarily freed from threats of retaliation and danger, battered women in shelters could display their long-ignored energy, rage, and coping abilities and reveal their similarity to all women. Any theory of violence against women that failed to account for the extraordinary personal transformations that occur in shelters would distort the truth about battered women.

My vision of this book deepened as I began to interview former battered women and movement activists. As we discussed their organizing efforts, I grew increasingly concerned that the thousands of stories about the creation of shelters, hotlines, and coalitions would go unrecorded, especially as "founding mothers" left the movement. I decided to chronicle the grueling, often mundane tasks women undertook to start and sustain institutions in the face of hostility and with few resources. I wanted to capture the radical feminist, grassroots, and democratic spirit underlying most of the earliest movement efforts. As non-feminist professionals joined shelter staffs in larger numbers, I was afraid that the movement's inspiring history would disappear behind official institutional accounts written by later generations of experts.

In the two years that I have worked on this book, some of my worst fears have been confirmed. In the Foreword to *Sheltering Battered Women*, a national survey of battered women's refuges published in 1981, Nancy Humphreys, the president of the National Association of Social Workers, fails to mention the grassroots and feminist efforts that led to the creation of services for abused women.

Instead, she attributes the national recognition of battered women's plight to "society."

> The battered woman is not a new problem. Rather, it is society's awareness of this problem that is new. Society's recent interest in, and sensitivity to, the issue of violence...has made it possible for the many victims to come forward and seek help.[1]

The president of the National Association of Social Workers is wrong. "Society" did not recognize battered women; feminists and grassroots activists did. Nowhere in her introduction is this fact acknowledged, so, unwittingly, her statement rewrites the history of the battered women's movement.

Over the last several years, sociologists, government bureaucrats, and professionals have appreciated the importance of services for battered women. Yet at the same time they have transformed the issues and insights that feminists and grassroots women pain stakingly raised. For example, by 1977 activists had forced the words "battered women" into public consciousness. Soon thereafter funders, researchers, and professionals began to proclaim a "spouse abuse problem;" in their false notion of equality, men were the victims of violence as frequently as women. This change from battered woman to battered spouse masked the radical political insights about male domination that feminists had forged. This renaming is one that the movement must fight so that battered women are not made invisible again.

My fears that the accomplishments of the battered women's movement would go unrecorded or be distorted increased as a reactionary government took office, intent on restoring the traditional male dominated family, slashing social welfare programs, and upwardly redistributing wealth. In a column entitled "Beating Up on the Family," Jo-Ann Gasper, President Reagan's Deputy Assistant Secretary for Social Services Policy at the Department of Health and Human Services, unashamedly stated that:

> ...the concept of domestic violence was so vague that it can mean "any form of 'belittling' or 'teasing' or 'failure to provide warmth' (whatever that may be—I guess if you don't set the electric blanket high enough in the winter)."[2]

The indifference to the pain and danger in women's lives and the trivializing of violence, mutilation, and death are shocking reminders of the plans of the current administration. Battered women's services can expect no assistance from this federal government, and they will also face cutbacks from their states over the next several years. As of this writing, some shelters have already closed. Their short-lived victories remind us that an active feminist and progressive movement is necessary to save what we have won.

Seven years ago, battered women were not the "clients" that they are in some programs today, but rather participants in a joint struggle. A feminist movement had played a central role by providing new theoretical insights about violence against women, an ideology of sisterhood, and the inspiration and support that led thousands of women to work ceaselessly, often for no money. In writing this book, I wanted to applaud the energy that literally created a movement out of nothing.

In a very brief time span, activists built a practice that offered battered women meaningful help for the first time. They also started and maintained institutions, negotiated with the state, and accrued resources. They tried to maintain their visions, politics, and sanity as they dealt with constant crises, violence, and poverty in battered women's lives and sometimes in their own. Here I try to record all the levels of this work.

I hoped to capture the movement's roots partly so that women new to the struggle could understand their histories. With too much work, the first generation has often neglected to transmit its vision, politics, and leadership skills, and this has come back to haunt the movement.

This story is told from the perspective of a socialist feminist who is trying to show the striking accomplishments of a movement and at the same time detail the similarities, differences, and tensions within it. As I did research for this book, visiting shelters and coalitions and speaking at conferences, I learned that I knew less about the battered women's movement than I had originally thought. I discovered that the movement was much more diverse, complex, and rich than I had assumed. In many places feminist activists started the movement, but in other localities former battered women, neighborhood women, or professionals initiated it. Nationally, the movement was begun and sustained largely by feminist leadership, yet its base of support extends far beyond feminist networks. While I try to respectfully record these diverse contributions and the differences among the participants in the movement, I, like all others, am a biased observer. I want to take stands, provoke debate, and accord feminism its rightful place.

Although very limited in scope, non-feminist services have

traditionally existed for battered women. Some professional groups have also been aware of the existence of abused women for years. Religious organizations were sheltering battered women long before the movement mobilized in the 1970s. Closely allied with Al-Anon, programs like Rainbow Retreat in Phoenix and Haven House in Pasadena served battered women who were married to alcoholic men as early as the 1960s. Child abuse reformers and researchers had made the family an arena of public scrutiny, and by 1966 every state except Hawaii had passed a child abuse reporting law.[3] However, none of these efforts catalyzed a movement on behalf of battered women. Only an environment in which women were organizing on their own behalf—a feminist political presence—could create and mobilize this new movement. No other explanation adequately accounts for the proliferation of services and reforms in the 1970s. Yet once a movement began, it spurred many groups with varied beliefs and political assumptions to help battered women.

This book is an attempt to provide an overview of the central achievements of and issues within battered women's services and organizing efforts. The first eight chapters examine the roots of the battered women's movement, the founding of shelters and coalitions, and the movement's reform efforts. Chapter nine offers a theory of violence against women in the family. Here I hope to provoke interest in one of the original feminist concerns that began the movement—why are women battered? By exploring the social conditions that maintain and perpetuate battering, I attempt to target ways in which the movement should organize to end the tormenting physical and psychological abuse of women. I hope that theory will help guide the movement's discussion of future practice and directions, the topic of the book's last four chapters.

The final chapters explore the current strategy dilemmas and problems that the feminist part of the movement faces. Just as I feel a responsibility to bolster and praise feminists, I also feel compelled to explore our shortcomings and political weaknesses. The book takes a critical look at issues that divide the movement internally, like racism and homophobia. While working on these later chapters, I was painfully aware that what I wrote could be used against activists or individual shelters. This is not my intention. Rather, I hope to strengthen the movement by encouraging discussion of critical issues.

Caught up in daily survival and the need to build institutions, activists have sometimes lost sight of the political visions that inspired the formation of a movement. In the final chapters of the book, I argue that shelters need to view themselves simultaneously as services and as movement organizations. Only by maintaining this tension will the spirit of progressive social change continue to inspire women and help mobilize them for the fight ahead to keep shelter doors open. This book offers a countervailing political ideology through which the radical spirit and experimentation of the movement can be sustained. Without an ideology and a practice based in the hope of liberation for all women, including those who face the greatest discrimination and have the fewest resources, a movement will flounder and move in more conservative directions.

The history of the movement that I preserve here is far from complete. It would take volumes to tell the stories of the hundreds of women's organizations that have emerged in the last few years. Moreover, some estimates suggest that religious, traditional grassroots, and professional social service organizations now provide at least 50% of the services available to battered women. These institutions are clearly underrepresented in this book. Further, my recounting is biased in favor of feminist activity in those states where women organized early. It is also molded by the fact that financial constraints kept me confined to the east coast and the midwest, although conferences and long distance phone calls provided a chance to talk with women from the far west and the south.

The experiences of the battered women's movement offer insights into the commonly chosen feminist organizing activities of fighting for reforms or providing services and illustrate many of the tasks and dilemmas common to what is labeled "single issue organizing." The strengths and weaknesses inherent in operating shelters, hotlines, and safe homes projects for battered women will sound familiar to those involved in rape crisis centers, women's health clinics, and displaced homemaker programs. Just as shelters helped battered women in grave danger, they also allowed feminists to start their own institutions, put forth their views, and gain legitimacy and respect from a much wider community. Yet maintaining large, expensive institutions took a heavy toll on the politics and spirit of many. The battered women's movement suggests some hopeful possibilities for building a movement where diverse groups of women work together at the same time that it illuminates the complexity and difficulty of such an undertaking.

The battered women's movement has never mobilized tens of thousands of people in large demonstrations. In this sense, it is different from other social movements. Yet it offers many valuable lessons to progressive organizers. Small groups, often ten to thirty people, radically altered the treatment of battered women in their hometowns. Larger networks, bolstered by other feminist, neighborhood, and professional organizations, changed laws and public consciousness. It is clear that the small group organizing activity, so typical of the women's movement, has sometimes radically restructured the power dynamics between the sexes.

As an activist, I have spent the last several years, first part-time and later full-time, gathering information for this book, mainly from other activists. I have interviewed over seventy women and men formally and talked to hundreds more in workshops and meetings. Many activists read continuing drafts of the manuscript, and where I discuss a shelter or coalition in detail, at least one woman has read the section that pertains to her organization's work. Although this book is heavily biased by the stories of identifiable or public movement leaders and founders of programs, I also interviewed the staff and residents at several shelters where I stayed. I talked with board members, former battered women, and women who have left the movement both satisfied and dissatisfied. I tried to interview a diverse group of third world women as well as white women.

I feel an enormous debt to all those who have shared their insights, victories, and hurts so generously with me. Without their help, this book would have been far less, again reminding me of the richness that comes through collective participation. I hope that the book will spur a continuation of our many dialogues and a recognition that the ideas and participants within the movement continue to grow through their interactions with one another.

I write with the benefit of involvement in many of the events I describe and the weakness of being too close to them and sometimes too busy to absorb them. I am aware that my assessments may be premature at times, or may sometimes simplify a complicated reality. If the reader considers them as attempts to encourage dialogue about the movement's past choices and future directions, my intention will be understood. The shifting political realities of the early 1980s make an evaluation of the movement even more difficult and strategies more complicated to delineate.

As I wrote this book, it became increasingly clear that the choices a movement makes, especially in a time of limited radical political activity, are filled with contradictions and are tightly circumscribed by political and financial constraints. As a result of these insights, I have grown more generous toward the battered women's movement. I hope that other activists, exhausted by too much work, frequent defeats, and financial cutbacks, will share my awe at the movement's accomplishments as well as my belief in the need for gentle yet pointed criticism.

Despite the large odds against the battered women's movement, its achievements have been highly significant. Whatever its shortcomings, the battered women's movement has fought to save women's lives in a way that attempts to respect the dignity and strength of all those involved. Activists and battered women have shown their courage, persistence, and ingenuity in multiple ways, and as a result they have changed many lives unalterably, including my own. I am deeply grateful to the women in this struggle.

PART I

Building a Movement

CHAPTER 1

Before the Movement:
The Socially Induced Silence

The Hidden Violence in Women's Lives

Until recently, the millions of American women of all classes and races who are beaten annually had virtually nowhere to go. As late as 1976, New York City, with a population estimated at more than 8 million people, had 1000 beds for homeless men and 45 for homeless women.[1] In Minneapolis-St. Paul, there were only a few beds available before the first battered women's shelter opened in 1974.[2] A 1973 Los Angeles survey revealed 4000 beds for men and 30 for women and children—none of these 30 beds was for mothers with sons older than 4.[3] In various states, social service or religious organizations provided minimal programs or temporary housing for displaced persons, "multi-problem" families, or the wives of alcoholics, but there was no category, "abused women."* Since 1975, the ongoing struggle of the battered women's movement has been to name the hidden and private violence in women's lives, declare it public, and provide safe havens and support.

As battered women's shelters opened in hundreds of towns

* In this book, abused or battered woman will be used interchangeably with battered wife. Because women who are not legally married are also beaten, the legal terms "wife" and "husband" will refer to married and non-married couples, unless specifically noted.

throughout the United States and women declared themselves sisters in a movement to end male violence, a seemingly obvious yet unprecedented challenge was hurled at centuries of male domination. In contrast to just one decade earlier, battered women are no longer invisible. Their stories, retold here, convey the experiences of generations of women. They also offer a painful glimpse into the lives of women, who, in 1982, are still abused and frequently find no help. Although violence against women has now been declared unacceptable, it endures pervasively. By 1981, the 5 New York City battered women's shelters, filled to capacity, turned away 85 out of every 100 callers asking for refuge.[4]

One woman shares with us a story that is horrifying because of the regularity with which women repeat it. Pronounced isolation, commitment to her marriage, and determination to cope mark her life as typical. Married in 1964, she ended her marriage in 1974, two years before the first shelter opened in her hometown.

> Even before we were married, there was this feeling that he was right. No matter what he said. There was no violence; you just didn't get him mad.
> When we were married, if I didn't agree with what he said, I'd get pushed or told, "You're not thinking right; sit down and think about it." I'd think, "Of course, he's right." When he started drinking the same thing would happen. If I disagreed with him or if I wanted to do something else, I'd get hit. You know, one Father's Day...he didn't want to go to my family. He said, "just tell them you're not going." I said, "I want to go." I got slapped in the face and he said, "now call them and say we're not going." So, of course, I called. I was very scared.
> He pushed me and slapped me a lot; I was never badly beaten. Once he ripped two nightgowns off me. He ripped one off and pushed me into the hallway—naked. I got back into the apartment and he ripped off the next. I can't understand why the neighbors never said anything.
> Usually, it didn't take much to get me in my place. You'd say to yourself, "I don't want this to continue." So I'd say, "I'm sorry; I made a mistake. I didn't mean to say that. You're right."
> We were together ten years. In the beginning, I was pushed once a year. In the last five years, I was in a constant state of worry. My whole life revolved around him and keeping things quiet. I'd make the kids be quiet. I'd say to people, "Please don't call when he is home." I had one friend. I never wanted anyone in the house because I'd never know what he would say or do. When he went to work, everything had to be done. The shopping and the laundry had to be done when he wasn't there so that I could sit and listen to him when he got home. I was on automatic pilot those last five years. I would ask him to leave and get his own apartment and he would blow up. God forbid, I should mention separation or divorce.
> I remember when we were first married I called my mother and she

said, "You're married now, you deal with it." I thought it was my fault. I considered it *my* problem. I was afraid everyone would say, "You didn't do a good job so that's what you get. You weren't a good wife." I believed that if I only did better, it would stop. My father never hit my mother. I just said, "I'm doing something wrong." I never thought his violence was right or wrong. I thought that he was crazy. But I also thought that this is where I have to be. I married this person. However he treated me I had to cope with it. My strength was in coping. No one ever knew. I did a good job. I was a really strong person. I was doing what I wanted and I did a good job in protecting myself. I look back and get angry at myself for staying, but I was in a crazy situation and I did a great job with what I had to work with.

I said "no more" when I got punched and had hair pulled out; there were big clumps in my hands. He threw chairs at me. I remember being on the floor screaming. It was a nightmare. It happened over a book we wrote. I say "we," but I wrote it and he took all the credit. I told him that I was rewriting it and he told me to leave, but the kids had to stay. I remember getting hysterical saying, "Where am I going to go? I have nowhere to go." His response was, "You stay here and do what I say," and he attacked.

I ran to my neighbor. She let me in which is amazing. He banged and screamed on her door until the police came twenty minutes later. The neighbor told him, "Get away from my door; you have no right banging on my door." But her daughter kept saying, "Let her out; she doesn't belong here; let her solve it." I knew he was going to kill me and she was literally pushing me out the door.

The police arrived and said, "Did anything happen?" The house was in pieces; chairs were broken everywhere, and my hair was out of my head, hanging on my shoulders, and the cop said, "It looks like nothing happened." Finally, they took him to the hospital.

I decided not to let him back in. He would come and cry and then he'd come and threaten. I couldn't take it. The terror brought me to that decision. I didn't want to please him anymore. You can only live so long being afraid. I was afraid for so many years but then to be terrified on top of that was too much. Up to that point I had the idea that I could control it. If he was yelling or hitting the kids, I could get in front of them and get hit. That was my control. If he started yelling, I could pick out the right thing to say and calm him down, and that was my control. But the last night there was nothing I could do to stop him. I couldn't control him anymore.

I never talked to anyone. I never thought that anyone else got hit. Nobody else had to hang up the phone when her husband came into the house. I was just very alone. There were no movies about battered women. This was my private responsibility. If I had knocked on a neighbor's door for help, it would be like saying, "Listen, I failed." I had the idea that I'm doing this for him. I'm coping; I'm controlling the amount of abuse I'm taking. I must be a good person. The importance I got was what I was doing for him.

When I locked him out, I got support from my family. I just said, "He tried to kill me." They were emotionally helpful. I was on the phone constantly; I needed to ramble on and on. Financially they were great. Shoes and clothes would just appear.

At first, I was not scared about income; he was working and I was so happy without him. At first he gave us money. Then when I got a Family Court Protection and Support Order, he stopped giving money regularly. Sometimes I would get it and sometimes for weeks I would have no money. I went to welfare and I couldn't get welfare because the court order said I was getting enough money. Welfare said, "Court has to make him pay." They sent me back to court. In the meantime I had nothing. This went back and forth for a year between him and court. It took a year to get welfare.

We were so relieved. If we wanted to go for a walk at 8 p.m., we could go for a walk without having to report in and tell him where we were going. It was such a relief not to get hit. The financial thing...I love to cope. It's been a challenge to get through. I just wanted to be left alone.

But he sometimes still comes around. I call the police. If I hear a noise in the hall, I'm still jittery. I think I'll have this all my life. I'm afraid he'll hit me and be out of control. Thinking about it upsets my stomach.[5]

Brutality is not necessarily confined to hitting, pushing, and pulling out hair. Its extreme, yet not infrequent, forms often leave women severely scarred, physically and emotionally. Terror and intimidation, experienced by all battered women, reach unbearable proportions for some. In the next story, tragedy is faced alone while its cause lies deeply embedded in centuries of male domination. Mary McGuire was accused of trying to have her husband killed in 1976 after five years of abuse. In those years, institutions such as the police not only offered her no help but actually supported her husband's violence. They, not she, bear indictment, yet their actions seemed guileless and their role hidden until the battered women's movement uncovered their complicity in maintaining sexist violence.

I know the horrors of beatings; of being shot at and pistol whipped; of being tied up to watch while my grave was being dug; of having my husband hold a gun to my child's head demanding obedience and threatening to pull the trigger; of trying to prevent my 12 year old daughter from being raped by my husband, while Father laughs and states, "I am the king of this house and can do as I damn well please." I and my children have received many beatings. I have had cigarette burns on my arms, a broken nose, cracked chest and ribs, a concussion, and a cracked pelvic bone. My children were terrorized by their father's attempts to run over my 4 year old son, and by his act of beheading our pet horse. I tried separation but was brought back to the house at gun point. He has told me repeatedly that neither my children or myself would ever be free from him and that he would stop at nothing to destroy us.

And everytime I went to the authorities, they laughed at me stating that they, the law, would have to see my husband kill one of us before they could help. Intolerable isolation, extreme fear and a desperate need for help are realities in my life. Should any human being have to be subjected to this brutality? Where do the solutions to tragic domestic situations lie?

The general public needs to become aware of the problem...the other side of the story needs to be brought out. A woman who is faced with a physically brutal and psychologically tormenting situation actually has no where to go. If she goes to the law enforcement officials, she is usually told that she is the cause of her own problems and that the law is not responsible for settling domestic quarrels. What is the difference then whether she goes to the law or takes hers and her children's lives into her own hands?

At the present time there are a lot of women in correctional facilities because they just couldn't stand any more of this abuse. These women need help now and if they had been able to obtain help some time ago they probably would not have ended up as they have. I am one of those victims. I am now spending time at the OWCC because I had no where to turn. I had gone to the law many times and been turned away. I tried what I believed to be every possible solution but nothing worked. I finally took steps on my own to prevent my children and myself from being killed. I was charged with soliciting, the act of trying to hire someone to kill my husband, and while I serve my time—five years—in the State Penitentiary, my husband is still continuing to harass me and my family. Is it justice that I continue to be punished for my husband's abuse?

Where is the justice that this country is so proud of? Is it justice when the woman ends up in prison, taken from her children, while the man she has been tortured by is still running free?

There are many more stories than just mine. Other women are here on murder charges for either doing away with their husbands or obtaining help to do so. They also could not get anyone to help, so they took the law into their own hands. Sure, we all knew that it was morally or legally wrong but it meant our lives and our children's, or his.[6]

In the 1950s and 1960s, cases of women being killed by abusive husbands were rarely recognized for what they were. Headlines such as "Husband Goes Berserk and Shoots Estranged Wife" masked the reality, and we will never know how many battered women died. Although these are the most dramatic examples of the horror of battering, they reflect the brutal isolation, wasted lives, and private suffering endured by many.

In other cases, family members, friends, or professionals helped battered women change their lives. Or women left their husbands on their own, secretly and courageously planning minute and detailed escape plots. In still other situations, women stayed and made the best of their impossible burdens.

Current estimates suggest that approximately two million women in the United States are battered annually.[7] Yet in 1970, there were supposedly few abused women. As late as 1974, the term "battered woman" was not part of the vocabulary. Interviews make it clear that even the founders of battered women's programs were unaware of the magnitude of the problem they had uncovered.

When recognized, battered women and their abusers were labeled as deviant and considered psychiatric cases. Even today, many people do not comprehend the extent of the problem nor the quality of battered women's lives. Both supporters and detractors sometimes suggest that the movement exaggerates the amount of abuse. When activists speak about battered women, even sympathetic audiences continually scrutinize the victim's behavior, moral "failings," or "stupid" reactions, returning repeatedly to the question, "Why do these women stay?"

Examining who battered women are is a first step in understanding both their invisibility before the shelter movement and the judgmental reactions of contemporary observers. In spite of psychiatry's determined efforts to convince us otherwise, battered women are not all the same, nor do they fit into any one personality type; they are as varied as any random group of women in the population. This frightening fact helps explain the readiness with which we distance ourselves from battered women and label them as different.

Detailing and analyzing the violence in battered women's lives is another necessary step in unraveling societal attitudes, especially the tendency to blame the victims of abuse. Many women are beaten for years. Violence often begins or escalates during pregnancy, but it does not stop there. Most battered women experience various kinds of abuse. Slapping—which in itself is capable of badly breaking a jaw—pushing, and shoving are common, and violence often escalates into punching or kicking. An English study of 100 battered women reported the following injuries.

> All women had the minimum of bruises caused by a fist, but 59 claimed that they had been kicked and 42 said a weapon had been used in the attack. In 8 cases a belt with a buckle had been used. Lacerations were present at some stage in 44 instances, usually healed at the time of interview but a scar could be shown. In 17 cases attacks had been made with a sharp instrument—knife, razor, or broken bottle. Burns and scalds occurred in 11 instances, usually due to the violence having taken place in the kitchen, with hot water or utensils being thrown or knocked over. Strangulation attempts were made in 19 cases;...[8]

Battered women are often subject to two other forms of abuse—rape and verbal assault. When asked, many women recount that they were forced to have sex with their husbands after a beating. Forced intercourse need not mean a gun was held to their heads; the fear of another beating is an adequate threat. Battered women consistently complain of degrading verbal abuse: "You are the dumbest woman I've ever met;" "You can't do anything right;" "How could I have ever married a pig like you!" Verbal assaults, like physical ones, may go on for hours in a relentless attack on a woman's sense of dignity and self worth and almost always include threats: "I'll cut your throat from one end to another;" "If you try to leave me, you're dead." In one study, all subjects thought they could be killed by their husbands.[9]

Although the details of the assaults are shocking, their meaning lies beyond the deadening statistics documenting the severity and frequency of violence. Violence signifies crossing a boundary in which violation and degradation, previously unacceptable in a loving relationship, are now used as tools of power and coercion. Battering is far more than a single event, even for the woman who is hit once, because it teaches a profound lesson about who controls a relationship and how that control will be exercised.

Battering, whether or not it is premeditated, is purposeful behavior. According to R. Emerson Dobash and Russell Dobash, "the use of physical force against wives should be seen as an attempt on the part of the husband to bring about a desired state of affairs."[10] These authors elaborate on this in their excellent study, *Violence Against Wives.*

> The altercations relate primarily to the husband's expectations regarding his wife's domestic work, his possessiveness and sexual jealousy, and allocation of the family resources....When a husband attacks his wife he is either chastising her for challenging his authority or for failing to live up to his expectations or attempting to discourage future unacceptable behavior.[11]

Self-consciously exercised, violence temporarily brings a man what he wants—his wife acquiesces, placates him, or stops her demands. As a form of terrifying intimidation, violence signifies that the man's way will prevail even when the woman struggles against this imposition. Leaving her in a constantly vigilant state, violence forces a woman to worry about the time, place, or reason for the next attack. As trust is destroyed, life is never quite the same again. Because the basis for intimacy is trust, the entire nature of a relationship is changed through violence, especially repeated violence.

The fear of being hurt makes all of us deeply anxious and partially accounts for the distancing anger directed at battered women. For those of you who are skeptical about this assertion, I ask that you spend five or ten minutes thinking about an experience in which you were victimized. If you cannot remember such an event, imagine a major trauma, an accident or death. Focus especially on how you felt or think you would feel during and after the event.

For those who seriously engage in this exercise, the feelings that consistently surface include fear, shock, shame, anger, distrust, sadness, guilt, and helplessness.* In robbery attempts or dangerous accidents, everyone reports the same chilling reaction: "I thought I was dying." The terror of confronting the possibility of one's own death is all-consuming. Shock and denial are most often manifested in statements like "I was numb" and "it didn't seem real." After life threatening or traumatic situations, we cope in the best ways we know, often flatly and unemotionally proceeding with our daily life. Additionally, most victims feel degraded or shamed. Many rape victims take repeated showers, trying to wash away the violation; robbery victims call themselves stupid. At some point in their healthy coping processes, victims blame themselves in statements like "I shouldn't have left the door open" and "I shouldn't have gone for a walk by myself." In these usually erroneous statements, people are attempting to regain control over random events by blaming themselves rather than accepting the arbitrary chaos of violence. Some people start to feel paranoid and "crazy." For those who have faced severe violence, carrying out daily routines such as caring for children or attending school may be temporarily impossible. In violent experiences, victims have their control and dignity stripped from them. Assault makes people feel helpless, immobilized, and overwhelmed with feelings of vulnerability. The violation of one's body or physical space is enraging and depressing. As victims of violence, we suffer multiple losses. Frequently, we are left with an insight that we would prefer to ignore—life let us down. We wonder, "why did this happen to me?" We search for an explanation, even a self-blaming one, that will restore control and order to our lives.

Unlike other examples taken from the literature on violent

* This is based on having completed the exercise with hundreds of individuals and groups; these consistent reactions are very similar to those of battered women.

victimization, battered women face unique circumstances because they live with their victimizer. Each woman must face the horrifying truth that the person she most trusted, hurt her. As a couple, they may have shared many years together, including many good times. The children probably love him, and they will also be a tie that means ongoing contact. Similar to other forms of violent victimization, battering is more devastating. The home is supposed to be a place of compassion and love and, according to sexist ideology, the woman's role is to ensure this tranquility. When her husband violates this norm, not only has he betrayed trust and love, but he also asserts that his betrayal is her fault. The battered woman feels shame for her "failure;" she also feels particularly isolated in her victimization because of the cultural notion of the privacy and sanctity of the home: no one is to know what goes wrong in the family.

Even more terrifying and debilitating, battered women face a fear of revictimization that few other victims confront. According to one study of 109 women, "a majority...experienced at least two attacks a week. Twenty-five percent said that the violence usually lasted from 45 minutes to over 5 hours; the other 75% reported that the physical attack lasted 30 minutes or less."[12]

The battered woman who decides to leave her violent husband confronts the fear of retaliation, as well as other major obstacles. Imagine her fleeing home with nothing but the clothes she is wearing, the money in her pocket, and her children. Returning for furniture or cherished objects is impossible, for now. If she is lucky, there will be housing provided tonight and for the next several weeks. The children will change schools. If her husband is particularly violent, she may be advised to hide out and refrain from contacting family or friends who might give him her address. As a single mother with children, she will have trouble finding an apartment.

Add to this set of practical burdens the emotional awareness that, for a woman, a failed marriage raises potent and lingering doubts about her capability and even her decency. Frequently, her self-blame is reinforced by other family members, friends, and institutions. Many consider her responsible both for causing her husband's violence and for not stopping it by leaving immediately; yet no one wants to help her depart. It is her fault that she is beaten and, in a double-barreled attack, it is her fault if she feels too ashamed to ask for assistance.

If we are not too frightened to remember our experiences as victims, we can recognize the discomfort and pain of our own helplessness and loss. Because helplessness is one of the most uncomfortable feelings humans endure, most of us, like most battered women, prefer to forget these moments. Battered women force us to confront this potential loss of control over our own lives. Angry at them for the reminder, we blithely say, "I'd never take it," pretending we have none of the same practical, emotional, or economic vulnerabilities. Often we blame battered women and judge them harshly, distancing ourselves from their pain and our memories of vulnerability. Since any woman might be battered, it is a fear that we can only pretend not to know. Soberly and chillingly, the existence of battered women compels all women to deal with the possibility that intimate relationships with men are not safe.[13]

Sympathetic friends, family, and observers expect battered women to leave their husbands instantly. They forget that women weigh their alternatives and constantly make choices; any woman might decide to stay after asking herself, "What is it like to be beaten twice a year compared to living alone with two children, penniless?" If aid is offered and turned down, friends are angry; few are able to understand or feel sympathy for the woman who is ambivalent about leaving her husband. When people do not know what to do or lack resources to meaningfully assist, their helplessness may turn to anger, not always at the circumstances, but at the person requesting help. They cope with this anger by blaming the victim.

Yet most people feel ambivalent when ending a long-term relationship. Major change is always difficult, often slowly and haltingly undertaken. We recognize this generally, but fail to see how it applies to battered women. Instead of acknowledging battered women's strength, persistence, and survival skills, we call them weak or passive. We deny them the compassion we accord to other victims. Acknowledging our discomfort with victims of battering can help us to understand why battered women remained hidden for so long. An even more compelling explanation for the invisibility of abused women emerges from an analysis of psychiatric literature and institutional practices.

Blaming the Victim: The Logic of Sexism

From its inception in 1939 through 1969, the index of the *Journal of Marriage and the Family* contained no reference to "violence."[14] In other forums, when battered women were discussed, conjecture passed for evidence. A 1964 article in the *Archives of*

General Psychiatry, a journal of the American Medical Association, unselfconsciously reveals professional attitudes toward battered women. In "The Wifebeater's Wife: A Study of Family Interaction," Snell, Rosenwald, and Robey speculate about the wives of thirty-seven men charged with assault and battery. The women, who are seen in a psychiatric clinic attached to the court, first turn to the police after 12-20 years of marriages marked by abuse, and the psychiatrists want to know "why now?" They discover that the intervention of an adolescent child into the violence often leads the worried mother to search for help. This "discovery," however, is interpreted as a disturbance of "...a marital equilibrium which had been working more or less satisfactorily."[15]

Snell *et al.* cite a case in which an older son intervenes to stop the violence inflicted by a husband who drinks too much and then makes heavy sexual demands on his wife. The wife enters psychotherapy. The psychiatrists concur with her husband that she is in control of her family's life, including the violence.[16]

> The husband stopped drinking shortly after his wife began treatment, and the violent arguments practically stopped. This improvement, *while not lasting* (emphasis added), was impressive to him and his wife, and they both felt, for different reasons, that it was due to her treatment. He took it as confirmation that she had been the "cause" of his behavior; she felt that it was because she was learning how to "handle" his behavior. We felt that the initial improvement was due to the venting of the wife's hostility and manipulative behavior out of the marriage, taking pressure off the husband.[17]

The authors report that the wife later dealt with her "frigidity."

> It was about this time that the wife began dealing in treatment with her great hostility toward her husband, alcoholic brothers, and men in general. She talked more about her alcoholic father and his pattern of violence in the home, but it remained difficult for her to translate the hostility she so clearly felt toward other men into terms of her feelings toward her father.[18]

Perhaps the authors believe there is no good reason for her hostility toward an assaultive, alcoholic husband who demands sex when he is drunk. To them it is her feelings toward her father which are most significant.

At no point in the article are the authors outraged by the violence directed against battered women. They suggest that, like the wives of alcoholics, these wives have a masochistic need that their husbands' aggression fulfills.

The essential ingredient seems to us to be the need both husband and wife feel for periodic reversal of roles; she to be punished for her castrating activity; he to re-establish his masculine identity.[19]

According to the authors, these women were generally "aggressive, efficient, masculine, and sexually frigid."[20] As evidence, they note that all but one of them later regretted taking legal action and the one woman who said she would do it again was "the most masculine of all."[21]

There are profoundly disturbing implications to this article. By never condemning the violence, the authors sanction it. The husband's main problem is his weakness, not his assaultiveness. Moreover, the woman not only deserves the violence because of her own aggression and coldness, but also needs and causes it for her psychic well-being. If she only fulfilled her feminine role more adequately and demurely, she would not provoke his rage. One could conclude that if women were sexually "giving" when their husbands were drinking, never said a public word about being beaten, and certainly never called the police for protection, all would be fine. The stories of thousands of battered women who did just that and were beaten even more brutally belie these conclusions.

By 1974, although writings on battered women had become less overtly hostile, they were still permeated with sexism. In an article that originally appeared in *Medicine, Science and the Law*, M. Faulk, a psychiatrist, describes twenty-three men who are in custody for seriously assaulting their wives. He categorizes their five types of marital relationships: 1. dependent passive husband; 2. dependent and suspicious husband; 3. violent and bullying husband; 4. dominating husband; 5. stable and affectionate group.[22] Some of these categories seem to suggest that men are now held accountable for their violence. However, a description of the most common type, the dependent passive husband, reads:

> In this type of relationship the husband characteristically gave a good deal of concern and time to trying to please and pacify his wife, who often tended to be querulous and demanding. The offense was an explosion which occurred after a period of trying behavior by the victim. There was often a precipitating act by the victim.[23]

The author adopts, without question, the husbands' perspective on the marital dynamic. According to this view, the husband loses control because of his wife; he has neither the will to resist her "provocation" nor responsibility for his behavior. The author colludes in this justification of violence and leaves the reader sympathizing with the man and blaming the woman for causing the problem.

Only nine of the twenty-three men went to jail while five, including two who had been charged with murder, were placed on probation.[24] Informing us that most of these men were responding to strain or were severely mentally ill, Faulk notes the courts' sympathy for them and their "tragic situations."[25] The extraordinary fact that two women died and their murderers were placed on probation goes almost unnoticed.

These articles are part of a growing body of sociological, psychological, and criminology literature focusing on the woman's participation in her own victimization. Faulk's principal category draws on a theory of victim precipitation by which the victim does something to "cause" the assault. Snell *et al.* conclude, "one cannot hope to understand the offender and his offense without having some understanding of the people with whom he has to deal."[26] In this literature, the families involved are often described as problematic or exceptional. In a totally unsupported thesis, it is proposed that victims and victimizers display unique characteristics or personality problems that lead them to find or provoke one another.

These articles define women's subordination and compliant behavior as legitimate and desirable. Women who attempt to assert their humanity and equality by negotiating with their husbands or demanding what they need are labeled provocative. She, rather than he, has a problem. The literature assumes that:

> She has little or no right to engage in any behaviour, no matter how innocuous, of which he disapproves, and that she should not challenge his decisions. If the woman goes beyond these limits, she is said to be "provoking" him and this supposedly explains or justifies the violence she receives from her poor "beleagured" husband....The idea of provocation is a very powerful tool used in justifying the husband's dominance and control, and in removing moral indignation about his use of force in securing it, maintaining it and punishing challenges to it.[27]

Husbands' historic, legal, religious, and culturally sanctioned rights to correct, chastise, or beat their wives are ignored. Disregarding hundreds of years of history, these arguments incorrectly assume equal power between men and women in intimate relationships. They fail to recognize that violence cuts off all discussion, makes its victims fearful and intimidated, and graphically demonstrates "who is boss."

Theories of victim provocation will never explain why women

are battered in their sleep or raped after they have been beaten to a pulp. Common sense tells us that all people who know each other intimately irritate each other: irritation does not cause violence; it is an excuse offered by a man who believes he has the authority and right to beat a woman. Victim provocation theories leave sexist behavior and ideology unquestioned. They keep us scrutinizing the victim's behavior and, as a result, remove responsibility from the man, the community, and the social structures that maintain male violence.

Victim provocation theories are not confined to academic journals and psychotherapy. Their assumptions are echoed by medical, law enforcement, and social service institutions, and thus have a profound impact on battered women. In 1976, researchers examined the entire medical histories of all women who came to the surgical emergency room at a large metropolitan hospital in December of 1976. This pilot study, analyzing the medical records of 481 women, found that "of the more than 1400 injuries these women had ever brought to this hospital, physicians had identified 75 abusive incidents, although an additional 340 or 24 percent fell into the "probable" or "suggestive" categories of this methodology."[28]

The findings suggest that battering is perhaps ten times more frequent than physicians acknowledge.[29] Equally disturbing is the response to battered women when, for example, their x-rays and lab tests are normal but their complaints persist. Flitcraft, Stark, and Frazier found they were "labeled 'neurotic,' 'hysteric,' 'hypochondriac,' or 'a well-known patient with multiple vague complaints.' One non-battered woman in 50 leaves with one of these labels; 1 battered woman in 4 does, and is given tranquilizers, sleeping medication, or further psychiatric care."[30] This study is important not only because it suggests how widespread battering is, but also because it traces how the real issue—violence—is hidden, and the woman herself labeled the problem. Especially before 1975, this response was common. Even supportive professionals or friends were likely to suggest, through a quizzical stare or a pointed question, that battered women were somehow responsible for the violence directed against them.

Battered women consistently found that institutions were unwilling to help them and to deal with the real problem, as this report from a Legal Services attorney indicates.

> ...The former wife called the police on 5 consecutive days. She had a visible "black eye" from an attack the week before when the officers

arrived on the first day. She showed them her lease, which was for herself and three children, and stated that she was divorced. They said that without a copy of the divorce judgment they could do nothing. The former husband heard them say this. He returned every day for the next 4 days and heard different responding officers repeatedly state they could do nothing for this woman because this was a family matter. He forced the lock on the apartment door and slapped or punched and threatened to kill his former wife each day. He left each time when the police came. On the fifth day the former husband was standing in the kitchen when the woman and their three children arrived home with groceries. He threatened to kill her. She told him to leave. He picked up a serrated steak knife and cut and stabbed her in the face, arm, and side. The neighbors heard the children's screams and called the police. The officers arrested the man for attempted murder.[31]

In case after case, women recounted that the police did nothing to help and often made the situation worse by encouraging the man's violence or by minimizing and trivializing her injuries and fears. Police officers frequently walked the husband around the block and then sent him home, leaving the woman vulnerable to his fury because she had dared to phone for help. One battered woman stated that the first time she called the police, "they said they would arrest _me_ for harassing a disabled veteran. It was his home." The second time they arrived, "the police told me to leave because my husband owned the house." Arrest generally occurred only if wounds required stitches or if the violent husband turned on the police, challenging their right to control the situation. For women of color and poor women, sometimes even severe injuries were met with indifference, if the police bothered to arrive at all.

The stories told about judges resembled those about police, as this former battered woman recounts. ·

I'll go to Criminal Court first. Simple battery. A five day beating with fist, feet and a shoe and he is charged with simple battery. Oh I see, he would have had to use a gun or knife on me in order to be charged with anything more serious. How much did you say he'd have to pay to get out of jail? Just one hundred dollars and he'll be out in a few hours....

A continuance for one month. His lawyer is out of town. Back to Criminal again. Another continuance for one month, new lawyer.

Back to Criminal Court again. This is it, the final continuance. And I'm ready. I've got four hospital reports. My only witness, my twelve year old daughter. And the shoe he beat me with. _Dismissed?_ I couldn't have heard you right! Dismissed for lack of evidence. Oh, a discrepancy in the dates. I see.

Well, I finally got the Writ of Detention. Now, he'll get what he really needs. Psychiatric help. Everyone who knows him knows he has a problem. A problem that I am just realizing I can't solve for him. "No, your Honor, I don't feel as if *I* am sick. I stayed so long because I wanted to keep my family together at whatever costs and I believed that I could help my husband because I love him."

So, your Honor, your final decision is that he is a paranoid schizophrenic with an explosive temper, but not recommended for commitment.

Sir, he has in his possession an M-carbine, two shotguns, and a black belt in Karate, not to mention the fact that he broke out of *this* mental institution the day after he was admitted. And you don't feel as if he needs psychiatric help? Well sir, *who* can I hold responsible if he hurts me or our children? *You're* sorry you can't help me. Well, so am I.[32]

Judges minimized the problem and frequently intimidated battered women with statements like, "But you wouldn't want him to go to jail and lose his job."

Battered women who turned to institutions acted logically, appealing to an outside authority to end the violence. Women did not necessarily want their husbands jailed; they wanted the violence condemned and stopped. The logic failed, not because of the women, but because the institutions sanctioned male violence and communicated that violence was unimportant or deserved, that women belonged at home under the control of their men. These institutional responses often left battered women feeling shocked, helpless, guilty, crazy, and wrong for seeking help. Men learned that there were no major consequences to their behavior unless they maimed or killed their victims.

R. Emerson Dobash and Russell Dobash cite statistics that are a damning indictment of the institutional treatment of battered women. According to their research, 109 women reported a total of 32,000 assaults during their marriages; only 517—less than 2%—were reported to the police.[33] Clearly some women were stopped from reporting abuse by their husbands, and some had other reasons for not turning to the police; most, undoubtedly, had learned the futility of such an act.

Battered women are victims of sexist economic, political, and social institutions. In the 1980s, many of them remain trapped, both practically and emotionally. Yet prior to the battered women's movement, their predicament was even more impossible. All women, but especially the unskilled majority, knew that if they left their husbands, they might not be able to find safety, jobs, and housing. Unmarried women, beaten by male companions, were viewed by institutions as immoral and unworthy of help. A married battered woman seeking help might have found compassionate friends and professionals, but she was also reminded that her proper place was in the home with her children and their father. Those who sincerely wanted to help could offer little of what battered women needed most—inexpensive housing, jobs with decent wages, day care facilities, support networks for women living alone or in nontraditional households, and safety.

The police, courts, hospitals, and social service agencies cooperated, although not conspiratorially, in defining the abuser's behavior as legitimate or insignificant and the victim's behavior as crazy, provocative, or reformable. Prior to the 1970s, supposedly only a few sick women who acted up were beaten—and they deserved it anyway. Perhaps a few inhuman men went too far; they needed help or incarceration. Had abusive behavior been generally declared illegitimate, then a woman's right to leave and exist as a separate and independent person would have been supported with government services and resources. Women's right to safety, equality, and autonomy in the family would have been validated. But this would have amounted to an acknowledgment that the family is not always a safe place, that it is sometimes preserved at a devastating cost to women. Before the women's liberation movement, there was no room for such declarations.

CHAPTER 2

The Roots of the Battered Women's Movement: Personal and Political

Raised Consciousness

In the early 1970s, it sometimes seemed as if the issue of battered women came out of nowhere. Suddenly feminist lawyers, therapists, and women's crisis and anti-rape workers were reporting hundreds of calls and visits from abused women desperately in need of housing and legal assistance. No mere accident, this groundswell was the result of the changing political consciousness and organizing activity of women. The emerging feminist movement painstakingly detailed the conditions of daily life that would allow women to call themselves battered. A fundamental assertion of the movement, women's right to control their bodies and lives, and one of its practical applications, women's hotlines and crisis centers, provided a context for battered women to speak out and ask for help. These courageous first steps, by battered women and activists, led to the formation of shelters, houses of refuge where battered women and their children can stay. Later, larger informal feminist networks and state and national meetings, like the 1976 International Women's Year Conference in Houston, provided the settings in which women found one another and created a national battered women's movement.

The feminism which engendered the battered women's movement was itself the product of prior influences. In the 1950s and

1960s, the civil rights, anti-war, and black liberation movements challenged the nation. Although not all women who would become feminist activists were involved directly in these struggles, the movements of the 60s deeply affected the development of feminism. Efforts to win equality for blacks set precedents for women's struggle for equality. As in the 19th century, women working against racial oppression came to question their own position—and gained political experience that would help them in building a feminist movement.[1]

Many activists in both the civil rights movement and the new left valued participatory democracy, honesty, and equality; they distrusted hierarchy. These ideals, however, were not necessarily applied to male/female relationships, nor to the structure of movement organizations, and women began to chafe at this contradiction. Their recent experiences had helped prepare them for a struggle; many middle class women had spent time working with poor women, who had taught them much about strength and survival. And by 1968, hundreds of thousands of young women had participated in some form of political protest—a march, a sit-in, a rally.[2] Gathering courage to criticize male dominated organizations and build their own models of freedom, these women formed one segment of the new women's liberation movement.

There were, however, many other influences operating upon those who would start or join the feminist movement. Published in 1963, Betty Friedan's *The Feminine Mystique* captured the discontent of a whole generation of middle class women, caught between aspirations for fulfillment and an ideology that consigned them to the home. Feminism was influenced, too, by women's participation in the paid work force. Throughout this century, increasing numbers of women worked for wages, which gave them more options to fight against male domination and feel their own power. Yet they faced severe discrimination. Low salaries, limited opportunities, and dead end jobs—juxtaposed to a rhetoric of equality and social justice and their families' economic problems—compelled many to scrutinize their own situation as women. From another direction, thousands of women, committing themselves to fight against poverty through welfare rights organizations and government agencies like the Office of Economic Opportunity or the Peace Corps, began to apply newly acquired political insights personally. As women saw others define the solutions to their life problems as political, they were inspired to act.[3]

By the late 1960s and early 1970s, feminism itself had developed into two major branches, a women's rights feminism, exemplified by organizations like NOW, and a women's liberation movement, embodied in socialist feminist and radical feminist groups, and small, autonomous organizing projects working on issues like abortion, women's schools, day care and prisoners' rights. Women's rights activism focused mainly on gaining access to the rights and opportunities held by men. Women's liberation encompassed this goal, but went far beyond it, exploring the unequal gender division of labor and women's lack of control over their bodies, sexuality, and lives. As a result of its analysis, women's liberation demanded a total, egalitarian restructuring of male/female relationships and society. In the early 1970s, both camps agitated and organized around multiple legal, political, social, and personal issues, changing the consciousness and practices of a generation.

Both branches of feminism were responding to the material discrimination and subordination women experienced. In 1968 fully employed white men earned $8,014 annually compared to $4,700 for white women while minority men earned $5,603 and minority women, $3,677. Women not only failed to gain equal pay for equal work but the majority also found themselves in low paying, sex-segregated jobs. The average female college graduate earned the same salary as the average male high school graduate. While increasing numbers of women were forced to work out of necessity, the ideology that women work for "pin-money" or supplementary income was used to justify discriminatory treatment. Moreover, women who worked outside the home generally worked two jobs since they remained responsible for caring for children and doing household tasks. Yet these mothers rarely had access to pregnancy leave, adequate, affordable child care, or time off to attend to sick children.

In addition to fighting discrimination, the women's liberation branch of the feminist movement declared that the private and the social were no longer separable categories. By claiming that what happened between men and women in the privacy of their home was deeply political, the women's liberation movement set the stage for the battered women's movement. Through small consciousness raising groups, women, often in fear or shame and then exhiliration, found that what they felt was "petty" or "private" was widely shared. Some of the most energizing topics for consciousness raising focused on previously undiscussed "personal" problems—feelings of isolation in maintaining a home or caring for small children, a sense of physical weakness, intense concern about appearance, the guilty feelings of never doing enough for men and children. In the early women's liberation anthologies and newsletters, articles proliferated on the unequal division of labor within the household, women's responsibilities for child care, the maintenance of rigid sex roles, the internalization of oppression expressed as women's self-hatred, low self-esteem and need for male affirmation, the socialization of women for passivity and caretaking, the continual and degrading sexual objectification by men, and the repression of female sexuality.

Although many political, strategic, and ideological differences were evident in the developing women's liberation movement, women agreed that men held power and privilege over women in personal life. Domination was uncovered operating, not only in the public political world, but also in the private political sphere of the family. This analysis moved women closer to a collective realization about violence. If women were dominated by men both outside and inside the family, women and men no longer had identical interests even within the family unit. Claiming conflicting interests, husband and wife were no longer "one." The importance of this message was twofold. First, women had rights as autonomous human beings which meant that their psychological and physical dignity could be asserted. Secondly, no longer could women be blamed for their own vague sense of dissatisfaction or for their husbands' unhappiness. Women's right to verbalize their pain without self-blame created an environment in which discussing violence was less shameful. In some consciousness raising groups women talked about violence,[4] while in others violence was too deeply buried or too painful to surface as a common element of many women's experiences.

As early as 1970, reference is made to male violence in the family in several of the women's liberation anthologies. An article in *Sisterhood Is Powerful* states that "the other crude and often open weapon that a man uses to control his wife is the threat of force or force itself....In this circumstance it is difficult for a woman to pursue the argument which is bringing about the reaction, usually an argument for more freedom, respect, or equality in the marital situation."[5] And *Voices From Women's Liberation* suggests that "few radical women really know the worst of women's condition....Few have experienced constant violence and drunkenness of a brutalizing husband or father."[6]

Although violence is acknowledged in these anthologies, its extent and impact, especially in middle class families, is understated. There are articles about self-defense and references to violence, but *Sisterhood Is Powerful* and *Voices From Women's Liberation* contain no articles about rape. It would take another year or two for the anti-rape movement to emerge; the battered women's movement would not begin for four or five more years.

The women's liberation movement not only helped create an atmosphere where women could understand and speak about battering; it also influenced the organization of work in the battered women's movement. Because male domination often inhibited women from talking and taught them to doubt their abilities, the women's liberation movement emphasized egalitarian and partici-patory organizational models. Rules for consciousness raising groups included "going around the circle" until each woman had commented on a subject. Consensus decision making became an important political tool for some groups and organizations. Many early women's liberation groups believed in starting autonomous projects which would define issues for themselves with no central organization determining each group's direction.[7] Work or issue groups stayed small and were connected to other projects through elected representatives. As a result of the abuse of power experienced in male dominated organizations, the women's liberation movement developed a strong suspicion of hierarchy and leadership. Hierarchy only seemed to create differentials in power which could be misused either through acquiring personal privileges and status or through misrepresenting the group. Leadership was also suspect, so women's liberation organizations developed the idea of rotating leadership. The ideal insisted that many women were to be exposed to leadership positions and encouraged to develop skills in new areas. Having expertise was a dubious distinction, often negatively associated with a professionalism that deeply hurt women by labeling and excluding some at the same time that it elevated others. Egalitarian forms of working gave strength to the battered women's movement. But these new ideas, sometimes only vaguely formulated, would inevi-tably come into conflict with traditional concepts of structure and organization.

The influence of the women's liberation movement on the battered women's movement is illustrated concretely in hundreds of shelters and women's crisis centers in the United States. In St. Paul, Minnesota, Women's Advocates, one of the oldest shelters solely for battered women,[8] began as a consciousness raising group in 1971. Later wanting to move beyond their own small group experience, these women dreamed of opening a house for themselves and for any woman who needed a place to go. This house was to be a liberating, utopian community. Their early vision of a home never encompassed a battered women's shelter, although this is what it would become.[9]

The first Boston shelter, Transition House, was also influenced by women's liberation ideas. Although the two women who started the shelter were former battered women, they were soon joined by two former members of Cell 16, one of Boston's earliest radical feminist groups. Women using the house were encouraged to explore their personal lives, learning the political parameters of "private" problems. For the activists at Transition House, physical abuse was not an isolated fact of daily existence. Battering was an integral part of women's oppression;[10] women's liberation its solution.

The Influence of the Anti-Rape Movement

In the 1970s, applying feminist principles, women created hundreds of autonomous service and organizing projects throughout the United States. One of these projects, the rape crisis center, developed into an important movement that merits special attention here, both as an illustration of the large-scale feminist organizing that preceded the battered women's movement and as a path-breaking model for that movement.

In some cities, like Chicago, women active in anti-rape work formed part of the group that would later demand help for battered women. In Boston, close personal contact without organizational affiliations existed between feminists in the anti-rape and battered women's movements.[11] In still other places, women's crisis centers that originally provided rape counseling and anti-rape education added battered women's concerns to their tasks.

Although many activists in the battered women's movement never did rape crisis work, the battered women's movement maintains a striking and obvious resemblance to the anti-rape movement and owes it several debts. The anti-rape movement articulated that violence is a particular form of domination based on social relationships of unequal power. Through the efforts of the anti-rape movement, it became clear that violence is one mechanism for female social control. Today this sounds obvious; ten years ago it was a revelation. The anti-rape movement changed women's consciousness and redefined the parameters of what women would individually and collectively tolerate.[12]

Susan Brownmiller, the first author to document the history of rape, described how unaware people were of the magnitude and significance of rape, noting that "few outside its victims thought it might be an important subject to explore. No one considered that it might have a history, and only a handful believed it was going to become an issue of international feminist concern."[13] Yet in 1971-72, Bay Area Women Against Rape formed;[14] in June 1972, the first emergency rape crisis line opened in Washington, D.C.[15] Soon after, rape crisis centers appeared all across the country, started by former rape victims and active feminists.

The anti-rape movement first exposed the mythology that helps maintain rape: women like to be raped; women mean "yes" when they say "no"; women seduce their attackers through "provocative" clothes or gestures; rapists act impulsively; rapists are sex-starved; most rapists jump out of the bushes on dark streets to attack their victim; most rapists are poor and black. The Chicago Women Against Rape (CWAR) statement of purpose read in part:

> Rape violently reflects the sexism in a society where power is unequally distributed between women and men, black and white, poor and rich....In rape, the woman is not a sexual being but a vulnerable piece of public property; the man does not violate society's norms so much as take them to a logical conclusion.[16]

The anti-rape movement not only exposed the mythology but also showed how it served to blame women for rape, let rapists go free, and provide ideological justification for legal and medical institutions to treat victims and people of color with hostility or indifference. It declared that rape reflected socialization patterns in which women learn to be passive and men learn to be dominating; rapists, the movement explained, were psychologically no different from most men.

Throughout the country, anti-rape groups conducted extensive educational campaigns. They distributed myth and fact sheets, with facts often based upon the one large-scale study of rape available, Menachem Amir's *Patterns in Forcible Rape*. A typical sheet explained:

> **the myth:** Rape is predominantly an impulsive act.
> **the fact:** In three quarters of the cases the rapist(s) planned it. Group-rape—90% planned; pair rape—83% planned; single rape—58% planned.[17]

In addition to establishing the facts, anti-rape literature interpreted them in a new way. One of the first and most profound explanations, Susan Griffin's 1971 "Rape—The All-American

Crime," broke the choking hold of terror and shame and articulated a theory of rape.

> I HAVE NEVER BEEN FREE OF THE FEAR OF RAPE. From a very early age I, like most women, have thought of rape as part of my natural environment—something to be feared and prayed against like fire or lightning....
> RAPE IS AN ACT OF AGGRESSION in which the victim is denied her self-determination. It is an act of violence, which, if not actually followed by beatings or murder, nevertheless always carries with it the threat of death. And finally, rape is a form of mass terrorism, for the victims of rape are chosen indiscriminately, but the propagandists for male supremacy broadcast that it is women who cause rape by being unchaste or in the wrong place at the wrong time—in essence, by behaving as though they were free.[18]

The anti-rape movement unearthed the multitude of ways in which victims historically had been blamed for the crime and silenced. Hundreds of articles about rape, many of them in mainstream journals and magazines, detailed this discovery, describing how, "the vast majority of victims fail to report the crime out of fear—fear of vengeance, of police, of publicity, of courtroom hassles—and out of shame. The fear is sensible. The shame is not, but it has been bred into our bones....Women who go to the police often bitterly regret that they didn't keep their mouths shut. For at every level of our legal system they may find themselves treated like criminals, and worse: a murderer is innocent until proven guilty; a rape victim is guilty until proven innocent."[19] Exposing victim-blaming not only produced new theoretical understandings of rape but also laid the groundwork for pushing institutions to change the treatment of victims. Perhaps most profoundly, it gave women a way to relieve shame and guilt. Almost any rape crisis worker can recount the stories of women who phoned "just to talk." When asked the date of the rape, the caller would respond, haltingly, "Oh, twenty-five years ago." Painfully and bitterly, they told of agonizing guilt and loneliness, of sexual and personal relationships destroyed.

Recognizing victims' needs for emotional and legal support and the movement's need to document and change sexist abuses in police stations and courts, rape crisis centers trained women to become legal advocates. Lay advocacy, as it was called, first meant that the rape crisis center staff or volunteers, often with the help of a few feminist lawyers, mastered the intricate details of local police and court procedures as well as local and state ordinances or laws.

Based on its understanding of how institutions revictimize

women, the anti-rape movement demanded legal and institutional reforms. Activists insisted that women on witness stands not be grilled about their sexual behavior. Throughout the United States, women worked to overthrow laws that required corroboration of evidence by someone other than the victim. They focused on improving police arrest and evidence gathering procedures and some worked legislatively to change criminal sentencing procedures. Hospital policies that included administering dangerous drugs like DES to prevent pregnancy or that failed to provide privacy or concern for the victim were also targets of reform. With the help of rape victims, advocates painstakingly documented abuses; in large cities, simply keeping track of them was an enormous task. These difficulties often led to the formation of task forces to study the problem and implement change; NOW organized more than 300 local and state rape task forces.[20]

Institutional reforms, clearly needed, were won through years of effort. Yet even as they pursued their immediate, daily struggles, many women understood that reforms within a racist and sexist society would not protect all women, nor would they eliminate rape. "Rape is not an isolated act that can be rooted out from patriarchy without ending patriarchy itself. The same men and power structure who victimize women are engaged in the act of raping Vietnam, raping Black people, and the very earth we live upon....No simple reforms can eliminate rape."[21] Throughout the anti-rape literature there is a recognition that the system sometimes helps "legitimate" victims—white, married women who fought their rapists and were visibly injured. "Illegitimate" victims—women of color, poor women, single women, women who dared to be out drinking or walking the streets late at night, prostitutes, women raped by judges or doctors—would never be consistently helped. Nor would the racist use of the rape charge, which helped whites brutalize the black community, ever cease without major social transformations. Exactly how rape was to be eliminated remained a difficult question. Those advocating feminist revolution sometimes acknowledged that profound social struggle would have to attack the sexism, racism, and class domination in capitalist society in order to end rape. Thus while the anti-rape movement recognized that institutions needed to be changed, much of it also felt compelled to take an oppositional stand toward these same institutions.

In addition to replacing a sexist ideology with a feminist one and pushing for institutional reform, the anti-rape movement brought together thousands of women who continually developed new skills.

Activists educated themselves and others politically. The Feminist Alliance Against Rape (FAAR) newsletter, started in 1974, was the movement's political sounding board and brought inspiration to hundreds of women, often working in isolated groups. Later it played a role in encouraging the battered women's movement to engage in the same kind of political and skill exchanges. The anti-rape movement spent and continues to spend thousands of hours on community education work. Speaker's Bureaus, often providing extensive political training for their participants, became part of many rape crisis centers. Rape crisis centers offered self-defense courses, rape prevention seminars, support groups for victims, and training seminars for professionals on how to provide emotional and practical support to victims. Educational materials—bibliographies, political overviews of rape, counseling techniques, rape prevention strategies—were written, rewritten, and distributed to thousands of people.

By 1977, searching for more militant and public forums, thousands of women around the country marched annually to "Take Back The Night."[22] During this single evening, they walked unafraid because of the collective presence of women. Turning individual fear into mass anger, women felt strength and temporary psychological liberation even as the number of reported rapes increased.

Borrowing ideas from the women's liberation movement, the counseling developed in rape crisis centers focused on the victim's need to retain control over decisions affecting her life and often used self-help methods. The victim was to decide whether to report the rape and who she would tell about the experience. Insisting that feminists and women who had experienced rape were the experts, rape crisis workers were often suspicious of professionally trained therapists who traditionally had blamed women for male violence. Although disagreement existed over the role of professionals in the work of rape crisis centers and tensions heightened as mainstream social service agencies or hospitals became involved, the idea of self-help and victim control remained primary to many feminists.

In rape crisis centers, women learned essential lessons about beginning and sustaining organizations. Workers in rape crisis centers formed boards of directors, set up by-laws and work procedures, wrote funding proposals, coordinated hotlines, and negotiated with bureaucracies. Like the battered women's movement, the anti-rape movement relentlessly searched for funding and never secured enough money to keep all the needed autonomous feminist organizations alive.

At the height of the anti-rape movement in 1976, there were approximately 1500 separate projects—task forces, study groups, crisis centers, "doing something about rape." Of these, perhaps 400 were autonomous feminist rape crisis centers.[23] Survival was difficult. In a survey published in 1978 of eighty rape crisis centers which were autonomous from any public agency, 39 spent less than $100 per month and 5 operated on over $4000 monthly; another 36 had budgets in between these two figures.[24] Today it is impossible to estimate the number of feminist rape crisis centers because as funding became available, professionals increasingly became involved in providing services. Now, many rape crisis centers include a combination of feminist and professional staff and influences.

How one evaluates the long-term victories of the anti-rape movement depends on what is being weighed and who is making the assessment. As in the case of the battered women's movement, any judgment may be premature. The decline in the number of autonomous feminist rape crisis centers fails to tell the whole story. The anti-rape movement continues to transform women in unquantifiable personal and political ways. A rape crisis worker typically comments, "I'll never be the same again. I've learned so much about myself, women's lives, violence, and men that I could never be who I was." Experiencing or simply hearing about male violence temporarily topples women's belief systems. Listening to victims can be agonizing, but the anti-rape movement helped overcome the pain by creating a collective context for understanding and fighting rape.

> We were not alone because thousands of other women were doing the same thing we were all across the country. And we were not alone because we got so much from each other. Four of us shared an office and every injustice or outrage was discussed. Every painful story told to one of us with tears or rage was retold. So much women's pain came out in that building, but so much caring and attention were born. The energy was unceasing. The process intertwined the details of our daily lives with lovers and children, our struggles as women with the daily lives of other women, and the institutional and social horrors they found. We were always angry.[25]

The anti-rape movement has given women mastery and hope as well as a chance to acquire and teach political and organizational skills. Politics, advocacy strategies, and community organizing tactics are debated and fought over. Women often disagree among themselves but no one else cares like the movement does and no one, therefore, is able to do so much. Even with many defeats, the anti-rape movement has won important victories; hospital, police, court, and psychiatric practice have been changed. Rape victims are treated differently by many people.

The anti-rape movement also produced important and painful lessons about single issue organizing. By focusing on the relationship between men and women, the anti-rape movement dissected the meanings and dynamics of rape. At the same time, however, it ignored or downplayed the other political dynamic involved—the racist use of the rape charge. A 1978 article, "Rape, Racism, and Reality," in the Feminist Alliance Against Rape newsletter notes that while anti-rape organizers exposed myths about interracial rapes, and developed outreach programs to black, hispanic, chicana, Indian and Asian women, they developed no unified analytic position on racism and rape.[26]

This and several other critical articles urged the feminist movement to consider the racist use of the rape charge. "Rape laws were designed to maintain the property rights of white men and to control blacks. The law made rape a capital offense only for a black man found guilty of raping a white woman. A white man who raped a white woman could receive a maximum sentence of no more than twenty years, depending on the state. Nowhere in the law was the rape of a black woman considered a crime."[27] In a 1975 paper, the Socialist Women's Caucus of Louisville cited statistics to prove that the rape charge has been used as a systematic weapon of terror against the entire black community. "In the last 40 years alone, 455 men have been executed for rape; 405 of them were black, and 398 of the executions took place in the south. No white man has *ever* been executed in this country for raping a Black woman."[28] Such terrorism is not over. Since the United States Supreme Court's death penalty decision in 1972, 69% of the rapists sentenced to death row have been black[29], and men are still arrested for rape, not because there is any evidence of their guilt but because they are black.[30]

In "A Second Open Letter to Southern White Women," activist Anne Braden suggests that women's efforts to expose rape are of primary importance and yet also have seriously neglected to talk about racism and rape. She rightly criticizes Susan Brownmiller's widely read *Against Our Will: Men, Women and Rape,* which thoroughly fails to understand the racist use of the rape charge. When Braden quotes a black woman's question to Susan Brownmiller, she captures the problem of adopting an exclusively gender-based analysis: "What you are saying may help me protect myself, but how can I protect my son?"[31] Ignoring the connection between racism and rape means that the history of black women's rape by white men is also ignored. Speaking of this history, Angela Davis declares:

> As females, slave women were inherently vulnerable to all forms of sexual coercion. If the most violent punishments of men consisted in floggings and mutilations, most women were flogged and mutilated, as well as raped. Rape, in fact, was an uncamouflaged expression of the slaveholder's economic mastery and the over-seer's control over Black women as workers.[32]

The anti-rape movement has repeatedly been criticized for failing to deal with racism and rape, yet only some anti-rape groups have responded by analyzing personal, historic, and institutional racism. Ignoring racism and failing to condemn it has meant negating third world peoples' histories and unique needs and has set back efforts to build a multi-racial women's movement.

Government co-optation was another unresolved problem for the anti-rape movement. In 1976, the Baton Rouge district attorney, administering a Law Enforcement Assistance Administration (LEAA) grant, ordered the director of the Stop Rape Crisis Center to eliminate services to victims who did not report their rapes to the police and to those whose court cases were concluded. When the center's administrator objected, the district attorney fired her. Subsequently, the entire staff resigned and was replaced by employees of the criminal justice system. Although feminist activists fought against funding stipulations like these that denied women control over the decisions affecting their lives, they sometimes were left penniless.[33]

Feminists lost out in other ways too, as "Learning from the Anti-Rape Movement," an article written for the _National Communication Network for the Elimination of Violence Against Women_, indicates.

> What happened when the National Center for the Prevention and Control of Rape was established at NIMH [National Institute of Mental Health]? Did the money go to community, feminist rape crisis centers who had brought the issue to the fore? Were anti-rape activists given control of the budget after expending so much time and energy on revising the bill which created the National Center? Well, not exactly. Money has gone primarily to professionals, often through universities, to explore research questions and to produce materials. For example, the University of Alabama received $79,213 to produce an annotated bibliography and literature review.[34]

To the anti-rape movement, the money allocated for bibliographies and research was staggering. Drastically understaffed and under-

funded, the anti-rape movement never felt it needed more bibliographies and literature reviews. Women, unpaid for their labor, had
produced them at the beginning of the movement.

With infuriating speed and seemingly out of nowhere, traditional agencies and professionals showed up to work on rape.

> We had done the work, raised consciousness, killed ourselves over long
> hours of learning how to provide help, mastering how to work within
> the courts and police, manipulating money here or there to stay alive,
> and then when LEAA money or some other source opened up—groups
> who had never helped a victim and often weren't feminists, although
> some women inside them called themselves feminists, appeared. A key
> difference between us and them was our accountability to a movement,
> our deep involvement with women victims, our politics, vision, and our
> simultaneous belief in and skepticism about making institutions work
> better for women.[35]

Many rape crisis centers had to affiliate with YWCA's or
criminal justice institutions to survive. Others thought it expedient
to do so for funding or believed that hospitals or district attorneys
offered needed expertise and legitimacy; only too late did they see
that some of these same agencies advocated providing services for
victims but refused to acknowledge a feminist analysis of rape or
uphold individual and collective rights to self-determination. "Co-optation" happened before many women understood the meaning of
the term.

Because a multitude of problems and issues had to be tackled on
low or non-existent budgets, women were forced into taking money
with strings attached. Activists learned the problems inherent in
simultaneously trying to run oppositional organizations, often based
on principles of collectivity and consensus decision making, and
keeping services funded through government grants that stipulated
hierarchies and professionally trained staff. Moreover, when conflicts arose, the movement was sometimes too weak—because of
underfunding, too few paid staff or volunteers, and exhaustion—to
respond effectively. As a result, several urban areas now have city
administered Victim/Witness advocacy programs that offer far less
competent or compassionate services than those that previously
existed and never mention the politics of rape.

Like other feminist organizing efforts, the anti-rape movement
has not satisfactorily resolved the dichotomy between services and a
political movement. In order to gain legitimacy and funding, anti-
rape work had to focus on the plight of the victim. In many ways this
focus is justified because violence brutalizes individual women. Yet

overemphasizing victimization creates the potential for a concomitant deemphasis on political analysis and organizing. Women could receive sympathy and funds for victims without ever mentioning male domination or its feminist challenge. Indeed, this happened frequently as more radical feminists left or were pushed out of rape crisis centers.

The anti-rape movement operates on many levels and never has adequate resources. It tries to help individual victims, change the social conditions that perpetuate and create violence, develop violence prevention strategies, and, in some places, ensure the survival of democratic, alternative institutions. In spite of defeats, in ten short years of anti-rape work, enormous transformations have occurred. Many feminists remain active in the movement and they can justly claim major victories. Laws have been altered and striking attitudinal changes, undreamed of in 1970, have been implanted in the American psyche. As one anti-rape activist declared, "When I started in the early 1970s there were married women who were raped and their husbands just left them as a result. It is mind boggling. Today eighteen year olds have no idea rape crisis centers didn't exist. For them, of course, you talk about rape."[36]

The feminist anti-rape movement has not only laid the foundation to change public consciousness, but also has built organizations and networks of politically sophisticated and active women. The anti-rape movement has unmasked the domination that violence maintains, has torn away a veil of shame, and shown that women can aid one another, transforming individual silence and pain into a social movement. Such work handed ideological tools, collective work structures, and political resources to the battered women's movement. Without this precedent, the new movement might have faced far greater resistance and hostility from bureaucracies, legislatures, and the general public. By 1975, it was clear that since rape and battering had the same effects upon their victims and depended upon similar sexist mythology, battering had to be declared socially, not privately, caused.[37]

Ideological and Personal Diversity Within the Movement

Women who started battered women's programs were motivated by diverse ideological and personal experiences. The meaning of this diversity, often invisible at first, became evident only later and partially accounts for tensions within the battered women's movement today.

A respectful caution must be exercised in untangling the ideological threads within the movement. Ideology played a significant role early in the movement, but not always a primary or articulated one. Necessity and the sense of belonging to a women's movement, rather than theory, motivated most women to organize. The humanist or feminist philosophy of women helping women, spurred on by battered women's pain and lack of resources, necessitated a unity which was reinforced by sexist ridicule and the public attention this new work evoked.

Examining ideology is meant neither to simplify reality nor to determine the most "correct" form of feminism. It is clear that women who use the same label, like radical feminist, ascribe different meanings to the words and often disagree with one another over practical decisions. And some women who work tirelessly for what are generally considered feminist goals do not feel comfortable calling themselves feminists. Moreover, many women's political positions and orientations changed over time, influenced by movement experiences. Yet political ideology, the way in which the power relations within society, including women's oppression, are explained, has important implications for understanding the history of the battered women's movement.

Different ideologies, personal motivations, and political circumstances meant different answers or approaches to a key set of questions: Why are women beaten? Why are men violent and what role does violence play in women's oppression? How should women organize to end violence against women? How are relationships of male domination and female subordination transformed? What, if any, is the role of a political movement to help battered women? Who should this movement belong to—battered women, feminists, or social service providers? What form of organization and programs best support battered women? Are questions of organizational structure important in a struggle to end female subordination? What is the appropriate relationship between the battered women's movement and the state? What is the role of a shelter? Should it exist solely to provide safety? Should the shelter experience serve to change women's personalities or self-image? At the beginning of the movement, the questions were not so clearly laid out. Nonetheless, daily work revealed and reinforced unstated beliefs.

Feminists in the battered women's movement did not always agree on the meaning or implications of feminism. In its broadest sense, feminism means women's individual or collective rights to autonomy, to define their lives as they see fit. It thus suggests equality between the sexes. For some, the women's liberationists, feminism is both an analysis of how women are oppressed as a gender category and a commitment to organizing to end that oppression, gaining power and autonomy on many levels. Non-hierarchical organizational structures and interpersonal relationships are the embodiments of feminist theory.For others—those who are part of the women's rights branch of the movement—feminism primarily implies making the society better through winning concrete changes in the law and within institutions. In both of these large categories, analyses varied; and women did not necessarily label themselves as being in one or the other branch of the movement.

Those who entered the battered women's movement from a women's rights perspective often came with a social work or legal background. They assumed that equality with men would be gained through reforming the existing social system. While some women's rights activists defined their goals more broadly, most were primarily committed to ending discrimination. Questions of organizational structure and process were secondary; most often hierarchy was the preferred model in order to perform tasks quickly.

Unlike women's rights activists, radical feminists articulated a theory in which specific non-hierarchical organizational forms and self-help methods were a logical outcome of an analysis of violence against women. In many programs, locally and nationally, radical feminists organized first, setting the style and practice that continues to dominate in much of the battered women's movement. Radical feminists believe that historically and structurally the division of labor and power between men and women became the basis for other forms of exploitation, including class, ethnic, racial, and religious ones. Patriarchy is seen not only as a system that oppresses women, but also as one that structurally and conceptually creates, sustains, and justifies hierarchies, competition, and the unequal distribution of power and resources on an endless variety of levels.[38] While some radical feminists embrace this analysis, others label the source of women's problems more broadly as male power, especially the advantages men gain through their control of women's labor and childrearing in the patriarchal family.

Theoretically, radical feminism claims women to be a class, challenging Marxist categories.

No matter what social and economic class a woman's husband belongs to, when she leaves her husband she is leaving the money behind. In this sense all women are of one class: they receive no money for their work, put in unlimited hours of service, and can be beaten mercilessly on the whim of their masters.[39]

For some radical feminists, feminism implies socialism; social revolution, including a complete redistribution of wealth, is necessary to end women's oppression[40] and its first target must be the elimination of male supremacy.

A radical feminist analysis of battering suggests that "the present organization of home and family, whereby the husband wears the proverbial pants, and the wife and the children are commonly viewed as his dependents and his property, is a primary cause of the high incidence of wife abuse. It [battering] happens whenever a man perceives that a woman is either stepping out of her role, that she might be contemplating stepping out of her role, or even to insure that she would never dare so much as reflect on the possibility of contemplating stepping out of her role."[41]

From radical feminist theory emerged a specific practice. Collectivity was the assumed work structure; decisions belonged to the group through its use of consensus rather than voting. Radical feminists emphasized the need to organize autonomous women's programs, separate from male control or influence, where women would be encouraged to express their anger at men. Radical feminists combined caring for women with self-help methods, egalitarian work forms, and a staunch commitment to politicize women's understanding of personal problems. Adding an enlivening, celebratory tone to an overworked movement through dances and music, radical feminists also helped many appreciate the importance of women's culture for a political struggle.

Socialist feminists who worked within the battered women's movement joined an analysis of male domination to one of class and race oppression. They grounded women's oppression within material reality: the unequal division of labor between the sexes inside and outside the home, female responsibility for childrearing, and women's work maintaining home and family. For socialist feminists, although male domination predated capitalism, class and race oppression could not be reduced to or explained by patriarchy. Each form of oppression had its unique historical foundations. Class and gender domination were intertwined through the benefits that both the capitalist class and individual men received from women's unpaid labor. But there were also ways in which men and women had interests in common, fighting against their exploitation as workers and as members of communities and families. Socialist feminists urged an examination of the changing nature of the family and the state under capitalism, refusing to label all women as one class and asserting that differences among women by class and race were as important as similarities. Like radical feminists, socialist feminists saw more than economic and political discrimination against women and believed that only profound transformations would end violence against women. At moments, socialist feminist analytic and strategic formulations sounded similar to those of radical feminists.

For socialist feminists, women's vulnerability to violence was a result not only of male domination in the family but also of a social system that sanctioned male violence and privatized the family, exploited women at home and at work, and left them few viable alternatives to escape from violence. Ending such conditions required that a movement against violence unite with other progressive movements for radical social change. This analysis meant that although socialist feminists argued that women needed to organize autonomous, women-only shelters, their anger at men often was more muted than that of radical feminists.

No analysis of battering has ever been explicitly labeled a lesbian feminist one. Because many lesbians also define themselves as radical feminists or socialist feminists, the distinctions blur. In the battered women's movement, lesbian feminist ideology speaks less to the analysis—which relies heavily on radical feminism—and more to the form of working with women. As a group, ideally lesbians represent women living happy, satisfying lives with women. To battered women, they demonstrate that women are able to take care of themselves and other women as they reject sexist injunctions to nurture men and feel responsible for them. Lesbian feminism expressed a primary, deeply felt commitment to women. For some it represented a political choice as well as a personal one. A 1972 article explained, "Woman-identified Lesbianism is, then, more than a sexual preference, it is a political choice. It is political because relationships between men and women are essentially political, they involve power and dominance. Since the Lesbian actively rejects that relationship and chooses women, she defies the established political system."[42]

In many locations, lesbian feminists were among those initiating battered women's services. Committing themselves to help women and children live free from terror and pain was their goal. As

one woman said, "Lesbians were able to look at violence and its
political ramifications and not freak out about its meaning for their
relationships with men. If you live with men and work with battered
women, you have to find a way to deal with anger and rage."[43]

Although few women entering the battered women's movement
were lesbian separatists, separatism exists as a strand within the
feminist movement. Some lesbian separatists label men as the
enemy while others see them as irrelevant. Sometimes, women are
classified as superior and their cultural, personal, and political life is
ideally developed separately from men's. Separatists believe in
creating a loving, sisterly nation of women. In this view, lesbianism,
as a sexual and political expression of women loving women, is the
best and most correct form of feminism. Although some lesbian
feminists prefer a form of separatism, especially through living in
all-female cultural and political environments, their analysis is
distinct from that of separatists who define permanent separation
from men as the only solution to ending women's oppression.
Separatists do not agree with most who view the need for autonomous women's organizations as a strategy rather than the long-
range goal of the movement.

Third world feminists brought their own diverse experiences
and political ideologies to the battered women's movement. Although their ideologies overlapped with the categories described
above, their unique histories of cultural and racial oppression shaped
their politics. The Combahee River Collective—a black feminist
group whose members have worked on diverse projects and issues
including sterilization abuse, abortion rights, rape, health care, and
battered women—defines its goal as developing "a politics that was
antiracist, unlike those of white women, and antisexist, unlike those
of black and white men." They go on to say:

> We also often find it difficult to separate race from class from sex
> oppression because in our lives they are most often experienced
> simultaneously. We know there is such a thing as racial-sexual
> oppression which is neither solely racial nor solely sexual, e.g. the
> history of rape of black women by white men as a weapon of political
> repression.
> Although we are feminists and lesbians, we feel solidarity with
> progressive black men and do not advocate the fractionalization that
> white women who are separatists demand....
> We realize that the liberation of all oppressed peoples necessitates
> the destruction of the political-economic systems of capitalism and
> imperialism as well as patriarchy.[44]

Other black feminists had different analyses and different politics. However, almost all third world women within the battered women's movement asserted that their experiences as women were different from those of white women. Some also explained third world male violence in a different way.

> The soil of this cruelty, maiming, and murder is the racism of the Great White Society. This country has systematically discriminated against, humiliated, and degraded certain of its people. These battered people, the poor and powerless, the ethnic minorities, the disenfranchised are the real abused children of the white patriarchy ....These powerless men inflict violence on women and children, the only people who are even more powerless than themselves.[45]

Feminist ideology and diverse experiences of women in the movement were not all that determined practice. Circumstances influenced the form the battered women's movement took in different locales, and how it expressed its politics. Some rural, more conservative communities translate feminism into "women who just want to break up families." Rural women had to tread even more carefully than their urban counterparts who were forced to exercise substantial caution but who, at least, had more potential allies. It is a stark understatement to suggest that circumstances forced feminists to work in less than ideal environments and to downplay, if not modify, their politics.

In fact, there was rarely adequate time to develop consistent ideological positions. Philosophy was hammered out in between emergency phone calls or meetings with local bureaucrats offering a few thousand dollars so that a shelter might open. Philosophy was formulated by drawing on experience in previous movements and jobs or by watching someone else succeed or fail. No one had ever done this work before and everything had to be mastered at once, often during long work weeks of seventy hours.

If feminism is broadly defined, then the battered women's movement is a feminist movement. The goals of the movement are feminist as is the leadership in most, though not all, locales. However, women who do not consider themselves feminists have played a very significant role in the battered women's movement. Women who reject the label feminist have started shelters and worked in shelters; they have served on Boards of Directors of explicitly feminist shelters. Most important, battered women themselves are, obviously, not always feminists. Their political views cover a broad spectrum from feminist to anti-feminist—and like those of other women in the movement—are not static. But whatever specific political label, if any, battered women use, they brought what one woman called "gut-felt" commitments into the movement. In the middle of heated political disagreements, they often have reminded their non-battered sisters that the focus, helping battered women, was disappearing. Whenever they spoke about their lives, people changed, growing more respectful. Their experiences, strengths, and scars were the force that started a movement. While romanticizing former battered women and their pain is unacceptable, understanding their contribution to building and maintaining programs, from nothing, is central. They have been determined and persistent fighters who saw themselves as improving the world for women and for their communities. They have worked with feminists and with women who do not consider themselves feminists but who share the goals of helping battered women, starting shelters, and changing indifferent social attitudes and behavior.

Among women who were not feminists, the analysis of the causes of violence against women varied as did personal backgrounds. At the beginning of the movement, although some were professionals, most were not. Generally they found common ground with many feminists when they insisted on organizational autonomy, egalitarian treatment, and self-help.

Professionals within the battered women's movement sometimes had a different perspective. Although some professionals within the movement saw the cause of violence against women residing in family pathology and others viewed it as a result of female oppression, those most professionally identified tended to emphasize providing traditional, "quality" services to women based on separations between helper and client.

However, generalizing about professionals is dangerous. Early in the movement, before government funding began, the primary motivation of most professionally trained women was a political or personal commitment to help battered women. Many professionals within the movement were feminists who worked as dedicated organizers for the first battered women's programs and later helped create legislative and social change in most states. Feminist attorneys and therapists often brought needed grant writing, lobbying, and group facilitating skills to the movement along with contacts for money within funding agencies. Or as some professionally identified women report, simply working with battered women and movement activists radicalized their views and changed their commitments. Maintaining both a professional and a movement identification created its tensions. The struggles of one socialist feminist social worker, described in her personal journal, are not unique.

> A personal theme in those early days was my commitment to a movement and my own desires for recognition. It is an incredibly complicated issue, one that I feel guilty thinking about and certainly writing about. This individual/collective contradiction is one that I think many women in the movement experience and where you come out on the continuum probably depends on many issues: your class background, political beliefs, career aspirations, financial needs.
>
> So many of the arguments in the movement reflect all the shades of difference along the professional/movement organizer continuum. I found myself pushing and being pushed more and more into the organizer camp. This continuum determines so many of the debates and struggles in the movement, i.e. Are we a service for women or a movement to end violence? Do we mainly focus on changing professionals, laws, and institutions or do we organize women? Is service the key to a "quality" shelter or is politicizing the women there the key? Do battered women exist because of inadequate service delivery systems or because of women's oppression?[46]

In practice, the answers are far more complicated than these dichotomized questions, but the personal, moral, and political challenges they provoke are real.

For women of all races and classes, for feminists and non-feminists, for professionals and activists, reasons for joining the battered women's movement were and are complex and varied. Particular individual experiences, as well as feminist ideology, brought women into the movement. For many, a decisive factor was contact with a battered woman, as evidenced in the responses of a group of Pennsylvania women from diverse battered women's programs to the question, "Why did you first become involved in the issue of battered women?" One woman's motivation to take battered women into her home came from "radical church teachings that her family was not only her immediate family; from counter-cultural ideas that things don't have to be the way they are; that people must do what they believe in; and from women who came to the women's center with nowhere to go." Another woman, who had been adopted at six weeks and had felt the importance of a family taking her in, was also deeply influenced by the women's center and the homeless battered women she met there. One activist had been a battered woman herself and as a VISTA* worker in a low-income housing

---

* Volunteers in Service to America, a domestic peace corps which is now part of the federal agency ACTION.

project she had also seen the lack of resources available to poor women. Another woman volunteered at a women's center out of a desire to reenter her former professional field, social work. A mother with two children, she sought paid part-time work at the center. Unable to find this, she volunteered and became deeply committed, first to the women's center and then to the shelter that emerged from it. Still others "fell" into the work by answering a few crisis calls at a women's center. Drawing the connection between one's own life and that of the woman calling was often a relatively easy step. Since women of all classes, races, and ethnic groups are battered, everyone heard a story that was hauntingly close to her own circumstances.[47]

Once a part of the battered women's movement, women's analyses and understanding grew and changed over time, as they found themselves transformed through shelter and movement life.

CHAPTER 3

The Emergence of the Battered Women's Movement

No Place To Go

After you have participated in this conference...be ever mindful of the hundreds of women who may *never* see their children again because...after taking as much abuse as they could...they've protected themselves by killing their husbands and are now serving prison terms.

And don't forget the countless women who have died at their own hands, rather than live in fear of death at the hands of their spouse.

Also keep in mind the endless women going in and out of mental institutions because they just can't deal with the reality of having an abusive husband so they relinquish their rights to reality.

Do you have any idea of how many battered women there are out there? Women who could live normal lives and be productive members of our society.

Many of these women would leave in a minute if they had a place to go and the help they needed to get on their feet and live in peace.[1]

Although a former battered woman spoke these words in 1979, she captured the pain and rage that motivated hundreds of women to organize in the mid-1970s. Earlier in the decade, no one knew the staggering statistics that soon would emerge on wife abuse; there was no reliable data, even within police departments, on a crime labeled insignificant. Soon, however, documentation substantiated the claims of battered women and feminists. In 1979, extrapolating

from a sample of Kentucky women, researchers estimated that
80,000 women in that state were victimized by their spouses during
the preceding twelve months, 33,000 of them seriously.[2]

Although the programs for battered women that emerged in the
1970s articulated a multiplicity of philosophies, they shared one
common belief: battered women faced a brutality from their husbands and an indifference from social institutions that compelled
redress. This theme stimulated networks among thousands of
women and programs throughout the United States, Canada, and
Europe. Even in 1982, the experiences of battered women often shock
a politically diverse movement back into recognizing the unity
imposed by violence, social indifference about that violence, and the
desperate lack of services.

The brutal institutional experiences battered women endured
are recorded in several excellent books and thousands of pages of
testimony that read like the following.

> A woman who had experienced 14 years of beatings from a husband...
> had gotten 1-year Family Court injunctions against his assaults seven
> times. Frequently, when the police responded they told her to file a
> violation petition, requesting the court to hold her husband in
> contempt. They did not arrest him until the night they found her dazed
> and dripping blood from a large head wound. Her husband had
> smashed her in the head repeatedly with a chair. He had inflicted
> several stab wounds with a screwdriver....As the officers arrested the
> man for attempted murder, he protested, "But she's my wife."[3]

Unofficially, the police concurred, further isolating and stigmatizing
the woman and lending support to her husband.

Courts generally ignored the problem, consigning it the status of
a minor, family squabble. In Washington D.C., in 1966, prosecutors
issued only 200 arrest warrants to the 7,500 women who requested
them.[4] Although 50% of the problems in Chicago's Domestic Relations Court were family assaults, in those cases that received a
hearing, "the most common disposition was an unsecured, unrecorded, blank, fake peace bond." Even when men pleaded guilty or
were found guilty, the official court docket almost always read
"discharged for want of prosecution."[5]

The extent of the harassment was shocking.

> One of my clients pressed criminal charges against her husband. The
> judge asked her if this was the first time she had been beaten up. After
> observing court proceedings that morning, she knew that if she
> answered "yes" like all the other women had, her husband would be
> released with virtually no penalty. So wisely she answered, "No, this is

not the first time." The judge dismissed the case, responding, "Well, it sounds like you must enjoy getting beaten up if it has happened before. There's nothing I can do."[6]

Women were also harassed if they attempted to leave their husbands. In Chicago in the early 1970s, as in many cities, battered women who left were denied welfare. Still legally married, their husbands' income made them ineligible for assistance. Without welfare, however, women had no money to rent apartments or pay moving expenses. The Chicago housing alternatives for those women without family members or friends to shelter them were revealed in 1976 by the newly formed Chicago Abused Women's Coalition.

1. The Salvation Army Emergency Lodge
   Description: Crisis Intervention, 24-hour telephone service, emergency housing, casework counseling available.
2. Pacific Garden Mission—Unshackled
   Description: Has limited housing for women with or without children. There is no charge. However, women are expected to attend Bible lessons.
3. Gospel League Shelter
   Description: No smoking, drinking, and women must attend Bible classes.[7]

In most cities, fire and catastrophe victims, alcoholics, and battered women found themselves in the same shelters. Often full, these facilities had to turn women away. And those who found shelter were sometimes made to feel responsible for their families' problems and their husbands' violence. No specialized assistance was offered nor was violent behavior labeled unjust. In most shelters operated by religious or charitable organizations, women were left to untangle their "personal" problems within a social and political context that extolled family unity and legitimated male dominance.

Prior to the battered women's movement, a few isolated shelters were formed to house victims of alcohol-related violence. For example, in California in 1964, women from Al-Anon opened the first shelter for battered women, Haven House. Outraged that beaten women were sleeping in cars with their children, Al-Anon women rented a large house in Pasadena. Although the shelter was specifically for victims of alcohol-related violence, many battered women simply arrived, asking for and receiving help. Between 1964 and 1972, using peer support and self-help, Haven House sheltered over 1000 women and children, surviving on a shoestring budget and the determination of grassroots women who believed in "women

helping women." In 1972, because of new, strict fire codes, Haven
House had to close, reopening in 1974 with a much larger budget and
staff.[8]

In most cases, however, battered women truly had nowhere to
go. Shelters were almost nonexistent, and medical, social service,
and law enforcement agencies rarely provided battered women with
the kind of support they needed. Although not all institutional
personnel treated battered women badly, a pattern of hostility
existed, leading many women to conclude: "No one wants to get
involved," or "I guess I'll have to be dead for them to stop his
violence."

The First Positive Responses

In the 1970s, feminists, community activists, and former
battered women increasingly responded in a new way, providing
emotional support, refuge, and a new definition of "the problem."

Feminist women's centers, like Women's Center South in
Pittsburgh, sometimes offered a safe place for women in crisis. This
women's center, with a kitchen, a place to sleep, a reading room, and
an information center, had someone in the house 24 hours a day.[9] In
an 11 month period in 1975, "the center logged 191 women sheltered,
86 children, and 839 visitors arriving to talk, create, nap, plan, work,
or just be themselves. Incoming phone calls climbed to an astro-
nomical 4961."[10] Two other Pennsylvania shelters, Women Against
Abuse in Philadelphia and the Domestic Violence Service Center in
Wilkes-Barre also evolved from women's centers.

Former battered women or women who had seen violence in
their families of origin were among the first to reach out. In Boston in
1976, "Chris Womendez and Cherie Jimenez opened up their five
room apartment as a refuge for battered women....At the time, they
supported Transition House as well as themselves and two children
on their welfare checks and small contributions from friends."[11]
Cherie Jimenez's earlier stay at Interval House, a Toronto program
primarily for battered women, influenced her decision to found the
Boston shelter. "I had never seen a place like that before...I had never
seen women helping each other out like that."[12] When asked whether
they had considered themselves feminists, Chris Womendez responded, "Cherie was more than I was. I never thought much about
it then. I identified myself as a lesbian more."[13]

Marta Segovia Ashley, whose mother was murdered by her

stepfather, describes the earliest discussions among the six women, both feminists and violence victims, who founded San Francisco's La Casa de Las Madres.

> In sharing the violence in our lives, we began to see that we were equally oppressed. There would be no separation between staff and resident....
> We did not want the social worker/white missionary establishment to run La Casa. We wrote into the original proposal that the residents would,hopefully by the end of the first year, become staff at La Casa and that we would work ourselves out of jobs.[14]

As a result of discussions during 1973 and 1974 in Harrisburg, Pennsylvania, battered women in Al-Anon organized a shelter. Their motivation was to help themselves and other women. In their view, battered women needed the support of their peers rather than professional help which often made them feel judged or disabled. The women did not see themselves as part of a feminist movement, although their first staff person did, and "a loving struggle developed between the feminists and the Al-Anon women." The feminist notion of "empowerment" and the analysis that blamed male domination for violence were foreign to Al-Anon women, but self-help and treating women as adults, important concepts for the women's liberation movement, were central to their philosophy.[15]

During late 1974, a multi-racial group of women in Boston's South End began meeting to plan a shelter for neighborhood women and their children. They were concerned about the complete lack of bilingual services for Latina women in crisis and the absence of any Latina controlled organization for women in the city of Boston. The founders of Casa Myrna Vazquez explain further.

> The origins of Casa Myrna Vazquez Inc. and the development of its philosophy and structure was not only influenced by the desire of these women to help other community women using a self-help approach (particularly Latina women and other women of color), but it was also closely tied to the fight being waged in the neighborhood to preserve the right of long-term residents to remain in the neighborhood and determine the quality of life there. At the time the South End was a neighborhood undergoing transition and change brought on by urban renewal and public and private interests and capital; people of color, poor people, new immigrants and the people speaking different languages were being rapidly displaced by the affluent. These people were fighting for the right to continue to live and own property in this neighborhood and exercise community control of their space. In keeping with this spirit, these neighborhood women wanted to create and maintain community-controlled services for women and their families to ensure that their work would remain a part of the people receiving the services.[16]

Casa Myrna Vazquez was to become one important model of help
emanating from neighborhood based rather than feminist models of
organizing.

In the early 1970s, as they listened or reassessed their own
experiences, women did more than provide housing for battered
women. In a social climate alive with feminist organizing and
community self-help projects, these women also uncovered, inch by
inch, the sexist ideology that declared nothing wrong with battering
a woman unless the violence went too far. Until the 1970s, "mild"
forms of chastisement were still considered necessary and even
helpful to keep a woman in line. A little slap was a sign of love. Most
Americans grew up with ideas like "real men keep their women
under control;" "she needed to be brought to her senses;" or "women
like men who dominate." These ideas are a shared and assumed part
of the culture. Social workers, probation officers, judges, or police
often eagerly recount knowing beaten women who enjoy the violence, offering as evidence, "You know. They always go back."
Activists had to assert that such attitudes deny women options for
escape and give men permission to beat. They declared it brutal and
misleading to label behavior masochistic or enjoyable when a person
has no perceived options.

Activists learned to challenge the ideology that preaches the
subordination of women, extols the moral superiority of men, and
logically assigns husbands the duty of chastising their wives.
Another specifically American form of ideology asserts the belief in
freedom. "Women are free to go; why don't they just leave?" This
definition of freedom ignores the fact that many women have
nowhere to go and no money to stay there once they arrive. A third
form of ideology focuses on the battering of poor women and women
of color and asserts that for them, violence is an accepted and
expected way of life and therefore need not be considered a problem.
This is a racist and class biased distortion of reality which
invalidates the suffering of poor and third world women while it
hides the violence directed against white, middle class women. As
they learned to help battered women, activists had to fight these
views within themselves and within the community.

Shelter Life

From the beginning, shelters for battered women have assumed a variety of forms. Perhaps 20% share space in YWCA

residences or use institutional settings, like motels or abandoned orphanages. Most often, shelters are old houses with many bedrooms where battered women and their children can stay for a few days or a few months. Although the buildings are often run-down, shelter staff become expert at repairing almost anything, valiantly attempting to keep them homelike. Capacity is usually five to ten families although size varies. Many women bring two or more children. Together women residents divide house chores, cook, and clean. Women may rotate tasks; for example, each woman chooses one or two meals that she will prepare for the entire group during the week. In many settings, each woman and her children share one bedroom; in others, because of severe space shortages, families double up in one room. Each shelter has rules about safety, drugs, curfew, care of children, and attendance at house meetings to discuss problems and chores. Often, length of stay agreements are made with residents.

Simply getting used to the shelter is an overwhelming task. As one woman described it, "the shelter is a hard place. Women like it but they also don't want to be here. It's just not home. Some women love it and still others hate how overcrowded it feels." As this Puerto Rican advocate explains, "Puerto Rican women who come to the shelter are very scared. They don't want to leave their community and come to a new place. They may have language problems. They don't drive. They may never have paid bills or done a budget. They particularly dislike having to share rooms with other people, both black and white women. They have never lived this way before. They're not used to living collectively or sharing apartments like white women do."[17]

During a shelter stay, women often pass through several stages. At first they are frightened and nervous, both about the decisions they have made and about their new environment of fifteen or more strangers. For the first several days or weeks, women are constantly busy with court proceedings, welfare applications or job hunts, medical appointments, and the search for affordable housing so that the next endangered woman can take her place at the shelter. After the initial flurry of activities, women wait for apartments and court proceedings, and at this point may feel intense doubts, fear, and pain. Women struggle with ambivalence, self-blame, and guilt as they contemplate their relationship ending and attempt to make sense of what happened. An Ojibwe resident at Harriet Tubman shelter describes how women cope.

— pulling together all your psychological know-how in getting along with people and still wondering if you're going to make it.
— feeling pain and confusion and not knowing if it's yours.
— having nightmares and wishing that they would go away...
— going out with other residents and thinking about your man....wanting to be with him....
— seeing your own people, feeling ashamed, and hoping to God things don't get out....
— not being able to talk at home and turning into a blabber mouth here....
— giggling with your roommate....
— abruptly remembering that you're single....
— wondering why the staff and volunteers still act so nice to you when you feel and act so out of sorts....
— connecting—being understood.
— wanting to forget....wanting to forget....wanting to forget.[18]

Many women describe the shelter's assumed but most significant advantages as time and safety to think, free from coercion and violent interruption.

Support from staff and other residents sustains women during moments of doubt. Although there is rapid turnover in residents, relationships among women form quickly, based on similar experiences, common living spaces, and the necessity of accomplishing major tasks. Support often comes through sharing food or coffee at the kitchen table. At a discussion with residents at Women's Survival Space in Brooklyn, one woman remarked, "Being here—you feel safe and that's *very* important. But you also don't feel alone. Group sessions help you relieve things that build up inside of you. It feels good inside." When asked what they get from the shelter, three women responded consecutively.

> A lot of women here give you courage. At first I asked, "Did I do the right thing? Is it me?" Now I say, "I don't have to take this. We, women, are in this together."

> From being here I get courage to face people and I won't let them make me feel low and degraded.

> Here everyone is in the same situation. Here women understand how I felt. At the city shelter, in the welfare hotel, everyone was lonely. I went home.[19]

Receiving more than courage from one another, women transform their understanding of why they were beaten. They hear repeatedly that the beatings were not their fault, and some take the first step toward freedom by rejecting responsibility for male violence. "Liberation" describes the experience of watching one shelter resident after another nod her head in recognition of another woman's plight, confusion, and eventual rage.

Shelters are havens, but they are not utopias. The atmosphere within a house varies, depending on the current group of residents, staff morale, and shelter organization. One resident describes typical problems in her shelter.

> Cliques seem to form here and as a newcomer I'm pretty uncomfortable. The older residents boss the new ones around. The women seem to be bored, complaining about missing men and sex. I wish there were more support groups, more to do.[20]

Often, however, this tension dissipates when women share with one another in groups or at house meetings, forming close bonds at least temporarily.

Because American society is so racially segregated, a shelter may be one of the few places women live interracially. Battering, living in a shelter, and starting over with nothing are the common experiences among sheltered women; racial and ethnic lines are crossed through mutual aid. Because no one escapes the racism in this society, differences and tensions are common.

> The kitchen becomes a battleground of ethnic righteousness. Women wrinkle their noses in disgust at each others' food or out-right refuse to eat. The children sit watching and listening, learning well the lessons of prejudice....The kitchen is where everything happens. Women support each other, there they cry with each other, there they prepare the food and eat....
>
> Food is an issue that people can relate to easily. It's an emotional issue, and compounded with women from different races and class backgrounds can be a very explosive one.[21]

Coming from extremely isolated areas, some rural women confront different problems.

> Isolation is intensified when there are not neighbors to hear her scream, when she has no car and there are no buses that come within 15 or 20 miles of her house. She may have no phone. There may be four feet of snow. Furthermore,...tradition dictates that one does not bring family problems to anyone external, particularly in a small town where once one's business is known by a few, it is known by all.[22]

Just getting to the shelter may be an overwhelming task.

> Recently in Nebraska, a woman tried to walk to a shelter for battered women that she had heard about. It was 150 miles from her home. She had walked nearly half way with her small children on back roads when she came to a town that had a volunteer task force on domestic violence which arranged for transportation...[23]

Once at a shelter, rural women may have to adjust to using indoor plumbing or washing machines for the first time. They may be members of a white ethnic minority in the community that is scorned by some women at the shelter.

For rural women and urban women, for women of different races and ethnic groups, shelters offered a chance to escape an unbearable situation. They created an environment in which diverse women came together to live, rebuilding pained lives. Finding the best way to do this would not be easy; few models existed and financial resources were always limited.

Shelter Philosophy and Structure

As shelters formed, they began to develop their own philosophies and structures and deal with the troubling question of their relationship to the state. Focusing on two of the first shelters, Transition House in Boston and Women's Advocates in St. Paul, highlights early shelter activity and helps clarify the philosophical differences that would emerge in the battered women's movement as it expanded.

The founding of Women's Advocates and Transition House were real and symbolic victories in the struggle of women to free themselves from male violence and domination. Their stories suggest the richness, complexity, chaos, and energy of the early battered women's movement. Women's Advocates emerged from a consciousness raising group which, in 1971, set itself the goal, typical in the early women's liberation movement, "to do something."[24] This determination led the group to produce a divorce rights handbook and organize a legal information telephone service, staffed by volunteers and two VISTA workers assigned to Women's Advocates through a Legal Aid Office.

> ....what to do next. The need for emergency housing was the one urgent and recurring problem for which there was no referral....The immediate need of so many women moved us toward turning our vision into a reality.[25]

They began by asking friends for pledges toward the down payment on a house and for operating expenses. By 1973, monthly pledges of $350 helped pay rent for a small apartment and the cost of a telephone and answering service. Calls for help exceeded room in the apartment, and advocates soon took battered women into their homes. After three months, Women's Advocates was evicted from its apartment because of neighbors' complaints about the children. Their office then temporarily moved into the home of one of their VISTA workers.

> Several women needing emergency housing stayed together at her home that summer while her family was on vacation, and we realized the importance of women being together in one house, sharing their experiences, and getting support from one another.[26]

They also learned a lesson about how women together can transform fear. Searching all over town for a woman whose kidneys he had damaged in a beating, a pimp threatened Women's Advocates. At that moment, "there was another woman with four children, a woman with one child, and a single woman in the house. We had a meeting about this man. I remember one volunteer argued for everyone leaving the house because of the potential danger. The whole group decided to hold their ground and take shifts, staying up all night in case he showed up. It was the first time I felt that kind of power."[27] In this summer experiment, staff and residents had participated equally. Advocates maintained friendships with the women they were sheltering; staff were not just helpers.[28] Staff had seen the strength of battered women, which gave them the courage to move ahead and open a house; they had also experienced the reality of sheltering when women stole from them or did not like one another. Having sheltered women for eighteen months, Women's Advocates moved into their first house idealistic but seasoned, aware of the satisfaction and dangers ahead.

Women's Advocates' philosophy had been hammered out early in practical debates about whether a hotline worker should tell a caller what to do. Battered women's rights to self-determination, including the decision to leave or stay with their husbands, were to be respected; if sexism robbed women of control over their lives, Women's Advocates would work on methods for returning it, even if no one quite knew how. Outside agencies also forced a clarification of values. When the first funding sources suggested that Women's Advocates change its name to something "less inflammatory," the collective refused to compromise on its basic philosophy.

> We have never called women needing help "clients" or "cases," and this has not prevented effective communication with the professional community. When we were told that only trained and certified professionals could run the house, we insisted that professional credentials not be included as job requirements. We asserted our belief

that women in need of shelter were not sick or in need of treatment, emphasizing instead their need for safety, support, and help with practical problems.[29]

The importance of a collective, rather than a hierarchical, model of work was emphasized as the shelter founders drew the connection between theory and practice.

> We want women to be able to take control of their own lives, and to share in an environment which supports their doing just that. For many women and children, being at the shelter may be the first time they have been outside of the controlling authority of an abusive relationship. Each woman who lives and works in the shelter is encouraged to trust herself to make decisions which are best for her, and to participate in determining what is best for the shelter as well. Here, there is no boss who has the answers. It isn't easy, but together we are learning to trust in ourselves, and in each other, to determine what is best for us.[30]

At Women's Advocates, all major decisions are made by the collective, usually through consensus. Sometimes voting has also been necessary, but "a slim majority...never carries a decision. When the collective is split on an important issue, we set it aside, placing it on the agenda for the next meeting."[31]

One of the central issues for many shelters is whether the shelter belongs to staff or residents. Often this question surfaces in discussions of rules. When Women's Advocates opened in 1974, they had no house rules. Immediately, however, they found they had to set limits. The first rules centered around mandatory house meetings, signing up for jobs so that the house could function, and a "no drugs" policy. One founder commented, "on the first day we declared that there were no pets; on the second, no drugs; and on the third, no furniture storage."[32] Rules were made on the basis of experience, often negative ones, and sometimes the collective had to remind itself or be reminded by the residents that it had created too many restrictions.

For most shelters, a vexing consideration was what relationship to assume toward the government and funding agencies. *Women's Advocates, The Story of a Shelter,* an excellent description of the shelter's organizing activity and history, captures women's ambivalence toward the state.

> For the first two years the shelter was in operation, we made no active effort to affect legislation. Although we were acutely aware of the inadequacy of current laws available to battered women and the need

for funding for shelters, we were less certain of the benefits of legislation than we were of its potential dangers. As the only shelter or program of any kind for battered women in our state, we were isolated and in a state of political infancy. Before approaching state politics, we needed to be stronger—to know clearly what we wanted, and to know how to go about getting it without losing what little ground we had gained.[33]

Cautiously, Women's Advocates later took foundation funding and one local mental health grant that allowed them to preserve their autonomy. They hired a small staff and depended heavily on volunteers. State funding was to come later with the passage of legislation.

Working in isolation, but relying on feminist insight, battered women's input, and common sense, Women's Advocates learned through experience how to best help battered women. In the process, the advocates also found themselves transformed. As one shelter founder explains:

We discovered our politics in the process of discovering ourselves. When we saw how totally the traditional system failed to meet the needs of battered women, we rushed in to save them. What kept us from being a bunch of Lady Bountifuls was that everything learned from the women themselves, and our struggles with policy, direction, and with each other, was moving *us* off that continuum from victim to survivor. The personal was political. Personally, I didn't call myself a feminist when we started. It sort of snuck up and embraced me as I lived it.[34]

Members of the original Advocates collective had neither the extensive experience with violence themselves nor the theoretical commitment that motivated several women at Transition House, the first east coast shelter. In both cases, however, experience led them to the creation of shelters with similar ideologies and practices. Transition House was born in 1976 in the apartment of two former battered women. Believing women together could pool their resources to help others, Chris Womendez and Cherie Jimenez, with determination and no money, simply declared their home a shelter. Betsy Warrior and Lisa Leghorn joined their work as did other radical feminists. Since 1974, Leghorn and Warrior had talked about battering and women's slavery in the home as a core part of women's oppression.[35] These politics informed the philosophy of Transition House.

We are concerned not only with providing physical and emotional refuge from domestic violence, as a short term goal. We are concerned, more basically, with helping each woman who comes through here to discover that she is not alone, that the craziness she's being forced to deal with isn't unique to her and her children, but that it's a political issue which touches all women directly and indirectly.

Using informal consciousness raising techniques, the women at Transition House emphasize the political nature of the work.

In doing support and advocacy work for her, we are telling her that as sisters, her plight is our plight, and that the only way we can fight these battles and hope to win is by working together and supporting each other in every way possible. As soon as a woman comes into Transition House for the first time, we talk with her about her experiences, share our own experiences with her, play her tapes we made of other women who've come through the house talking about what they'd been forced to deal with and how they came out of it, and we give her articles and news clippings which address the problem of wife abuse as a political issue.

Transition House clarifies the desired, liberating outcome.

First of all, she gains a political awareness by viewing her own suffering for the first time in a social and political framework. And secondly, she discovers that the most effective way to confront the entire social, political, and economic system whose expressed interests are to keep the family with all its trappings of male supremacy and male privilege intact at her expense is to join together with other women and address the issues in a political way.[36]

From the beginning, Transition House has emphasized women's opportunities to share with and support one another. The growth of all women who pass through the house, battered women and staff, is seen as important. As one staffer* explained, "we are part of a liberating process of women helping each other. We are all sharing pain and through that similarity we grow. Often we forget to share our lives and we become objects of services. When we share, there is a continual transformation of our own lives."[37] Transition House staffers understood that the process of giving to others makes women feel stronger. Resident strengthening resident, a primary goal of the shelter, was considered more potent than staff helping residents.[38]

Because Transition House did not want the experience of staff to be vastly different from that of residents, women declared hiring former victims a priority.[39] According to Lisa Leghorn, peer support,

* At Transition House, volunteers and paid staff are all called staffers.

especially among battered women, worked better than other models because it gave hope, power, and validation to women. She explains the Transition House philosophy further.

> We were not providing social services. As staffers, we were not different from the women except that they were in crisis. We only gave people safety and information. We emphasized women have to make their own decisions. Support came sitting around the dining room table and while doing advocacy. Our advocacy model was a woman who went to welfare yesterday taking another woman today...If you caretake, you don't give a woman what she needs. Shelters where women went back to their husbands were often shelters where they had been taken care of as opposed to being helped to develop survival skills. This didn't prepare the woman for living on her own in an often hostile world.[40]

Initially, Transition House was crowded and chaotic. Speaking of the early days in the apartment, one staffer recalls, "we had beds everywhere and lofts and a closet stuffed with mattresses that we took out at night....People that did stay were extremely battered and really needed it. They had absolutely no choice....."[41] Under the circumstances, it was difficult for a work structure to evolve. When Transition House rented its first house, conditions improved and more structure was created. Paid staff were added. Three working committees were formed—maintenance, fundraising, and outreach—and a whole wave of unpaid staff was recruited from a Boston Women Support Women rally that focused on violence against women and drew 5000 participants.

Initially, rules came from the women staying in the house. Then new women would arrive, and, furious at old restrictions, change the rules. The short-term interests of women staying in the house for a few weeks and the long-term survival needs of the shelter were sometimes in conflict. Eventually, the power to make rules and decisions came to reside primarily with staffers through committee work and collective meetings; any resident willing to make a longer term commitment to the shelter was invited to be part of the decision making process and Board of Directors. However, rules could be changed by residents, except those that applied to the long-term needs of the house—like keeping the location confidential and maintaining safety precautions.[42] Rules were based on residents' experiences together. One staffer emphasized, "Transition House is for the women who live there and for the women who will come, and this dual focus has to be maintained."[43]

Women working at Transition House had to be tremendously

flexible. Change happened continually in a house holding ten women and their children, most of whom stayed six weeks or less and were instantly replaced by new women and children. There was no "correct" approach to the work, and at times the chaos and problems were overwhelming, especially when women had to confront the fact that "not all women are just wonderful." As one staffer said, "women have had to learn survival skills and some of these are negative. They may hurt other people and one has to learn this. It's a tough issue."[44] Learning to live with intense anger was also difficult for many. Staff had to explain why hundreds of women experience so much brutality from men, why the institutions seemed indifferent, and why women were trapped by financial, housing and child care problems.

Despite the pain and exhaustion that shelter workers sometimes felt, they were politicized through battered women's experiences and strengthened by the courage so many displayed as they reclaimed their lives.

> Running a shelter is very taxing...It goes back to mutual sharing, being there for each other...The shelter is a big connecting point between classes. I've changed being there...We get involved, excited, and have great respect and love for women we never would have met otherwise.[45]

A founder of Women's Advocates echoes these sentiments.

> As an advocate you got depressed and discouraged from hearing all the pain. The number of women, the severity of their problems, what they faced when they left the shelter—it weighed me down. What kept me going was that the shelter allowed the women's power to emerge. Listening to them was so moving...The women's options often seem hopeless but their spirit rises above hopelessness and gives me hope.[46]

Through redefining a social "problem" into a social movement, women from Transition House and Women's Advocates helped other shelters begin and served as catalysts for state, regional, and national coalitions. Using the self-help methods, egalitarian philosophy, and collective organizational structures developed within the women's liberation movement, these two groups discovered and then articulated a grassroots, non-professional view of battered women's needs. Through their struggle to define a feminist "shelter," they gave birth to one more alternative, democratic women's institution. Although their efforts and ideology were not always replicated in other cities, Transition House and Women's Advocates became respected and often copied pioneers.

Organizing Through a Coalition

Although providing shelter for abused women is a top priority of the battered women's movement, groups in the movement have organized in other ways too. In some cities, women representing a variety of organizations met together and decided to form coalitions. In Chicago, for example, in the spring of 1976, women of the Loop Center YWCA convened a meeting of women's organizations and individuals whom they knew to be concerned about the lack of services for battered women. Over thirty groups were represented at the initial meeting and expressed interest in combining resources for public education on the issues, support groups for the victims, and agency accountability for missing programs.[47]

Women who attended this and subsequent meetings decided to plan a fall conference to found the Chicago Abused Women's Coalition. To the surprise of the organizers, 300 women came to the October conference. The coalition, which defined opening a shelter as an essential goal, also identified other needs of the movement and worked simultaneously on many fronts. Several task forces—shelter, legal, agency accountability, counseling, and publicity—were established and became the core working groups of the coalition. They emphasized the need for creating services and making concrete change. Two elected delegates from each task force formed the steering committee of the coalition, and met together frequently.

The Chicago Abused Women's Coalition's efforts to work on a range of projects is typical of organizing in other locales as well. In many places, women start with a hotline or counseling project and slowly build local support for a shelter. In others, as a result of circumstances or choice, they never open a refuge but continue ceaseless support for battered women through their hotlines, crisis counseling, legal advocacy, public speaking, and transportation to shelters in other towns.

Initially, the Chicago coalition itself offered no services and had no paid staff. Member organizations, specifically the YWCA and Women in Crisis Can Act (WICCA), divided day, evening, and weekend hours to become a crisis hotline for the entire city and sometimes suburbs, answering hundreds of phone calls each month from women with nowhere to go. The Women's Services Department at Loop Center YWCA, with 2½ paid staff, answered all daytime calls from rape victims and battered women. WICCA operated as a collective with no paid staff and answered its phone on specified weekday evenings and weekend hours. Reflecting on these experiences at the YWCA, I later wrote:

> All I can remember is phone calls, constant, never-ending calls from battered women with no place to go and with endless stories of institutional indifference. I can remember just wanting to cry and cry. There were moments I dreaded talking to another battered woman. Working with battered women and not being able to help them find what they concretely need creates a panic, a steady stream of adrenaline that continues until help is found. Where would she go for now; what would she do if the local shelters for homeless people were filled; would she be safe; where would the kids be; what would her husband do if he found her; were there weapons involved; did she have money to buy food; did she have carfare to get to the Salvation Army; where were the birth certificates and medical records for the welfare office or hospital. The details are endless, but they must not be forgotten. We had to assess safety, give her support and information, and help her weigh alternatives. Maybe for shelter workers who can offer a safe place, the feelings are different, but all we had was a crisis phone.[48]

Early work of the shelter task force revolved around defining a philosophy; what emerged was similar to the values articulated by Women's Advocates. Learning about shelters for homeless women in the community further clarified the direction in which the task force would move. A former battered woman, who stayed at one of these shelters, testified about the experience.

> Oh, you're my social worker. It's nice meeting you. Oh, no, I don't have any money with me. But I do have a job. Do you mean I'll have to quit my job to receive your services? A leave of absence? Don't you want me to work? My job will be our only source of income now and I've only been on this job a short while. Well, O.K., I'll see if I can get a leave of absence for a month or so.
>
> Welfare! Yes, I guess you're right. If I'm on leave from my job, I will need money.
>
> Leave town! No, I hadn't thought about that. Change our names?[49]

Women on the shelter task force, all volunteers, worked tirelessly to raise money through pledges, legally incorporate, write grants, and find a building. For over a year, financial pledges from individual women were the only source of hope, but were never enough to open a shelter. Discouragement was constant. The city of Chicago did much to obstruct progress through unkept promises of funding. The task force eventually approached religious organizations that owned buildings, and one house was secured in 1978, after the Chicago coalition and other Illinois shelters received funding through state Title XX grants. Two years of persistent work finally achieved results.

In the meantime, the legal task force moved forward. The first Chicago Abused Women's Coalition newsletter, published in December 1976, defined four primary goals of the legal task force, all of which were accomplished over the next several years. The first goal was to mobilize around proposed state legislation that would provide temporary injunctive relief, protective orders, and custody and property determinations for women who had not filed for divorce; would allow women to sue their husbands for damages; would require police training and statistics gathering; and would declare spouse beating a specific crime. The three non-legislative goals included working with the police to develop new procedures in wife abuse cases, developing a court watch program that would document the problems within the States Attorney's office and Domestic Relations Court, and establishing a court advocacy program for victims.[50] Not only were these goals accomplished but the first Legal Center for Battered Women in the United States was funded by a grant to the Legal Assistance Foundation of Chicago. For two years, the Legal Center advocated for thousands of individual women, forced the Chicago police department to change its practices, and kept close watch over all local and state legislative and criminal justice systems developments. A legal center specifically geared toward meeting battered women's needs and changing legal practices had been defined as a necessity; its closing after two years due to lack of funds was a major loss to the battered women's movement.

Changing social attitudes and generating concrete assistance through educational efforts has been a primary organizing strategy of the battered women's movement. In its first two years, members of the Chicago Abused Women's Coalition spoke to hundreds of community groups, women's organizations, and professional agencies. Early coalition discussions served to clarify the analysis as well as the methods for conveying it. Almost every speaker shared battered women's stories, explained the significance of violence, detailed how victims are blamed and violence is sanctioned, dispelled common myths, and challenged her audience to help battered women and look at the broader social conditions that create abuse. Social attitudes toward battered women were painfully obvious through these efforts as audiences searched for "characteristics" of abusers and battered women. Professionals in particular hunted for pathology and a "battered woman syndrome," locating the cause of violence in women's personalities or their families of origin.

In addition to numerous speaking engagements, the Chicago Abused Women's Coalition, through a grant from the Illinois Humanities Council, co-sponsored three conferences in 1976 and 1977—one in the downtown business section of Chicago; another coordinated by latinas as a Spanish-speaking conference with the first locally translated materials; and a third in the black community on Chicago's westside.

Community education efforts provided an alternative and a challenge to dominant views about violence against women. Although audiences revealed their prejudices, they were often deeply moved and supportive of coalition activity. The movement's ability to balance moral outrage about battering with a deep concern for its victims and a vision of a better world led many to join in the struggle. For example, hospitals and social service agencies began to increasingly ask the coalition to provide their staff with in-service education and training. Some institutions became highly supportive of coalition activity, writing endorsement letters for coalition grants and, in some cases, starting their own services for battered women. These outreach activities had their effect on battered women as well. They heard the messages: "You don't deserve to be beaten; it's not your fault; you are beaten because society sanctions his behavior, not because of anything you do wrong; evidence suggests that no matter how many times you change your behavior to respond to his criticisms, you will probably be beaten again; through the years, violence grows more severe." Battered women reacted by reaching out for help and by involving themselves in the movement.

Activists in the Chicago Abused Women's Coalition developed skills as speakers, lobbyists, and planners. A core of fifteen feminists—lawyers, social workers, psychologists, and activists—fought for essential services. Ideological and political differences were muted until decisions had to be made about applying for government funding, cooperating with religious organizations, or working with men. At this point, after years of hard work, one of the most radical women left in principled and caring disagreement over the choice to work with religious organizations that oppress women. Repeated around the country, sometimes with far greater bitterness and divisiveness, are the stories of many hard working women who never saw the opening of the shelters they had envisioned.

To the Chicago women, shelter was only one step in a long-range, dimly articulated plan to stop violence. Battling with the bureaucracy and raising money for more than two years before a shelter opened, however, were trying. Working on the legal task force, doing community outreach—all took enormous time and energy. Although many women participated in the coalition on a sporadic basis, most of the work was done by a small group of approximately fifteen. In the rush to make concrete change, women stayed task oriented; no one stopped to see herself as an organizer for the coalition itself. In the constant push to respond to battered women and organizational emergencies, there was no time to build the organization's membership, a familiar story within the movement. When several key coalition members "burned out" or moved, the coalition and its newly opened shelter faced difficult days.

External Influences on the Movement

Even in its infancy, the battered women's movement had to contend with more than its own internal dynamics. It faced contradictory external reactions and pressures. The media, for example, was both help and hinderance. At first, the plight of battered women—like that of rape victims—made "good news stories." Women reporters, working cooperatively and thoughtfully with battered women's programs, often produced excellent and thorough articles, drawing attention to institutional hostility to abused women and the lack of services available to them. These stories brought more calls from battered women and supporters and also legitimated the need for services and institutional change. A message challenging hundreds of years of male domination reached many. This kind of coverage, combined with the movement's extensive outreach to women's organizations, sometimes led to concrete support from traditional women's clubs or women's auxiliaries who "adopted" shelters, furnishing rooms or coordinating fundraising benefits. Sometimes, however, publicity was counterproductive. Reporters produced sensationalized accounts which made battered women look foolish; worse, they sometimes revealed the addresses of shelters, thereby endangering staff and residents and forcing groups to move after they had spent years finding housing.

Government and community agencies could help direct important resources toward the movement, although, as in the case of the media, the movement's relationship to such groups was ambivalent. Sometimes, a key individual made all the difference.

In 1974, the Ramsey County Mental Health Board,...made a grant of $35,000 [to Women's Advocates]. A woman member of the board, with several years of experience as a social worker in the county mental health program, worked very hard to get that grant for us because she was impressed with the nontreatment approach of the advocates and the effect it had on women. In her own experience as a social worker she decided that depression was the appropriate response to the situation in which most women found themselves trapped. Moreover, the tools of the treatment system were authoritarian, fostering dependence. The new model seemed to her to be a way out for women.[51]

Simply recounting the experiences of battered women sometimes brought the desperately needed first grants; in other cases, funders changed their original negative responses after they visited shelters.[52] One or two key people, some of them feminists, within welfare departments, community or county planning boards, or United Way agencies, made the issue theirs, pushing others to support programs that had no legitimacy, credibility, or fiscal strength. In Pennsylvania, Ken Nealy, a state legislative aide who was later tragically killed in an automobile accident, invited several women from around the state to attend hearings so that grassroots groups might have an impact on pending state legislation. After a day of testimony, these women, none of whom had previously met, formed the first core working group of the Pennsylvania Coalition Against Domestic Violence.[53] Women from around the country tell of anonymous donors or key progressive legislators, male and female, who made a real difference in the early years.

Often, however, outside agencies' impact on the movement has been more negative than positive. Bureaucracies, especially local welfare and legal ones, constantly harassed battered women and their advocates.

We work with the county welfare department a great deal and have had almost every kind of disagreement and misunderstanding imaginable arise between us, but we have worked many things through. For example: women living in our house used to wait for weeks for an intake interview at welfare, trying to exist with no funds for personal expenses.[54]

Zoning boards and county governments wrought misery upon programs searching for affordable property that met the criteria for shelter. The Pittsburgh shelter experienced a series of disasters with zoning boards and realtors denying them access to one house after another. County governments and fire departments withheld funds or licensing approval for a series of nitpicking reasons. Sometimes community members packed public hearings, insisting that they did not want violent husbands in their neighborhood, and successfully blocked a shelter's opening.

As in the anti-rape movement, once the issue of battering gained legitimacy and funding was made available, more established organizations took over the issue that grassroots women had worked so hard to raise. One writer describes how this happened in Seattle.

> Prior to the funding hearing, the Salvation Army had worked cooperatively with feminist and other community groups in making the public aware of the need for a shelter for battered women. Since then, however, the Salvation Army and the Women's Commission have disagreed bitterly over the program plan, and the Commission and feminist groups have withdrawn their support. The Commission had been willing to support the Salvation Army as the sponsoring agency provided a Sub-Advisory Committee...was formed to assure that the program meet the needs and basic concerns of the community....The Salvation Army refused to make such an agreement, chose to act unilaterally, obtained United Way funds, and now plans to open in June 1976 a newly purchased facility...[55]

Competition over limited dollars allowed conservative private and governmental bodies to direct funds toward traditional, non-feminist agencies.

Generalizing about agency and governmental responses to the battered women's movement is difficult. In some locations, agencies like the United Way, offering funds or legitimacy, or the YWCA, giving its space or staff time, were extremely helpful; in others, similar agencies turned their backs or actively set up barriers to prevent grassroots groups from encroaching on their "turf." Battered women and their advocates had pointed out that established agencies were not meeting their needs; some of these agencies moved to redress the complaint while others reacted with discomfort and fought back with intense pettiness that caused long delays in shelter openings. Issues of power, control, and funding were often at stake, and newcomers, especially those with anti-professional or non-professional biases, were not necessarily welcome.

The Early Sustenance of the Movement

Battered women's shelters have, from the beginning, operated under extremely difficult conditions and been subject to many conflicting demands. Living and working in a shelter implies crises for all involved. In addition to dealing with the overwhelming problems of shelter residents, staff had to face daily pressures. Since there was never enough money, women had to learn quickly how to write grant proposals, lobby, generate publicity, speak on radio and television, apply for loans and mortgages. They also had to learn how to organize staff and develop work procedures. At the same time that shelter work and its accomplishments were exhilarating, the strains were wearing. In the early years especially, worker "burnout" was common, and some staff literally destroyed their health or personal lives.

In a few places, women encountered yet one more pressure. While community groups or individuals might sympathize publicly with battered women, "feminism" did not necessarily evoke similar reactions. Feminists were sometimes accused of hating men, and of being lesbians who were out to seduce battered women. The real purpose of these accusations—to divide collective efforts, undermine women's activism, and scare battered women away from the shelter—was often obvious. Although most women ignored the attacks and used their anger to continue organizing, some were diverted by this tactic. Bigotry and anti-feminist sentiment caused a few lesbians and heterosexual feminists to suffer through ugly, discrediting power struggles and ultimately lose their jobs.

In the midst of uncertainty, women turned to one another for multiple forms of sustenance. Women uniting, working cooperatively against huge odds, caring about one another and struggling together successfully carried small, isolated programs through the worst days. For many, a feminist analysis of wife abuse that placed the roots of male violence in domination could not be separated from a feminist process that actively struggled against recreating hierarchies and domination among women.

> We listened to and respected each other's opinions. We did not act for ourselves; we were acting for our group and accountable to it. You never dared make a major decision without using some accountability mechanism. You were, therefore, never alone or isolated. You relied on the collective intelligence; you trusted that you would get to the correct solution if you had all the information and you could continue to discuss the issues together. It felt great. I grew so much politically during the days we debated which funds to seek, how to negotiate with police, or how to address a psychiatrist's attempt to blame the victim.[56]

Close friendship networks developed in early battered women's groups. As one shelter worker explained, "The work becomes all-consuming. You live and breathe together the battered women's movement—the horrible things that happen to women, power struggles with other agencies. I think this is why so many women in the movement become such close friends. The movement is your life."[57]

When asked how their programs started or how their work progressed, early movement organizers instead described each group member's unique skills and personality. With both positive and negative outcomes, the personalities involved were as important as the strategies chosen, and in assessing the movement, women organizers consistently interwove these two topics, insisting upon their inseparability. The energy needed to maintain impoverished shelters often was generated by close, caring relationships which sustained women through demeaning encounters with the police and daily demands from battered women in need of non-existent housing, jobs, and protection.

In feminist shelters, women created a new morality which was in sharp contrast to the ethos within competitive, male dominated organizations and the "heartless" bureaucracies around them. They developed their own organizational forms, celebratory events, music, and measures of success. As a reaction to isolation and as an affirmation of women, activists tried to form a sustaining sisterhood, a community with new cultural norms.

Feminist process, however, with its somewhat unspecified standard of conduct, could be problematic. Early groups, often politically and racially homogeneous and driven to accomplish a task, sometimes experienced or expressed few conflicts. Although differences tended to remain hidden for some time, when they emerged they often did so with great force and venom. Participants in the early movement, overworked and under severe strain, were ill prepared to deal with such problems. The close bonding among women which sustained the movement also made political and personal conflict extremely painful and hard to resolve. Power struggles, difficult in any organization, took trusting feminists by surprise and left them paralyzed or unwilling to resort to tactics that were politically abhorrent to them. Some dedicated women were driven out of the movement by "trashing"—vicious attacks on a woman's character and political motivations. In a few places, shelters or groups came precariously close to dissolving, and important work was sometimes left unfinished.

Despite difficult times, most women in the movement were sustained by their relationships with others, by the knowledge that their work was essential, and by the ways in which they worked. Many speak of personal transformation and growth.

> Doing the work gave me unknown strength. I did so much that I'd never done before, things I never expected to do. We made real changes for battered women in the city. I knew my work was competent and

respected. What is important for us in the movement, or some of us, is to recognize how much we have been given, how much gratification we get from our work.[58]

Another woman remarked.

It helped my low self-esteem to help others. I didn't articulate this to my co-workers. What an incredible thing I was doing in my own life bridging all these differences between women. I just basked in their energy, their sense of humor. I got so much. It changed my life completely. It was a gift. There is a thrill in seeing women's strength.[59]

Individual growth also signified taking personal risks. Many women recount that friends avoided them when they joined the movement. Others rejected long time friends because they found them too "petty;" it is hard to work with battered women all day and then hear friends brutally criticize welfare recipients. Still other women left their marriages when husbands could not tolerate their wives' personal success or autonomy. Children sometimes resented mothers who were not always available for them. Some women lost much, but most insist that their self-respect has been a far greater gain.

For women in the movement, participating in something far larger than oneself was exhilarating. Depressing moments were overshadowed by a sense that one was helping to change the world. Each battered woman who moved from depression into anger and pride sustained that belief. Every phone call or scribbled note that said, "thanks for being there," or every woman who said, "you're the first person that I've ever told this story to, so please don't laugh at me," brought sustenance. Watching shelter residents strengthen one another and come back to join the movement reminded all that the world was different.

Being part of a larger national and international movement also energized activists. Initially, informal networks—women traveling from one city to another—conveyed information, strategies, and support. For example, friendships among women from Carbondale, Illinois and Pittsburgh influenced the founding of the Pittsburgh women's center.[60] Women's Advocates recalls that after the shelter opened in October 1974

notes and letters began to trickle in from women who had heard about what we were doing and wanted information to help establish shelters and safe housing in their own communities. We tripped over each other in our eagerness to connect with other women with similar purpose, sending encouragement, along with our proposals, budgets, and forms.

> Our sense of isolation dissolved with this spontaneous network of
> women, many of whom we would meet years later through organized
> networking efforts, incredibly as part of a national movement.[61]

Personal contacts were but one way that women in the
movement were linked nationally and internationally. The British
battered women's movement, which began approximately four years
before the U.S. movement, was known through Erin Pizzey's
pathbreaking *Scream Quietly or the Neighbors Will Hear* (1974). In the
U.S., women found their work legitimated in the journal of the
Feminist Alliance Against Rape (*FAAR*) and later in the first
newsletter of the battered women's movement, the *National Communications Network* (*NCN*). Even before a movement was publicly
recognized, activists like Betsy Warrior and Lisa Leghorn wrote and
distributed pioneering literature on battered women.[62] In 1976, the
first edition of Warrior's invaluable directory of individuals and
groups helping battered women, *Working on Wife Abuse*, was
published. That same year, Del Martin's *Battered Wives* became a
major source of information and validation for the movement. It
legitimated the view, already put forward by local feminist shelters,
that violence against women was caused by sexism. This analysis,
no longer the "ravings" of a few individuals or groups, was the
framework adopted by thousands.

Finally, women were sustained through their commitment to
end male violence and female subordination. Helping battered
women was, for many, part of a broader struggle for women's
liberation. Testifying before the U.S. Civil Rights Commission,
Monica Erler from Women's Advocates declared helping individuals
insufficient.

> A last thought. All that I have said describes a Band-Aid measure.
> That is what our work is. The violence goes on. With Marta Ashley we
> say, "Don't ask why she stayed; ask why he beat her."[63]

For women to have real alternatives to abusive relationships
and for men to stop their violence, major social transformation
would be necessary. The battered women's movement forged an
analysis and a practice that would be an essential part of that
struggle. The very existence of the movement announced that the
world was different and that women together would not rest until
changes were made.

CHAPTER 4

Growing Pains

Shelter Services Expand

Battered women's shelters, safe homes projects,* counseling, and hotline services appeared in hundreds of locations after 1976. Rarely, however, did services exist for all who needed them. A 1977 survey of 163 programs revealed that "46,838 battered women were served by these programs....approximately four times as many of the clients were served on a nonresidential basis as were housed. During that same period, 14,473 children were sheltered in program facilities. Unfortunately, the average capacity of a shelter program was 15 persons, including women and children, and program directors report that they often have to turn women away because of lack of space."[1] According to a 1979 survey, in the state of Minnesota, 70% of the women requesting shelter had to be turned away because of lack of space.[2]

The less than ideal circumstances under which service was provided are as noteworthy as the statistics. In one study, "of the 138 programs which responded to this question, 93 (57 percent) indicated

---

* In these programs members of the community take a battered woman and her children into their home for a specified number of days while an advocate helps coordinate legal and welfare problems and plans for the future.

that at least half of their workforce was comprised of volunteers. Without CETA* funding and extensive volunteerism, many programs either would not exist or would be unable to offer the surprisingly wide range of services currently available."[3] Volunteers outnumbered paid staff by almost three to one in these programs.[4] Services included twenty-four hour crisis hotlines, counseling, medical or job assistance, legal and welfare advocacy, and child care, often for sheltered and non-sheltered women alike.

Unlike Transition House and Women's Advocates, many groups wrote proposals and received funding before they housed battered women. The Women's Transitional Living Center, Inc. was one such shelter. A description of the center which was included in a 1977 White House briefing packet on battered women captures the diversity of the emerging battered women's movement.

> The Women's Transitional Living Center, Inc. (WTLC) grew out of a NOW Task Force on Family Violence....
>
> With the need for a shelter firmly established, the Task Force sent letters seeking support to a broad range of community resources such as the departments of Public Social Services and Mental Health, Police, attorneys, law centers, doctors, schools, women's centers, hotlines, and prominent business people in the community....
>
> A 10-month revenue sharing grant for $72,000 in January 1976 was followed by an 11-month grant of $85,000 in late 1976. Smaller amounts of money have been raised from membership contributions... sporadic donations from private foundations and corporations, and small client fees....The center also received funds from C.E.T.A....for two paid staff positions.
>
> The WTLC has four full-time and two part-time paid staff members. In addition, two consultants are retained: a psychiatrist spends 20 hours a week at the center, and a counselor spends approximately 11 hours a week.[5]

As new programs were born, old programs expanded their services by acquiring more substantial government or foundation support. The Domestic Violence Service Center (DVSC) in Wilkes-Barre, Pennsylvania, finally gained a breathing space after two years of subsisting with no secure funding base. In 1979, "the DVSC, with the support of the United Services Agency and United Way of Wyoming Valley, was able to obtain its first Title XX grant." One activist recalls, "this marked a milestone in our agency's history: our grass roots struggle had found community support and acceptance.

* Comprehensive Employment Training Act, a Department of Labor job training program.

Battered women in Luzerne County would be assured a safe refuge..."[6] After operating on so little, the agency's $50,000 a year budget seemed a windfall. Many programs recount similar stories, developing from an all-volunteer or mainly CETA funded staff to a six to ten person staff financed through grants. Many programs, however, had to continue relying on CETA and VISTA to keep their shelters operating the necessary seven days a week, twenty-four hours a day.

Almost every project contended with renewable grants, guaranteed for no more than one or two years. At any time, limited foundation or government funds might be allocated to other pressing problems. Many shelters watched their funding come and go. Expansion of services to battered women rarely followed a smooth path; just as some programs received state funding that offered partial security against extinction, others would close temporarily or permanently. Testimony before the United States Senate revealed the extent of the problem.

> In Claremont, New Hampshire the 13 shelter employees earn an average of $309 per month. They are funded by CETA. The CETA contract will end in August, 1980. Absent unforseen funds, the shelter will close.
>
> In Morgantown, West Virginia the crisis center closed during the summer of 1979 because of a lack of funds for maintenance and repair of the shelter. This is one of the oldest shelters in the state of West Virginia and is known for its aggressive fund raising efforts.[7]

As late as 1979, fewer than fifteen state legislatures had enacted laws funding shelters and less than half of all shelters received any state or federal monies.[8] Federal legislation to fund battered women's services, introduced first in 1977, has failed to pass the Congress.

Shelters, old and new, flourished nevertheless, and by 1982 estimates place the number of shelters and safe homes projects somewhere between 300 and 700. There is enormous variation from state to state in the number of shelters; in 1980, for example, Arkansas had four shelters and California sixty-eight. While Maine had five shelters and three safe homes projects, Kansas had three of each and New Hampshire four refuges and five safe homes networks. Minnesota reported seventeen shelters, all of which provided hotline services, as well as four separate crisis hotlines for battered women.[9] Across the country, the labor of thousands of women has made possible the development and expansion of essential services.

The Search for Legitimacy and Funding

As the movement grew, shelters with diverse philosophies and goals faced some common tasks and problems. Local groups had to convince sometimes skeptical communities and funding agencies that their shelter legitimately represented battered women. Maneuvers to gain credibility reveal a flexible, strategically astute movement aware of the odds it faced. As strategies are detailed, it must be kept in mind that political and economic circumstances varied extensively from state to state and from rural to urban areas. Activists knew that a feminist analysis of violence against women might win support in Boston or Chicago while the same views would destroy all possibilities of ever opening a shelter in a rural area. For example, in Boston, a strong, diverse women's movement existed years before Transition House opened and was able to organize resources and networks quickly on behalf of battered women. California had sprawling, lively feminist and grassroots political movements, whereas in other states, where support for social services was minimal, it was difficult to keep even a few shelters open. Success was never solely dependent on the women involved and their skills, nor were choices necessarily rooted in philosophical ideals.

> Our strongest support has to come from conservative organizations in our community—the Baptist Church, the Y, the United Way. Public funds aren't available in our town except for the police and fire departments and small services. We simply had to become part of the local Y to survive. We had to call the problem family violence, not battered women. Program development consists of taking what you can get and going with it. We don't have the luxury to choose our resources.[10]

Publicizing the experiences of battered women as victims of male violence and social indifference was the most commonly chosen form of legitimating the need for a shelter. As one woman stated, "No one is in favor of domestic violence."[11]

Throughout the country, women's groups tell animated stories about efforts to legitimate their activities. Some groups moved into buildings, declared their need, and squeaked by for months on courage, hard work, and the intense energy they generated. Their efforts moved people to respond. Others, the majority, spent years lobbying, testifying, and writing grants. Almost all relied heavily on educational forums, public hearings, radio, and television to reconceptualize the issue and explain its parameters, stressing that woman abuse was a community responsibility rather than an interpersonal "problem." Often, months or years were spent gathering allies among legislators, agency directors, and foundation staff and convincing them that a problem and a constituency existed. Elected officials and the many state and local Commissions on the Status of Women held hearings which legitimated the issue. Battered women came forward along with activists and professionals to testify repeatedly to the desperate need that mandated shelter funding. In many cities, women's clubs, the Junior League, or the National Council of Jewish Women responded as needed allies during hearings and supplied small grants or volunteers.

For change to occur, strategies had to be matched by persistence, skill, unpredictable luck, and even tragedy. In one state, feminists spent three years constantly lobbying their Public Welfare Department for funding with no results; the next year, a supportive woman became director and substantial funding was granted immediately to programs statewide. In another, as legislators debated the first domestic violence bill and women lobbied around the clock, two battered women were murdered by their husbands. Legislation was enacted rapidly. As one activist recalls, "Our local Junior League had a member whose husband killed her right after she had complained about him at a Junior League meeting. They became immediate supporters of the shelter, helping us enormously."[12]

Because women's groups established services long before other organizations offered any help to battered women, many funding agencies and community institutions were moved, sometimes begrudgingly, to trust them and use their programs. In huge numbers, battered women also turned to these new organizations which, unlike other agencies, provided the concrete assistance needed. The fact that most shelters stayed full from the first day they opened spoke most eloquently in the search for legitimacy and funding that continues to this day.

Acquiring and transmitting skills at a breathtaking rate, shelters moved to gain as much as possible for battered women from sometimes recalcitrant, endlessly delaying bureaucracies. Persistence and hard work were crucial as were patience and self-control in the face of condescension and sexist jokes about abused women and the cute "girls" helping them. The following description reveals the picayune, time-consuming work done to master bureaucratic detail and gain enough funding to keep the doors open.

> The county has a vendor system that pays Women's Advocates $5.50 per day room and board per woman and $2 per day per child up to 30 days. This is an emergency housing measure paid from county welfare emergency funds....
>
> We also receive purchase-of-services funds under Title XX, for which residents qualify as persons who suffer from "neglect, abuse and exploitation." We are considered providers of counseling and advocacy services. These kinds of funding entail paperwork, but we have been able to devise reporting methods that maintain confidentiality.... Our concern for the safety of the residents made it necessary for us to work out procedures with the welfare department that do not reveal a woman's whereabouts to anyone.... The job is never done. New people join the department and we have to explain again....
>
> Our house has been designated a day-care center, which makes us eligible for funding under the Minnesota Child Care Facilities Act. We are also a group family day-care home, which entitles us to food commodities through a U.S. Department of Agriculture program...[13]

The most basic, seemingly trivial, but lifesaving, systemic changes had to be negotiated. For example, in some states, women were not legally allowed to live in communal facilities with their own children. The public schools caused nightmares, as La Casa de Las Madres notes.

> As soon as they find the new address, they will give it to the father,...the principal most of the time is a male and will call up the fathers and let them know where his children are.[14]

Efforts to buy and finance buildings to serve as shelters were foiled again and again.

> After making the downpayment on our house, we owed $24,000....we found that we were unable to qualify for any kind of home mortgage. We finally secured a conventional loan for $24,000, due in 2 years, interest rate about 12 percent. Our search for funds to pay off the mortgage began immediately. St. Paul HRA met with us and discovered they did not have a definition for emergency housing that would cover us. Eventually Urban League, Migrants in Action, and Women's Advocates, aided by the St. Paul Community Development Office, prepared a joint emergency housing proposal for community development block grant funds. Women's Advocates' share was $36,000.[15]

Almost universally, the expansion of shelters continues to entail a draining search for money. Even after years of persistent activity, Women's Advocates reported it was still chronically short of funding.

Raising capital funds, which is money to purchase and maintain building, furniture, and equipment, has been very difficult, and has created unnecessary hardship. Energy that could go into the program for women and children is used for bare survival in an overcrowded, inadequate house.[16]

In addition to providing room and board for victims of abuse, shelters worked to protect battered women's rights, a more difficult and elusive task than it would seem. Advocates were forced to know more than the local welfare or police bureaucrats who often ran circles around uninformed clients, denying them their legal rights through technicalities. Any shelter resident might find herself in Family, Criminal, or Divorce Court; she might need welfare benefits or have to sign up on a waiting list for a low-cost apartment from the Housing Authority. At any moment, if criminal charges were pressed or injuries noted, the police, the Bureau of Child Welfare, and a hospital might also become involved. Staff and volunteers were extensively trained in advocacy and spent a substantial amount of time accompanying battered women through court or welfare centers, writing letters for them or making phone calls. As one advocate said, "You have to do a million things to get one woman help."

Once activists mastered the details of various bureaucracies, they worked to convey the information to battered women, shelter advocates, and the constant stream of professionals who called for advice. Literally hundreds of legal rights, welfare rights, and counseling manuals were written, revised constantly, and distributed through battered women's shelters. In New York, 85,000 copies of *A Handbook for Beaten Women*, written and published by South Brooklyn Legal Services' staff, were distributed in a twelve week period during 1977.[17]

Not only did women in the movement help individuals through the bureaucratic maze, they also spent much time attempting to change regulations and establish new procedures. Shelter staff have negotiated with and lectured to thousands of personnel in hospitals, police departments, and social service agencies. They often met with success on this front, and new regulations eased the situation for battered women. In large cities, however, change is difficult to monitor and maintain and so has generally been less effective.

Confronting Key Issues

As funding became more available and more staff was hired, shelters could begin to plan more extensive programs. Finally, there was time to write brochures, pamphlets, newsletters, and additional grants. Hotline and shelter shifts were more smoothly coordinated, easing the seven day a week, twenty-four hour a day burden on some. Records could be maintained and systems developed for coping with the hundreds of inquiries that arrived monthly. Community education specialists might plan education and prevention efforts within the neighborhood, reaching out to other community agencies as well as to battered women. As staff expanded, most shelters, if they did not already have them, instituted regular staff and program planning meetings and continued the house and resident support group meetings. Often, courses or "rap" groups on topics like parenting were introduced for current or former residents.

With room to examine important concerns, certain key issues emerged. One of them related to children, who comprise *at least* 2/3 of shelter residents in most cases. It became increasingly evident that children, living with multiple forms of stress, had pressing needs and felt intense guilt, confusion, and fear. Fleeing from violence and seeing their mothers brutalized, they also have left familiar ways of operating, their homes and neighborhoods, cherished possessions, and sometimes fathers they love.

Initially, shelter workers tended not to be focused on the children.

> A lot of staff and volunteers don't see the kids, don't think about them, avoid them, or are fearful of them. You need to prepare volunteers. Sometimes volunteers think that working with the kids is a lesser task than working with the women. If you are really supportive of the women, you've got to deal with the kids.[18]

The deeper reluctance to work with children emerged poignantly in another conversation, where an activist recalled that some of the shelter workers found it too difficult to consider the needs of the children because it brought back the pain of their own childhood experiences, which included physical abuse. She comments, "This was a clue; we had to look at and learn from the negativity we had experienced as kids so that we would not in turn perpetuate it." This shelter worker went on to describe how they tried to sensitize staff to the children.

> Now in all our training, we ask people to think about a time when they

were hurt or in a tough situation as a child. We ask them to imagine assisting themselves as a child in a bad spot and we share and write on the board all the things children wanted. It's very powerful. They could remember what kids needed. It gave insight and confidence about what to do with kids, the rights of the mother, and it gave dignity to the role of being a friend to the child. They saw they were important as non-parents.[19]

Many battered women's shelters now coordinate some form of children's program, including child care for pre-schoolers and afternoon programs for children when they come back from neighborhood schools. In one locale, foster grandparents watch the children during the day while their mothers are in court or apartment hunting. This shelter had used a child care specialist but recently had lost funding. In many places, children's advocates are now an integral part of the shelter.

The children's advocates offer a supportive and creative child care program every weekday. Three mornings a week mothers meet with the child care staff to discuss special needs and issues. The children's staff works with both the mother and her children to try to provide support for their relationship. Assertiveness training is integrated into contact with the mothers and their children. Child care workers are alert for signs of child abuse and offer counseling or referral when appropriate.

The children's advocate also serves as a liaison with community agencies. She may make contact with the schools, help mothers find child care or temporary foster care, and put women in touch with single-parent resource centers or support groups.[20]

In many shelters, difficulties arise over how to deal with violence directed against children. One activist describes the complexity of the issue.

I wrote the first non-violence policy for the shelter...The first confrontation I had with a woman who hit her kid with a belt was horrible. All the residents were angry at me. I realized I needed a relationship with the woman to deal with these heavy issues. To do good by the kids I really needed to know their mothers.

Out of this conflict we got a discussion going on taking frustrations out on kids and it was good. Parenting discussions happen regularly now, but we don't just talk about parenting; we are dealing with relationships between people.[21]

Although many advocates had to ferret out their own motivations, scrutinize middle class value systems, and face the difficulty of intervening in a family at a time when the mother is most vulnerable, gentle confrontations about child abuse have become a standard part of most program's policies. Nonviolence has been taken seriously as a way of living in most shelters, even as confusion reigns about its exact definition and parameters.

Within shelters, conflicts between women can come out through their children. Some children intimidate their peers and others arrive enraged. Racist comments become a way for children to cope with terrors about their new environment. Special programs help integrate children into the shelter, allowing them to adjust and express their worries, just as parenting discussions alleviate some of the intense anxiety mothers experience about raising children alone.

In shelters, staff and residents also must learn to live together. In many cases, workers initially tried too hard to make the house nonpunitive; then when problems erupted, they would react by drawing up endless lists of rules. Residents sometimes hated the restrictions and complained bitterly.

> Oh my goodness, those awful house rules! I began to think I was in a branch of the armed forces. The rules were to be enforced without exception. At seven a.m. the residents had to get up and get themselves and their children downstairs for breakfast at seven-thirty. At noon, lunch was served, and don't be late![22]

In this large shelter, rules were strictly enforced. However, size and chaos are only two explanations for the proliferation of rules. One activist notes that

> you often don't have control over your work in a shelter. Everything happens at once; women come and go so you make rules to deal with the lack of control. For some people who can't stand paradox and conflict, they get rigid or turn on the residents by making rules. It is a way to distance and control people without getting at the real issues. Some residents are favorites and others can't do anything right. For some reason, we don't feel comfortable and don't admit it. Maybe it's a kind of fear of getting hurt; maybe it's burnout and being too needy ourselves; maybe it's our classism or racism.[23]

Power and authority battles, sometimes unrecognized, abound within a shelter. Rules embody the question of who owns the program—the staff or the residents? Many residents can articulate areas over which they feel control and those they know belong to the staff. When uncomfortable issues come up, like asking a woman to leave who has constantly violated curfew or repeatedly abused a child, rule enforcement almost always falls on the staff who already have accrued more power. Because the staff usually determines a woman's admission or rejection, at best a fine balance is maintained between the shelter's rights and the residents' rights. Sometimes the balance shifts too far in the direction of staff and the shelter becomes like any other bureaucratic institution. Residents express anger when they sense that the shelter is trying to change them or the way they parent their children. One battered woman complains.

> You talk about empowering women but how many residents do you include in the power developing through the unity of the shelter network conferences?...How can you decide how to run a shelter without including battered women, women who need and use shelters?...
>
> Exclude us from your organizing, your unity, your conferences, and you will lose us. You are then only sheltering yourselves from our pain, our reality, our growth. You are then only using us, capitalizing on our pain and needs.[24]

In shelters, third world residents and staff have often felt misunderstood or tokenized. Poor women and women of color see the world differently and some have far fewer options than do white, middle class women. They may, for example, define the criminal justice system as an enemy to their community as well as protection from a violent man. Because of racism, relocating in a new town may feel impossible; walking around the strange neighborhood surrounding the shelter may be frightening, not exciting. Yet, painfully, these realities have often been ignored by white women.

Frequently, third world staff felt that they had to downplay their commitment to their own communities. They criticized feminism for claiming that all men are the same oppressive enemy and thereby ignoring the discrimination and lack of power experienced by third world men. For some third world women, newly hired in shelters, feminism seemed to mean "individual women striving to get ahead." Racial tensions erupted all over the country.

> I came to the issue with skills, not with a political analysis. They needed women of color. The crucial issue of bringing third world women into organizations is isolation and tokenism. When you bring a woman of color into a group, it says you are about change. It felt like to me, "everything was fine until you got here." Often, white women view racism as an isolated topic—"don't raise it now; it is not the appropriate time; save how you feel for the larger conversation, the biggie."
>
> In retrospect, I was in a lot of pain. There were allies in the organization I worked in. Yet I often felt I had to make a choice between being a black woman or being a woman in a feminist collective.[25]

As a result of early struggles against racism, some shelters' staff now reflect the ethnic and racial diversity of its residents. These programs have regularized racism awareness workshops as a mandatory part of all staff and volunteer training. One shelter reports that

> new CETA positions are enabling us to increase our training efforts, especially for non-white women and ex-residents. To ensure this transfer of information and skills, we now have a 24-month limit on employment here, during which time training will be on-going....In addition, we have struggled hard to deal with our own institutional racism and feel proud of our achievements in having a predominantly non-white and bicultural/bilingual staff.[26]

In many places, however, little has changed.

For shelter workers, the difficult issues are not only the ones that can be given clear labels, like racism and child abuse. A central dilemma is maintaining the precarious balance between being supportive and caring and yet avoiding smothering or infantilizing a battered woman. Workers often experience self-doubts about their effectiveness and they sometimes feel torn between the need to help individual women and the ongoing work of keeping the shelter functioning. Worker after worker, however, emphasized that "no matter what, the women must stay our focus; we must be flexible and caring."

In response to the question—"If someone were taking a job in a shelter, what would you advise?"—a woman who had worked in a shelter for less than a year reports her struggles.

> I would clue you in to the ups and downs. You get self-doubts, feel like you aren't doing enough. You get frustrated when women go back to their husbands. It's a whole different pace here. I used to feel I wasn't getting any work done...Sometimes I feel when a woman goes home that I could have done more. Someone at court treated her badly; she lost self-confidence and went home. I could have gone with her.

This worker went on to describe the ups and downs of shelter life.

> Fights blow up. Tensions come out around cleaning and disciplining kids, but they often are about anger, hurt, and loneliness. We have a house meeting after the blow-up; there is enormous support. Women say, "We're upset; I went through what she's going through, too." Discussions bring the women back together. It's the best part of the shelter.
>
> The most pressing part of the daily work is meeting women's needs. It's so hard because so much else also has to be done—training, supervising. I can never get my work done.[27]

Compare her comments to those offered by a battered woman who stayed in the same shelter and then went on to volunteer there.

> Coming here was the best thing that ever happened to me. I thought
> the shelter was going to be a building with lots of beds, but instead it's
> like home. You have time to think. People here helped you, but you
> knew when you did something it was your idea.
> We came here with 57¢ and the clothes on our backs and it was the
> best thing I ever did. I had to ask him when I could go to the bathroom or
> when I could use the phone.

Shelter life is difficult and sometimes terribly depressing.
Although renewed energy comes through watching women change
or give encouragement and hope to others, shelter workers live with
the knowledge that at any time, a woman who has lived in the shelter
might be hurt or killed by her husband.

> Millie Davis, a woman who had stayed at Transition House last winter
> and then left to live with her mother, was brutally murdered in March
> by her former batterer, a man she had not seen for months and
> probably thought she had finally escaped.[28]

Many workers worry about the women who leave, seemingly safe,
and those who are hounded by their husbands or return to them. As
shelters, filled to capacity, turn away battered women, workers
must cope with the sense that they are never doing enough.

Over time, shelter staff, with the assistance of residents, have
come to learn how to help women live together successfully. So many
levels of communication occur at once within a shelter that good
group and interpersonal skills are extremely important. For example, fights explode over a child's behavior when in reality each
mother involved is frightened and upset as she fantasizes about her
unpredictable future. Or a resident forgets to cook and twenty
women and children are angry, without dinner. Staff become experts
at sensing tension and aiding women to sort out the real reasons for
conflict and unhappiness.

Money, the Mixed Blessing

After subsisting on minimal amounts of money for six to
eighteen months, most shelters concluded that government funding
was imperative. Monthly pledges and foundation grants could not
pay bills based on expanding staff, programs, and the larger facilities
sought as shelters. Funding, though never adequate, brought many
advantages to battered women's shelters. Some women could be paid

regularly for their work and staff and volunteers could be trained more effectively. Problems could be met with consistent and systematic responses. Most importantly, the shelter received external support and validation. Police, judges, and welfare workers were forced to listen more carefully because shelters now asserted a reinforced claim as legitimate community institutions. It no longer seemed that the doors would close at any moment. Survival carried with it the hope of building institutions that could respond credibly to the myriad problems battered women presented.

Money, however, was not the unmixed blessing it originally seemed. A larger funding base sometimes undermined important movement principles. Shelters that chose to expand often saw themselves transformed in unpredictable, unwanted ways.

> I've seen this house go through many changes. The staff was originally all volunteer, deeply committed, and collective. At the beginning there was no money. As we got a little, I always knew how the house was run and how decisions were made.
> Then a director was hired who was here during the day. Lots of volunteers dropped out and now only work at night and on the weekends. We have more staff. I don't feel in control of the whole at all. I worry we are becoming another social service agency. We have debts for rehabilitation and we're tied to needing money.

This advocate details changes in the division of labor and in resident-staff interactions that are repeated throughout the United States in those programs that have expanded.

> There is a split between administrative and service work. We all have separate offices, which we never had before, and work specializations.
> We have communication meetings for staff to deal with their feelings about their work once a week. This is a positive development but you also worry about forming a "professional" skills attitude. You have to remember where you came from—battering could happen to me. Now we have formalized case reviews. In some ways it is useful because you pay attention to individual women and staff perceptions of each woman are examined. It's good because personal feelings get involved all the time. All of us are racist, judge other people, and sometimes treat them poorly. A more formal process can control gossip and help you understand yourself. But it can also create distance between you and the residents.

Increased specialization transformed more than the organizational structure.

> I don't feel we are part of a movement to end violence against women

any more. People are hired only to do specific jobs, not to be part of a movement. I don't want to be split off. If you know how to do everything, you feel more in control. If there is no strict division of labor, it's better.[29]

Changes sometimes occurred because there was too much to be done and hierarchical structures appeared to be the solution to overwork. At other times, however, funding sources explicitly influenced organizational and structural changes.

> We desperately need money and need to institutionalize. United Way criteria, however, mean having a board that sets policies, a director who directs, and salaries based on title, not need. We have never operated that way. Staff resents that salaries and policies will be determined by the board. The staff and board are becoming very separate. Staff is furious about losing control. Until now, salaries have been based on need, one criteria being the number of children each staff member has. It's ironic that we've never been on more solid ground financially and more unhappy. I can't sleep at night. The board is pushing me one way and raising lots of money, and the staff is pushing me in another.[30]

In approaching funders and community groups, activists encountered charitable and professional values that emphasized helping the "needy" and often unwittingly assigned to women the permanent status of helpless "victim." The pervasive influence of psychological explanations for social problems was seen as funding agency after funding agency defined battered women as a mental health issue.

As funding increased, even the most politically sophisticated programs noted subtle changes in their treatment of women residents. For example, when individual shelters fought for and won welfare or Title XX reimbursements, they also had to fill out forms and account for "units of client services." Many of these "units" are credited according to the individual counseling and advocacy sessions provided. As a result, worker after worker has commented that she slowly and unconsciously started to call battered women "clients." Greater attention was paid to the individual woman's counseling needs and less to group sharing, peer support, and teaching battered women to advocate for one another.

In many cases, the funding agencies downplayed or discouraged social change. Federal Title XX funds can be used for services only, not for community education. Helping victims was tolerable while changing the social conditions that created these victims was far less desirable, measurable, or fundable.

In the constant search for legitimacy and credibility, hiring professionals seemed like one way to placate the funding sources. And in some states funding agencies required that a social worker with a master's degree supervise all paid staff. Other states are beginning to demand similar qualifications, although in many areas such requirements have not been placed on battered women's programs.

It was easy for external pressures to turn into internal ones. Many shelters decided that social workers and lawyers not only had needed group and organizational skills, but also might make funding negotiations less arduous. Many women felt bullied by bureaucracies or their own boards of directors or worried about their competence in working with battered women or their legitimacy within the social service "community." Uncertain about how to proceed, they gave in, changed their structures, or hired more professionals, sometimes later regretting these choices.

Usually, funding agencies did not consciously intend to undermine the work of the battered women's movement. They simply expected battered women's programs to respond like every other social service organization. The movement held different views, and clashes and compromises from both sides would occupy significant movement energy for the next several years.

However, funding agencies not only influenced the battered women's movement, but were also prodded consciously and forcefully by it. One group explains:

> We consider fundraising one form of class advocacy for battered women. In 1973, there were no funding rules, regulations, or guidelines which mentioned the needs of women who suffered physical abuse in their homes. Our class advocacy and fundraising were nearly always inseparable because we had to explain the problem before any money was given to help us in our work.[31]

A further description of how one group mobilized to obtain a Community Development Block Grant to pay for shelter services underscores the importance of organizing. Asking the Minnesota Housing Authority for $57,500 out of its $12 million budget, employees, uniting in their own Women's Union, found that:

> the Commissioners (six men and one woman) rejected the proposal because it was "sexist" in that men would be excluded from using the proposed shelter. The vote was six to one against.

The women refused to accept the absurd decision without a fight.

The Women's Union continued to work to gain key support for their proposal with the intent of presenting it again to the Commissioners. Since the Housing Authority had received its CDBG funds through the City Council, the Women's Union decided to ask all members of the Council to write letters of support; seven of the thirteen members did. Legislators instrumental to the passage of legislation proposed by the Housing Authority were asked to write letters of support; over a dozen did. In addition, members of several well organized and powerful neighborhood organizations were asked to contact the Commissioners representing their respective communities urging them to accept the proposal; four of the six Commissioners received a number of calls from neighborhood leaders.

The stakes escalated. As a well organized opposition, planning its strategy carefully, women forced the Commissioners to reconsider.

Attending the board meeting with members of the Women's Union were "credentialed professionals" from the city attorney's office, counseling programs, hospitals, child abuse teams, churches, the League of Women Voters, Women's Advocates...and dozens of other groups and agencies which provide services to battered women. Over thirty people gave brief but powerful presentations clearly demonstrating how lack of affordable emergency housing perpetuates violence against women. The presentations ended with that of a legal aid attorney addressing the question of suits against the authority because of sexism, pointing out that state law permits operation of housing programs for special populations. As newspaper reporters, TV cameras, and radio microphones edged to the front of the room, a motion was made to grant the $57,500 to fund the Women's Union proposal; the motion carried unanimously...[32]

In some states, individual shelters still face these kinds of struggles alone; in others, like Pennsylvania and Illinois, statewide women's coalitions now receive grants that they distribute to their member programs. In still others, like Massachusetts, grants are made to individual shelters, but the statewide coalitions serve as strategy making bodies and as negotiating buffers. In all these cases, the fear and reality of cutbacks have forced grassroots groups to mobilize every year. At any time, one conservative legislator or bureaucrat can introduce damaging fiscal or regulatory amendments that might undermine shelter autonomy. In many states, hundreds of hours are spent strategizing as well as establishing and maintaining relationships with state agencies. The Community Development Block Grant story cited earlier describes best how obstacles are turned into challenges. Despite victories like this however, the government (as the stronger party) has forced shelters, often subtly, to modify practices and procedures. When women made the choice to provide costly services, the deck was stacked against them, particularly in those places without powerful enough feminist or progressive coalitions.

Decisions About Structure

Because shelters started small, structure seemed to take care of itself early in the movement. With expansion, however, came complex questions about how to best organize work and decision making. Some shelters chose to work collectively, others organized on a hierarchical basis, and many developed structures that are modified versions of collectives or hierarchies.

Hierarchies are organizational forms which limit access to information and resources to a select group, or, conversely, give specific people, like directors, more information, status, and resources. For a variety of reasons, most groups within the battered women's movement have moved toward some form of hierarchical structure. The advantages of a hierarchy are that power and accountability are presumed to be clearly and honestly acknowledged, and work appears to be accomplished more efficiently. Workers who are not movement activists find their tasks and commitments clearly delineated. And, perhaps most important, hierarchy is the most familiar organizational form, and so seems to be the simplest to implement.

Despite these advantages, many in the battered women's movement find hierarchies problematic. Multiple leadership potential is often squashed, participation may be discouraged, and workers tend to identify with their job or organization, rather than with the movement. Since access to information is limited, power belongs to a few. Uninteresting jobs may be assigned to volunteer workers or new staff. The political goal of ending domination is frequently obscured as the organizational leadership develops a vested interest in remaining unchallenged. Women as a group learn fewer skills, gain less self-confidence, and must again defer to the authority of others—a poor model for battered women.

Those who have worked successfully in collectives evaluate their strengths compared to hierarchies. Collectives create a model of women working together and respecting one another which inspires battered women and demonstrates an alternative to the domination they have experienced. Work is far less alienating because thinking and planning are not separated from doing.

Autonomy and skill development are encouraged, as are high levels of participation in the organization. Many have the opportunity to exert leadership. Collectives encourage individual initiative; at the same time, through consensus, they allow "the wisdom of the group" to emerge.

Those with unhappy experiences in collectives cite the potential tyrannies of the model. Although power is supposed to reside with all, it almost always accrues to a select group, those with more time to give or more skills, who can then deny they have it. The pretense of equality frequently leads to hidden power struggles and "trashing" and can feel more oppressive than hierarchy. Collectives have been criticized for poor internal accountability mechanisms, for failure to accomplish administrative work, and for spending inordinate amounts of time on "process," rather than on accomplishing tasks. Consensus decision making, a feature of most collectives, works only if there is substantial political agreement and respect. One person can easily sabotage the process, and collectives have been notoriously bad at confrontation and conflict resolution.

One of the most difficult problems is worker accountability. Some successful collectives say that ensuring accountability lies with the task group or committee; others designate an individual supervisor; and still others publicly list all tasks and responsibilities, reviewing them each week at staff meetings. Most agree that there is a need to publicly state penalties for failure to perform tasks, time lines for completion of work, and evaluation criteria for all workers, paid or unpaid.

Today, collectives face a persistent dilemma whose resolution is central to the survival of feminist organizations—how to deal with different skills within the collective and the values socially ascribed to them. For example, fundraising has more status than grocery shopping. Collectives must learn to face the competition among staff for leadership, power, and recognition; they must attempt to allow individuals to learn new skills while still making sure that work is accomplished.

Collectives that have survived tend to reexamine their work structures, plan directions, set long-range goals, and build in accountability mechanisms. Women's Advocates explains one of its restructuring decisions.

> Allocating time to the business work of the shelter was a radical departure from our idealistic struggle to keep business from infringing on our real work....We finally gave in to the need to provide adequate time for these tasks and to support each other in learning these

necessary survival skills.
Each staff advocate is a member of one of the three principle task forces. Her time and energy are focused in either the Women's Program, Children's Program, or Business work of the shelter. We may move from one task force to another whenever exchanges are possible. Task forces meet weekly to organize and coordinate their work.[33]

Some programs that now function as hierarchies point out that they would have preferred to run collectively, but had little or no experience with this form. Without prior knowledge or training, chaos reigned and sometimes became overwhelming and destructive for residents and staff. Staff responded by adopting more familiar and internally manageable forms. Other women had to start their shelters within traditional social service agencies where collectivity was actively discouraged. At present only a small number of shelters operate as collectives.

Most women, confronted with difficult circumstances and pressures, expressed their feminism in interesting ways by creating what they label "modified hierarchies" or "modified collectives." On paper, the organization may resemble a traditional hierarchy. Information, however, is openly shared and staff and residents alike have input into decision making. Consensus decision making processes are still the ideal, although not always the reality. Within these modified hierarchies, cooperation and shared decision making keep alive the feminist vision.

But sustaining a feminist perspective within a traditional structure is not always easy. Most often, a shelter that moved toward a hierarchical structure hired a director or coordinator and created a board of directors that retained policy making power over the shelter. The board often took active responsibility for helping shelters incorporate, setting up personnel policies and procedures, determining budgets, raising funds, and writing job descriptions. Board members often provided expertise and committed themselves to the shelter's survival, including volunteering at it. Many boards continued to respect the importance of internal democracy by leaving most policy and day to day decisions to the staff and residents. Disagreements between shelter staff and boards, however, have exploded frequently. Many board members stopped working within the shelter or indeed were invited to join boards without any knowledge of nontraditional organizations or battered women. Many people without the direct experiences in shelters that politicized early supporters were sought as board members; they had valuable contacts for fundraising or essential skills which shelters

could never afford to purchase. Their personal and political resources and connections to mainstream institutions were essential
to insure shelter survival.

Some shelters failed to recognize that boards could wield
considerable power. Clashes were inevitable and often erupted in the
middle of a fiscal or personnel crisis when the board, seeing itself as
legally responsible for the shelter, moved to "straighten out the
mess," as they perceived it. One director describes months of
agonizing board/staff conflict, which she claims as the worst
problem of her four year old shelter.

> The staff and board spend lots of time at odds. The board uses a lot of
> guilt and blame instead of constructively dealing with problems by
> asking why they happened in the first place.
> The board thinks it has to be in control of a staff that works
> cooperatively and doesn't see the conflict this creates.
> The board doesn't recognize that this is new for all of us. Many board
> members are coming from a non-feminist, helping professions model of
> work. How can they be involved if they can't identify with the problem?
> The board has a good philosophy but they don't understand what this
> philosophy means in practice.[34]

In one shelter, the board demanded that the director "keep her staff
in line" while the director asserted that staff had the right to
participate with full access to information. In other cases, however,
staff found themselves insisting on their rights while the director
and the board formed an alliance against them. Disagreements also
emerged over models for helping battered women, with the board
emphasizing traditional counseling approaches and the staff stressing self-help.

In her dissertation, "Battered Women and the Shelter Movement," Kathleen Joan Ferraro points out that board-staff conflicts
were not necessarily between feminists and non-feminists. Rather,
some conflicts were simply bids for power among women who
professed the same politics. In her study she observed that, "the
alleged formalization and professionalization of the shelter was a
guise for promoting individual interests...What happened at the
shelter was a product of interaction between individual interests and
the structure imposed by the funding agency."[35] We can conjecture
that in some shelters women used staff and board positions to insure
that their political views prevailed, but in others they were used to
acquire power for its own sake. These problems became more visible
as shelters expanded.

Especially in very large shelters with thirty or more residents and fifteen or more staff, expansion meant that every aspect of work had to be renegotiated. Shelter founders and directors often became full time administrators, a role that some of them disparaged, avoided, or were ill equipped to handle. Boards had to assume frightening responsibilities for finances and the shelter's future. Residents were sometimes lost in the shuffle. With so many paid staff, resident control slipped away as did volunteer involvement.

Expansion raises questions about which jobs should be salaried and who should be hired. Is priority given to volunteers, to professionals, or to former battered women? In answering these questions, shelters make decisions about who and what they designate as most important. When organizations reach this stage, they often find that volunteers feel mistrust and anger at paid staff, who, in addition to earning money, seem to accrue more information and skills while volunteers lose power. One activist speaks of the need to guard against the tendency for paid staff to control the shelter.

> We face the danger that the place gets run by paid staff. Our core coordinating meeting had been during the day and now it is at night so volunteer staff can come. There is a constant tension between control by paid staff and control by the people who work less. If volunteers aren't on committees, things aren't going well. This is how we evaluate the shelter. It's a continual process. How do we keep it young?[36]

Growing organizations must frequently decide how to devise or modify a board structure. Some groups designate two simultaneous boards: one a working board composed of shelter volunteers, former residents, staff, and community members and another an advisory board of professionals who provide legitimacy and skills but are allowed no real policy making power. Some grant a board authority as a court of appeals for staff conflicts and as a fundraising body but leave policy making in the hands of residents and staff. Whatever structure is agreed upon, it is imperative that contracts between a shelter board and staff designate areas of control and responsibility; a commitment to empower battered women must be part of these agreements.[37]

Not all feminist shelters have had to confront problems of expansion. Through a lack of funding or by choice, many shelters stayed small. Even in these, however, struggles over politics or between staff and boards have emerged. A scramble for funding and survival keeps these shelters endlessly busy and frustrated. Yet with a small staff, interactions with battered women remain more personal, less governed by rules; trust and shared understandings among staff are maintained more easily. Residents in these settings must assume substantial responsibility for the shelter's daily functioning; staff simply do not have the time.

Despite the pressures that come with growth, some shelters have retained egalitarian work structures even after major expansion; women's political commitments have helped them through hard times. Transition House and Women's Advocates are still collectives; within them, old-timers. worry about specialization or staff's assumption of too much control, but equality is still the goal. Here too, funding and daily crises occupy too much time and sometimes community outreach and education efforts suffer. Yet these shelters continue to serve as models, and in the 1980s, throughout the country, women are again talking about the feminist roots of the movement and how their vision was sometimes shoved aside in the push to provide essential services, build organizations, and endure.

Collectives remind themselves that if a commitment to democracy and participation is to be lived, then the criteria for success is not just the accumulation of programs and money. They recognize how quickly efficiency replaces participation and build in mechanisms to challenge the abuse of authority and power. They encourage many women to get involved in committee and house meetings. The task is not easy, especially for those shelters honestly working to incorporate diversity among women.

> Our philosophy is that violence perpetuates women's lack of power. But how do you live out an empowering norm when women are coming together collectively for the first time from different backgrounds, classes, and races. Some women are street wise; some aren't. The shelter itself has to be kept running. You need a basis of operation, which is a political issue, but how do you make it happen with constant crises and staff problems?[38]

Diversity and Tensions Within the Shelter Movement

As shelters hired more staff, women with diverse political and personal motivations found themselves working together. Any one shelter might include radical feminists, feminists with a professional perspective, former battered women, non-feminist professionals, and women who viewed their work primarily as a way to earn a living. The bond that held this diversity together was helping battered women. Yet early movement organizers, who erroneously assumed that everyone still shared the same goals and perspectives, frequently felt betrayed when they found themselves in angry, unexpected confrontations over values and politics. One shelter founder laments: "As the staff has expanded, the primary question has become, can we even trust each other?"[39]

With staff expansion, common assumptions about the shelter are sometimes lost. In separate interviews at the same shelter, divergent views were revealed. A veteran staff person described the organization as "a feminist emergency shelter for women based on ideas of self-determination and empowerment." The newly hired staff person disagreed and commented that "the staff still thinks of this as an emergency shelter; the problem comes out of the name itself. We [the staff] should be about evaluating particular families at particular times and deciding what needs to happen—whether they stay longer."[40] This new staff person, coming with professional therapy training, interacted compassionately with battered women, but for her, the shelter was not just a safe place; it was a place where battered women could and should change their "unhealthy" patterns. It is not surprising that in this rapidly growing shelter, common understandings would be reached but would then quickly evaporate.

Often differences between shelters surface over the role of battered women within service projects. The Nebraska Task Force on Domestic Violence believes that "ex-victims can sometimes be effective workers but they must be screened very carefully to be sure they have worked through all their problems and conflicts related to abuse."[41] This policy contrasts sharply with that of Transition House, which encourages "every woman, both while she is at the house and after she has left, to become part of the collective, which means maintaining the house and sharing experience and knowledge with incoming women."[42] Even among those who labeled themselves feminists, unanimity was impossible in the search to define the "appropriate" relationship between helper and victim and the proper role of battered women in the shelter movement. The Nebraska Task Force has a feminist analysis of the causes of violence against women, yet some of its policies, like those of many feminist shelters, reflect a professional bias.

> Often, however, a woman will not have resources of her own or if she does, not have money with her at the time of the crisis. Some groups

maintain an emergency fund to help women in such cases, often with the understanding that she will reimburse the fund when she can. *However, never give money directly to a client. If she needs gas or groceries, a task force member should make the purchase.* (emphasis added)[43]

How far diversity can extend, strengthening rather than undermining a feminist base of an organization or a movement, is continually being tested. Within and between shelters, and crisscrossing ideological camps, debates are raging as battered women's services confront internally encouraged and externally imposed differences. In some shelters, as definitions of legitimacy were increasingly influenced by funding sources, expediency, and professional identification, the original staff—radical feminists—were pushed out and nastily discredited.[44] In other shelters, more open dialogue seems to have eased the problem, and in still others, the struggles continue.

Although women in the movement often do not label themselves, most would fit into at least one of three categories: feminists, professionals, and grassroots women. Some Idaho shelters provide an excellent example of a type of non-feminist grassroots service developed by and for battered women. In Idaho, out of a strong belief in local autonomy, and neighbor helping neighbor, as well as an awareness that the state government would provide little financial help, women have maintained volunteer-managed shelters for three to five years. Most of these programs, with yearly budgets from $700 to $5000 per shelter, have no paid staff. Twelve to thirty local women take responsibility for the shelter's survival and advocacy for its residents. Unlike many feminist programs, these shelters have no overnight staff. Self-help and peer support is the service model. As one organizer explained, "although we offer support, battered women have been taking care of themselves before they came to the shelter; why should they be cared for in the shelter?"[45]

Committed to helping victims and ending violence against women, these organizers stay focused on battered women's immediate needs. Often they oppose introducing feminist concerns like abortion or equal rights into their work. Circumstances also affect their views. Noting the difference between Idaho and other states, one woman stressed, "We turn to the community for help; we find housing and jobs for women in our towns. We can get tougher court orders now."[46] Because of the ease with which they effect change and their belief in self-reliance, these women do not see the connection between struggles to help battered women and those for women's liberation or socialism.

Some grassroots women established shelters based on principles of cooperation, egalitarian treatment, and caring self-help that closely resemble those of radical feminists. In practice, these two kinds of shelters often share more with each other than they do with those administered by feminists who have strong career or professional motivations guiding their choices. Labels themselves can make this acknowledgment impossible as do disagreements over ideology and strategy.

In some locations, out of expediency, grassroots, feminist, and more traditional groups have united, warily admitting that without cooperation a shelter might never open. Because working with battered women tends to politically challenge and radicalize people, these cooperative ventures have sometimes proven mutually beneficial. In other places, feminist or grassroots groups keep a guarded distance from more traditional organizations or from each other. Privately and sometimes publicly, women's groups have railed at state agencies for encouraging more traditional groups to apply for funds, thus creating competition over scarce resources and supporting the development of non-feminist analyses of the issue. In spite of intense hostility, many groups put aside differences to lobby for money and increased legal protections for battered women.

As state and local governments funded battered women's services, more professionals "joined" the movement, as did professional social service organizations. As of 1982, three shelters in New York City were administered by agencies like the Henry Street Settlement House and the YMHA; a fourth, operating out of a welfare hotel, is managed by the City of New York; only one shelter in the city belongs to an autonomous women's organization.

In shelters controlled by professional social service agencies, feminism plays no stated part, although its influence is felt programmatically and through individual feminists who may join the staff. Battered women's plight is recognized as serious, even if "clients" are defined solely as recipients of services. The need for advocacy and social change, especially to facilitate women's leaving or ending violent relationships, is acknowledged although sometimes minimized. Women's weaknesses, as well as their strengths, are carefully scrutinized. These shelters often provide decent counseling, advocacy, and group supports, but place heavy emphasis on the need for individual therapy with professional counselors. Frequently, male responsibility for violence is relegated to secondary importance while a woman's personality takes center stage as the desired focus for change.

Professionals, joined by those who work within religious shelters, frequently complain that feminists, while stating their belief in battered women's right to self-determination, act differently. Feminists are accused of pushing battered women to separate from their husbands. Feminists retort that while they do not want women to reunite with violent men, most feminist shelters try to be respectful of an individual's choice to return to her husband. Because institutions most frequently encourage battered women to go home, feminists state that women have the right to hear alternative views. They add that now many professionals also want battered women to separate from abusers, but professionals are better able to mask this preference because of their seeming objectivity. In spite of overlapping views, some professionals and others angrily dismiss all feminist shelters as man-hating agencies that want to break up the family.

Feminist and grassroots activists offered persistent criticism of professionals. At the start of the movement, professional arrogance and indifference toward battered women helped mold the antiprofessional biases still operating in some programs. Feminists were the first to analyze violence against women as part of the power dynamic operating between men and women in a sexist society. By their persistence, feminist and grassroots activists forced the words "battered women" into public consciousness. Professionals then moved in to claim violence as a mental health or criminal justice problem. The political analysis disappeared, was changed, or was considered beyond the scope of professional concern.

While professionals ignored or refuted a feminist political analysis, they depended heavily on feminists' skills and information. Feminist activists had come to understand what battered women needed, and sometimes professionals used that information to start programs and gain funding without ever acknowledging its source. As professionals established "family violence" as their realm of expertise, their feminist colleagues were discredited as "not professional enough" and labeled irrelevant.

The emphasis on professionalism has created several simultaneous, contradictory tasks for the feminist battered women's movement. Shelters had to lay their claims to expertise in order to ward off competition from more traditional agencies and obtain funding. This expertise, however, had to be defined as non-professional if shelters wanted to avoid having standards placed upon them that would alter egalitarian relationships with battered women and destroy a democratic movement. Adding more difficulties, funding agencies, boards, and some staff advocated or demanded the hiring of professional directors or counseling staff in order to acquire the expertise needed to survive and help battered women. To provide services, staff needed to accrue and teach advocacy, counseling, and legal skills. As time went on, the directors of most battered women's programs were hired from the ranks of the legal and social work professions, and movement leadership became increasingly professional. Sometimes, imperceptibly, staff lost their connection to a movement in the process of learning their complicated jobs and becoming experts.

Within the feminist movement, there is disagreement over the role of professionals. Some worry, realistically, that without professionally degreed staff their agencies will suffer in grant competition. On a personal level, professional status can provide dignity to the worker as well as a sense of mastery and specialized skills. Although some middle class feminists rebuff the hierarchical privileges and higher salaries attached to professionalism, working class women often want and need the skills, money, and control over their work that professional status can offer. For these women, middle class ambivalence toward professionalism is confusing. In third world neighborhoods, some professionals have played a protective role, bringing to the community urgently needed information. Yet professional status permits and encourages domination just as it allows those who reject such privileges to share skills within an oppressed group.

Within and among shelters, conflicts grew between professionals and non-professionals and between feminists who primarily identify as professionals and those who define themselves as activists. Politics versus expediency became a source of perpetual tension. For example, many professionals urge the movement to accept any funding available while activists want politics to be kept primary in these choices. With the advantage of administrative positions and verbal and writing skills, professional women have sometimes squelched debate over political issues or manipulated fears by suggesting that without expanding programs or funding, shelters would close or lose credibility.

Differences between professionals and feminists or grassroots women also emerged over the issue of self-help. In self-help, staff were seen as organizers, not providers. Staff relationships with battered women were to be based on personal caring, honesty, and mutual growth. They saw that battered women's growth process was like their own, slow and halting, especially in relationships with men. One worker described her work as "pushing women to grow without ever telling them what to do. We express sisterly concern about what she is going through. We let her know what we're worried about."[47] Still another worker described why self-help works better for staff.

> You give information, role-play difficult situations, and support her. Staff are consciousness-raisers and educators. That way, when she gets turned down for an apartment, you can say: "It's not your fault. It's the landlord; he turned you down because you're a single woman with kids." If you play a caretaker role, you burn out.[48]

Self-help, closely related to definitions of "empowerment," is described as a process through which women, experts about their own lives, learn to know their strength. "Empowerment" combines ideas about internalizing personal and collective power and validating women's personal experiences as politically oppressive rather than self-caused or "crazy." In a feminist political context, empowerment signifies standing together as a community just as it means supportively enabling a person to take risks. Its premise is to turn individual defeats into victories through giving women tools to better control their lives and joining in collective struggle.

Citing the example of Edinburgh Women's Aid during its first year without any paid staff, Del Martin notes that self-help is not a perfect model.

> Idealistically, they had assumed that once freed from their violent home environment the residents would soon regain their self-respect and, with the occasional assistance of social workers, establish a mutual support system among themselves....
>
> The difficulties were at their worst when one of the refuges was occupied by three families with acute problems. One woman who was a manic-depressive attempted suicide; another had five children, three of whom were delinquent; the third had been released after a prolonged stay in a psychiatric ward and was incapable of controlling her three children.[49]

Most battered women do assume responsibility for themselves, their children, and the shelter. As this example points out, however, self-help only works for women without severe emotional or chemical dependency problems.

Both self-help advocates and professionals generally agree that shelter workers should be empathetic listeners who can initiate gentle confrontation while being supportive. But professionals and self-help advocates disagree on how skills should be acquired, who is the expert, and what kind of experience heals. Self-help advocates stress that battered women, those who know what it is like to be beaten, are the experts who can best help one another. While some professionals agree, many claim that specialized knowledge and status gives them authority over their clients and means that they know best.

Self-help, unlike most professional counseling models, emphasizes politicizing women's understanding of violence.

> I think shelters can politicize women and I think they should. Women have to know why violence happened to them and not continue to search to blame themselves.
> Support groups in shelters are real important. You can talk about women not trusting women, how friendships are essential, and why their isolation happened...Also you give people a language in which to talk about their problems...Battered women want to depend on themselves and know that they are whole people in charge of their lives. They feel that has been taken away from them. Women realize this and get *angry*. They say, "Damn, why am I here instead of him?"[50]

Feminist or grassroots battered women's shelters do not advocate giving political lectures to residents. Unlike most traditional agencies, however, they believe strongly that articulating the nature, extent, and meaning of male violence against women heals, stops self-blame, and offers unprecedented tools to women in their personal search to change life's seeming chaos into intelligible events.

Feminists, however, need to avoid "trashing" those who aspire to professional status or those who have attained it. A norm might be developed in which professionals are expected to share knowledge in ways that will benefit the movement and that will empower as many women as possible. Accountability to the group one represents might be the standard for anyone purporting to speak for the movement. Acquiring professional expertise should be a method for bringing skills to a movement, rather than an automatic mechanism for accruing power or leadership. Extolling professionalism and according it higher status will serve to alienate or intimidate many women and hamper efforts to build a broad-based, participatory battered women's movement.

For many in the movement, differences also surface over whether groups and individuals define themselves as providers of services, part of a women's movement, or both. Calling itself both a service and movement organization, and using a specific definition of

movement, Women's Advocates pinpoints the tension in these two
roles.

> We were driven away from the main issue, which is: How are we going
> to stop violence against women?...
>   Are we going to change the situation? Or are we just going to build a
> social service to meet the needs of abused women only to a point; we got
> that far and no further.[51]

Although shelters themselves testify to and extend political and
material changes in women's lives, many activists want more. They
assert that a movement is necessary to end violence against women,
to keep the energy and anger of shelters alive, and to remind the
government and men that a collective power is watching. Shelters
that define themselves as part of a movement, however, lament that
they have spent most of their time providing services and maintaining buildings and organizations. The need to make more
demands on the system disappears, evaporating in the daily grind.
However, the vision and the movement, defined as women helping
women and organizing to stop violence, remain emotionally and
politically primary for many shelters.

   Those who prefer not to identify with a movement say that
"quality" service should be the only goal. Helping means giving the
best possible care to each woman using the shelter and bears no
connection to building a women's movement. They believe that
"politics are messy and unnecessary. In fact, they might hurt us as
we try to reach our goals. We might unite to share skills, find more
resources, and reform institutions and laws to enhance the quality of
battered women's lives, but we are not part of a women's liberation
movement." The need for a radical challenge to the current
structured power relations between the sexes, races, or classes is
usually minimized.[52]

   Those who want to build a movement see the necessity of
challenging the status quo and reordering a society in which women
currently lack power and control over their lives. Shelters that want
to build a movement define themselves: "We as women all face a
common oppression. Millions of women are beaten and we must keep
organizing to help them; our shelter only holds thirty people at once;
it is not enough. The only way to change the system is to build a
strong women's movement that will organize and demand change.
Battered women only exist today as a social category because women
united. We must continue this work or we will lose what we have
won. Caring services are part of our vision, but providing "less" and

helping women organize themselves is the most effective long-range challenge to women's social subordination."

Although differences between and within shelters are very real, they are clearer and simpler in writing than in reality. Most women's political analysis is not so clearcut or static. A supportive shelter community enriches residents' lives with new ideas and models just as it sometimes shocks, jolts, or horrifies them; staff, living in protective women's communities, are forced to grow as they learn about realities different from their own. No one stays the same. And while diversity means that political disagreements frequently e-merge, accomplishing concrete tasks and helping women sometimes mutes divisiveness and restores cohesion. How long the unity holds, how deeply the political differences can extend, and at whose expense unity is maintained remain to be explored.

CHAPTER 5

The Movement
Organizes Itself:
State and Local Coalitions

The Pennsylvania Example

In 1976, women traveled hundreds of miles across Pennsylvania to testify at the state capitol about pending legislation affecting battered women. One woman, two years later named director of the Pennsylvania Coalition Against Domestic Violence, describes this first meeting of strangers.

> It was like instant sisters. It was like people struggling through a storm. We decided to meet every six weeks around the state to see each other's programs. I've never missed a meeting![1]

By 1982, the Pennsylvania Coalition Against Domestic Violence administers approximately two million dollars a year in state Title XX funds to its member programs, trains police and district justices around the state, administers a five-state coalition building grant and, most importantly, brings its membership together continuously for support, skills sharing, and political discussion.

In forty-eight states[2] and many large metropolitan areas, women have built coalitions, organizations comprised of groups— sometimes exclusively feminist groups and sometimes a mix of organizations—concerned about battered women. Coalition purposes are multiple and their structures and accomplishments diverse, but their importance to the movement as a whole has been immeasurable. Coalitions have provided an essential, sustaining "free space" in which workers can relax, talk, and find validation as well as solutions to perplexing problems. They are the vehicles through which lobbying and organizing have proceeded. Based on feminist principles extolling decentralization, local autonomy, and self-determination, many coalitions delicately balance the need to build a women's power base with the problem of mediating conflicting political perspectives among individuals and member organizations.

From 1976 to 1978, with no paid staff, the Pennsylvania Coalition maintained a twofold purpose: to support women from around the state who were working in isolation, and to implement the recently passed Pennsylvania Protection from Abuse Act. Pennsylvania women were determined that this new legislation, later used as a model around the country, would be enforced according to their will.

Sharing information about their programs and themselves provided the first basis for unity among this diverse group of women.

> It was an amazing emotional release to hear we weren't working in a vacuum. We spent hours just listening to each other. We all stayed in each other's homes; this was key, people had no money. We would drive through snowstorms. We wanted to stop violence against women. We formed committees; we worked hard. Magic was created. Each meeting was bonding, celebrations, healing, and empowering. Tasks were not onerous.[3]

Testifying spontaneously to the early importance of the Pennsylvania Coalition, one member stated:

> The coalition provided us with very helpful information—how to train volunteers, how to incorporate, how to start a hotline. All of this was done with no money. If there were no coalition, there would be no program in this town. We experienced the same level of support as battered women do when they come to a shelter, find out what their resources are and then make things happen.[4]

Early experiences set important ground rules for later work; trust building and sharing were viewed as central, not secondary to the coalition's success. Women saw that they could learn best from one another, rather than from supposed experts, and they came to believe that compatible goals would emerge by insisting on the continued use of democratic processes.

The Pennsylvania Coalition moved from an initial membership of seventeen organizations and no paid staff in 1976 to its 1981 figure of thirty-three active members—including twenty-one shelters—fourteen pending members, and a staff of nine. Only organizations with policy-making bodies that are "autonomous and governed by a majority of women" may be members.[5] The right of battered women to control their lives and of individual programs and the state coalition to control as much as possible on behalf of battered women have been the central tenets of organizing work, or, as one woman declared, "our essence."

The coalition's early focus on winning gains from the state and supporting its members has remained. When the Pennsylvania Department of Public Welfare allocated an original 1.7 million dollars through Title XX funds for services to battered women, the Pennsylvania Coalition, using its expertise, credibility, and years of lobbying efforts, became the grantee. This designation meant that the state coalition determined program standards as well as allocations and monitoring criteria for all battered women's services in the state receiving Title XX funds. A coalition Title XX committee reviews all funding applications, from those of members and nonmembers. An individual member organization must comply with coalition criteria; for example, its governing body "shall be representative of the community that it serves, including the population at risk."[6] Because the battered women's movement, rather than the state, allocates funds and monitors programs, an unprecedented amount of control is placed in the hands of grassroots women's organizations.

The coalition defines one of its primary purposes as "the elimination of domestic abuse of women and their dependents in the Commonwealth of Pennsylvania." Membership, by organizations only, must be committed to: 1. providing services to the victims of domestic violence; 2. exposing the roots of violence in the institutionalized subservience of women in this culture; and 3. providing quality service statewide through cooperative, non-competitive means.[7] To accomplish these purposes, the coalition has developed an elaborate working structure. Voting members come only from service organizations that are primarily women-governed. These member organizations each select a delegate to the coalition board of directors, the policy-making body. Coalition staff members are responsible to the board, to the coalition director, and to one another as part of a commitment to consensus decision making. The coalition staff provides skills and resources, such as legal or community education training, to local programs, but sees its primary role as helping member organizations turn to one another for assistance.

To carry forward a purpose like "exposing the roots of violence
in the institutionalized subservience of women" requires political
vision. Within individual shelters, plagued by constant service
demands, clarity is not always easy to attain. Coalition meetings are
a time for political discussion and serve as a vehicle in which to
stay "righteous, clear, and angry."[8] Describing a statewide coalition
retreat, one activist captures what happens.

> The fusion of service delivery with political activism for battered
> women,...was like a strong fiber woven through each retreat session....
> Rather than having participants choose from a list of prearranged
> workshops, we sat together and identified the issues most in need of
> exploration....And I found that when we broke into small groups, we
> were motivated to talk about specific topics in the light of the rest of the
> concerns of the group. Nothing that we discussed could be isolated
> from the whole consideration of the Vision of service and the
> Movement.[9]

In 1981, the Pennsylvania Coalition decided to hold regional
retreats and meetings in addition to statewide ones. Travel distances
within Pennsylvania are large and regional meetings make broad
participation easier. Regional meetings are seen as a way to involve
more women, as a mechanism for internal education, and as a tool to
build support in local programs for coalition activity. Through these
meetings, local shelter staff not only learn from one another, but also
directly experience the need to support their program's commitment
to coalition activity. As a vehicle for rooting women in the same
political analysis, the coalition exposes many to strategy sessions
and thereby develops skills vital to the movement's future. Learning
from feminists' errors in other states, Pennsylvania activists are
eager to preserve their base of support through involving the
membership.

Recently, one region spent its meeting exploring whether shelters truly empower women and then discussed the significance of the
larger women's movement for the battered women's movement.
Other statewide and regional coalition meetings have included
workshops on child snatching and the maintenance of confidential
records; counseling battered women; setting up community based
safe homes networks; community education; grassroots fundraising; working with men who batter. Training needs are defined by
the membership. In skills sessions, lively discussions flow as the
political meaning of each topic is analyzed.

The coalition newsletter is another vehicle for sharing information and analysis. One newsletter, for example, explained that

> PCADV has drafted a piece of legislation which would make communication between battered women and shelter/hotline paid and unpaid staff confidential;...
>
> PCADV members have recently had a flood of subpoenas served on shelter workers. Most of these have been directed to oral communications as well as records. The potential for widespread use of subpoenas to harass shelter workers and battered women has become apparent.[10]

The Pennsylvania Coalition newsletter not only adds to the discussion by analyzing pending legislation or detailing the latest Title XX or food stamp problem, but also reports on national battered women's movement news, self-defense cases, and important political issues like racism. Moreover the coalition has produced its own manuals on counseling, police training, shelter fiscal management, lay advocacy, and program development—useful aids for new as well as old programs.

The Pennsylvania Coalition uses every opportunity available to organize women on their own behalves and to change public consciousness. For these women, legislative change is important in and of itself, yet it is also a means for women to organize themselves and gain resources to use for other, self-defined purposes. Through working within existing legal parameters, Pennsylvania women not only win more for battered women but also, inch by inch, broaden women's collective power. Although these women, too, must deal with co-optive bureaucracies and the growing administrative tasks that funding entails, their unity brings them the strength to challenge systemic abuses and remain advocates at the same time that they use funding to proceed with their own political agenda.

Pennsylvania women attribute their success to the time they spend together, to hard work, and to careful attention to structural details. The Coalition Board of Directors meets every six weeks, and for continuity and accountability, the same member-selected representatives must attend each meeting. All committee work is done by the membership with coalition staff support. In this way the members assume responsibility for the organization and the staff is not scapegoated for coalition problems. Two-day statewide coalition meetings every six weeks are the norm. At these meetings a celebratory dinner is always followed by dancing no matter how many hours have been spent working.[11] Pennsylvania activists probably expend more time on coalition activity than women in any other state, but the rewards have been worth the effort.

Pennsylvania women admit they have far to go. Some of their

new programs, joining the coalition primarily for funding, do not subscribe to the broader political purposes. Even with a pledge to cooperate and avoid funding competition among programs, one member organization recently applied for the same source of funding as the coalition. It is difficult to hold members accountable if they are not committed to the political principles involved. Many new members share neither the political ideology nor histories of struggle common among founders. As one woman described it, "old members were always running out of money and being kicked out of buildings; we were always in crises like battered women were and the closer we are to struggle the closer we are to understanding what battered women need and what we must do politically."[12]

Individual programs and the state coalition continue to face major challenges; two million dollars, a small amount for thirty-three programs, covers only the cost for direct services, not education, advocacy, or social change. Thirty-three different programs must learn to work together and develop the same trust, sharing, vision, and group affirmation that the original seventeen programs once experienced. Moreover, as the funding conduit for state grants, the Pennsylvania Coalition now faces the unanticipated tensions inherent in being both a support system to its members and concurrently the body to which member groups are programmatically accountable. But women in Pennsylvania believe they are engaging in a unique experimental project. They are helping to set up and control high quality services, and at the same time, they are creating models of help and forms of organization based on a practice of democratically empowering those involved. A commitment to grassroots democracy and constant political discussion sustains the Pennsylvania Coalition, holds diverse groups of women together, and for now, allows them to determine the future of battered women's services in their state.

Striving for Unity in Massachusetts

In its excellent manual, *For Shelter and Beyond*, the Massachusetts Coalition of Battered Women's Service Groups explains its purpose for forming a coalition.

> Coalition building is an important step in moving beyond simply providing battered women and their children with shelter, toward finding a way to eliminate male violence against women. By coalescing, we can reach across the lines which divide us: race, class, culture, age,

and sexual preference. Our work is not simply to provide service, though that is in itself an enormous task; we need to change attitudes, raise consciousness, and take action (whether through demonstrations, direct action, lobbying, etc.). We need to gain immediate reforms while also working for long range changes. We need to build coalitions with other groups,...By coming together to share our strength, by working together to make our voices heard, and by sharing with each other what we know, we strengthen our movement.[13]

The Massachusetts Coalition affirms in its principles of unity that: 1. it is a coalition of individuals and community-based women's organizations run for women in crisis and their children; 2. it is committed to helping women acquire the information and skills necessary to control their own lives; women will not be encouraged to remain in or return to violent situations; 3. its model of working is based on self-help. Welfare and courts are not seen as solutions to battered women's problems, but as necessary aids; 4. it is committed to a violence-free society and to combatting racism, sexism, classism, heterosexism, and ageism inherent in the system under which we live. The coalition commits itself as a group and as individuals to struggle with these issues, build trust, avoid competition, and make power and leadership available to all women.[14]

Formed in June of 1978 with eleven member organizations from around the state, the Massachusetts Coalition grew to eighteen members by 1981. Although Massachusetts programs receive Title XX funds, these funds are granted through the state bureaucracy to individual programs as part of a general "women in crisis" fund. Unlike the situation in Pennsylvania, individual programs receive no money from the coalition itself. The Coalition's primary functions have been to help members set political direction for their programs and the movement and to offer a forum for sharing and developing skills. Between 1978 and 1980, an eight person coalition staff, funded through a federal Community Services Administration (CSA) grant, helped carry forward these purposes. In addition to statewide meetings, bi-monthly workshops were held in four different regions.

The extraordinary range of skills and political issues explored by the coalition is reflected in the 1981 publication of *For Shelter and Beyond*. This manual details the philosophy, tasks, skills, and information needed to effectively help battered women in shelters. It includes material about empowerment and self-help; racism awareness for white women; dealing with welfare, the police and courts.[15]

The Massachusetts Coalition performs its work through committees, which are open to any "woman who staffs in a member program," agrees with the principles of unity, and works five hours per month on any one of the following committees: fundraising, inservice training, legislation, EEO/Anti-Racism, Community Education, Membership/Ethics, Legal, Fiscal, or Personnel. An executive committee is responsible for overseeing all ongoing work, and a steering committee, consisting of one representative per group, meets quarterly and makes long-range policy decisions. General membership meetings occur approximately four times a year.[16]

In 1978, the Massachusetts Coalition defined several key areas on which to focus attention: the need for resource sharing, the need for input into the Welfare Department's new allocation of $250,000 of Title XX funds for battered women, and the need for new legislation. Women wanted to support one another and not compete for money and recognition. By 1980, much of this work had been accomplished, although women must continually keep watch over funding and legislative developments. New goals were formulated by the general membership in 1980; in effect for two years they are: 1. to help member groups develop sound internal structures and practices; 2. to support, encourage, and recognize the leadership of third world women in the community, in shelter/service groups, and in the coalition; 3. to strengthen each group's sense of itself as an organizer of a political movement; 4. to insure that work is equally empowering to all women. Emphasis should be redirected toward helping battered women use peer support and empower themselves. 5. to keep woman abuse in the public eye.[17]

In practice, these goals are not always easy to implement, and the relationship between feminism and third world women continues to be painfully struggled through by this coalition. As one black woman notes:

> My issue with this coalition is a need for a third world base of support in the shelter movement. Shelters are too white on all levels. Individual shelters need to look at outreach to third world women. People agree but little happens; the coalition has made attempts in its own hiring. However, the *member groups* of the coalition need to make a more serious commitment to actually doing this.[18]

As in Pennsylvania, issues like racism, empowering battered women, and co-optation are not of equal importance to all coalition members, although the coalition's existence creates a framework from which to raise these concerns.

The Massachusetts Coalition, like others, confronted the danger that staff, not members, would control the organization and set its direction.

> We face a contradiction. The members employ us but the staff has the vision. The staff doesn't know what it can or cannot do. What does it mean to provide leadership. Direction should come from members but it doesn't always.[19]

In 1981, the coalition's CSA funding ran out, and staff has been reduced from eight to two. The coalition must rebuild its base more strongly in local programs, and the burden is back on the membership—also beset by CETA and other state funding cuts—to define its direction. Regional meetings will be relied upon more heavily and membership criteria have evolved to include individuals as well as organizations in the hope that more battered women, working class women, and third world women will join the organization.

The Massachusetts Coalition offers a challenge to itself and to the rest of the battered women's movement. Can it forge a progressive, anti-sexist, anti-racist political agenda, remain internally united, and keep services open? Political circumstances and women's organizing activity will provide the answers over the next several years.

Diverse Coalitions

Coalition staff is a luxury that only some states enjoy. Since 1977, shelters have met monthly as the membership of the New Jersey Coalition for Battered Women. Since its inception, this coalition has had neither staff nor funding. Its focus has been on legislation, sharing skills, and monitoring member programs to insure quality service.[20] Its funding and legislative accomplishments, carried out solely through mobilizing its membership, are typical of the direction most state coalitions have taken, sometimes not as successfully as New Jersey.

> The NJCBW secured the inclusion of funding for battered women's programs in the Comprehensive Annual State Title XX Plan, ensured the provision of SLEPA* funds to shelters in 1980, and initiated actions which resulted in...additional money for shelters in the New Jersey Fiscal Year '81 budget....
>
> Chief among the Coalition's accomplishments to date are the passage of the Shelters for Victims of Domestic Violence Act...and an amendment to the municipal zoning ordinance statutes which allows

* State Law Enforcement Planning Administration

the establishment of shelters in residential areas....As a client of Legal Services of New Jersey, the NJCBW has been working on developing an Act Concerning Domestic Violence,...which is a comprehensive bill addressing current shortcomings in the implementation of available legal remedies.[21]

Six of its twelve member shelters started as grassroots, autonomous organizations; four are run by YWCA's. According to a former coalition president, feminist philosophy is assumed rather than explicit. Her explanation is typical of programs without budgets.

> We have not had extensive philosophy discussions. Individual programs are focusing on political issues now that they are not worried about toilet paper. There is no coalition staff to do work. There is a range of philosophies within the organization. As long as the service to battered women is respectful and nonjudgmental, member organizations work well together.
> There has never been time to do outreach to more women. Whoever comes—you work. We only have one day a month for our business. Only twenty active people do all the work. We don't have to know a lot about each other in order to be comfortable together and to respect each other.[22]

Because of their capacity to mobilize hundreds of women in lobbying efforts, state coalitions often prove their strength in legislative campaigns. Even before a statewide coalition existed, women from Minnesota worked carefully on every appropriation bill and legislative act concerning battered women; the first state funding bill in 1977 was formulated jointly by a state senator and a Consortium of Battered Women. Later, lobbying efforts were coordinated statewide.

> A system was established for informing and notifying organizations across the state of impending legislative action. Educational materials on all bills, lists of legislators in each region, and an information sheet were distributed. In each region, shelters or community education/advocacy groups established their own network of constituents. Every state representative was visited by constituents....[23]

In 1977, the Minnesota legislature appropriated $500,000 for four shelters and $50,000 for community education projects; in 1978, $100,000 was appropriated for two more shelters and $25,000 for mandatory data collection from state agencies and professionals. In 1979, the legislature allocated three million dollars for fifteen shelters over a two year period.[24] This increase was orchestrated carefully by the feminist advisory board and the first director of the

Minnesota Department of Corrections Battered Women's Program, the monitoring agency for state funds. When the first $50,000 in community education funds were allocated in 1977, these activists contacted women's groups in eleven state planning districts, few of whom were operating services for battered women. Distributing $2,800 to each of these groups for community education, a base was built throughout rural Minnesota where legislative support for larger appropriations would be critical. In eight months, these groups educated 20,000 people about battered women and, accumulating their names and addresses, turned to them when the legislature voted on appropriations in 1979. In this way a large statewide constituency was built.[25] Today, not accidentally, the Minnesota Coalition has a membership of approximately thirty-eight grassroots feminist organizations that receive 3.7 million dollars in state funding.

Many other kinds of state coalitions also exist. A well-traveled organizer described one as "composed mainly of professional social workers operating shelters in conjunction with mental health centers. These men and women see themselves as providers of services and therapy to battered women who are defined as disabled."[26] In this case, individuals formed a coalition of all interested parties, including government agencies, in order to gain funding, credibility, recognition, and skills. They viewed themselves neither as advocates who change bureaucracies like the police and courts nor as organizers who work to redistribute power for women. Another coalition is described as a group of professional women who dislike feminism but who enjoy working together and understand the political significance of violence against women.[27]

From state to state, coalitions have unique histories and structures. In 1980, the California Alliance Against Domestic Violence formed with three representatives from each of the following groups: the Northern California Shelter Support Services, the Southern California Coalition on Battered Women, the Central California Coalition on Domestic Violence, California Women of Color Against Domestic Violence, and the Western States Shelter Network.[28] This effort is described as "bottom-up" rather than "top-down" organizing. The California Alliance sets its own goals as does each member coalition. For example, the thirty-two shelters—organized mainly by feminists and/or community women—who belong to the Southern California Coalition, share skills, information, and support. Its seventeen member shelters in the Los Angeles area recently agreed to ask the county for equal grant allocations for

each program even when the government encouraged local competition. The Southern California Coalition also helped these seventeen programs organize to keep their funds when many traditional
social service agencies began to compete with them after the
California legislature passed a marriage license tax which funded
shelters.[29]

Until 1981, Wisconsin had two politically disparate organizations, one feminist and one not, which maintained an uneasy
private relationship but a respectful public one. It seemed as if the
two groups, the Wisconsin Coalition Against Woman Abuse and the
Domestic Abuse Prevention Council, were polarized by political
differences, but in reality neither group was well organized or active.
In the spring of 1981, the Wisconsin Coalition Against Woman Abuse
hired two staff organizers who discovered widespread interest
among at least twenty of the state's thirty-three battered women's
projects in building a unified organization of groups whose primary
focus is domestic violence.

The Wisconsin example suggests the importance of using
experienced organizers who are able to patiently build from the
bottom up and untangle old disagreements. Without these efforts,
Wisconsin service providers fought with each other and often were
ignored by state agencies that determined policies affecting battered
women. As a result, several important battles were lost. For
example, even though the Wisconsin legislature allocated one
million dollars in 1980 and 2.8 million from 1981-1983 for battered
women's services, the legislation, viewing unmarried women without children as "unworthy" victims, specifically prohibits reim-
bursing shelters for their stays. Now Wisconsin women are uniting
to overturn this legislation and demand accountability from state
agencies who can no longer ignore this growing statewide power
base among women.[30]

Prodded by coalitions, some states have introduced their own
innovative legislation or included funds for battered women as line
items in an agency's budget. Setting a precedent, in 1978 the Florida
state legislature placed a $5 tax on marriage licenses, predicting
$600,000 to be raised that year for shelters. Each qualified shelter
would be entitled to receive up to $50,000.[31] During the last few
years, fourteen states have legislated marriage license fees and many
more are considering them. Montana receives $14 from each license;
North Dakota—$19; and Ohio—$10.[32] From another direction, in
1979 the state of Washington appropriated one million dollars for a
two year period to the Department of Social and Health Services,

$700,000 of which was to be used for shelters.[33] Despite these important gains, approximately thirteen states have refused to allocate any state funds to battered women's services, and in those where appropriations have been made, funding could be lost at any moment.

Only some coalitions have successfully pushed states to utilize federal funding. For example, federal Title XX funds provide for a broad range of social services to low income families and to special populations such as children and adults in need of protection from harm or neglect. As of September 1981, it was estimated that approximately twenty-five states allocate federal Title XX or Emergency Assistance funds for battered women's services.[34]

Today, coalitions face many challenges in addition to the weighty task of saving services hit by budget cuts. One is the lack of involvement from member program staff and battered women. Shelter directors are the major participants in most state coalition activity. If this continues, women collectively will have fewer experiences that demonstrate the value of organizing together; to many, the "movement" will stay a vague abstraction at a time when it most needs widespread support.

If regional or state meetings were rotated from shelter to shelter and staff and battered women worked together on committees, many more women could meet one another, creating the space to define their own needs and build networks. In Minneapolis, the Battered Women's Consortium staff recently helped former battered women organize their own conference. Although these efforts consume major staff time, they are mandatory if battered women are to become meaningfully involved in the movement. Shelter boards of directors and executive directors, however, will have to face the sharing of power that such participation signifies.

Another worrisome issue facing statewide coalitions is the definition of their constituency. To retain control over decision making and political direction, most coalitions have stayed based within service organizations. However, in order to build strong, more diverse constituencies for lobbying and to include battered women and third world women, some coalitions, like the one in Massachusetts, have created categories of affiliate or supportive membership. Questions remain, however, about how power should and will be shared. Service organizations need to determine their own policies; yet battered women and third world women are unlikely to be active coalition members unless they have some real power.

The issue of who should be permitted to join feminist coalitions is complex. As noted earlier, some groups want to join state coalitions solely for access to funding. Others have diverse motivations for joining. Most coalitions evaluate prospective members, but criteria are loose and difficult to measure. The impulse of most coalitions has been to include a wide range of groups so that political discussion and struggle can take place and so that feminists and activists can keep watch over those who might sabotage their purposes. In some instances, this has created tensions as members have demoralized coalitions by failing to participate or by undermining collective efforts. While some activists regret this inclusionary choice, most believe it was necessary and often productive, since diverse women have much to teach one another. Many activists suggest, however, that it is appropriate and useful to have clear internal program standards and monitoring devices that help in establishing policy for coalition membership. It might be possible to develop standards that respect diversity and local conditions but also force groups to honestly confront their commitment to coalition work and their philosophy of helping battered women. One activist in a coalition with large state funding suggested that new applicants not receive funding through the coalition for at least one year after they join.

The potential problems of a diverse coalition have emerged dramatically in a few states where feminists organized coalitions very quickly. They established exemplary principles of unity based on ending racism, sexism, and class bias without doing persistent education and organizing to make sure that all who joined the coalition were truly committed to the same goals. Major ideological and personal fights have erupted, splitting coalitions and leading to bitter in-fighting. As one early activist commented, "radical women organized and yet many others felt left out." She explains what happened in her state.

> This coalition was begun by women with a vision of collectivity and empowering women. But there was never enough time to educate women new to the movement about these principles. Some members believed in self-help and others in professional help. Then, before the coalition really jelled, funding became an imminent possibility. Because we didn't have a unified grassroots base, funding came too soon and divided us further. We chose what seemed at the time to be an urgent priority of gaining adequate funding, thinking, among other things, that the paid staff would enable us to do necessary consciousness raising and education within the coalition. But the choice to seek funding represented an emphasis on expanded high quality services rather than the strengthening of the political base of the movement.[35]

Yet the problems are not easy to avoid. As another woman asks, "how do you go slowly and integrate new members when the government is acting so quickly and you are forced to respond?"[36]

Some states have successfully incorporated diverse groups in their coalitions.

> In Southern California, Haven House, started by Al-Anon women, and Sojourn, a radical feminist collective, set a tone of cooperation. By respecting each other and staying task-oriented, we avoided the bitter splits caused when a radical analysis is rammed down people's throats. Only in 1981 did we define principles of unity but it was easy because now we trust one another. "Bottom-up" organizing means that women own and assume responsibility for the organization.[37]

These states illustrate two poles of an extremely complicated continuum of organizing problems. The question remains: can widely diverse political philosophies and styles coexist without destroying feminist principles or even the more limited goals of lobbying for funds or legislation? In what contexts can women with different ideologies coalesce and under what circumstances should such work be avoided? How can feminists preserve a base to put forward their own interests, both inside and outside of statewide battered women's coalitions?

The Nightmare in New York City

New York City poignantly illustrates what happens when an autonomous coalition fails and an official city task force oversees battered women's services. Although the degrading and punitive services some battered women now receive in New York City result from far more than the failure of a grassroots coalition, they do suggest that the survival of autonomous, grassroots women's coalitions is a necessary, although not sufficient, condition to insure decent services for battered women.

In November 1976, the New York City Council passed resolution 491. Sponsored by Councilwoman Miriam Friedlander, this document urged city agencies to make concrete plans for providing specialized assistance to battered women.[38] At this point the city had shelter space for forty-five homeless women without children. Given that subsequent studies estimated that 1000 shelter spaces were needed to adequately serve battered women,[39] the city, on the brink of bankruptcy, confronted a monumental service problem. A task force of city council and agency personnel was formed that pressured the city's Human Resources Administration (HRA) to fund the first shelter. This Manhattan demonstration project was a collaborative effort of two agencies: Henry Street Settlement, which provided shelter, and Abused Women's Aid in Crisis which provided screening and follow-up. In addition, the task force succeeded in having welfare procedures changed so that battered women could be designated emergencies and shelters reimbursed on a per diem basis for their stays. The first shelter, serving only eighteen families who were welfare eligible, opened in July 1977 and offered battered women refuge in apartments.

Concerned personnel within HRA felt that the city itself needed to provide more services, yet the city had no money. The "trick," as one person called it, was to do it without money. In October 1977, the city opened a shelter in a hotel that accepted per diem welfare payments. The program staff was pulled from a variety of city agencies since no new funding was made available to hire workers. This "shelter," in a hotel near Times Square, the pornography center of New York, had neither cooking nor child care facilities. The planner involved had found day care space, but no one ever followed through to see it provided. As she put it, "We worked under severe agency and fiscal constraints to see a shelter open. Compromises were made on everything no matter how hard you fought. No one took the issue seriously. Only a handful of people in the agency helped. It was like guerilla warfare in your own agency."[40]

As these two shelters were being planned in Manhattan, a third was under discussion in Brooklyn. Early in 1976, many New York City groups interested in starting a shelter had hoped to receive the $200,000 appropriation from the state's 1976-1977 supplemental budget that Carol Bellamy, then a State Senator, had included for a shelter. These groups attempted to work out their differences and avoid competition over these limited funds, but their attempts ended in failure.[41] Eventually, a Brooklyn based coalition of the National Congress of Neighborhood Women, the YWCA, and the Mayor's Task Force on Rape formed the Center for the Elimination of Violence in the Family, received the $200,000 appropriation, and opened the first Brooklyn shelter, Women's Survival Space, in March 1977. Thirty-six women representing these three different organizations sat as its board of directors. Soon Women's Survival Space—the only autonomous women's shelter in the city—was internally divided. Women self-consciously tried to resolve the differences; the process was an excruciatingly painful one that ultimately failed. Women's Survival Space thus added to the nightmare that was beginning in New York City.

In February 1977, the American Friends Service Committee (AFSC), with the help of an advisory task force, sponsored the first New York City Conference on Battered Women. With 500 people attending, AFSC announced the formation of the New York Coalition for Battered Women under its sponsorship. For two years this group met, trying to overcome the political differences and distrust that had been fostered by earlier competition for extremely limited funding. It also faced problems inherent in a coalition without membership criteria, by-laws, or accountability mechanisms. All interested groups and individuals, whether or not they were providing help to battered women, could join. Political perspectives were extremely diverse as were participants. The coalition was a disaster. Only two unifying issues emerged in its two year history; its major campaign centered on demanding that HRA move its shelter out of a welfare hotel and out of Times Square. The coalition also attempted to investigate and mediate the problems at the Brooklyn shelter. Neither of these efforts were successful. By 1979, attendance at meetings had dwindled and after one angry meeting, called to resurrect the coalition but permeated with hostility and political differences, the coalition died.

For the last several years, no coalition has existed in New York City. The only group that meets is the City Council's Task Force on Domestic Violence, composed of city and social service agencies, elected officials, and battered women's organizations. It is jointly convened by City Councilwoman Miriam Friedlander, the director of the city's Victim Services Agency, and the director of HRA's Family and Adult Services, whose agency now funds all five New York City shelters.

Conditions have stayed the same or grown worse in New York City shelters over the last two years. HRA now interprets state guidelines so that only welfare eligible women are allowed to use HRA funded shelters. In the past, at least Women's Survival Space allowed working women to pay their own rent and supplemented the cost of their stay by private fundraising. In 1981, HRA disallowed this procedure and working women had access to no shelter in New York City. The city has destroyed the autonomy of shelter programs further by forcing each battered woman to be verified by a welfare center as eligible for shelter and by giving each shelter resident a two party welfare check which must be turned over to the shelter to pay for the residents' food and rent. As a result, the shelter becomes like a landlord rather than a trusted friend. In one shelter the bookkeeper

and director spend over half their time dealing with the city
bureaucracy.[42] Because per diem welfare funding provides no money
for staff training, travel, renovation, building maintenance, or equipment, the programs remain perennially short of funds. HRA insists,
however, that funding be used to hire certified therapists to provide
or to supervise all counseling services and that no counseling can be
provided to non-sheltered women.[43] Constraints like these exist in no
other city in the United States.

To force a woman to be verified as battered by a welfare center
before she can gain entry to a shelter and to create services but make
them unavailable to working women are but two of the many horrors
the Task Force on Domestic Violence has been presented with over
the years. In 1980, when the city had to move its shelter out of the
Times Square hotel because of financial problems, battered women's
organizations pressured HRA to find a safe, home-like setting.
Instead, the city shelter is in yet another welfare hotel which women
describe as frightening and dangerous. Staff warn residents to keep
their dressers against their doors at night.

Only rarely do groups within the Task Force complain, but
nothing changes; only a few programs—and no shelters—are left
which have a funding base independent of HRA. The main participants at monthly Task Force meetings, especially city bureaucrats
and politicians, continue to suggest that everyone present has the
same interest—"to help battered women." When an independent
feminist group, The Committee to End Violence in the Lives of
Women, staged a demonstration denouncing the conditions at the
HRA shelter and demanding that it be moved, a few of its members
were angrily attacked in a Task Force meeting for publicly subverting the city's "good intentions." While some city bureaucrats
have decent motives, they have absolutely no understanding of
battered women's real needs. Although the City Council Task Force
on Domestic Violence does little to truly help battered women, its
existence makes it look as if the city of New York is actively involved
in providing adequate services.

The failure of the New York Coalition for Battered Women
created a power vacuum which the city filled. Operating with no
understanding of or commitment to grassroots services, the Task
Force on Domestic Violence has legitimated one disaster after
another. It is not surprising that four out of five shelters in New York
City are part of much larger social service agencies. Most grassroots
groups left this struggle long ago, feeling hopeless to overcome the

previous problems of disunity and lack of funds to start programs. The New York City failure should provide a warning to those facing service cutbacks. It is clear that autonomous women's coalitions that have thoroughly discussed the meaning of cooperation and non-competitive funding and have struggled together toward shared goals are most able to avert such failures. They can act together as a potent force in creating services that preserve battered women's dignity and rights to self-determination.

CHAPTER 6

National and International Efforts

National Communication

What started as a Wisconsin Conference on Battered Women in October 1976 turned into an historic event when women from around the country began a national newsletter, *The National Communication Network for the Elimination of Violence Against Women (NCN)*. They also envisioned forming a national organization of grassroots service providers. Fears of co-optation, accentuated by warnings from the anti-rape movement, echoed loudly in Wisconsin as did hopes for unity.

> The dream was of a feminist national coalition grounded in state and regional coalitions. We would share responsibility and serve as a power base to support each other. At this conference Cathy Avina at Women's Advocates first articulated the idea of a National Battered Women's Corporation, to lobby for, collect, and distribute funds to local groups. We would determine eligibility for funding based on principles of self-help and peer support instead of competing with each other for federal and state funds. We needed to be large enough and work fast enough to become the national voice and avoid co-optation.[1]

After this conference women from Minneapolis-St. Paul tried to raise money for a first national meeting to organize such a coalition, but in 1977 the lack of funds as well as personal and political problems foiled their efforts. Because few state or regional coalitions existed at this time, a national grassroots effort from the "bottom-up" was premature.[2] However, the *NCN* published its first issue in April 1977, based on six months of volunteer labor.

The first five *NCNs,* compiled by women from Boston and Minneapolis-St. Paul, shared information from around the country and published articles on self-defense, co-optation, and the politics of the movement. As early as the first issue, a possible merger with *FAAR,* the newsletter of the Feminist Alliance Against Rape, was suggested. The logic of a merger was apparent to women in both groups, many of whom were in supportive contact with one another. Concerns centered on *FAAR* and *NCN* staying accountable to their constituencies and each retaining its own identity rather than submerging it.[3]

A national meeting was called for July 22-24, 1977 in Minneapolis-St. Paul to discuss the advantages and disadvantages of the possible merger. A careful plan, calling for two separate publications jointly mailed and then working toward a single publication with two major sections each retaining editorial control, was negotiated. Through the merger, *NCN* changed its editorial policy to reflect a feminist analysis of violence; earlier policy had provided no editorial control over material published. The broader political and historic importance of the merger was stated in the third *NCN.*

> With over 200 rape crisis centers already existing in this country, with shelters for battered women being organized rapidly, and with women protesting advertising which depicts brutalized women, the phrase, "violence against women" is becoming more commonplace. What this signifies is a change in women's consciousness—a growing awareness that we, as women, experience oppression in our daily lives, and that it is maintained by the threat and reality of physical violence. Redefining violence and weaving together forms of violence into a total system of social control are implicit in the adoption of the term, "violence against women...."if we conceptually link all forms of violence against women, then our fight, too, must be against the whole web.[4]

The first jointly published *FAAR* and *NCN* arrived in August 1978. Not only were rape and battering to be analyzed, but the new bi-monthly publication developed feminist perspectives on sexual harassment through the regular contributions of the Alliance Against Sexual Coercion, as well as on media violence, forced sterilization, and violence against women in prison and medical and mental institutions.[5]

By November 1978, the new magazine was calling itself *Aegis, the Magazine on Ending Violence Against Women.* For activists around the country, *Aegis* fulfilled many needs. It alleviated women's sense of isolation and offered inspiration. It provided insight and direction so that political women, sometimes ostracized, could define their community as a national rather than a local one and feel renewed. The magazine provided information and resources about legislation as well as political articles that formed the basis for local, statewide, and regional discussions. Much of the movement's political vision was articulated in *Aegis*, and its politics reverberated in shelter and coalition debates around the country.

Although *Aegis* is the only journal dedicated to preserving and building a feminist analysis and grassroots movement, it was not the only mechanism for sharing information. Three other publications served national audiences. *Response,* first published by the Center for Women Policy Studies beginning in 1976, focused largely on the criminal justice, hospital, social service, and federal responses to rape and battering. *SANEnews,* published by the Community Health Center of Middletown, Connecticut was concerned primarily with sharing information and legislative developments, and a *Monthly Memo* from the National Technical Assistance Center on Family Violence contained short news items. In 1981, however, because of funding cuts, the National Technical Assistance Center closed. *Response* and *SANEnews* continue although *Response* now operates at a reduced level.

Even more avidly than the printed word, thousands of women repeatedly sought out conferences to break their isolation. Literally hundreds of conferences have been held by the battered women's movement, some of them serving as internal political and educational forums and others reaching out to educate the professional or lay communities. In all kinds of forums, grassroots service providers have found one another, shared information, worked on problems, and, through mutual support, lessened the pain of daily service or organizing work. Conferences often concurrently served many purposes.

> In addition to newspaper, television and radio coverage of the conference, there will be a series of television programs on battered women. As a result of the conference, a legislative Task Force was formed and is working on legal reform....
> Important steps were taken at the conference towards the establishment of a network of battered women projects on the west coast. The participating projects want the network to provide a communications link and to enable the projects to send a woman to a shelter in another state if she needs to get away.[6]

Movement gatherings like the two National Conferences on

Violence Against Women held in Denver in 1979 and 1980, or the 1979 Chicago Confronting Woman Abuse conference interwove skills training and politics. The Chicago conference held workshops on organizing shelters, children's needs, police and court advocacy and change, and worker burnout. Keynote addresses focused on the "Analysis of Violence Against Women" and "Developing Future Movement Goals." Such conferences left women renewed and energized; young programs learned from older ones. And many women valued most the informal sharing and creation of personal ties that helped build an ongoing national movement.

Organizing a National Coalition

At the same time that the *NCN* was being published and conferences were being held around the country, the idea of a national coalition, first raised at the 1976 Wisconsin meeting, was becoming a reality. As the grassroots battered women's movement gained public attention, a governmental response set the stage for further attempts at national organizing. In 1977, Jan Peterson, formerly on the staff of Brooklyn's National Congress of Neighborhood Women and a co-founder of the Brooklyn shelter, was appointed Associate Director of Public Liaison at the White House. As Peterson notes, "at the time battered women were *the* major grassroots organizing effort in the women's movement; Midge Costanza, Assistant to the President, and I thought a White House meeting between the real experts, battered women and service providers, and federal agency personnel, could help the grassroots. We needed women on the inside and activists from the outside exerting pressure and supporting one another."[7]

On July 20, 1977, the first White House meeting opened with the testimony of battered women[8] and was followed by twelve carefully strategized statements presented by activists who were each allotted three minutes. Organized before the White House meeting, activists from around the country had divided key topics among themselves.

> This jointly developed, jointly delivered presentation started with a discussion of the issue of woman abuse and why it should not be lumped with alcohol and drug abuse or child abuse. We talked about what shelters are; why they are important and why they should be community run and autonomous. We discussed the need for shelters which were multi-cultural, multi-ethnic, and multi-racial and accessible to all women.[9]

As bureaucrats listened with respectful silence, activists offered suggestions about how specific federal agencies and legislation could be improved.[10]

Although no substantive decisions were made, the movement used this meeting for its own ends, building trust and support among an ever increasing number of grassroots activists, previously strangers to one another. One woman, central to early national organizing efforts in Washington D.C., describes the impact of the White House meeting. "The feelings of unity and success that grew out of this provided additional incentive to struggle across 3000 miles in order to form a national coalition." She explains further, that "at the time of the first meeting, the movement was new and almost all grassroots. In my mind, this was the essential ingredient that allowed us to work together well and to build unity quickly."[11]

The International Women's Year conference in Houston, November 18-21, 1977, provided the next unanticipated opportunity for grassroots groups from all over the country to organize themselves. Besides the official workshops and resolutions devoted to the issue, a Caucus on Battered Women met three times and decided again to develop a national feminist coalition based in local autonomous grassroots programs.

Two months later, on January 30 and 31, 1978, the United States Commission on Civil Rights sponsored a _Consultation on Battered Women: Issues of Public Policy,_ fulfilling its statutory mandate to investigate the denial of equal protection of the law based on sex. Although the purpose of the consultation was to inform the Commissioners, hundreds of activists arrived in Washington to listen and organize. Federal legislation authorizing funds for services to battered women had been introduced several months earlier, and activists were anxious to affect its course.

Although women actually formed the National Coalition Against Domestic Violence (NCADV) during this consultation, its birth was the result of much previous work and careful organizing by feminists around the country and by two women in Washington. In preparation for the consultation, the U.S. Commission on Civil Rights contracted with the Women's Legal Defense Fund to conduct research and recommend an appropriate structure and speakers for the consultation. Using Betsy Warrior's directory, contacts with a few activists in other states, and word of mouth, two staff members, working on this contract, called women in every state, hunting for information about shelters, hotlines, model state and local legislation, and other law reform projects. Informing concerned organizations all over the country of the upcoming consultation, they recommended a number to testify before the Commissioners. They wanted to include women from different regions, from rural and urban areas, and from shelter and non-shelter programs as well as to ensure that testimony was heard from women of diverse racial and ethnic backgrounds.[12]

One of these women, Valle Jones, further catalyzed a national organizing effort by sending post cards to all grassroots groups and individuals registered for the Civil Rights Commission Consultation, inviting them to meet the evening before the Consultation to discuss federal legislation and to organize nationally. Approximately sixty women attended that meeting. For the next several days this growing group met at every meal and throughout the evenings to create regional caucuses, an interim structure, and a statement of purpose for a national organization. Two steering committee members were elected from each of ten federal regions, and nine working task forces were formed until a national meeting could be held. The goals of the new organization were similar to those articulated in Milwaukee, with emphasis on gaining financial aid for shelters and grassroots services, on sharing information, and supporting research beneficial to the movement.[13] Consensus decision making was the norm and, if not possible, a two-thirds vote could decide issues. Each committee was to strive for representation that crossed age, race, economic, and sexual preference boundaries.[14]

These decisions were not easily made; some felt excluded when a grassroots feminist coalition organized on its own behalf. Others were wary of being explicit about feminist politics. Few women knew one another, and pronounced geographic and political differences only heightened the tensions. These conflicts were to haunt the newly formed National Coalition Against Domestic Violence.

The Civil Rights Commission hearings did far more than provide the space for women to start a national organization. They legitimated the needs of battered women, prodding the conscience of some federal agencies and introducing them to a new constituency.

> Arthur Fleming, The Chair of the Commission, said he had never seen such intense interest and enthusiasm on the part of those attending a consultation. The audience sat and listened to every word, staying to the very end. Their commitment and dedication were very strong and most people outside of the movement are not used to seeing it.[15]

Describing the sense of power and excitement as incomparable, activists found themselves surrounded by hundreds of women doing similar work. A movement had been born and was now recognized.

The new steering committee was given three directives: 1. set up a structure; 2. hold a national conference; and 3. impact on national legislation.[16] A projected national conference for 2,500 women to be held in Minnesota in the fall of 1978 never happened. But during the two years between the Civil Rights Hearing and the first national meeting in 1980, substantial work was done and major problems faced.

The task of defining a purpose, structure, and goals was particularly difficult for an organization with no paid staff, little money, and interim representatives who had to travel across the country in order to meet as a whole body. All the old shelter debates reemerged. For example, the steering committee asked itself: Are we to call ourselves an organization dealing with battered women or domestic violence? Is our purpose to get money or to build a movement? Is this a grassroots and professional organization or only a grassroots one?[17]

Some members of the steering committee were uncomfortable with a strong feminist position, which affected the work of the coalition in many ways. For example, although the _NCN_ section of _Aegis_ was originally seen as the voice of the National Coalition Against Domestic Violence, some steering committee members saw the _NCN_ as too radical. Since _NCN_ was strongly committed to maintaining its feminist autonomy, a link between the two organizations was impossible.[18]

One movement activist reflects on the earliest problems.

> We wanted the national organization to look like the coalition now developing in Pennsylvania. But everything happened too fast. We were racing to keep up with the government instead of defining our own priorities. The government had stepped in at the same time that feminist activists in Boston and Minneapolis-St. Paul were swamped by maintaining NCN and their local programs. Worse, between 1976 and 1978 we could not raise money for a national meeting.
>
> Then in 1978 problems emerged among individual coalition members who had appointed themselves as National Coalition representatives at the Civil Rights meetings in D.C. until a national meeting could be convened. Problems of abrasive and dogmatic personal styles, combined with the radical feminist and lesbian baiting politics of some individuals, alienated and discouraged many local programs from participating in the newly formed coalition. These conflicts set back the organization's efforts for months, if not for years.[19]

Internal disagreements and mistrust led to excruciatingly slow decision making processes.

By late 1978 the steering committee had decided upon goals, including:

1. To monitor and impact legislation relating to domestic violence and family policy.
2. To aid in the development of state and regional coalitions.
3. To develop a national network of shelters.
4. To educate the public to a non-acceptance of violence and to strive toward the complete elimination of violence in our society.
5. To support and initiate change in traditional sex-role expectations for women and men.[20]

Active voting members had to be independent, community based organizations providing direct services to battered women and their families. The steering committee, meeting approximately four times a year, was responsible for recruiting members and carrying information between the membership and the national organization.

In the meantime, pending legislation and federal bureaucratic plans for battered women demanded immediate attention. Because of constituent pressure and in some cases, personal interest, during the 95th Congress Congressman Newton Steers (R.-MD) and Lindy Boggs (D.-LA) in the House and Wendell Anderson (D.-MN) and Edward Kennedy (D.-MA) in the Senate had introduced the identical bill, the Domestic Violence Prevention and Treatment Act, proposing to establish a research and demonstration program within HEW. The Anderson-Kennedy Senate bill was assigned to Senator Cranston's (D.-CA) Child and Human Development Committee and later became known as Cranston's legislation. Almost simultaneously, Congresswoman Barbara Mikulski (D.-MD) introduced the Family Violence Prevention and Treatment Act, which proposed to create within ACTION a National Center for Community Action Against Family Violence.[21] Wary about HEW and especially NIMH's* use of rape funds for research rather than service and aware that ACTION** would be more amenable to grassroots influence, Congresswoman Mikulski hoped to see Congressional hearings on these bills. As her legislative assistant notes:

> These bills were never regarded as competitors. The Steers-Boggs bill took a research-demonstration grant approach, the traditional way to run a program through HEW. Mikulski introduced her bill because she hated HEW and still does. She saw the issue as one for a community-

* The National Institute of Mental Health, a branch of HEW.
** The federal agency that incorporated VISTA and the Peace Corps.

based operation; HEW has never run a good community-based program. Steers, Boggs, and Mikulski saw these bills as talking points— excuses to hold hearings.[22]

Through the House of Representatives hearing process, H.R. 12299, the Domestic Violence Act of 1978, was reported out of committee and authorized $15 million for fiscal year 1979, $20 million for fiscal year 1980, and $30 million for each of the three following fiscal years.

On May 23, 1978, by invoking a special "suspension of rules" procedure that necessitated a two-thirds majority, this bill failed to pass the House by a vote of 205 to 201. Reports indicate that many Congresspeople were in favor of the bill but were angered by the special procedures used; others were confused by the legislation's title, assuming it referred to terrorism.[23]

Expecting no action until the next year, domestic violence advocates were surprised when the Senate, by voice vote and without major political debate, passed the legislation on August 1, 1978. In an unprecedented effort, the House Rules Committee reconsidered the legislation and finally moved it out of committee. With just one day left before adjournment, however, the bill's persistent House critic, John Ashbrook (R.-OH), read thirty-five amendments into the Congressional Record and effectively killed the legislation.[24] The victim of indifference, domestic violence legislation, which would have allocated a piddling amount but also would have created a significant precedent of federal support, almost sneaked by the 95th Congress.

The 95th Congressional session taught the emerging battered women's movement several lessons. As one activist commented, "the important aspect of the early federal legislation...was that we gained experience working together, building unity and coalitions. We also learned a lot about the federal legislative process."[25] The first efforts not only offered an education for grassroots activists, but also for the Congressional representatives, many of whose aides turned to the National Coalition to provide expert testimony and information in the next session.

Throughout this Congress and into the 96th, members of the National Coalition offered extensive critiques of pending legislation. The National Coalition and its grassroots affiliates constantly worked to reshape the legislation. Notes from the files of Barbara Hart, the National Coalition's legislative committee chair, indicate the messages feminists and grassroots activists repeated hundreds of times.

1. As much funding as possible should be earmarked directly to community-based groups for advocacy and services.
2. Federal, state and local bureaucratic involvement must be minimized: at the state level no new domestic violence bureaucracies should be created. A federal Domestic Violence Council within HEW is permissible if community-based, women-centered groups have a majority of the policy and decision making responsibility.
3. NIMH is an unacceptable federal overseer.
4. Research grants should be limited to those helping local groups meet particular programmatic needs.
5. Grassroots groups should retain as much control as possible over the grant review process.[26]

As a "bottom line" negotiating strategy, activists fought to define domestic violence broadly so that all women, including unmarried ones, could be provided services; records would remain confidential; no licensing requirement would be imposed on shelters; and no fees would be required of shelter residents. Activists understood well that they needed not only to fight for the best legislation but also to monitor the entire implementation process to avoid losing all they had lobbied to create.

During the 96th Congress, the National Coalition redoubled its efforts to see federal legislation passed. Unexpectedly on December 12, 1979, the House voted on H.R. 2977, the Domestic Violence Prevention and Services Act. Because the National Coalition had expected the House bill to be voted on in February or March, a November phone call from Rep. Mikulski, saying that the bill was coming up, took everyone by surprise. Working out of the dining room of one of the staff recently hired to coordinate the first National Coalition conference, women from Washington D.C., Maryland, and Pennsylvania undertook a massive organizing effort between late November and December 12th. On minimal and sometimes nonexistent salaries, Morgan Plant, Mary Morrison, Diane Pellicori, and Dane Russo, National Coalition temporary staff, worked tirelessly on two major efforts—lobbying and planning a conference. Dividing tasks, one group polled members of Congress while the other designed a massive state by state wall chart of the House of Representatives and called every known local contact, using the recent mailing list developed for the first national conference to be held in February 1980. An effective network had been formed through two years of steering committee meetings which brought women together from around the country. Contact people in key districts represented by undecided legislators mobilized supportive phone calls and letters, while each shelter took responsibility for generating ten telegrams from its program. As one woman noted, "we had people calling their grandmothers and their representatives." Other women's organizations—the General Federation of Women's Clubs, Business and Professional Women, Women's Equity Action League, and the National Women's Political Caucus—played central roles in mobilizing constituencies.[27] Over 60 organizations supported the legislation and, just before its passage, with 292 votes for and 106 against, President Carter endorsed the bill in a personal letter to the House.

The Senate battle over the bill would be a long and difficult one. Meanwhile, however, on February 27, 1980, a three year dream came true as 600 women from 49 states came to Washington for the National Coalition's first official membership conference. Visiting the Senate was a key part of that four day event, but a Senate vote would wait for agonizing months, held off through the summer election campaigns. The conference, as designed by the steering committee and temporary staff, focused heavily on information sharing and skill building. How-to workshops were held on obtaining and using Title XX and HUD Community Development Block Grant funds; building coalitions; formulating legislation; lobbying; and developing community education programs.

A slide show celebrating the "herstory" of the movement, a tear-stained, moving speakout about the personal meaning women attached to the movement, and a benefit concert by Sweet Honey in the Rock followed by a joyous, raucous dance bound together those present and, even as tensions simmered, emotionally reminded them of the importance of shared struggle among women.

Organizing this conference with temporary staff and almost no money or membership base had entailed creative work. As late as October 1979, the coalition minute book listed its active membership at twenty-six groups and its supportive membership at seventeen. By late 1980 the numbers had risen to 123 active members and 167 supportive ones.[28] The first national meeting, a membership conference, enticed grassroots groups to join, but their impoverished programs generally needed financial help to send representatives to Washington. The national staff frantically wrote proposals, raising $20,000 to support travel scholarships, and devised a political formula so that money could be equitably distributed.

Private foundation grants, individual contributions, and registration fees slowly trickled in; eventually $122,034 was raised for expenses and travel. Staff and activists negotiated major contracts with federal agencies to prepare for the skill building workshops. A

$30,000 research grant was awarded by HEW's Office on Domestic Violence to develop a handbook and workshop on Title XX services to battered women; HUD provided a $15,500 grant to develop a handbook and workshop on the use of CDBG funds to purchase shelters; another $10,000 came through the Office on Domestic Violence's clearinghouse for a manual and a workshop on state domestic violence legislation.[29] Women who facilitated the workshops underwritten by grants ploughed money back into the conference to be used as scholarships. Not only did these funds support the conference but also, in the usual style of the battered women's movement, the excellent manuals supplied tools for local women to navigate through the bureaucratic maze of state and federal regulations.

Throughout the conference, participant-initiated workshops and caucuses created room for the diversity and disagreements within the movement to surface. On the last morning of the conference, caucus statements came from women of color, feminist socialists, rural women, handicapped women, and from individual states like California, complaining that the representational formula for steering committee delegates did not address their needs or concrete problems. Women of color, who had been asked to lead the racism awareness and minority women's workshops, complained of the National Coalition's failure to use their talent and leadership in skill building workshops and in the conference planning. The feminist socialist caucus statement, whose seven points of action were ratified by the majority still present by late Saturday morning, reflected some of the concerns downplayed by the conference:

> We ask that the NCADV membership ratify the following work priorities, and that the NCADV leadership submit to the membership a work plan to implement these tasks by January 1981:
> 1. A plan for concrete anti-racist work, to be incorporated at every level of our analysis, our programs, our reforms, our hiring practices and our outreach.
> 2. A plan to develop the participation and leadership of former battered, third world, rural, handicapped and low income women at every level of our organization.
> 3. A recognition of the leadership and activity of lesbian women in the movement and an active public stance against homophobia and lesbian baiting.
> 4. An analysis of the dangers of cooptation at all levels of our work including organizational structure. A recognition of the ramifications of our accepting government funding and an analysis of working in the criminal justice and welfare systems and their tendencies to implement punitive and degrading services for

battered women.

5. Ongoing discussion among our membership which addresses the complexities of gender, race, and class as they operate in our daily work. That this analysis and the strategies and skills that result from it become the major focus of our next national meeting.

6. A plan to share with the membership of this organization community organizing skills so that we can effectively build our movement and mobilize on a grass roots level.

7. Priority be given to building alliances with other struggles in the women's movement and with those progressive forces working in housing, daycare, civil rights, jobs, welfare rights, and labor organizing. It is only through the development of these alliances that we will create a mass, large-scale movement that will struggle to create a society which will end violence against women.[30]

Recreating state and local organizing problems, the caucus statements revealed that agreement over the meaning of feminism and the goals of the battered women's movement clearly did not exist. One southern woman comments, "Feminism is a dirty word in many communities....On a state level we talk about counseling, advocacy, and coalition building, not racism and class."[31] Some conference participants were appalled by the idea of publicly mentioning lesbians in the movement. While these differences provoked important political dialogue and helped participants recognize the important variations in local conditions, they also painfully highlighted the problems inherent in building a national movement. The 1980 conference increased the skills and personal contacts desperately needed by isolated grassroots groups; yet the political discussions that many women hungered for found their expression unofficially and inadequately through caucuses and at the last plenary meeting. It would be left to the steering committee to design a plan to help women develop skills, vision, and a political analysis and, at the same time, hold a diverse membership together and keep them involved.

Participants generally evaluated the National Conference positively. Simply sitting in a room with 600 other women dedicated to the cause of ending violence against women moved activists to redouble their efforts. Using national legislation and lobbying efforts as a unifying activity, women crossed state and political lines to work together. The Southeast Coalition Against Domestic Violence, incorporating eight states, dates its inspiration and founding to this first national meeting.[32]

With the Domestic Violence Prevention and Services Act still in the Senate, legislative work provided significant Coalition direction

for the next eight months. First, the National Coalition urged
Senator Cranston's staff to bring the bill to the floor for a vote before
the potentially controversial White House Conference on the Family
convened in June. As majority whip, Cranston, however, never
seemed interested and made none of the careful effort to work with
the National Coalition that Representatives Mikulski, Miller, and
Boggs had.

Between February and May, President Carter's budget slashing
deeply affected women, and feminist organizations demanded a
meeting with the Office of Management and Budget (OMB) to stop
these projected cuts. Mindful of the need for unity, the National
Coalition called a strategy session hours before the OMB meeting.
Thanks to this careful planning and the fact that all the feminist
groups attending the OMB meeting viewed the domestic violence
legislation as a priority, it was the only new women's program left in
the budget. Only with the help of other organizations, especially the
Women's Equity Action League and the National Women's Political
Caucus, did the bill remain funded at a projected $45 million
dollars.[33]

By summer, two major problems had arisen. Even if the Senate
passed the bill, it would go to a conference committee in order to
resolve Senate-House differences and would then have to be passed
again by both houses before the end of the session in November.
Would there be enough time? Worse, Jerry Falwell's Moral Majority,
gearing up for the Presidential election and its anti-abortion fight,
targeted the Domestic Violence bill for defeat.[34] During the summer
Senators received hundreds of pieces of mail, many of them form
letters, that opposed the legislation stating, "This legislation would
not allow me to spank my child and I oppose it;" "battered women's
shelters make women promise to divorce their husbands in order to
enter the shelters;" "don't meddle in family matters." Lies abounded.
Senator Gordon Humphrey from New Hampshire, opposing the
legislation and perhaps infuriated by the Civil Rights Commission
hearings, inserted these comments in the Congressional Record.

> The Federal Government should not fund missionaries who would
> war on the traditional family or on local values....
> The money is almost entirely devoted to the creation of more
> bureaucracy and more indoctrination centers for women with family
> difficulties.[35]

Distortions, typical of reactionary attack, had begun even earlier as
Phyllis Schafly, a leader of anti-abortion and anti-ERA forces,

asserted:

> Under questioning, many of the experts in domestic violence concede that the principal problem in domestic violence is alcohol, with other drugs close behind. They also concede that most wives who are beaten by their husbands return to them after R and R at a shelter, and that a large percentage of wives return repeatedly.[36]

To imply that a stay in a shelter is like a vacation is an extraordinary cruelty. For Senator Humphrey and Ms. Schafly to suggest that they care about the family, as millions of women within it are beaten and have nowhere to go, reveals their actual horrifying disregard for human life.

Several senators, whose support appeared guaranteed in the summer, had changed their vote by September, but the bill squeaked by the Senate, 46-41, on September 4, 1980. A conference committee met later that month, resolving the House and Senate differences in a way the National Coalition desired; and the House approved the conference report 276-117.[37] Just as National Coalition supporters at the local level kept up their efforts, the opposition continued its attack. After the November elections, when Senator Cranston brought the bill up for a vote, opponents threatened to filibuster and the Senator withdrew the bill, effectively killing it. Although Representative Mikulski has already reintroduced it in the 97th Congress, few remain hopeful about its passage in a more conservative Congress.

Most analyses attribute the failure to pass domestic violence legislation to a right-wing mobilization. Although acknowledging the damage done by this kind of opposition, the National Coalition Against Domestic Violence blames its liberal senate "allies" and the White House, as well as a Washington budget slashing climate, for the legislation's demise. The National Coalition suggests that, unlike his peers in the House of Representatives, Senator Cranston neither shared information with grassroots groups nor aggressively pushed the legislation forward. Unnecessarily waiting until Reagan's victory hurt the bill's chances even more. Moreover, key liberal supporters, while paying lip service to the bill, neither showed enthusiasm nor jockeyed for the legislation. During February and March, the Coalition unsuccessfully asked the White House to send an endorsement letter to the Senate. In August, when President Carter was in reelection trouble, Coalition staff were suddenly invited to the White House, but as one woman noted, "It was too little too late; for victory, the White House had to move earlier, but only its female staff cared about this legislation."[38]

June Zeitlin, the former director of HHS's* short-lived Office on Domestic Violence, adds another assessment of the legislative defeat.

> It is a tribute to the National Coalition that this legislation got so far. It is very unusual that women's legislation is taken up so fast. From perceiving a problem to enacting legislation is usually a far longer process.[39]

Although this defeat was a major loss, the National Coalition and the battered women's movement had successfully used legislative organizing to publicly educate thousands of people around the country. Most significantly, federal legislation prodded the battered women's movement to organize internally. Hundreds of women first learned to lobby and build local and statewide networks in their efforts to pass this legislation. As they coordinated a state by state effort, National Coalition staff came to know, first on the telephone and later in person, hundreds of women who either joined the National Coalition or turned to it for assistance.

Even as the legislative effort consumed major time and energy, other work proceeded. Throughout 1980-1981 the organization attempted to redefine itself, and "it was agreed that coalition building and services to membership should take priority along with leadership in political thinking/visioning and political education in the immediate future. NCADV needs to work hard to help battered women and workers in the movement come out of isolation into a sharing/empowering dialogue with sisters across the nation."[40] Although there was not enough money to finance another large membership conference until the summer of 1982, the National Coalition declared October 17, 1981 as a national day of unity on behalf of battered women across the country.

The Coalition continues to work on many fronts. In an effort to analyze and organize around serious issues, the coalition has solicited position papers on topics such as co-optation; alliances with other movements; the role of battered women in the movement; and the concerns of rural, third world, and lesbian women. As of this writing, few papers have been produced. However, at least three task forces are working on some of the key issues. The Rural Women's Task Force has asked each state coalition to designate a rural caucus

---

* Health & Human Services, formerly the Department of Health, Education and Welfare.

representative; as a first activity, a questionnaire has been circulated asking rural programs to detail the special problems they face. The Lesbian Task Force has developed a national plan of action for combatting homophobia through educational training and organizing activity. And in the fall of 1981, the Women of Color Task Force, working collaboratively with the steering committee, received an eight month Ford Foundation planning grant to research employment training models targeted at women of color and low income and rural women who have been battered. The possibility of developing small businesses, as both training sites and income generating sources for shelters, will be explored through this grant.

Today the coalition continues to define itself as a monitor of public policy and a watchdog for the interests of grassroots groups, a critical national role. By bringing together twenty-five women from all parts of the country, the steering committee is a useful forum for sharing political and "state of the movement" information, mobilizing networks to stop harmful developments and capitalize on beneficial ones.

Not only have women shared skills, program ideas, and support, which are then redistributed throughout each region, but, with mixed results, they have also experimented with feminist organizational forms to see if principles of non-competitive fundraising, cooperation, and consensus decision making can be applied to larger efforts. The coalition hopes to build a non-hierarchical national organization which works effectively and, at the same time, develops into a multi-racial feminist organization. And at least among themselves, delegates have replicated the joy and strength that women continue to feel at local levels.

But major problems that are common for national organizations with a grassroots base prevail. The membership declined significantly after the national conference. A major membership drive in the summer of 1981 again raised membership to over 500 and dues helped keep the national office open. With little money and no legislative direction, it is difficult to know how to best reach and involve the membership. Since the National Coalition is politically and geographically diverse, its membership has varied needs. Some relatively well funded member groups, who belong to strong coalitions and have a fierce commitment to grassroots autonomy, want the National Coalition to focus solely on federal initiatives. Others, isolated and with extremely limited resources, ask for technical assistance in their local and state legislative, coalition-building, and fundraising campaigns. Noting an additional dynamic, the National

Coalition staff commented that most members call desperate for advice about their financial problems whereas some steering committee representatives see their role as preserving the movement and its vision.

For the immediate future, the work of the National Coalition may be redefined by necessity. The introduction of the Family Protection Act and the Human Life Amendment, two right-wing bills, and the cutbacks in federal grants suggest that the National Coalition will have to use most of its energy and resources to prevent federal disasters.

An International Battered Women's Movement

On March 4-8, 1976 in Brussels, 2000 women from 33 countries came together for the International Tribunal on Crimes Against Women.[41] For four days, women heard testimony, held workshops, and shared information about rape, battering, forced sterilization, mutilation, and economic and legal crimes against women. At this historic event, organized by and for women, the workshop on battered women proposed the following resolution which was sent to the governments of all countries.

> The women of Japan, Netherlands, France, Wales, England, Scotland, Ireland, Australia, USA, and Germany have begun the fight for the rights of battered women and their children. We call for urgent action by all countries to combat the crime of woman-battering. We demand that governments recognize the existence and extent of this problem, and accept the need for refuges, financial aid, and effective legal protection for these women.[42]

On April 14-15, 1978, 128 women from 13 western nations met at the International Conference on Battered Women in Amsterdam, concluding their conference with the following press release.

> Although individual refuges in different countries face different practical problems of housing, finances and government policies, we agreed to the fact that women being battered is rooted in an international acceptance of the subordination of women.

Revealing the similarities in an international movement, workshops explored the use of paid and nonpaid staff, refuge structure and organization, research, publicity, fundraising, and a feminist analysis of battering.[43]

In 1981, women from twenty countries held yet another international meeting and today the Women's Aid Federation, England's national coalition of battered women's groups, reports contacts with organizers from Europe, Asia, and Africa, all searching for information and support.[44] Although most international movement information available in the U.S. comes from England, usually through journals or personal contacts, women from these two countries have not had formal meetings, except for the large conferences mentioned above. News from Japan, Israel, Australia, Germany, and France is even less frequently received and distributed.

The knowledge of an international movement, however, continues to bring encouragement, support, and advice to women in the U.S. And, in a time of cutbacks and increased concern about the political direction of the movement, the need for mutual strategizing is urgent. Movements in different countries offer comparisons that illuminate our own strengths, weaknesses, and struggles even though comparisons do not always adequately account for differences in historical and material conditions between countries.

Shelters around the world confront similar questions, and as in the U.S., sometimes come up with diverse answers. As late as 1979, one of Amsterdam's first refuges, Blijf van m'n lijf, founded in 1974 and housing ninety-seven women and children in an old mansion, refused to solicit government funding. It placed the highest importance on autonomy. Only one worker is paid; the collective that established the shelter donates labor on a rotating basis.[45] An Oslo shelter, also based on principles of self-organization and self-reliance, accepts government money and still maintains a non-hierarchical collective structure.[46] In most countries, not all shelters are feminist. Ninety-seven out of 135 English shelters belong to the feminist Women's Aid Federation.[47] In heavily Catholic Quebec, some shelters are run by religious orders, some by feminists, and the remainder by professional social service agencies.[48]

Although only approximately 25 of Australia's 100 refuges are feminist, feminist influence reaches far beyond what numbers suggest. For example, in New South Wales, one of Australia's seven states, the government adopted feminist guidelines for refuge provision. These include that the shelter must be organized as a collective of staff, residents, and ex-residents; that its workers allocate time to political organizing around women's concerns in their community; and that the shelter staff remain non-professional.[49]

Started by women squatters, Elsie, the first Australian refuge, uses its government funding to support a large staff, including four child care workers and one ex-resident worker who helps organize women who have lived at the shelter. Elsie runs a food co-op for itself and former residents, as well as a second hand clothing store where everything sells for twenty cents. Child care is offered twenty-four hours a day to alleviate battered women's burdens and to encourage residents to relax and spend time outside the shelter.[50]

In Marickville, Australia, women have acted on their feminist beliefs in another way. After carefully helping an ex-resident group build its strength and skills over a period of years, the feminist collective recently gave shelter control to the ex-residents.[51]

In 1982, Australian feminists face a difficult fight. For seven years, with a progressive Labour government, shelters received federally earmarked dollars for operating expenses and salaries. With the election of a right-wing government committed to social service cutbacks, all federal funds are now passed on to the states as general revenue sharing. As a result, shelters are forced to negotiate with state governments for their funds. The outcome is uncertain; New South Wales' shelters were recently refunded, although in states with more conservative governments, shelters may find stronger resistance. Seeing strength in numbers, shelter workers across the country have organized, demanding an adequate wage and refusing suggestions to use volunteers until the shelters are sufficiently funded and staffed.[52]

Reports from England, Scotland, Northern Ireland, and Wales suggest that individual shelters and national organizations in these countries face many of the same issues as the movement in the United States. A 1979 Annual Report from Scottish Women's Aid, the national organization with which many shelters affiliate, documents individual shelter's complaints of having neither a long-term secure funding base, nor enough shelter space for all the women who need it.[53] Additionally, shelters are harassed by inconsistent responses from local police, social work departments, and housing authorities. Safe, decent housing for relocation often is unavailable and refuges are constantly in need of repair. The British movement has targeted legal reform, second-stage housing for women who have left the shelter, and fair implementation of their Homeless Persons Act as crucial areas in which to work.

As in the United States, for significant portions of the British movement, democratic and cooperative work structures are the ideal. Sometimes, too, these preferences come into conflict with those of traditional agencies. Most groups in England, Scotland,

Wales and Northern Ireland form non-hierarchical support groups. Support groups are of nonpaid community women who take long-term responsibility for the refuges. They help battered women, maintain the refuge, and nurture one another. They are women working with women for women.[54]

A former coordinator of National Women's Aid Federation* in England described how local groups are recommended for national membership, further clarifying internal refuge politics.

> Collectivity is the desired work form for most of us. Decisions should not be made by paid staff but rather the general meeting of three groups—women living in the house, women paid to work in the house, and the support group, or when there is no paid staff, of two groups— women living in the house and the support group. They decide if a resident should be kicked out, how the house runs, and admissions policy. Many residents don't come to general meetings so the shelter support group of twelve or so women is often dominant. Conflicts about expectations of all three groups are common. Women in the house think workers don't do enough for them. Workers and the support group have conflicts over who will do the work which is often more than the whole group can handle. Battered women see the shelter as a service and some of us see it as our political work. We also have to look out for its long-term interests.[55]

Debates within the British movement, locally and nationally, have been echoed in shelters throughout the United States. One such debate ponders the effect of earning a salary for work that has been defined as a political commitment rather than as a career. Although some refuges are still run by unpaid workers, most local women's aid groups feel they need proper funding to continue. Needing more funds has, predictably, raised the concern about co-optation—losing control of the shelters and the movement.[56] A second major debate has centered on the role of men in the movement. A third tension within the British movement focuses on the relationship between Women's Aid and Women's Liberation. The 1979-1980 Scottish Women's Aid Annual Report summarizes the point being contested.

> *In support:* ...that Women's Aid should be aligned with the Women's Liberation Movement as the main organisation fighting women's happening.[57]

---

* The name "Women's Aid" can be confusing to American readers since it refers both to local refuges and to national organizations of refuges. Originally, the National Women's Aid Federation included women from England, Wales, Northern Ireland, and Scotland. By 1980, each country had its own National Women's Aid Federation.

from the Women's Movement.

Against: Several groups were unhappy about a public identification with the Women's Liberation Movement as they felt it would alienate officials and potential volunteers in the small towns and rural areas. Inverness pointed out that they had experience of this happening.[57]

The debate over the relationship between feminism and the battered women's movement had, earlier, precipitated an ugly battle between Erin Pizzey—a key figure in the movement—and many other groups. As the founder of the first English refuge, Chiswick Women's Aid, Erin Pizzey demonstrated an unrelenting determination in the battle to secure shelters for battered women in the early 1970s. Her pioneering work was invaluable. However, according to the National Women's Aid Federation, four years later in 1975, at a conference of over thirty groups, Pizzey fought against the establishment of a national feminist organization. Angered by her defeat, she sent the following letter to every Social Service and Housing Department in the country.

We are particularly worried and unhappy that there are groups who seem to be trying to use Women's Aid as a platform for Women's Liberation and Gay Women's Liberation.

We would strongly advise Social Services and Housing Departments to look very carefully at the groups in their areas who are offering to set up refuge before giving them your support. If in doubt please feel free to contact us at Chiswick for any information.[58]

This letter's effect varied by locality; in some places groups had to face questions about their politics and a few suddenly had their requests for refuges turned down.[59] But despite Pizzey's efforts, the Women's Aid Federation of England grows.

The problems, however, continue. One activist talks of the difficulty of dealing with the media.

We have very limited coverage in the press as a direct result of our not being prepared to produce bloodcurdling stories to keep the papers happy. Neither are we prepared to produce individual women as 'stars' for them; they therefore continue to refer to the 'star' they already have created in Ms. Pizzey who is also prepared to give the blood and guts stories they want.[60]

As in the United States, financial problems plague the movement. As of 1981 in England, out of a total of 135 refuges, 70 are not government funded. Voiunteers and the residents meet weekly to solve problems, but no daily service by paid staff can be provided. In shelters with paid staff, funding is spread out so that a few women receive small salaries. As one woman noted, "you earn just enough to live on. Many staff women live in groups. You can't make this your career. In most of our refuges the paid staff is small."[61] In Women's Aid refuges, it is rare for staff to stay overnight. Residents would experience this behavior as an invasion of their space.[62]

In England, many women now live in refuges for as long as nine months because of the housing shortage. Housing issues are thus a major focus of Women's Aid agitation. In 1977 a Homeless Persons Act, which establishes a battered woman's legal right to housing, was passed through the efforts of a large housing coalition. As a result, when no shelter space is available, some local authorities now put women in hostels or Bed and Breakfast hotels. Women's Aid groups believe that adequate housing, one long-term solution to the plight of battered women, needs to be raised as a national demand.[63]

Because of financial constraints and political decisions, Women's Aid groups generally provide far less comprehensive service to battered women than their U.S. counterparts. Mental health services are offered only as referrals, and for the most part, professionals have expressed little interest in being included in the movement.

When the National Women's Aid Federation was established in 1975, its thirty-five founding groups agreed on the following aims:

1. To provide temporary refuge on request, for women and their children who have suffered mental or physical harassment;
2. To encourage the women to determine their own futures and to help them achieve them, whether this involves returning home or starting a new life elsewhere;
3. To recognize and care for the emotional and educational needs of the children involved;
4. To offer support and advice and help to any woman who asks for it, whether or not she is a resident, and also to offer support and aftercare to any woman and child who has left the refuge; and
5. To educate and inform the public, the media, the police, the courts, social services, and other authorities with respect to the battering of women, mindful of the fact that this is a result of the general position of women in our society.[64]

Like coalitions in the United States, national organizations help new groups, provide a forum for skill and political sharing, and wage legal and other reform battles. Although it is difficult to estimate because shelters open and close continually, by 1981 there were approximately 135 refuges in England, 97 of them affiliated with Women's Aid. There were 37 shelters in Scotland, Wales, and Northern Ireland affiliated with National Women's Aid Federation; another 20 such refuges were in formation in these countries in 1981.[65]

For some women, working with their National Women's Aid Federation is a major political commitment. Jo Sutton, the first National Women's Aid Federation coordinator, sums up the radical emphasis of the national organization.

> The title 'Women's Aid' makes no mention of battering nor of any form of violence against women. Women's Aid was aware from the outset that a woman injured by her husband was only a physical symptom of the social position of women.[66]

Social Change on Behalf of Battered Women: Reforming the Criminal Justice System

Changing Police Practices

One survey reports that in almost half the violence cases, women turn to no one,[1] a shocking reminder of the depth of their isolation. Thousands of battered women, however, do ask for assistance. Many turn in desperation to the police, the only "helping" agency open twenty-four hours a day. Before the movement began, the typical attitude toward intervention on behalf of battered women was recorded unashamedly in the Michigan Police Training Academy procedures.

    a. Avoid arrest if possible. Appeal to their vanity.
    b. Explain the procedure of obtaining a warrant.
       1. Complainant must sign complaint.
       2. Must appear in court.
       3. Consider loss of time.
       4. Cost of court.
    c. State that your only interest is to prevent a breach of the peace.
    d. Explain that attitudes usually change by court time.
    e. Recommend a postponement.
       1. Court not in session.
       2. No judge available.
    f. *Don't* be too harsh or critical.[2]

The failure to weigh the seriousness of assault and its potential for escalating into homicide had grave consequences. In a Kansas City study of domestic assault, the Police Department found that "they had responded to disturbance calls at the address of homicide victims or suspects at least once in the 2 years before the homicide in 90 percent of the cases, and five or more times in the 2 years before the homicide in 50 percent of the cases."[3]

At the beginning of the movement, battered women complained frequently that the police simply would not come when called. If they did come, they would refuse to arrest, saying: "There's nothing we can do. It's a family matter; go to Family Court tomorrow." Or they would side with the husband, walking him around the block or joking with him about the violence. Police refused to escort women to hospitals or to wait and protect them as they gathered their children and clothing. Continually looking through sexist blinders, the police failed to acknowledge that this victim was often frightened and intimidated because she lived with her assailant.

James Bannon, Commander of the Detroit Police Department, corroborates battered women's stories as he explains the procedures police used.

> The second example of a not atypical strategy is what has become known as "call screening." Some years back, calls for police service exceeded the department's ability to respond. The decision was made not to respond to certain types of calls. Wouldn't you know that the first calls screened out were family troubles.[4]

Bannon describes how battered women's cases "disappeared" as they proceeded through the criminal justice system in Detroit.

> In 1972 for instance, there were 4900 assaults of this kind which had survived the screening process long enough to at least have a request for warrant prepared and the complainant referred to the assault and battery squad. Through the process of conciliation, complainant harassment and prosecutor discretion, fewer than 300 of these cases were ultimately tried by a court of law.[5]

Calling this treatment malfeasance, Bannon offered his explanation for why only 300 out of 4900 assaults were tried.

> It is my view that police, and later prosecutors and courts, contribute to domestic violence by their laissez-faire attitudes toward what they view as essentially a "personal problem." This is made even more problematic because police are socialized to regard females in general as subordinate.[6]

Laws against assault and battery existed in every state before the battered women's movement began. Assault and battery is always a crime, either a misdemeanor or felony, depending on the seriousness of the attack. But, as Del Martin notes:

> Usually, in misdemeanor cases a police officer can only make an arrest on the spot if the act is committed in his presence or if a warrant has been issued....
>
> When a felony has been committed, an officer is authorized to make an arrest on "reasonable belief" or "probable cause," that is, if he has sufficient reason to believe that a felony has been committed and that the person identified by the victim or witnesses committed the crime. But this provision, being the most subjective and also the easiest to ignore, is rarely invoked in wife-abuse cases.[7]

Although laws vary significantly from state to state, the battered women's movement worked legislatively to see that wife beating was treated as a crime—a social, not a private matter. The movement argued that battered women deserved the same rights as any other crime victims, and worked with the police, legislators, and courts to enforce already existing laws or to create new ones. Additionally, parts of the movement asserted that because this victim lives with her victimizer and faces recurrent intimidation and danger, police arrest powers should be expanded. As one lawyer noted, "in battered women's cases, the police tend to view serious attacks as misdemeanors rather than felonies so you must specify in legislation that the police may arrest without a warrant for a misdemeanor offense."[8] As a result of the movement:

> Twenty-seven of the recent state laws on domestic violence expand police power to arrest in domestic abuse cases. In twenty-one states, arrest without a warrant is permitted where a police officer has probable cause to believe that an abuser has committed a misdemeanor. In fourteen states, police may arrest without a warrant if they have probable cause to believe that an abuser has violated a protection order. (Eight states allow probable cause arrest in both cases.)...
>
> Almost half the statutes impose some duties on police responding to domestic disturbance calls, including transporting the victim to a hospital or shelter, informing her of her legal options, staying until she is no longer in danger....[9]

In much new legislation, the emphasis is on enforcing the victim's rights, increasing her legal options, and protecting her from further assaults.

In Oakland and New York, the battered women's movement decided that the best way to deal with recalcitrant police was through legal confrontation rather than legislative change or bureaucratic negotiation. In October 1976, battered women filed a class action suit, Scott v. Hart, against the Oakland Police Department, and in December 1976, battered wives leveled a suit, Bruno v. Codd, against the New York City Police Department, the New York City Department of Probation, and the clerks of the Family Court.[10] In New York City, the Litigation Coalition for Battered Women charged the police and courts with gross failure to comply with the law. One plaintiff's deposition stated that the police refused to arrest her husband even though he was still hitting her when they arrived and they had to pry his hands from around her neck. Another woman, beaten many times, was told by Family Court personnel that she would have to bring her husband with her to the court's family counseling program before she could get an order of protection.[11] In an unstated admission of their guilt, the police settled the NY suit before it went to trial. The agreement stipulated that the police must: 1. arrest men who commit felonious assaults; 2. send out officers for every call from a battered woman; 3. arrest in misdemeanor cases unless there is justification not to arrest; 4. arrest where the husband has violated a Family Court protection order; 5. assist the woman in receiving medical help; and 6. search for a husband who has fled the scene of the crime as the police do in other cases.[12]

Lawsuits were one tactic that dramatically focused national attention on the institutional complicity that kept women battered. The examples provided by activists in New York and Oakland encouraged women in New Haven, Chicago, and Atlanta to threaten their police departments with lawsuits and inspired Los Angeles women to sue in 1979. Although only a few lawsuits were filed, their impact reached far beyond the departments sued. As one activist noted, "some of us...have been able to use the leverage of other cities' suits to get our police departments to review their policies, procedures and training..."[13]

Time is needed to fully assess the impact of these suits. They helped activists find one another across the country, share information, strategize, and build a movement. Locally, the early lawsuits brought together lawyers, grassroots groups, and battered women in a joint effort to reclaim women's rights. Where these coalitions have remained organized to monitor the police, abuses, while still frequent, have decreased. In one New York City neighborhood with an active grassroots service program, police compliance with the law is significantly better than in neighborhoods with no watchdog agency. In general, change is described as small, based on individual officer's attitudes. In evaluating the lawsuits, a veteran feminist lawyer cautions, "don't do lawsuits unless you are in this for life. Police attitudes are embedded in centuries of sexism, and if you don't have an organized movement behind you, lawsuits won't help."[14] Another activist lawyer notes, "litigation can be used for social change. It is not a change agent in itself but rather a public relations tactic that gives the movement power to negotiate."[15]

A final focus of statutory or regulatory change was police training procedures. One Michigan study revealed that although almost half of all police calls for assistance are about domestic violence, only 3 to 5 out of 240 hours of police recruit training are spent learning to handle domestic violence complaints.[16] While hailed by many, police training legislation can be problematic unless carefully written and monitored. Because so many police officers are killed answering "domestic disturbance" calls, it is in the interest of the police to protect officers, mediate the conflict, and leave as soon as possible. Training can easily fall into teaching the police crisis intervention and mediation techniques. These skills, while helpful to officers, leave battered women in a vulnerable position. In a context where one person unpredictably resorts to force to get his way, "mediation" offers no safety for the victim. It holds no legal sanction. The victim learns nothing about her rights. Because of these problems, the battered women's movement has often opposed mediation and pushed for very specific training legislation that encourages officers to arrest the batterer and to assist the victim. One example from Washington is cited as a model.

> All training relating to the handling of domestic violence complaints by law enforcement officers shall stress enforcement of criminal laws in domestic situations, availability of community resources, and protection of the victim. Law enforcement agencies and community organizations with expertise in the issue of domestic violence shall cooperate in all aspects of the training.[17]

Even model legislation, however, can be ineffective without monitoring by women's programs. Police training mandates can be easily ignored and subverted, and behavior can stay remarkably fixed in sexist patterns.

Court Reform

Courts, like the police, reflect sexist values and often provide little aid to victims of battering. Court orders are supposed to protect battered women.

> A protection order (also called a restraining order or temporary injunction) is an order issued to an abuser by a court requiring him to change his conduct. The court may, depending on state law, order an abuser to move out of a residence shared with the victim, to refrain from abuse or contact with the victim, to attend a counseling program, or to pay support, restitution, or attorney's fees. The court may award child custody and visitation rights or may restrict use or disposition of personal property...[18]

At the beginning of the battered women's movement, in many states such protective orders were available only to women filing for divorce; as of 1981, twelve states still granted such injunctions pending only divorce, separation, or custody proceedings.[19] For religious, economic, moral, or emotional reasons, many battered women will not file for divorces; such women were, and in some cases still are, without civil court protection.

My observations as a battered women's advocate in 1978-79 in Manhattan Family Court, a civil court, suggest typical problems battered women's groups have sought to remedy. This Family Court offers women Orders of Protection, pieces of paper that order the abuser to refrain from harassing, menacing, or assaulting the petitioner for one year. Failure to comply with such orders can result in six months in jail, although in my twelve month experience, only one husband, violating a court order for the eighth time by throwing his wife from a second story window, went to jail. His sentence was thirty days.

The law states that the purpose of Family Court is to keep the family together. Twisting the law to their own ends, probation officers used this mandate to keep women out of court. As noted in the New York City lawsuit, Family Court probation employees—those who interview each court petitioner before she sees a judge—denied women access to court by illegally coercing them into family counseling. Unlike the potential inherent in a court order of protection, family counseling offers neither protection nor any enforcement mechanism to punish men if further abuse occurs. As a result, battered women felt the seriousness of their cases denied. Heaping one abuse on top of another, hostile attitudes toward victims were commonly expressed; one probation officer carefully explained to me that battered women are generally, "shrewish, unfeminine, and crushing."

Even when granting orders of protection, judges urged counseling. Only rarely did they exercise their authority to remove an abusive man from the home; women and their children, therefore, bore the burden of leaving. Three or four week delays were common between the date of a woman's first court appearance in which she was granted a Temporary Order of Protection and a second hearing in which her husband was entitled to legal counsel. Long delays and adjournments often resulted. In the meantime, she might be beaten again and advised by the police to go back to court and file a violation of an Order of Protection; no arrest would occur. If her husband appeared for this hearing, he was usually verbally reprimanded. Many men learned that the court would do nothing to stop their abuse. Sometimes they even watched judges grant mutual orders of protection in which non-violent women were ordered to stop "harassing" their husbands. The humiliation was often unbearable for women.

Family Court can also grant visitation, support, and custody rights. Men who batter often use visitation as a form of tormenting their wives by failing to return children on time. Since most order of protection hearings, especially those without attorneys, last no more than minutes, few women ever have the chance to explain to judges their unique fears about further violence or their concerns about child snatching. In addition, if violations of visitation rights occurred on a weekend, women had no immediate access to the courts.

Legal remedies for unmarried women were even more problematic. In New York City, for example, Family Court serves married women only. Unmarried women are sent to a totally ineffective summons court or to criminal court if their cases are serious. Fearful of retaliation or protective of their men, many women do not want to use criminal court and find themselves with no civil court remedies.

In some states, where battered women's advocates were well organized, activists wrote, lobbied for, and helped implement state legislation that offers women more substantial remedies. A member of the Battered Women's Action Committee describes the provisions of the Abuse Prevention Act passed in Massachusetts in 1978 which is modeled on the Pennsylvania legislation enacted in 1976.

1. *Broad definition of abuse.* "Abuse" is defined as attempting to cause or actually causing physical harm, putting another in fear of imminent physical harm, or making another engage involuntarily in sexual relations by fear, fear of force, or duress.
2. *Greater availability of emergency protective orders.* Unmarried people living together, as well as women married to their abusers, may request emergency orders. Married women are eligible for emergency

orders whether or not they choose to file for divorce or separation. These emergency orders include protective orders as well as those for custody and support. The request is made on a simple complaint form which is free and can be filled out without the assistance of an attorney. Orders are issued the same day; a hearing will be held within 5 days to give the abuser the opportunity to respond. Local police stations can advise women of judges available on a rotating basis during hours when the court is closed.[20]

The Massachusetts law mandates that victims can request compensation for injuries, moving expenses, and loss of income; that violation of the order is a criminal offense; that police must take whatever steps necessary to prevent further abuse. Police must arrest the attacker if a felony has occurred, if a misdemeanor has been committed in their presence, or if a protective order has been violated. And finally, "recognizing that jail is not a solution to violence,..." the law suggests referrals to counseling, a residential treatment facility, or probation officer in sentencing while contact with the victim of abuse remains restricted.[21]

Although courts have had the judicial right to evict a violent man based on legal precedents of just and fair treatment, they never offered this option to battered women. This inequity was partially corrected as state legislatures passed laws specifying that the abuser, not the victim, bears the burden of leaving. In some states where these laws are in effect, women hail them as significant reforms. For example, rural service projects, without local shelters, often successfully use court vacate orders and then support women in their efforts to stand firm against their husbands' recurring threats. Thirty-two of the new protection order laws have eviction clauses which give victims a right to their homes.[22] From surveys done around the country, however, it is clear that courts are not consistently granting protection and vacate orders.

In assessing any criminal justice system changes, it is important to distinguish large urban areas from small towns. It is also crucial to recognize differences between coalitions and local programs that have allocated significant resources to police and court training and monitoring from those that have not. Reports from small towns, while very varied, generally are more optimistic than those from large urban areas. In small towns, police and judges have been confronted about their sexist behavior by advocates who are often their neighbors. Personal contact frequently allows ongoing discussion and has sometimes brought noticeable improvements in law enforcement. In some areas, judges and police have felt the weight of social criticism as women mobilize others in the community to condemn sloppy law enforcement. Even more marked changes are sometimes recounted by those coalitions, like Pennsylvania, that received grants to train police and district justices throughout the state. In one year, staff trained all 580 of Pennsylvania's district justices and 400 police officers, noting attitudinal and behavioral changes in many.[23]

Divorce, support, and child custody laws were also amended as a result of the activity of the battered women's movement. In states that maintain "fault" divorces, desertion is defined as one ground for divorce. Battered women who left their husbands to avoid abuse were sometimes found to have abandoned their families and thus could be divorced by their husbands. Facing the maddening logic of sexist double-binds, women then discovered that desertion charges were used against them in child custody battles. New Jersey, therefore, adopted specific legislation stating that abuse is a defense to any action alleging desertion.[24] In Illinois, a sixth factor was added to the five existing ones for determining the best interests of the child in custody cases.

> The physical violence or threat of physical violence by the child's potential custodian, whether directed against the child or directed against another person but witnessed by the child.[25]

Another Illinois statutory provision allowed victims, often harassed by their abusers even after they leave them, to avoid divulging their addresses on court orders if such disclosures might endanger them or their children.[26]

In their search for legal support in civil cases, most battered women, with access to few, if any, financial resources, found that courts were not the only cause for complaint. With some notable exceptions, like the Family Law Unit at South Brooklyn Legal Services, advocates bemoan the lack of help available through Legal Services, the agency mandated and funded to offer legal assistance to the poor. As several activist attorneys have remarked, "most lawyers see family law as the boring junk, or worse, the sphere that forces them to serve hysterical women." Although Legal Services is mandated to help anyone who fits into its eligibility criteria, each office chooses its priorities. Some offices subvert their mandate by including husbands' income in eligibility determinations and declaring battered women "over-income" and thus ineligible for services. In others, only routine divorce cases are handled, while emergency protective orders are not. Complicated cases—in which rights to protection, custody, and support are contested—may be passed on to the youngest, least experienced attorneys.

Poor legal treatment is not just the result of local decisions. The National Center on Women and Family Law, a Legal Services back-up center mandated to scrutinize the needs of women and disseminate information nationally, receives the lowest allocation of any Legal Services back-up center. It will be hardest hit by cutbacks, and probably will be the first center phased out by President Reagan. Women attorneys organized and pressured Legal Services to establish this Center, yet from the beginning, these attorneys were told that battered women were an inappropriate priority.

Like Civil courts, Criminal courts demeaned battered women and trivialized their experiences. Badly beaten women, desperate for protection, often saw charges reduced or dismissed by prosecutors and heard attorneys and judges alike recommend counseling or mediation. The constant taunts: "You don't want to lock him up; he'll lose his job; your kids need a father," greeted battered women who tried to prosecute. Prosecutors considered these cases a bother, demanding proof of severe injury, promises to follow through, and "character" checks to verify battered women's credibility as witnesses. Like rape victims, battered women often felt like the criminal.

Ten states have passed legislation making spouse abuse a separate criminal offense; this legislation creates no new substantive law but rather emphasizes the need for enforcement of criminal law and makes data collection easier.[27] Some states have passed legislation setting conditions for pre-trial release and deferred prosecution. These include orders of protection specifying that the abuser is to stay away from the victim. Michigan and California legislation has created diversionary counseling programs, ordering defendants to participate in counseling. If the defendant completes the program successfully, charges are dismissed; if he fails to comply with program criteria, criminal proceedings can be resumed.[28]

Some women have opposed mandatory therapy on the grounds that it deprives people of their civil rights; that mandated, rather than chosen treatment never works; and that men who batter should face serious consequences that only criminal sanctions bring. Moreover, some courts use counseling diversion as a way of throwing cases out. Many worry that court-appointed therapists hold sexist views about treatment. Focusing on keeping the family unit together, they fail to understand the seriousness of violence and have few skills to stop it. Men will not only be released unchanged but also might have their sexist views reinforced.

Other feminists, however, argue that mandated counseling should be tried because it is one of the only tools available to help men to change their behavior. For them, the important issue becomes the ideology and therapeutic practice of the counselors as well as the conditions for counseling that the court imposes. As a result of court demonstration projects that have tested mandated therapy, feminists have drawn several tentative conclusions about the nature of such counseling. These include that: 1. the victim retain the right to express her wishes about court diversion decisions; 2. men who have histories of repeated arrests and severe violent attacks should not be diverted to counseling; 3. abusers must participate regularly in a program in which stopping their violence is the treatment focus and alternative methods of handling anger are provided; the counselor's goal is to stop the violence, not to keep the family together. 4. if further violence or threats occur or the counseling contract is violated, prosecution will resume; 5. contact between the victim and abuser is restricted or if the couple is still living together, the counseling program must maintain a relationship with the woman to determine if further abuse is occurring; 6. the woman also is entitled to advocacy and support; 7. battered women should be informed that counseling is a long process that often fails with violent men. No woman should be falsely assured about the efficacy of counseling. Because men who batter minimize or deny the seriousness of their threats and assaults, counselor involvement with the battered woman is essential. Diversionary programs which do not meet regularly with the abuser or those that use traditional psychotherapeutic methods, like couple counseling, and refrain from focusing on changing violent behavior are ineffective and dangerous.

The battered women's movement has tried a variety of solutions to deal with the many problems victims face within the criminal court system. Women's groups have organized court watching projects, gathering evidence about battered women's experiences to use as leverage in negotiations for institutional change. Reminding judges that they are publicly accountable for their actions, some groups send large contingents to court, especially for trials involving women who were badly brutalized. And in some cases, attorneys advocate using criminal and civil remedies jointly, especially against those men who would rather see a woman dead than free.

At the same time that they serve as individual women's advocates, feminist attorneys and shelter workers attempt to educate court personnel about the seriousness of violence. These educational efforts have included formal training sessions for judges and police as well as informal meetings and discussions about the meaning and impact of violence. Many advocates report that frequently criminal justice personnel, including judges, have little awareness of and inaccurate information about family law. If the legislature has recently enacted new laws, ignorance tends to multiply. Heightening the problem, many judges hold stereotypic attitudes toward battered women, either seeing them as nags or as women who drop their cases. Education and training, therefore, are essential. Although reports from advocates in states like Pennsylvania are optimistic about the effectiveness of training, it is too early to assess long-term change, even where the movement has allocated significant resources to this work.

Sometimes advocates working to reform court procedures must spend time on petty matters. In Pennsylvania, for example, advocates not only had to oversee the development of new legal forms but also push each county court to buy them. Activists encounter infuriating resistance at literally every step in the process through which law is translated into practice. They are often forced to take their complaints back to the legislature and lobby over minor matters like who is mandated to distribute legal forms.

As in the anti-rape movement, a debate flares up repeatedly over whether to raise or lower the severity of criminal court punishments for violent men. The argument for increased severity suggests that to be taken seriously, violence against women must be labeled the crime it is and punished. Felony charges are a logical and necessary protection because of the unequal power context in which battered women operate. The reality is, however, that an overworked criminal justice system still largely sees women's problems, including violence, as inconsequential and a waste of police and court time. As a result, if the police are aware that abusers will be charged with felonies and punished more severely, they may simply stop arresting; similarly, judges might find fewer men guilty. The law's intention could be easily subverted. A more practical counter suggestion is to force the courts to treat family violence like other forms of assault with a range of penalties, higher for felonies and lower for misdemeanors. This argument recognizes that although education and monitoring are a continual necessity to insure that battered women's cases are even treated as assaults, it is more effective to declare battered women equal to others rather than make them a more protected class.[29] It also counters the alternative suggestion of lower penalties for all wife beating, including felonies, and suggests that such lowering feeds into the sexism that views battering as insignificant.

The battered women's movement currently faces major challenges about civil and criminal court legislation and proceedings. Because several potentially dangerous bills have been introduced within state legislatures, the movement must remain vigilant and mobilized to insure that seemingly "helpful" legislation fails to pass. For example, the New Hampshire legislature introduced a bill that required medical personnel to report all cases of adult abuse. In Kentucky, following the precedent of child abuse statutes, the legislature mandated not only reporting but also investigation of all adult abuse and neglect cases, turning battered women into children. An *Aegis* writer offered a critique of the New Hampshire bill.

> If legislation is to be passed, it should assist women in taking direct control over their lives: it should not sanction unsolicited intermeddling by doctors, social workers and judges. There are more than abstract issues of personal control, confidentiality and privacy involved here: battered women will probably be deterred from seeking necessary medical attention if the bill is passed.[30]

As one activist noted, "the movement has put out hundreds of such small fires. If successful, some of these proposed changes would have further robbed battered women or shelters of their autonomy. No one ever hears about these time-consuming, draining efforts but we have had to mobilize frequently to prevent disasters."[31]

Although advocates predicted long battles to see legislation implemented correctly, they never expected the numerous appeals and constitutional challenges that men have initiated. Fending off a backlash against women, activists have fought court battles successfully in Minnesota, Pennsylvania, California, and Ohio. In Pennsylvania, an abusive husband challenged the right of the court to grant a temporary order of protection, excluding him from his home; in Ohio, a defendant argued that issuing a temporary order of protection as a condition of bail was a violation of state constitutional rights and that ordering a man from his home denied him federal constitutional rights to travel. California law was challenged because it was limited to female victims.[32] Although new laws have been upheld as constitutional in these test cases, activists are forced to mobilize repeatedly, depleting movement resources, yet reminding us of the importance of an organized feminist community. Only a movement, advocating for women and monitoring legal change, insures that the altered power dynamics that are symbolized by new legislation will become a reality.

Women's Rights to Self-Defense

In October 1977, the third issue of the *National Communications Network for the Elimination of Violence Against Women*, carried the lead story: "Do We Have a Right to Self-Defense?"

> Across the country there are countless women sitting in jail awaiting trial, awaiting sentencing, or serving time...all with one thing in common...they are victims of acting in their own self defense! Their commonality is that they are victims of husbands or lovers who attacked them; they are victims of fear and stress produced by long term abuse; they are victims of the long standing failure of social service, the police, the courts and society itself, to provide alternatives to battered women....
>
> At root is the basic question, "Do we have a *right* to self defense?" Further, the legal definition of self defense is being questioned and challenged....
>
> Coming to light is the entire mental set of a woman who has been repeatedly physically and/or psychologically abused, beaten and thoroughly traumatized over a period of years—to a point where *her perceptions* tell her that, in fact, her life (and possibly those of her children as well) is immediately in danger...that, in fact, he *will kill her*.[33]

This issue of *NCN* and subsequent ones carried the stories of women murdered by their husbands and women who killed in self-defense.

> Item: Roxanne Gay—currently being held on $100,000 bail, awaiting trial on murder charges in the stabbing death of her pro football player husband...spent 4 years sustaining documented injuries from repeated beatings...
>
> Item: Gloria Timmons—23 year old woman serving a 20 year sentence in Washington State for the manslaughter shooting of her husband after numerous beatings and rapes, often in front of witnesses.[34]

Two years later, *NCN* was still documenting the violent horrors of women's lives. Serving fifteen to twenty-five years in jail, Jenna Kelsie was not unlike many battered women who kill; she had separated from a husband who continued to terrorize her.

> Jenna's attempt at self defense followed two years of violence—her ex-husband had forced her car off the road, invaded her home to abuse her sexually, beat and harassed her repeatedly while their divorce was pending. The police never actually saw him beat her, so they made no arrest. Her husband and his family wielded considerable power and influence in the area, so Jenna lacked serious support.
>
> Jenna began carrying a gun, ironically given to her by her husband's mother. She feared for her life. One night he attacked her savagely with

fists and teeth, attempting to scratch her eyes out while she sat trapped in a car. She shot him.[35]

In 1977, Claudia McCormick, superintendent of the Women's Division of the Cook County Department of Corrections, found that 40% of women in that prison system convicted of murder or manslaughter were women who had killed continually abusive male partners. Every woman had called the police at least five times; many had separated from the men. McCormick's study finds that "none had maliciously and with premeditated intent, committed murder" and concludes that prison cannot rehabilitate someone who has killed only in self-defense.[36]

Women's rights to defend themselves from male attack, based on the right to control their own lives and bodies, had been central to the work of the anti-rape movement.[37] Inez Garcia, Joan Little, and Yvonne Wanrow are just three of the many women whom feminists, third world groups, and anti-rape activists worked vigorously to help free. Yvonne Wanrow's case set new terms for the self-defense debate.

> The impression created—that a 5'4" woman with a cast on her leg and using a crutch must, under the law, somehow repel an assault by a 6'2" intoxicated man without employing weapons in her defense...constitutes a separate and distinct misstatement of the law and in the context of this case, violates the respondent's right to equal protection of the law.[38]

In *Women Who Kill*, Ann Jones notes that women are developing a new definition of self-defense, different from the legal precedents which focus on a *man* preserving his life. Men and women have different training in the use of their bodies and therefore face a different reality, one which Jones describes well.

> To acknowledge that a 110-pound woman might need a weapon against her 255-pound husband, or that she might try to catch him off-guard is not special pleading but facing facts. To a small woman untrained in physical combat, a man's fists and feet appear to be deadly weapons, and in fact they are...most women killed by their husbands are not shot or stabbed but simply beaten and kicked to death. The woman who counters her husband's fists with a gun may *in fact* be doing no more than meeting deadly force with deadly force.[39]

Repeated violence also creates a terror that is quite literally unimaginable to those who have never been through it, yet one that leaves its victim feeling as if she might die unless she kills.

Like every other aspect of battered women's institutional

experiences, murder trials are often imbued with sexist and racist practices. In the well-publicized Bernadette Powell case, the district attorney suggested that Powell was a masochist and portrayed her as nagging and manipulative. Powell, who is black, was convicted of second degree murder by an all-white jury. Only later did her supporters learn that the district attorney had been divorced by his wife, who, in uncontested divorce proceedings, alleged repeated violent abuse.[40] Agnes Scott's prosecutor failed to tell the grand jury that her estranged husband had attacked her in the street with a knife while he was under court order to stay away from her.[41] The prosecutor's goal was to see her punished for homicide. Judge James Ramsdell sentenced Sharon Crigler to ten years, announcing "that it was impossible for him to find any sympathy for her because she 'desired' to remain on welfare instead of going to work."[42]

Determined to defend women like these, battered women's advocates joined together throughout the country, forming committees to assist women in jail and those recently accused of killing their husbands. These groups organized letter writing campaigns and petitions, created a feminist presence at trials, helped raise the huge court and attorney's fees sometimes necessary, and consistently brought public attention to the plight of battered women. Defense committees served a major consciousness raising role. Until the anti-rape and battered women's movements, few people knew about the thousands of women in jail for killing their male partners. Respectfully and carefully, defense committees spent hours explaining battered women's unique needs and circumstances to sympathetic reporters around the country.

Defense committees paid particular attention to educating defense attorneys and sometimes helped them do their work. Because defense attorneys frequently have little interest in battered women, they interview women defendants inadequately. They fail to ask enough questions about the history of violence or about women's fears of being killed. Attorneys "forget" to interview witnesses who can verify that a woman was beaten brutally. Defense committees have spent hours interviewing battered women and possible supportive witnesses; through their work, case outcomes have been significantly influenced and attorneys and judges educated. In some cases, feminists have managed to see charges dropped before any criminal proceedings began.

Because battering creates so much stress, many attorneys have chosen to use temporary insanity rather than self-defense pleas in murder trials. Some make this choice because they perceive it as the only winnable strategy while others use it, as one attorney noted, "because they don't have a political analysis to think of battered women as anything but insane."[43] Many feminists argue that most defense attorneys have not vigorously pursued self-defense pleas nor adequately understood the issues involved. Because of sexist biases, legal education becomes a persistent necessity.

Around the country, women continue to develop legal strategies and then share what they learn with one another. Feminists have mobilized resources for trials and parole hearings, often enlisting the support of psychologists who were willing to testify as "expert witnesses" about battered women's psychological and social plight. Activists have found that each case must be carefully assessed for the circumstances of the event, the political climate in the town, and the wishes of the individual woman involved. Yet feminist emphasis on public consciousness raising and mobilizing political support among women does bring results. Many women state that the only reason they are free is because of the support and power of the women's community around the country.[44]

Many feminists have already noted the backlash beginning against battered women. Everyone is frightened by women "getting away with murder," the recent title of an unsympathetic CBS *60 Minutes* portrayal of a woman in jail. Some people are furious about women "getting off, unpunished," fearing permission has been given to kill men. Glibly, many now assert that women are liberated and can easily leave violent men; their logic suggests that if these women kill they deserve severe punishment. These arguments ignore that shelters are often full and that some violent men persistently hound and torture their wives and ex-wives, destroying women's attempts to live normally, free from terror.

The reality is that most women who kill do not "get off"; they are found guilty and go to jail. Moreover, the fact, not the fantasy, is that homicides committed by women declined somewhat in the last twenty years. The real horror is that four out of five women who are murdered are killed at home,[45] and that women are left with no alternative but to kill. Yet many people are fearful as women in general, no longer willing to be victims, assert their right to defend themselves.

Battered women who kill most often suffer from acute physical and emotional pain and guilt. They have been tormented for years by abusive men and they face sensationalized media coverage, jail sentences, and separations from children who have already endured too much. When they get out of jail or are freed before or after trials, they must slowly rebuild their lives, paying for the fact that a man repeatedly brutalized them.

As a result of the movements to end violence against women, these women are, for the first time, neither hidden nor viciously condemned. Although the battered women's movement faces skepticism and displeasure for its support of women who have killed, this work is essential.

> Any time the criminal justice system prosecutes a woman for fighting for her life and dignity, all women stand to lose.[46]

The Complicated Choices Ahead

Efforts to reform the criminal justice system are fraught with multiple levels of conflict. Debates continue within the battered women's movement over certain key questions whose answers shape the position one takes toward criminal justice reform efforts. For example, what should the movement's and society's response be toward men who abuse women? Is this behavior sick or an expression of the power men hold over women? Even if we agree that violence reflects power rather than illness, what is the most efficacious way to stop individual acts of violence—criminal sanctions, counseling, consciousness raising about sexism, or, as some suggest, a careful combination of all these things? And answering these questions is only a first step. The movement must also decide if its scarce resources are best spent searching for ways to control individuals or whether, instead, it should organize women and men to fight against the sexism that creates violence.

Another debate within the movement centers on the issue of modifying the behavior of police and court personnel. As women state, "No one is clear about what to do with the police. Do you change attitudes or make them act differently by forcing their departments to adopt new guidelines?" Some activists answer "do both," while others retort that sexism is so pervasive that almost all reform efforts are continually sabotaged.

Activists working to reform the system must also confront the issue of whether battered women should be treated as a special category of victim. Some see potential danger in this position, while others feel that given the sexist conditions under which institutions operate, special consideration is the only way in which a woman will gain leverage to stop her husband's brutality.

The question of who retains control over prosecution is another crucial concern. Increasingly, district attorney's offices, in their "improved" treatment of domestic violence cases, are making it difficult for a woman to drop charges or are threatening to prosecute without her cooperation, which, in reality, is often difficult. Some argue that such strategies force prosecutors to do their jobs by removing victim "non-cooperation" from their list of rationalizations for not proceeding with cases. Moreover, such actions demonstrate that the state is on the woman's side, eager to punish abusers while it protects her from intimidation. These activists argue that battered women do not really have a choice when they drop charges; because violent men control their wives with repeated threats and brutality, women are not free to decide if they will prosecute. In this situation, some advocates insist that the victim alone should not decide how to proceed. Rather, they suggest that police should arrest, attorneys should prosecute vigorously, and the victim should be treated as a witness rather than a complainant. They argue that when a woman fears for her safety, she should not appear in court; the prosecutor should find others who have witnessed her husband's brutality. Underlying these suggestions is the belief that it cannot be the woman's role to control her husband's violence. Instead, institutions must take responsibility for stopping the violence, using their power to declare that men cannot beat their wives.[47]

These arguments, however, are in conflict with those that insist on women's rights to self-determination. Advocates for this position believe that battered women must decide how to proceed. The essence of victimization is to strip women of control, and the criminal justice system cannot be given powers to further deny women control. Additionally, many believe that prosecutors will abuse their increased privileges by ignoring their clients' concerns for safety. A dangerous precedent can be set as prosecutors gain the power to shape women's futures. Many argue that battered women would not use community institutions, like the courts, if prosecution is automatically the result. Because of the narrowness of the solutions available in this society to stop violence, women's rights to free themselves from violent men may conflict with their rights to self-determination.

In working to reform the criminal justice—or other—systems, women in the movement are faced with difficult political questions about the nature of social change and the relationship between institutional reform and a social movement. Taken to its extreme, one position suggests that reforms are the solution to battered women's problems. The other extreme declares that police, courts, and welfare systems reflect a hopelessly racist, sexist, and class-dominated society and that attempts to change them or work within them waste time and are eventually co-opted. In fact, many movement workers see themselves caught somewhere in between these two positions.

> In the early days there was a horrible fear of being contaminated by the system. We saw ourselves as radicals. Even though our analysis was not always clear, we knew in our guts that you can't end violence against women under capitalism. And there we were trying to educate all the judges and social workers to make them do their jobs. On the one hand, we had to do all these things—how else could you help battered women. On the other hand, we were not sure if our work would really change most of them. Some people had to be forced to change and even then without very strong women's and progressive movements they won't modify their behavior. It is a horrible dilemma to hear the stories of thousands of battered women and then to say—can we really do anything? If you are a battered women's movement, you have to help and the reality is you both can and cannot.[48]

Most would agree that despite its contradictions, reform activity is essential and saves lives. If women do not leave their husbands—and sometimes even if they do—criminal sanctions are one of the only tools they have to attempt to stop abuse. Because so many batterers deny responsibility for their acts, blame their victims for the violence, and find their behavior supported by institutions that wish to keep the family together, criminal punishment is seen as one way to force men to assume responsibility for their actions. By making violence a crime, the movement offers psychological, symbolic, and actual relief to women in their search to free themselves from abuse and self-blame. Women's attempts to win justice through the courts is one important assertion of their dignity and control over their lives.

An example from Duluth, Minnesota illustrates the possible effectiveness of a comprehensive reform effort. There, by utilizing probable cause arrest when there is a visible injury, protective orders, eviction orders, court mandated counseling for abusers combined with stayed jail sentences, and shelter and support groups for women, activists report that for the first time, the onus is placed on the man and community institutions rather than on the woman.[49] The abuser must move out of his home, face a counselor who says he is responsible for the violence, and in approximately 25% of the cases a judge who will send him to jail if his wife or a counselor informs the court of threats or recurring violence. While this experiment proceeded, the Duluth shelter had empty beds for the first time.

Yet reform activities have severe limitations. In large cities, even legally won gains, such as increased protection, are often a brutal fiction. The Duluth project, in a city of 100,000 people, received special cooperation from the police and courts for its duration and was painstakingly designed and staffed by feminist activists. And even so, the project director notes that the day the research component ended, the Duluth police participating in the study stopped arresting batterers. To solve this problem, the police department issued an order that officers must arrest, and when they do not, they must write an explanation to their commander. This too failed. Now the department requires arrest as police policy.[50] With each solution that is developed and then undermined, feminist activists battle against the sexism which inhibits change.

In reality, the criminal justice system leaves many women frustrated. Even successful reforms only correct the problem for a limited number of individuals. They cannot end the conditions that create or perpetuate violence. Moreover, legal solutions have not provided battered women with the economic and social resources— jobs, child care, housing, and safe communities—that they need to free themselves from dependence on violent men. It is, however, sometimes difficult to recognize these limitations when one is immersed in the fight for reform; when a movement works toward reform, it must act as if the problem can be corrected.

Working within the criminal justice system is particularly problematic for poor and third world women. Like others, they turn to the system when they cannot stop their partners' violence. At the same time they use this system, they are aware that it can be as destructive as their husbands. Relationships of domination based on race, class, and sex are continually played out subtly and overtly within institutions. Scrutinizing or judging the behavior of poor women is a common pastime of court and welfare workers. Facing institutional discrimination, women persist in their search for justice, but they also know it to be double-edged.

Feeling the necessity of working within the criminal justice system yet recognizing its racism, most of the battered women's movement maintains an ambivalent stance toward the criminal courts. The issue of sanctions against abusers raises particularly difficult questions. For example, in states where constitutionally permitted police arrest power has been restricted, women debated whether these discretionary powers should be broadened in battered women's cases. As one shelter noted, "while we wanted to activate police protection for abused women wherever possible, we were hesitant to support the extension of discretionary powers of arrest, so open to abuse, particularly against Third World and low income people."[51] Twenty-one states permit arrest without a warrant when a police officer has probable cause to believe that an abuser has committed a misdemeanor.[52] Through this mechanism, theoretically, women are relieved from seeking a warrant and are protected from immediate harm. In reality, the provisions are rarely enforced, yet the fear lingers that if they are, poor and third world men will bear the brunt of increased police powers. Some suggest that forcing the legislature or police to mandate misdemeanor arrest and to specify the circumstances under which it must occur, rather than leaving it to officers' discretion, is one way to mitigate racist abuses and insure that battered women are protected. Some remain skeptical, however, convinced that third world men will be severely punished and that white, middle class violence will go unreported. Women are forced to make difficult choices, when in reality, the cause of the problem lies within a racist criminal justice system and society.

Because it is well documented that punishment in jail reinforces violence and bitterness, the movement's ambivalence toward the criminal justice system is further heightened. Yet most activists would support court-mandated, anti-sexist counseling and education programs in which batterers would be punished for second offenses. Even as they acknowledge the problems and limitations inherent in the criminal justice system, many feminists have learned painfully that most men who batter, bolstered by the power accorded them by sexism, feel so little guilt that criminal sanctions are needed to stop them. Most men who batter seek help either because they lose their wives and want them back or because they are forced to modify their behavior by more powerful authorities.

Even after much reform effort, failure to inform women of their legal rights, denial of service, and hostile treatment remain constant complaints from battered women and their advocates in 1982, especially in major urban areas. Criminal justice systems are overloaded, and they do not want battered women's cases. Institutional imperatives to keep caseloads down, to see that the agencies function smoothly, and to maintain control over clients all create barriers to battered women's search for protection and justice. As a Bronx judge remarked to a battered woman's attorney, "if the police will now be required to arrest when orders of protection are violated, this court will just start issuing fewer orders."

Like clients, workers within bureaucracies are often degraded, stripped of control and meaningful work. As a result, helping people disappears as a norm, replaced by "getting through" each painful day as uneventfully as possible. Unfortunately, battered women and other poor clients are caught in these bureaucratic power struggles and conflicting imperatives.

Without large numbers of individuals and organizations consistently and skeptically watching bureaucracies, many of the positive reforms struggled for on behalf of battered women can disappear. Pressuring institutions to change without maintaining a critical stance toward them easily leads to relegitimating their power and authority. A few minor changes or programs receive public attention. Bureaucrats tout how much they have accomplished, and sometimes the community believes them.

> The audience loved the police officer who spoke at the conference about how badly the police had treated battered women. By presenting the view of the enlightened police officer they make themselves look better. When one advocate in the audience pointedly asked, "How have you specifically changed your procedures," a totally evasive answer was given.[53]

With seemingly helpful responses from bureaucracies, it is more difficult to publicly assert that victims are turned away and denied rights. The movement faces the challenge of cooperating with institutions at the same time that it remains critical of them and mobilized on its own behalf.

Complicating this struggle between women and the criminal justice system is the double bind in which battered women's organizations are often caught. For example, as in many major cities, Philadelphia's Women Against Abuse Legal Center received 13,000 calls in one year and 4000 in-person visits from battered women.[54] As a result of excellent publicity done by the movement, thousands of women now want orders of protection and eviction orders which they believe will solve their problems. Yet small movement organizations with scarce resources cannot possibly handle the client demand. In many cities, legal programs and shelters have decided to assist only those women facing the most severe abuse with the consequence that others must fend for themselves. Denied help by battered women's organizations and feeling unsupported, these women view the "movement" like any other bureaucracy. Sometimes, a multi-tiered system of justice is created in which women with specialized advocacy from battered women's organizations are well treated while those without this service feel the cold brutality of a sexist and racist criminal justice system. As the movement screens out all but the most serious cases, courts and welfare departments are not only let off the hook, but also now have a social movement doing their "dirty work" by denying people service. Adding to the insidious quality of this dilemma, movement organizations are so inundated with calls for help that frequently they have no time to reflect and turn these new problems into demands for social change. In the frenzy of work, service organizations stop providing political explanations to battered women and the community, declaring requests for help "impossible" to meet rather than calling the system the culprit and demanding change.

Working toward social change provides common tasks and potential victories, central to maintaining the movement. Reform work helps to keep a movement united and angry. Without targets for possible change, frustration and defeat overwhelm individuals. Working toward more elusive goals, like ending violence against women, exasperates many. When changes occur in police departments or courts, results are visible and concrete; women feel collectively strengthened while the issue gains further legitimation.

The battered women's movement must continue its advocacy and social change efforts within the criminal justice system. At the same time, however, a fine tension needs to be maintained so that advocacy and reform are balanced with building a broad-based, well organized feminist movement and continuing community education efforts. Only in this way will battered women's organizations retain the power base and community support from which to demand institutional change. Although criminal sanctions to stop abuse are a vital part of a solution to battered women's immediate problems, in the long run, the community, not just the criminal justice system, must understand that violence against women is rooted in male domination. Only by developing a philosophy of and struggle for gender equality will a movement change public consciousness which in turn will force individuals and institutions to treat violence against women as a serious offense.

In evaluating reform efforts, criteria are needed which assess how much control women gain over the decisions affecting their lives. An additional assessment must weigh whether these options are actually available or are presently legal fictions.

One advocate suggests a position for the movement to adopt about reform work.

> We have to assert that battered women deserve the same protection from the system as anybody else. They are not an exempt category. On the other hand, the system is not a solution for them and they know it. Reforms aren't a solution to their problem.
>
> The movement must acknowledge winning reforms and the difference they make and say where they come from. This is the only way of dealing with the problem of just helping the system look good. We can't cloud over the motivations of institutions.[55]

If the movement allows institutions to claim reforms as a result of benevolence, then the movement loses the opportunity to acknowledge its strength and impact. This tension suggests another important criteria by which to assess reforms—are women brought together to participate democratically and struggle? If women gain new skills and a sense of power by working together on behalf of all women, then new strength and energy is brought to the movement. Reforms introduced to take control away from autonomous women's programs or from individual battered women must be defined as unacceptable.

Weighing reforms in terms of their impact on collective and individual self-determination is essential but not sufficient. Reforms that can be turned against women or other groups without power also need to be carefully discussed and possibly opposed. For example, preventive detention for batterers would give power to the police and courts that can easily be abused.

A series of questions might help guide an analysis of reforms.

1. How are social relationships of domination by sex, class, and race challenged or reinforced by each proposed reform?
2. How does this reform effect the male right to beat?
3. Does the suggested change further empower women or make them more dependent?
4. Which women of which class or race benefit or are harmed by this activity?
5. If there are racist consequences to specific work, can they be minimized, avoided or fought against?
6. Do women gain control by proposed changes? If not, who gains control or legitimacy, and in what way might this harm the movement?
7. How do specific institutions reinforce the subordination of women—through policies, practices, structures, lack of community control? Can the movement effect these different areas and is it worth the energy?
8. Does the fight help build the movement and organize women?

Feminist theoretician and activist Charlotte Bunch proposes five similar criteria to evaluate reforms so that women can gain the power to eliminate patriarchy and create a more humane society.

1. Does this reform materially improve the lives of women, and if so, which women, and how many?
2. Does it build an individual woman's self-respect, strength, and confidence?
3. Does it give women a sense of power, strength, and imagination as a group and help build structures for further change?
4. Does it educate women politically, enhancing our ability to criticize and challenge the system in the future?
5. Does it weaken patriarchal control of society's institutions and help women gain power over them?[56]

Because so many practices affecting battered women need changing, choices are difficult. Each must be defined in its complexity, facing the limitations and tensions within it. Equally important to measure is the fact that just as reform efforts build the movement by recruiting more women to work on problems, reforms can also unnecessarily deplete energy needed for other tasks, like community education and outreach to battered women.

In its assessment of reforms, the movement must ultimately face other layers of contradictions. Many women want to use neither shelters nor courts. They do not want police to arrest; they just want the violence to stop. For another group of women, leaving their husbands or communities is unthinkable, and going to court feels like cutting themselves off from their only base of support. In this case, the movement's necessary push to enforce battered women's rights collides with endemic problems within a male-dominated, capitalist society. The lack of community and social mechanisms to stop male violence or to support women staying within their neighborhoods meets a society that fails to provide many women with the decent incomes and housing that would free them from violent men. These failings cannot be solved within our current criminal justice system. To transform this reality, reforms must go far beyond the parameters currently defined by the police or courts; the need for a broad-based, progressive political movement, fighting to democratically redistribute resources, power, and control is clear and pressing if battered women are to be protected and violence ended. If we fail to win far reaching change, criminal justice and other institutions will continue to reflect the racism, sexism, and class bias of the larger society. Without a larger feminist community, supported by anti-racist and working class movements committed to ending oppression, the impact of the courageous and important efforts to secure battered women justice and autonomy will be limited.

CHAPTER 8

The Contradictory Effects of Government Involvement

Funding Through the Law Enforcement Assistance Administration

Examining the problems feminists encountered with Law Enforcement Assistance Administration funding illustrates some of the difficulties of working for change within the current system. As early as September 1974, the Feminist Alliance Against Rape (FAAR) offered major criticisms of the Law Enforcement Assistance Administration (LEAA), the funding branch of the Justice Department and the only major federal source of discretionary rape funding at that time. The partially completed findings of a NOW National Rape Task Force Investigation were shared as evidence.

> *Portland, Oregon;* $116,000 allocated to establish a rape reduction program in the office of the District Attorney....Victims who do not report or whose cases do not come to trial do not utilize the service. The stated goal of public education does not yet have a program. Likewise, the stated goal of personnel to accompany the victim to court has not yet materialized.[1]

Throughout the years, many similar criticisms have been raised by both the anti-rape and the battered women's movements. Grassroots feminist groups provide the data and analyses to LEAA consultants but their work is neither acknowledged nor compensated; funding is given to criminal justice bureaucracies, not the anti-rape or battered

women's movement groups who provide caring service and competent advocacy. The criminal justice bureaucracies, with a large
funding base, gain legitimacy and take over "victims" services in
their local areas, often providing victims with minimal service and
no understanding of why they were raped or battered.

The most fundamental critique pointed out that LEAA's interests lay in making the criminal justice system operate more
smoothly and in improving police weaponry and training, whereas
the feminist anti-rape and battered women's movements' interests
were in preserving victims' rights to self-determination as well as
ending violence against women. This critique gains legitimacy when
LEAA's budget is scrutinized. Although it is impossible to determine
how much LEAA Block Grant money allocated directly to states was
spent locally for anti-rape and battering programs, tracing the
discretionary grants distributed directly by LEAA's Washington
office reveals the tiny amounts community groups received. For
example, in 1977, $703,159 was granted to family violence projects
out of a discretionary budget of $55,256,000 and a total LEAA budget
of $753,000,000. By 1980, the last year of funding, family violence
programs received $2,922,075, the largest amount allocated by any
federal agency, while LEAA's discretionary budget stood at
$29,904,000, and its total agency appropriation at $486,463,000.[2]

LEAA's Victim/Witness Assistance Program focused on victims
of "sensitive" crimes: rape, sexual abuse of children, and intra-
family violence. By 1978, "violence in the home" had become a LEAA
"priority" and eleven grants were made during that year to agencies
providing a range of services.[3] In fiscal year 1979, sixteen projects
were funded under LEAA's Family Violence Program; nine more
were added in 1980 for a total of twenty-five projects funded under
federal discretionary grants for these two years until the program
closed in 1981.[4] With budgets averaging between $60,000 and
$200,000 per year, grants ranged from projects like the Alaska
Family Violence Program which provided statewide services including counseling, shelter, hotlines, public education, and professional
training to a program in Santa Barbara that operated shelters and
also collected data on the extent of violence, prosecuted cases,
referred appropriate cases to diversion and treatment programs, and
trained law enforcement personnel.[5]

All LEAA funded programs offered services, but as a part of
grant requirements they also had to improve the criminal justice
system and involve the "community," meaning criminal justice,
medical, and social service agencies. Testifying about the goals of the

Family Violence Program at the Civil Rights Commission Hearings, one LEAA staff person comments:

> The overall objective of these projects is to improve the treatment given to these particular crime victims and thereby increase the number of crime reports and number of successful prosecutions. Although these projects are aimed at criminal justice improvement, they are definitely social service oriented.[6]

LEAA brushed aside the fact that improving prosecution rates and helping victims are not always compatible, especially for those women who do not want to prosecute.

LEAA funding forced the battered women's movement to face the same issues the anti-rape movement had confronted. On the one hand, little federal funding was available, except LEAA discretionary funds, and battered women desperately needed and deserved services. On the other hand, the money served to legitimate LEAA and an ideology which suggested that criminal justice institutions could solve the problem of violence against women. Many grassroots programs heatedly debated applying for these funds. Some decided against applying, while others believed that their autonomy and views would not be compromised. In fact, most of the grassroots programs that accepted LEAA funding maintained their integrity by fighting for victims' rights to confidential services and self-determination. Several of these projects began shelters, hired large staffs, and conducted extensive outreach or training with the money. Many battered women received help and advocacy services as a result.

LEAA money did not go exclusively to grassroots women's programs, however. Several of the twenty-five Family Violence Project grants went directly to District Attorney's offices in LEAA's efforts to "improve the criminal justice system's response to intrafamily violence." One was given to a Rockland County, New York program to counsel batterers and provide a cost benefit analysis to determine "how frequently the program avoids formal proceedings, whether it saves resources, and if it is cost effective."[7] An Ohio grant hoped to develop a SUMMONS program which would enable police to summon violent repeat offenders to appear before an arbitrator. This program proposed to offer offenders and victims professional assistance in conflict resolution without the "adverse" effect of exposure to the court system.[8] The dangers to battered women inherent in such programs are as obvious as the unstated goal of ridding the criminal justice system of its "troublesome" cases.

Some of the problematic results of three years of LEAA funded criminal justice research are now emerging. For example, a recent summary of the experiences of LEAA Family Violence Projects, produced by the Center for Women Policy Studies which itself received LEAA funding, legitimates several potentially dangerous recommendations. The criminal justice system does receive its proper dose of criticism and the summary rightly suggests that mediation has been found to be an inappropriate remedy and that counseling and diversion must be done with the utmost care. However, it is advised that since many battered women drop charges, the prosecutor, not the victim, should press charges and victims should not be allowed to drop charges once they have been filed, unless there are exceptional circumstances.[9] No mention is made of what happens to the women in such cases. One program sends out warning letters to abusers when charges are not filed and states that while no systematic follow-up study has been conducted, subsequent violence appears rare.[10] The key question—how can these programs assert that violence is rare without follow-up studies—is not answered. Mandated counseling programs for men who batter are also suggested as important methods to stop violence but again no follow-up studies have been done to verify the "fact" that violence is halted over time. Although many people advocate testing a number of models to help men end violence, including counseling and invoking criminal sanctions to stop abusive behavior, it is dangerous and misleading to tout untested assumptions.

Undoubtedly, LEAA court projects to serve victims and witnesses increased police and court sensitivity. As one former staff person comments:

> Nothing these programs did hurt. They helped victims with transportation to court, babysitters and they gave them support. When you start with nothing, everything is an improvement.[11]

Moreover, LEAA pioneered a federal response to battered women and by its grants recognized the existence of family violence and women's right to safety. It pushed law enforcement agencies to take battered women's cases seriously and punish or condemn abuse.

At the same time, LEAA reclaimed law enforcement as the proper locus for solving the "problem." Subtly subverting a grassroots movement, LEAA funding and that of other federal agencies legitimated a new view of the problem. A "family violence" label masks the fact that the victims are predominantly women and children. Hiding behind a helping ideology, LEAA programmatic assumptions suggest that: 1. the problem is created within the "troubled" family rather than within male-dominated institutions; 2. social change means changing bureaucracies to make them work effectively; and 3. battered women's problems can be solved without fundamental social transformations.

LEAA's criminal justice findings may be widely disseminated and in well-funded, thoughtfully conceived programs that believe in women's right to self-determination, they may help some battered women. In the hands of overworked and underfunded court administrators and counseling services, they also may create havoc for battered women. Local battered women's programs and state coalitions now face a tough monitoring job to insure that the few thoughtful recommendations are carried out, and that the dangerous ones are not. For example, women will have to work diligently to see that funding is not diverted to help violent men or to ease the demands on courts while shelters, the priority need, struggle to even stay alive.

The Center for Women Policy Studies

Between 1977 and 1980, the Center for Women Policy Studies (CWPS) in Washington received approximately one million dollars in LEAA funds[12] to provide technical assistance to LEAA Family Violence Programs, to research and produce the *Response* newsletter, and to provide information to many agencies and groups through its Resource Center on Family Violence. For several years, *Response to Violence in the Family*, mailed free to a national audience, was published monthly and filled with useful information about LEAA projects, federal sources of funding for battered women, federal and state legislation, programs for batterers, general research findings in the field, and conference schedules from around the country. CWPS staff have also spoken at professional conferences, and hundreds of newly forming groups have looked to the Center for information, especially on funding, state legislation, and criminal justice intervention models.

Early in both the anti-rape and battered women's movements, the Center for Women Policy Studies, which was founded in 1972 to "identify, analyze and propose solutions to problems related to the status of women,"[13] was challenged about its role in these movements. A 1975 FAAR article criticized CWPS for its handling of a large rape research grant.

> By claiming to be feminist, such organizations as the CWPS gain certain credibility with funding sources seeking to fund token projects. These funding sources are responding to pressure generated by the feminist movement and its popular support by large numbers of women....While the CWPS identifies itself with the feminist movement, it has failed to seek the criticism and support of feminists organized against rape. Any group or individual that presumes to represent a particular constituency should attempt to make itself accountable to that constituency.

FAAR also blasted the politics of the CWPS grant report and its "use of loaded phrases that discredit feminist rape crisis centers." The report stated that rape crisis centers "may earn the reputation of being anti-male, anti-professional and difficult for more conventional groups to work with." As FAAR commented, "statements such as this reinforce the view that feminist groups should not be dealt with and cannot be taken seriously."[14]

Two years later, in the December 1977 NCN, yet another major criticism was raised about the CWPS' plan to publish a national listing of battered women's services after Betsy Warrior's widely reviewed directory Working on Wife Abuse had already been through four editions. Ms. Warrior writes about compiling the directory.

> Over the past few years I've managed to continue working on it and printing it by, at various times: borrowing money, working at other jobs, subsisting on welfare, etc....None of the work that's gone into it (which is a full-time job) has ever been paid for....

CWPS expressed an interest in taking over the directory and Ms. Warrior responds.

> I was surprised that CWPS would want to take over work that someone else had already invested so much time and effort into, had developed numerous contacts for, and voluminous files of resources and information—it would seem much more sensible to just support the work already being done. After my negative response to the CWPS proposition, I heard from them maybe once more, requesting the latest edition of the directory, which I sent. That was over a year ago....
>
> I have just heard again from CWPS...I've received a form letter from them saying that they are planning to publish a directory of programs and services for battered women (exactly what I've done four times already) and that they would like me to send them any information I have that they can include. Apparently, while I've been busy doing this work CWPS have been busy and successful in getting funded for it themselves.[15]

The CWPS directory was published, widely distributed, and seen as a useful resource by many organizations and federal agencies. Any protest came from individuals and grassroots groups. No concerted way has ever been found to stop efforts like these.

Defining legitimate movement spokespeople is a difficult dilemma in any national grassroots movement. The CWPS offers itself as experts on battered women, but it has no grassroots constituency and offers no direct services to victims. As a federally funded Washington-based women's organization, the CWPS can appear as an objective reporter of national news, unconcerned about local movement politics. But reality is more complicated than professed objectivity. In its seeming neutrality, the *Response* newsletter consistently conveys a politic. For example, its April, May, and June 1980 issues included supplements on programs for men who batter. These programs were printed and, in spite of grassroots concern, reprinted with no critical analysis of the ideology, politics, or treatment methodologies of the groups listed nor any criteria for evaluating them. The message conveyed nationwide is that all programs for men who batter are legitimate and helpful, a highly contested point. Moreover in *Response*, the interests of the battered women's movement and the criminal justice system are made to look the same. The ideology presented is "that we are all in this together to solve battered women's problems" and that we face no major disagreements or contradictions. In the pages of *Response*, the diversity, disagreements, and importance of the grassroots battered women's movement almost disappear. Political concerns are laundered and social change is made to look as if it happens in Washington D.C. and within bureaucrats' offices.

Some have described this process as co-optation of a movement. It is a difficult process to stop when organizations such as the CWPS have financial resources and reach toward professional or bureaucratic audiences uncritical of their views and often unaware of the differences within the grassroots movement. Funding for groups like the CWPS reveals a government deeply cut off from democratic grassroots movements for social justice. Such choices suggest that the government prefers to legitimate groups that ignore and sometimes discredit popular movements.

An Enlarged Federal Response

As the grassroots movement grew and battered women were classified as the newest "social" problem, the federal government responded. In 1978, a group principally composed of those interested in the few research and development grants that their agencies had allocated to domestic violence met regularly. When asked why this group formed, one career official responded.

> The grassroots made us aware of the pervasiveness of the problem. Suddenly there was an explosion all over the country and local groups told us of the lack of concern and money. Rape and child abuse legislation and programs set the stage and then the women's movement pushed for change.
>
> On a federal level, LEAA set a precedent for others by allocating funds. Our concern was to institutionalize by moving funding of domestic violence programs from Research and Development sources to regular program funding. If the programs are part of operational funding, it is harder to drop them. Also we realized domestic violence was a widespread problem and there was a need to find out what works and develop programs.
>
> Finally there was a federal response because the problem cuts across class and race. If domestic violence affected only poor women, it would have been dismissed.[16]

One year later, on April 27, 1979, President Carter created the Interdepartmental Committee on Domestic Violence, composed of representatives of twelve federal agencies, and of staff from the Office on Domestic Violence, a branch of HEW formed on that same day. With what would prove to be inspiring but empty political rhetoric, President Carter declared, "this administration is committed ultimately to the cessation of such violence and immediately to the relief of those who suffer its consequences." The Interdepartmental Committee was mandated to recommend to President Carter ways to increase government agencies' responsiveness to battered women and also to concentrate on the need for domestic violence programs in Native American and military families.[17] One active participant in the federal agency personnel group that had been formed a year earlier notes that most federal regulatory changes were first suggested by this group rather than the one later appointed by the President. Some bureaucrats as well as most activists describe the presidentially created Interdepartmental Committee as fundamentally a showpiece, part of a plan "to act as if the government was doing something without having to give anyone money."[18]

The newly formed Office on Domestic Violence (ODV) also had no mandate to directly fund services, although it was to have acquired the important role of fiscal conduit and monitoring agency if federal legislation passed. It was seen as a central locus for policy planning, information dissemination, and interagency coordination.[19] Because it had no statutory basis or appropriations, its programming effort remained small with a 1980 budget of 1.2 million and a 1981 budget of $240,000[20], allocated to technical assistance, education, and research. Without a legislative mandate, direct services could not be funded.

Many in the battered women's movement supported the establishment of the Office on Domestic Violence because it was seen as a potential federal advocate for battered women. During its brief existence, ODV worked hard for the passage of federal legislation. Activists and ODV staff worked together on legislative lobbying strategy and ODV brought an insider's knowledge to the grassroots and lent the legitimacy of its office to the struggle. It also helped fund a few resources useful for the movement's national conference.

Although activists saw the ODV as a conduit for funds that would "help the movement help itself," ODV had its own ideas, and the movement was never strong enough to control the relationship. ODV, in typical bureaucratic fashion, established yet another National Clearinghouse on Domestic Violence through which research findings were disseminated. The National Clearinghouse published a number of useful monographs, but also duplicated previously completed work. In 1979, ODV joined LEAA in funding the Center for Women Policy Studies' technical assistance efforts. With several other federal agencies, it jointly sponsored three demonstration projects to provide services to children in shelters and other family service organizations.[21] In 1980, the ODV sponsored a national survey of domestic violence, which was conducted by Louis Harris Inc., and prepared several training films and manuals. Movement activists consistently raised the criticism that producing manuals was not the most effective way to train staff, and that more surveys were a waste of money while battered women were being turned away from overcrowded shelters.

The history of the Regional Technical Assistance Centers on Domestic Violence first funded by ACTION and later jointly sponsored by ODV and ACTION reveals most clearly the contradictory effects of government funding. In 1979, battered women's programs from around the country competed to become technical assistance centers and ten were chosen. Each regional center was expected to hold conferences and meetings so that battered women's organizations could come together and share experiences. In some regions, these conferences focused on skill development; in others they provided a needed forum for political discussion as well as skill sharing. For example, in Boston the Casa Myrna Vazquez Technical Assistance Center sponsored a conference and produced an important booklet: *Doing Community Outreach to Third World Women*.[22] Some regional centers clearly saw their role as movement organizers and for several years insured that information, skills, and resource people made their way around the region. In other regions, centers adopted a narrower definition of their role or viewed movement building as too political.

After a year of funding, problems arose. The goals of second year funding, as defined by ODV and ACTION, became increasingly problematic. According to the government, each technical assistance center was "to demonstrate that existing resources can be used more effectively to meet the needs of battered women and their families."[23] Translated to the regional technical assistance centers, this mandate meant that after the second year no more funding would be available. During the second year, the regional centers were to bring together traditional and non-traditional service providers to insure that battered women received more help. That traditional social service agencies offer totally different models of help and have different politics was insignificant to the funders. Especially in their second year, some centers carried forward the mission of transmitting information to traditional agencies, potentially helping to expand services to battered women while, at the same time, strengthening those very agencies whose professional views might undermine the grassroots and self-help base of the movement.

Despite many problems, the work of ODV and most regional technical assistance centers has been valuable. Activists believe that ODV's usefulness lay primarily in its legislative lobbying efforts and its funding of the ten regional technical assistance centers. Federal agency personnel and the director of the ODV view its importance somewhat differently.

> The contribution of ODV was drawing attention to the problem inside and outside the government. Coordinating the Interdepartmental Committee meant that a problem existed that required a response. As a result, the Interdepartmental Committee put together a handbook of federal resources for battered women. The Clearinghouse answered several hundred requests each month.
> We also lent the issue legitimacy by talking to state and local

officials, professional groups and Congresspeople. For legitimacy, some people looked to ODV and others to the grassroots.[24]

With the election of President Reagan, the ODV was dismantled. Those bureaucrats staying in government moved to the National Center on Child Abuse and Neglect (NCCAN) also within HHS's (formerly HEW) Administration on Children, Youth and Families. Unlike ODV, NCCAN had been created through Congressional legislation in 1974 and by 1981 had a yearly budget of thirty million dollars. The few ODV grants remaining were monitored by NCCAN and if NCCAN survived the 1981-1982 Reagan budget cuts, its only funding to the battered women's movement would be for children's services. All regional technical assistance funding ended.

Along with closing the Office on Domestic Violence and moving a few staff to the National Center on Child Abuse and Neglect (NCCAN) came arguments correlating child abuse and "spouse abuse." The April 1981 National Conference on Child Abuse and Neglect, sponsored by NCCAN, opened with five minute debates on "major issues facing the field." The point on battered women, debated in front of 2000 participants, read:

> With data indicating a considerable correlation of spouse abuse with child abuse and neglect, it would be both cost effective and treatment effective to combine funding and programs for child protection and spouse abuse in a new framework of family violence.[25]

Weeks before the conference, it had been arranged that Jeannie Niedermeyer Santos, a NCCAN staff member, former deputy director of the Office on Domestic Violence, and a former LEAA Family Violence grant monitor, would argue in favor of this point, infuriating the grassroots movement. A male social work professor, Alfred Kadushin, was to argue against it. The grassroots battered women's movement mobilized and protested its exclusion from the debate. Then both original debaters withdrew, and the conference organizers had difficulty finding anyone willing to assume a pro-merger stance, reflecting the fact that "everyone knows that merging child abuse and wife abuse services will mean that battered women will be treated like children. No one in either field wanted this to happen."[26] At the conference, a strong declaration refuting the assumptions and politics of the merger statement was made on behalf of the National Coalition (see appendix).

Direct Support for Battered Women

Without devising new structures or offices, some federal agencies changed their regulations to ease the plight of battered women. As a result of testimony at state levels and federal lobbying, amendments to the Social Security Act now allow Title XX funds—one of the largest federal categorical grants for social services—to be used for emergency shelter at a state level.[27]

The push to change HHS's Title XX regulations may become irrelevant as a result of the Reagan Administration's plan to eliminate Title XX and fold its funds into State Block Grants. If this happens, social services will find themselves competing with each other for even fewer funds as states and localities gain far greater discretion over the use of government dollars. Without federal monitoring, it will be impossible to insure that funds are spent for the poor or those in danger of exploitation.

The Department of Housing and Urban Development (HUD) offers another example of regulatory change initiated by grassroots groups cooperating with women in government. Established in 1974, HUD's Community Development Block Grant Program was designed to assist localities to physically rehabilitate and revitalize urban communities. As of 1978, community development funds had been used to purchase and rehabilitate only one shelter in the United States.[28] By 1980, a close effort between activists and personnel within HUD's Office of Women's Policy and Program Staff had pushed that number to over fifty-three shelters, receiving more than 3.4 million dollars. One HUD staff member describes the process through which it happened.

> In 1977 HUD held a two-day meeting with women who were working locally on housing issues. The needs of battered women were listed by this group as a priority, and the Office of Women's Policy and Program Staff decided to adopt shelters as our priority. We were concerned and felt we could do something concrete to help.[29]

In 1978, HUD inserted specific language into its funding guidelines reaffirming shelters as an eligible category and then proceeded to distribute this directive throughout the country.

Whether or not local shelters received Community Development Block Grant funding depended on many factors, one of them being the level of sophistication about housing issues and organizing ability of the local battered women's group. In addition, local HUD bureaucrats' attitudes toward shelters—and their willingness to directly fund grassroots groups—varied enormously.[30] One activist, a former housing organizer, feels that most battered women's services, while comfortable fighting for social service funding, had little experience with housing grants. Often discouraged by local city planners and mountains of regulations, these women gave up. There is no data on the number of shelters that applied for local Community Development Block Grant funds and were denied them or that were discouraged early in the process by bureaucrats, although many suggest the number is high.[31]

Organizers assert that on a federal level the battered women's movement won little from HUD, partly due to the movement's lack of clarity over what to fight for. Women within HUD wanted the bureaucracy to be more responsive yet some activists felt conflicted about demanding that battered women be declared priorities for low-income housing, since most poor people wait for that designation for years. One organizer hoped to see HUD mandate that a percentage of Section 8 low-income housing be saved for battered women who faced housing emergencies, or that HUD allocate special funds for second-stage housing after women leave shelters. In a few places these experiments have proceeded.[32]

Unfortunately, by 1982 housing demands would be likely to fall on deaf ears. President Reagan eliminated the Office of Women's Policy and Program Staff. As HUD is reorganized and Community Development Block Grants are reduced, placed under local control, and subject to less federal regulation, many fear that the sole recipients of federal housing dollars will be private real estate developers rather than the battered women and poor people who desperately need them. The future of the Community Development Block Grants is uncertain, at best.

Until 1981, the Community Services Administration (CSA) was another source of aid to the battered women's movement. Both in 1979 and 1980 the Community Services Administration awarded two key grants, one to the Pennsylvania Coalition Against Domestic Violence and the other to the Massachusetts Coalition of Battered Women Service Groups, to be used for training and technical assistance for coalition member programs. As one former CSA staff person noted, "the Pennsylvania and Massachusetts Coalition grants were made because key grassroots women hand carried them around the agency and because women inside were sympathetic."[33] Because these grants funded coalition staff and were used to strengthen the movement internally, activists describe them as helpful. But as an agency committed to providing services or

referrals to family members in crisis, CSA funding went to help men
as well as women. In one CSA funded crisis center, the entire family,
including the violent man, was sheltered together. The battered
women's movement met this grant with a major uproar and organizing drive to stop it.

CSA grants illustrate well the level of government commitment to women's programs in general and battered women in
particular. In both 1979 and 1980, out of a total CSA annual budget of
500 million dollars for services to all low income people and a
Research and Development budget between 70 and 80 million
dollars, one million dollars of research and development grants were
allocated annually to *all* women's programs.[34] In these two years,
less than $500,000 annually was awarded to battered women's
programs. By 1981, no Research and Development funding was
granted to battered women's programs. A former CSA staff person
explains.

> In 1979 and 1980 a woman director of this agency made women a
> priority and she used women staff to help her. She noticed there were
> no women's programs. Without her, it would not have been done.
> Women's needs are not institutionalized here. Someone in power has to
> care. When this director left, women inside the agency had to push for
> women to even be an agency priority. Now women's issues are at the
> bottom end of the agency's *50* priorities. But worse in the Reagan
> Administration if you're into women's issues, it's the kiss of death.[35]

On October 1, 1981 the Community Services Administration was
abolished as a separate government agency.

At least during the Reagan Administration, the prospects for
federal funding are grim. In November 1981 a National Center on
Child Abuse and Neglect staff member, responsible for the few
remaining grants to children's programs in shelters and aware of
other agencies' efforts on behalf of battered women, could cite no
other federally funded programs serving abused women. When this
same bureaucrat worked for LEAA just 3 years ago, her office had
received over 300 proposals each year.[36] Cuts have hit every possible
avenue of funding for battered women. The Public Service Employment Program under CETA, a major source of staff salaries in
shelters which has probably "funded more battered women's shelters and programs than any other federal program"[37] has been
eliminated. The results will be devastating. Even though the
statistics are disputed, *Response* reports that, "as of February, 1981,
approximately 40 percent of 460 shelters...received some form of
federal assistance..."[38] Most likely much of it will disappear soon.

And individually, countless women and children will feel the effects of federal cutbacks as they face huge reductions in Aid to Families with Dependent Children (AFDC), food stamps, and medical benefits.

President Reagan's plan to shift much federal funding to State Block Grants poses a series of problems. One study of General Revenue Sharing, a block grant program in effect since 1974, revealed that only 2-4% of General Revenue Sharing funds were used locally for social service programs. Rather they are given to roads and transportation subsidies, public safety agencies like the police and fire departments, and sewage and sanitation.[39] As one article concludes, "whereas the categorical grant program very definitely specified how the funds were to be used, the block grant approach leaves it up to the discretion of the state and local governments." Only in those localities where community groups got together and exerted political impact, especially as coalitions, did a significant portion of General Revenue Sharing funds go for social services.[40]

This gloomy conclusion cannot be used to make previous years seem more rosy than they were for women's program funding. As this anonymous bureaucrat contends,

> Some of us cared deeply, but there was never a federal commitment to women. There were never enough women within agencies to even help with all the requests we received.[41]

Assessing Federal Efforts

In looking at federal reforms that aided the battered women's movement, the role of women in government, at all levels, must be highlighted. Many, out of a feminist commitment or a wish to aid battered women, lent their help without exacting any price. Most officials assumed from their positions of governmental authority that they and grassroots activists had the same political agenda. Often this evaluation was correct; everyone agreed on the need to actively support legislation, gain resources for women, and oppose right-wing or conservative anti-feminist legislators.

At other moments, however, these same women defined priorities differently as this comment illustrates.

> When the criminal justice agencies got more involved, the issue received a different kind of credibility. It showed a movement had come a long way. If you stay grassroots, you have a problem.[42]

Making expediency—an often necessary element in any successful organizing effort—the only important consideration, these women sometimes intimidated those grassroots activists who disagreed. One bureaucrat labeled feminist activists who opposed her agency's policies as "unsophisticated, abrasive, and immature," epithets used to discredit and erase the obvious political differences. In addition, some women in government had genuine problems with certain aspects of the grassroots movement.

> Local shelters' boards and staff had virtually no management experience. Shelter boards wanted to be in on everything; they wouldn't let the staff run the organization. Also, people wouldn't live with majority opinion—everything had to be consensus which can't always be achieved.
> Then when funding entered the picture, it created intense hostility among local groups.[43]

For the most part, however, women inside and outside the government worked well together and many insiders credit the grassroots movement for its compassion, sophistication, hard work, and ability to raise an issue so quickly. One government bureaucrat recalls that, "the grassroots women were very impressive and well organized. They used federal meetings and conferences to always put forward their own issues and arrange their own meetings. Women in government weren't wittingly funding this *movement* although they didn't disapprove of the movement using meetings for its own purposes."[44] For career women within the government, many of them feminists, the grassroots movement also provided an education. As one woman notes, "their notion of empowerment and their ideas of consensus decision making and doing business differently had an important impact on us."[45]

A far greater problem than the political differences between the grassroots and government women was the lack of power all women held. Almost every dedicated woman working within a federal agency concluded her assessment by saying, "we are just not a priority."

Because of the lack of local and state resources, the battered women's movement pressed its demands on the federal government. From the movement's perspective, a positive federal response would give battered women resources and would validate activists' earliest claims—violence against women was a national problem that necessitated wide-ranging reforms. Federal recognition of the issue was an important symbolic victory for the movement. It gave added weight to the movement's demands at state and local levels. Federal resources, especially CETA, temporarily sustained most battered women's programs and also allowed more poor women and third world women to become staff of local programs.

During the Carter presidency, because of a grassroots movement, the federal government was forced to respond, at least superficially, to women. While its plans, in the midst of a capitalist fiscal crisis, were extraordinarily cheap, for a brief moment battered women gained attention and credibility as a major social issue.

Just as the government bestows legitimacy on an issue, however, it can also change the parameters of how it is defined. In the pamphlets, brochures, and newsletters of the Office on Domestic Violence, HUD, and LEAA, battered women disappear to be replaced by spouse abuse and intrafamily violence labels, a form of professed objectivity and a renaming that masks the sexism a grassroots movement worked to uncover.

From the movement's point of view, activists often had little maneuverability, taking what they could get and working to stop dangerous developments. For example, a choice between criminal justice or mental health funding is not a large option; both redefine a social issue into an individual difficulty by labeling battered women, as the Department of Labor does, "another segment of the female population with special problems."[46]

Complicating the assessment of the federal government's role, however, is internal movement disagreement over the assertion that the government's actions were co-optive. An internal struggle about the appropriate role of the government and whether the ideology it explicates is helpful or damaging continues, based on unresolved debates over the politics and goals of the movement.

Women in the movement also disagree on strategy and tactics. Some believe the power of the movement will come through gaining credibility with the government, while others believe that power accrues as women organize themselves to demand more and the government is forced to respond. One activist writes:

> The Women's Resource Network,...provides consultation, training, and public education in the battered woman area. Becoming nationally oriented in scope and impact, we are currently working on proposals to LEAA in conjunction with James Bannon, Detroit Police Department....
> We are cooperating with the University of Wisconsin on research proposals which will lead to significant feminist control of policy recommendations at the federal level regarding appropriate treatment models and delivery of services to battered women....

> Our strategies are geared towards avoiding a repeat of the loss of feminist control of funds as has happened with rape.[47]

While this writer naively felt she could control forces far more powerful than her program, some women in the movement go to another extreme and say, "let's stay out of politics altogether and just help battered women." This latter stance allows more forceful voices, carrying the weight of governmental or professional legitimacy, to define the parameters of funding and ideological discussions without any grassroots opposition pushing them to modify their political stance.

The grassroots battered women's movement was compelled to seek resources from the federal government and to negotiate on behalf of battered women. Although the movement has had a major impact on federal policy, it was never strong enough to win adequate funding nor stop some of the government's co-optive plans. During the Reagan Administration, the movement can hope to win little. However, women are finding it helpful to reassess the impact of the limited government aid the movement has received. Although federal support is viewed as essential, activists are carefully weighing past choices to discover the best ways in which they might make future demands. How to recognize the subtle undermining of a movement's vision and how to resist it are growing areas of concern for a feminist movement to end violence against women.

Ellen Shub

August 1976 / battered women speakout and rally
City Hall Plaza, Boston, MA

Ellen Shub

August 1981 / Take Back the Night march
Boston, MA

March 1978 / International Women's Day march
Boston, MA

Ellen Shub

August 1978 / Take Back the Night march
Boston, MA

Ellen Shub

March 1979 / Emerge: reproductive rights rally
Boston, MA

April 1979 / memorial rally for murdered black women
Boston, MA

October 1981 / Women's Pentagon Action
Washington D.C.

PART II

Looking Toward
the Future

CHAPTER 9

Toward an Analysis of Violence Against Women in the Family

In speaking of the British battered women's movement, one activist declares that "those of us who work in the refuges have to fight on two fronts. The first is to survive, despite the widespread opposition. The second is to look for the next step that will ensure that a refuge becomes unnecessary because men no longer assault women."[1] This chapter considers that "second front" and attempts to analyze what causes battering to persist in the United States today and what conditions are necessary to end this form of abuse.

Theoretical explanations for battering are not mere exercises; by pinpointing the conditions that create violence against women, they suggest the directions in which a movement should proceed to stop it. Woman abuse is viewed here as an historical expression of male domination manifested within the family and currently reinforced by the institutions, economic arrangements, and sexist division of labor within capitalist society. Only by analyzing this total context of battering will women and men be able to devise a long-range plan to eliminate it.

Focusing on Individual Behavior

Those who attempt to develop feminist theories of battering must first contend with the theories that have already been constructed by others, primarily psychologists, sociologists, and criminologists. Current theories offer simultaneously helpful, confusing, and contradictory insights; in a potpourri of propositions, battering is attributed to alcohol, poor impulse control, personal or interpersonal illness, or a multitude of sociological "factors."

Before we proceed, clarity is needed about the question to be answered. Many sociologists and criminologists incorrectly assume that asking, "Why are men violent?" is synonymous with asking "Why do men beat women?" The former leads to postulating about woman abuse, child abuse, war, political assassinations, and psychotic behavior as if these phenomena had common historical roots and causation. Such theorizing tells us little about human behavior in specific contexts.[2] Examining why men are violent does not explain why men act violently toward a specific target, women, or within a specific context, their home, nor can it tell us why some men are violent solely to their wives. Only by studying social and historical relationships within the family can we reveal the meaning and purpose behind battering.

Even if it is agreed that the meaningful question is, "Why do men batter women?" most theorists fail to distinguish the different levels at which the question is being posed. Many assert that they are analyzing what causes violence, yet unwittingly they focus on why a particular man beats his wife and what makes a particular woman a victim. Instead of developing a social theory, they analyze individuals and call the sum of their insights about these cases social causation. For example, in "A Sociological Perspective on the Prevention and Treatment of Wife-Beating," Murray Straus declares that only small percentages of wife beating are caused by purely psychological factors like uncontrolled aggression, or purely cultural factors (rules that give spouses the right to hit each other), or purely as a result of the organization of society (unemployment, couples living apart from friends or family); rather, he suggests that a combination of these factors produces most wife beating.[3] In his theoretical work, Straus speaks to the question of why individual men may hit their wives at a particular moment. Analyzing this question is important, but it is not the same as designing a theory of why men as a group direct their violence at women. Straus and many other theorists, however, fail to make this distinction.

Self-assuredly, psychiatry offers a multitude of facile descriptions of men who batter. Such men are pictured as weak, insecure, inadequate, or dependent. They suffer from poor impulse control, poorly developed egos, and deprived childhoods. Some theorists suggest that they abuse because they are unable to express feelings. Psychiatry fails to see that men who batter are as diverse as the women who they beat. Some are likeable; others sadistic and mean. It is true that batterers often _feel_ powerless and that they bluster, bully, and threaten to cover up their sense of impotence and their inability to express their feelings. While psychiatric descriptions and personal experiences make us sympathetic toward individual abusers, they cannot erase the fact that batterers are dangerous and that they beat women and escalate their intimidating tactics as a way to regain what they believe is their rightful control of the situation.

In "Psychological Aspects of Wife-Beating," Natalie Shainess, a psychiatrist, maintains that men who batter may be under great stress and have no tools for handling it. Some of them are infantile, unable to tolerate frustration and therefore lash out.[4] Although the descriptions may accurately portray some violent men, they still fail to explain why these men choose their wives as targets. It is easy to read backward into deprived childhoods to find the cause of violence, but many "deprived" people are not violent. Indeed, men who were loved as children also learn to dominate and abuse women.

Stress is a totally inadequate concept to explain abuse. Under enormous stress, many men do not batter. Insecure women under stress do not beat up men in large numbers. Common sense suggests that heightened stress may be a factor in battering, but the concept of stress must be placed in a context. Most theorists have not done this, and stress is usually vaguely defined to include any kind of personal distress. The Emerge collective, however, suggests that in the case of battering, stress might be defined as threats to the ego and the ability to feel in control of one's life.[5] But, stress does not "cause" abuse; men choose to deal with stress in specific ways. The belief in one's right to use violence, batter, and dominate women is what causes a man to relieve his stress by beating his wife. One activist explains:

> When we become overwhelmed, we have a reason to act controlling where we can. When you feel powerless, you resort to what makes you feel powerful. Violence is controlling; control makes you feel better and it pays.

She clarifies further, "however, you don't have to experience a loss of control to want to be controlling; not all men are violent because they just experienced a loss of power or status."[6]

Personality theories suggest that battering is about illness and poor impulse control rather than power. Poor impulse control is a grossly misleading term; many men are only violent with their wives in the privacy of their homes. Sometimes, they carefully select which area of a woman's body to abuse. They usually do not kill. Some exercise substantial control and stop their abuse when they are threatened with jail sentences. Although they act "out of control," most batterers know what they are doing.

Many place the source of violence within conflictual couples or families. Straus, Steinmetz, and Gelles state, "It is clear that the more conflicts a couple has, the more likely they are to get into a physical fight. In fact, a persisting severe conflict over something crucial, such as disagreement over children, is almost sure to end in at least some violence."[7] Yet many couples disagree with each other nonviolently. Conflicts do not "cause" violence; the belief in the right to beat women and in the use of force do.

Many family therapists lose sight of the power differential available to the man to invoke violence as he sees fit. For these theorists, there is not a power dynamic in marriage; there are equals with problems. Or there are those therapists who define power as a symptom of illness, rather than a reality of domination, by saying, "some people are more powerful because their partners let them be."[8] Although the argument contains a grain of truth, it denies the intimidating quality of violence, and the superior material resources men can withhold from women, like money for food. These therapists incorrectly place the source of the problem within the family system, not within the person who beats, the traditions that maintain abuse, or the institutions that support male domination.

An equally misleading and attractive theory suggests that an intergenerational cycle of violence creates battering. Violence is learned in one's family of origin, either by watching father hit mother or by being hit oneself. Again, this theory must be recognized as an attempt to understand social causation by describing influences in individuals' lives. Even in this context, however, some of the conclusions of those who support such a theory appear suspect. Straus, Steinmetz, and Gelles note, for example, that "the more punishment one experienced as a child, the greater the rate of violence in marriages fifteen or more years later. One out of four or five of those who were punished the most hit his or her spouse during the year of this survey."[9] Although the authors state that physical punishment as a child increases the *likelihood* (emphasis added) of domestic violence, they then conclude quite emphatically that, "each generation learns to be violent by being a participant in a violent family."[10]

Childhood experiences do profoundly influence adult behavior and may be one factor in explaining why some men batter and why some women have difficulty leaving abusive men. For example, activists working in shelters report that a significant number of women who use the shelters were victims of incest. Incest victims learn a variety of "lessons," one of which is to keep family secrets. Often they feel intensely guilty and fear destroying the family. Some activists suggest that incest, a compelling "lesson" about male dominance and abuse, heightens women's later vulnerability to further violence.

However, the influence of childhood experiences of abuse on adult behavior is not mechanistic. While some men may learn that violence is a useful tool to get one's way and that women and children are acceptable targets, others may be repelled by violence. Many men who saw their fathers beat their mothers do not beat their wives. And one wonders if the fact that shelter residents experienced incest signifies a correlation between incest and battering or whether it may instead be one indication that incest is much more widespread than anyone has previously recognized. Using the example cited above from Straus, Steinmetz, and Gelles, it is possible to conclude, as they do, that a cycle of violence exists. On the other hand, one might just as easily look at their example again and conclude that three or four out of five who were "punished the most" did not hit their spouses. Similarly, the work of Russell Dobash and R. Emerson Dobash suggests that in many cases, brothers of violent men are not violent toward their wives or children. Yet presumably brothers raised in the same household experienced similar levels of violence in their childhood homes.[11]

Conclusions about the intergenerational effects of violence are premature until studies are completed of violent individuals and their siblings raised in both violent and non-violent households, and non-violent individuals and their siblings, raised in both violent and non-violent households.[12] To understand the relationship between incest and battering, one must study incest victims who are battered and those who are not. And if, as evidence suggests, 90% of all parents in the United States hit their children, careful, long-term studies must be done before any theories are developed linking family violence in one's family of origin to later violence.

Acknowledging that many men who batter come from violent households, the question remains—what do we learn from this fact? Straus, Steinmetz, and Gelles suggest that the family is a learning ground for violence in which everyone is a potential victim and aggressor. They imply that violence is somehow inherent in the family.[13] This emphasis has led many to conclude that husband battering is a serious problem, and a rash of articles like "Study Backs Up Suspicion Husband Is More Battered Spouse" appeared in 1977 and 1978. On the Today Show in February 1978, Richard Levy, co-author of *Wife-Beating: The Silent Crisis*, stated that husband beating affected twelve million American men. Less than two weeks later, the Today Show retracted this, noting that "Levy's statement was erroneous, having been based on Steinmetz's study of 47 couples, 5 of which had experienced *mutual* slapping and hitting."[14] Many scholars and movement activists critiqued the work of Steinmetz, offering evidence that refutes her findings. In an analysis of 3020 cases of violence in two Scottish cities, 1044 involving family members, 76% of the cases were husbands assaulting their wives and 1% were wives assaulting their husbands.[15] The Lafayette, Louisiana Task Force on Domestic Violence found that of 2000 domestic violence calls in 1976 to law enforcement agencies, 95% were from women victims.[16]

Statistics were not the only challenge to Straus, Steinmetz, and Gelles. Activists pointed out that their survey methods would never adequately explain the meaning of violence. A slap by a woman documented as "violence" may momentarily sting; a slap by a man has broken jaws. In surveys, as in therapy, men understate the amount of violence they perpetrate. Programs for batterers, like Emerge, claim that men who abuse constantly underreport the physical damage that they do to women. Far worse, in the Straus, Steinmetz, and Gelles survey no questions were asked about women's use of violence as a method of self-defense. From accounts by battered women, it can be suggested that self-defense is one primary reason for violence directed at husbands and male partners. Insight into the power dynamics between men and women and the meaning of violence is ignored by survey methods that rely on counting up the number of violent incidents. Nor do surveys reveal the consequences of violence; for example, women, not men, must flee from their homes in large numbers. A 1977 open letter to Suzanne Steinmetz emphasized the damaging ways in which her research had been used and declared, "You have a responsibility to publicly correct any distortions that have arisen and to clarify your analysis of the problem."[17] Confirmation, rather than clarification, came in 1980 with the publication of *Behind Closed Doors: Violence in the American Family*, co-authored by Straus, Steinmetz, and Gelles.

Although the authors acknowledge that wives are much more likely to be victims of repeated, dangerous, and injurious forms of violence and are locked into marriages to a much greater extent than men, they restate that many women are very violent, concluding meaninglessly, "It seems that violence is built into the very structure of the society and the family system itself."[18]

Straus, Steinmetz, and Gelles fail to see that the problem is not the family per se but the power relations within it. Men who counsel abusive men understand this dynamic well.

> Violence is a technique, a strategy of control. He needs to dominate; that is what he learned. He learned he had a right to dominate and control and violence becomes an easy method.[19]

The family is not randomly violent. Certain members, women and children, suffer much more brutality. Male children from violent families, following socialization and cultural patterns, may identify with the aggressor, learn to use physical force, and become violent. Female children may become withdrawn and frightened in families where the father is abusive. Yet in these cases, people are not indiscriminately learning victim and aggressor roles; they are learning about their proper place and the correct way to behave within a male-dominated family and culture in which violence has been institutionalized.

Feminists and mental health practitioners often disagree on the issue of whether it is useful to view socially created problems arising from power differentials as abnormal, with feminists saying no and mental health practitioners answering yes. When feminists suggest that violence is about neither sick psyches nor sick relationships, the reader should not conclude that they are dismissing psychology or ignoring violent individuals. They are stressing the need for a psychology that analyzes wife beating in its proper contexts, accounts for power differentials, and asks why women have been brutalized. Rather than label battering as pathology or a family systems failure, it is more conceptually accurate to assume that violence against women, like that directed toward children, is behavior approved of and sanctioned in many parts of the culture. Extreme cases in which women are mutilated by psychotic men are only one end of a continuum of violent behavior, the more moderate forms of which are viewed as normal. Many in this culture approve of hitting women.

Ideally, a theory of violence against women in the family will explain individual behavior adequately. However, here the priority is to understand why abuse is directed at women, not why each individual man abuses. Individual men who abuse have varied personalities. Clearly, their family histories, intimacy problems, stress levels, and alcohol intake will affect their behavior. In individual cases, such factors may contribute to abuse or heighten the likelihood of its occurrence, but they do not explain the consistent target—women. The task is to discover what social conditions produce this target generation after generation.

The Historic Legacy

The theory provided in this chapter is tentative, to be tested against historical, anthropological, and sociological data still being collected. It is based largely on evidence gathered from white Western European cultures. As such, it begins with significant biases. For example, as one black writer emphasizes, "it is important to note that sexual inequality between Black men and women has very different historical and cultural beginnings than the sexual inequality between white men and women. Consequently the present inequality is of a different nature..."[20] As third world women contribute more to theories about violence against women, feminist theory is undergoing important transformations.

The historical context within which battering has developed is that of male domination within and outside the family. Domination describes a social structure in which certain groups of people can determine and limit the spheres of activity of other groups. The power that a dominating group exercises carries with it the threat or the use of force to coerce compliance.[21]

Throughout most of Western European history, the patriarchal family was directly supported by the laws and practices of the larger society. The patriarchal family predates capitalist society, and so does violence against women within it.

> Patriarchal authority is based on male control over woman's productive capacity, and over her person. This control existed before the development of capitalist commodity production. It belonged to a society in which the persons of human beings were owned by others.[22]

Pre-capitalist and early capitalist patriarchal authority was based on the father's control of his household, which was the focus of daily life and productive activity for everyone.

In Western European pre-capitalist and early capitalist societies, battering was maintained by powerful legal and moral codes.

Christianity provided ideological justification for patriarchal marriages, and the state codified these relations into the law.[23] Marriage laws explicitly recognized the family as the domain of the husband, forced women to conform to the man's will, and punished men and women unequally for infractions of marriage vows.[24]

> To be a wife meant becoming the property of a husband, taking a secondary position in a marital hierarchy of power and worth, being legally and morally bound to obey the will and wishes of one's husband, and thus, quite logically, subject to his control even to the point of physical chastisement or murder.[25]

Under English common law, "the wife came under the control of her husband and he had the legal right to use force against her in order to insure that she fulfilled her wifely obligations, which included the consummation of the marriage, cohabitation, maintenance of conjugal rights, sexual fidelity, and general obedience and respect for his wishes."[26] Her status as wife excluded her from the legal process, placed her in the same category as children and servants, required obedience, and gave her husband extraordinary discretion over determining punishable offenses.[27] In their historical overview of wife beating, R. Emerson Dobash and Russell Dobash note that, "Through the seventeenth, eighteenth, and nineteenth centuries, there was little objection within the community to a man's using force against his wife as long as he did not exceed certain tacit limits."[28]

English common laws pertaining to marriage had a significant impact on later American law. Although not present in legal statutes in America, the husband's right to chastise his wife was upheld in the Supreme Court of Mississippi in 1824. The court ruled that a husband should be allowed to chastise without being subject to vexatious prosecution, which would supposedly shame all parties.[29] A North Carolina court ruling in 1864 asserted that the state should not interfere in cases of domestic chastisement but should leave the parties to themselves, to make up, unless there were permanent injury or an excess of violence.[30] Because wife beating was not specifically protected by legal statutes in the United States, battered women in search of justice took many men to court throughout the nineteenth century.[31] Judges, however, would imprison only the most violent men, and not until 1871 was wife beating actually declared illegal in two states, Alabama and Massachusetts.[32]

In England, husbands' absolute power of chastisement was abolished in 1829. Yet only the Married Women's Property Act of

1895 made conviction for assault a sufficient ground for divorce, and as two commentators note, "it was...very difficult to get a conviction for assault and the standard of proof was so high as to make a conviction almost impossible."[33]

These changes in England and America occurred in an atmosphere of general agitation from women who were demanding rights to divorce, separation, control of their property, and custody of their children. These changes slowly combined to loosen the legal and moral authority husbands held over their wives. In spite of these breakthroughs, violence persisted. Men were protected by institutions like the courts, while wives endured physical harm. Francis Power Cobbe's 1878 publication "Wife Torture in England" documented 6000 of the most "brutal assaults" on women who, in a three year period, had been maimed, blinded, trampled, burned, and murdered. Cobbe detailed the cases:

> Michael Copeland, who threw his wife on a blazing fire. Frederick Knight jumped on the face of his wife (who had only been confined a month) with a pair of boots studded with hobnails.[34]

Cobbe also explained why such horrifying abuse continued.

> The general depreciation of women *as a sex* is bad enough, but in the matter we are considering, the special depreciation of *wives* is more directly responsible for the outrages they endure. The notion that a man's wife is his *property* in the sense in which a horse is his property...is the fatal root of incalculable evil and misery.[35]

Although men no longer legally own women, many act as if they do. In her marriage vows today, the woman still promises to love, honor, and obey. Law and tradition continue to conspire to view the husband as head of the household, responsible for the support of his family, while the wife is in charge of housework and children.[36] According to sexist socialization, a woman is to nurture her husband, sexually respond to his wishes, bear and raise "his" children. Her needs are secondary to his, and his power inside and outside the family are unchallenged. He is still "king of the castle." Today, the patriarchal legacy intertwines with the needs of a capitalist economy, recreating the socialization patterns and institutional life that perpetuate male domination and violence. Men's status is upheld by a general division of labor outside as well as inside the home that makes women economically dependent on men. It is further reinforced by institutions—courts, police, hospitals, social service agencies—that either explicitly or implicitly support a husband's "right" to control his wife.

Battering as a Way to Maintain Control

Battering is one tool that enforces husbands' authority over wives or simply reminds women that this authority exists. As R. Emerson Dobash and Russell Dobash note, "all men see themselves as controllers of women, and because they are socialized into the use of violence they are potential aggressors against their wives."[37] Here it is important to distinguish between male domination in general and battering in particular. All men learn to dominate women, but only some men batter them. Violence is only one of the many ways in which men express their socially structured right to control and chastise. For some men, a sense of owning women is combined with a belief in the right to use force. For others, however, violence is a morally unacceptable way to maintain their dominant status. In still other cases men may not need to use violence to dominate. Verbal abuse, withholding affection, or withdrawing resources may suffice.

Men are not necessarily consciously aware of their need to dominate. Rather, they are socialized to feel uncomfortable when not in control,[38] and they turn to violence as a response to their discomfort. Even men who regret their violence insist that they need to use it to stay in charge. One man, recounting why he physically restrained his wife from leaving a family gathering, said, "I felt that she didn't have the right to make the decision to leave. Her decision to leave was not as important as mine to have her stay." As he later commented, "when all else fails, violence is the way to keep control, to maintain your identity."[39]

The right to dominate and control expresses itself in multiple, sometimes unfathomable ways. Battering is often used to punish or to teach lessons, even when women are unaware of the norms that they have violated. For example, if the house is cleaned "improperly" or if his sexual advances are rebuffed, punishment is meted out.[40] The dominator silently defines the parameters of unacceptable behavior and, as the aggrieved party, uses her broken "promises" to justify his abuse. His parent-like rationalization is often that she deserved the abuse for being "bad." Men will say, "she was acting like a child; I did it for her own good; this beating will teach her a lesson."

Often men batter to get their own way or stop a woman's challenge to their plans. As head of the household, some men, especially working class and middle class men, have control over the resources that their wives need and often women must negotiate for them from a disadvantaged position. In her interviews with battered women, R. Emerson Dobash found that if the woman tried to continue negotiating with her husband for money, for example, beyond a point he felt acceptable, he could always stop the process by force. As one woman described:

> The argument got too bad that he couldn't take it. He hated anybody continually arguing against him. Then he pulled me by the hair down these stone steps...and he hauled me out the back door and kicked me. Oh, he kicked me stupid.[41]

Forced to negotiate from a disadvantaged position, women sometimes find that the most basic, mundane requests evoke violent responses.

> Women who tried to persuade their husbands to spend more time with them or the children, or to convince their husbands to spend less money on themselves or their friends and more upon the family, or to get a social evening out were all subject to having their claims, requests or demands rejected.[42]

The women's just claims were then redefined by their husbands as nagging.[43] Nagging, of course, justifies a beating; she "provokes" him and therefore deserves punishment while he walks away "guiltless," compelled to beat her as a way to stop further insubordination or foolishness. One man who used to batter validated these insights.

> In an argument whenever she'd show me where I was wrong, I'd say bullshit—that's it, no more, you're wrong. I'd always end it. I'd say, "I can't understand your words." But it was very simple words she talked. I couldn't let her argue with me.[44]

Women's self-assertion through jobs or school particularly infuriates some men and many women describe how battering began or escalated when they made efforts to become more autonomous or received recognition for their work. Her separateness as a human being, her breaking the unstated vow that husband and wife are one and that the important one is the husband, is intolerable. This man who batters found his wife's self-assertion an undesired challenge to his expectations.

> If my wife had stayed the way she was when I married her, we wouldn't have had any problems...

Later in the interview he states:

> When I married my wife she was a pretty sweet girl who wanted what I wanted out of life. Or so I thought. Then she gets her consciousness

raised, and all of a sudden all that I'm giving her is not enough.[45]

Some men are infuriated by any sign of autonomy, as this same man, who broke his wife's arm and wrist, sending her to the hospital several times, suggests.

> I don't think most men want to go home to a lot of hooey about freedom and self-expression after eight hours in the real world. My wife always told me that I didn't own her. Like hell I didn't! I did own her.[46]

For those who blame violence on women's liberation, however, it is essential to remember that male violence in the family occurred long before women's liberation movements. It is primarily a sign of women's inequality, even when it is invoked to stop their struggle for equality.

Male domination is the expectation that men will be gratified by women and that they will get their own way. If a man feels entitled to deference and respect, any slight can produce ammunition for a rage. The slight and the resulting anger create the justification for an explosion. As Joseph Morse of the Emerge collective describes:

> He takes it out on her because she does something that he doesn't like. She is supposed to know about feelings and relationships. Women are nurturers and caretakers. Men expect this and when something bad happens, men blame women for it. If she can't figure it out, she isn't doing her job and she is hurting me. Men say, although not consciously, if I'm hurt, she did something wrong. If she loves me, she will understand me. If she doesn't understand, she's not doing her job; she's a *bad* wife.[47]

Although battering is purposeful behavior because it allows the man to remain in control at least temporarily, it is not always rational. Batterers often display irrational jealousy, for example, and then use this as a justification for a beating. Seemingly minor events can trigger battering, making it appear to happen "out of the blue." Gelles quotes one woman.

> We were having a birthday party and my father was there....Well, I had my son...help make the first cut. I had him give the first piece to my father because he had to go to work. My husband stormed out of the house...He came back loaded that night simply because my father had the first piece of birthday cake instead of him...That was the first time he broke my wrist.[48]

Battering may have no immediate antecedent at all. A woman may have done nothing obvious to insult her husband; she may be attacked when she is asleep. The hidden rationality in this seemingly irrational behavior is the unstated power dynamic and the restoration of male authority or sense of well-being.

Contrary to popular belief, battering does not always have a manifest sexist content; a man does not have to say, "I own her" to beat his wife. The process, beating, is the domination, while the actual issues being argued over may be irrelevant. Although verbal fights often center on women's "appropriate" duties in the home, the struggle to determine the nature of the relationship, not the issues, leads to violence.[49] To understand why so many different kinds of women are beaten, it is necessary to separate the sexist content of disagreements from the sexist process. Most people assume only "traditional" women who comply with rigid sex role stereotypes are beaten by their "traditional" husbands. However, many feminists with careers, political commitments, or personal autonomy are also beaten. A man beats to remind a woman that the relationship will proceed in the way he wants or that ultimately he holds the power.

In their research, R. Emerson Dobash and Russell Dobash found that the first violence is usually a single blow and is treated by both partners as exceptional; no one expects it to continue. The first violence, however, sets the stage for further abuse. Often, he rationalizes the attack by focusing on what she did wrong; she begins to scrutinize her behavior.

> She attempts to comprehend the violence in terms of her own behavior: to see her own 'guilt', and both to forgive her husband (for perhaps merely overreacting) and to seek a solution by changing her behavior so as to give him no further reason for hitting her.[50]

Such self-blame often lasts for years.

The attacks become more and more violent over time, and shock and horror continue. For her, fear, anger, shock, and humiliation intermingle with hope that he will change; eventually hope gives way to depression and anger. Her feelings of self-worth decline as her affection for him lessens. His remorse, if ever expressed, ceases.[51]

As violence becomes easier and easier to use, men fail to see the consequences of their behavior. As one counselor described it, "They don't necessarily see their impact or her fear; they minimize; they just act and they know they can get away with force."[52] In fact, if she tries to discuss the violence or share her pain and growing distrust, he may become angrier. To talk or not to talk about the violence becomes another control issue, and she may be beaten if she "pushes" him to discuss it. Placing her in a powerless, maddening dilemma, the man interprets her need to talk or her possible withdrawal as "punishing" and he retaliates.[53]

When women realize that their efforts will not stop the violence and that their husbands are uncontrollably brutal, fear, outrage, and and a sense of injustice grow larger but these feelings "cannot be sustained at a high level for very long, and between incidents the woman tries to cope simply by trying to ignore the problem of violence."[54] In this context, ignoring the problem is a coping mechanism although it is eventually self-defeating. Denial of the seriousness of his violence may help a woman feel that she can find help for him or that she can tolerate the abuse until she accumulates adequate resources to leave. This reaction, like that of hope, helps her to survive.

Paradoxically, the attempt to control through violence often destroys relationships and drives women away, but men continue beating. Those who work with men who batter describe violence as easy and efficacious.[55] Violence works in the sense that the violent person intimidates others and makes them act according to his will. Violence is practical; the violent person temporarily gets his way and he knows that he is frightening his victim.[56]

> Men like a woman's fear; they laugh about it. It is funny for him to see her grovel in her fear. Fear is a consciously used tool.[57]

The fear and intimidation take many forms, killing loved pets, destroying favorite objects, and sexual assaults.

Battering produces contradictory results. Men benefit from having placating wives; they do not have to bother with daily negotiations over children, housecleaning, or the allocation of each partner's leisure time. Some battered women insure that everything runs smoothly so that nothing irritates their men.

The control gained through battering extends far beyond violent events. Severe battering makes women afraid to challenge their husbands. As a result, often women know only what their husbands are willing to tell them about financial or family matters. Battered women often lack the information or freedom of movement most people take for granted. In this way violent men gain many advantages over women. However, as Jalna Hanmer points out in her important article on battering, the relationship being maintained is not primarily one of labor exploitation.

> The force is too often counter productive, not only may the woman be seriously injured but she may suffer nervous disturbance that makes it even more difficult for her to look after the children, prepare the

> meals...and she may end up in hospital...thus depriving the man of her services at least for a time.[58]

Hanmer defines the gain.

> It may be, or seem to be, necessary to kill, mutilate, maim or temporarily reduce a woman's ability to carry out services...in order to be in control. Prestige, self-esteem, a sense of personal worth is gained, expressed and made public by the acquiescence of others.[59]

Individual case examples make it clear that men use battering as a way to maintain or establish control. But men also abuse when they simply wish to display power for its own sake. Even though the motivations of individual abusers are unique, through battering men are making a statement to women about the kind of relationship they believe they are entitled to. In this sense, battering is a way of organizing a relationship so that men continue to feel superior to women.

Women's Inferior Status in Capitalist Society

We have established that battering results from an historically created gender hierarchy in which men dominate women. As long as this domination continues—in a capitalist or socialist society—men will batter their female partners. Yet capitalism itself creates unique conditions which leave women extremely vulnerable to violence. Analyzing women's position in the United States today helps us explore the other side of the dynamic of battering. First we asked—why do men abuse? Now we turn to the question—why do women stay with abusive men, and why can men get away with beating women?

In the United States, two dominant conditions of women's lives reinforce male domination and violence in the family. Under capitalism, women are primarily wageless or low paid wage earners and simultaneously, through an unequal division of labor, they are responsible for the maintenance of home and family. Zillah Eisenstein, a feminist theoretician, explains.

> Although this sexual division of labor and society antedates capitalism, it has been increasingly institutionalized and specifically defined in terms of the nuclear family because of the needs of advanced capitalism....With the rise of industrial capitalism, men were brought out of the home and into the wage-labor economy. Women became relegated to the home and were increasingly viewed by men as

nonproductive although many worked in the factories. They came to be seen solely in terms of sex roles....The work that women continued to perform in the home was not conceived of as work. Productive labor was defined as wage labor...[60]

Under capitalism, working at home and working for a wage eventually became separate phenomena. This made it seem as if women were detached from economic life when they did not labor for wages. As the home appeared to lose its productive functions and became more privatized, women found themselves in a degraded position, an easy target for male rage. A woman's "contacts with the outside world were dramatically constricted and her economic and to a considerable extent her social life mediated through her husband,"[61] setting up conditions that reinforced his power.

In manifold ways, the family is clearly not separate from the rest of society. Work performed within families, most frequently by women, reproduces the society. Women give birth to children, socialize them, clean, cook, and prepare everyone to go to school and jobs. Although referred to as private and nurturing, women's work is also socially necessary. In this sense, the family remains an integral part of the economy under capitalism.[62] Women nurture each generation of workers, and the capitalist class and individual men reap the benefits of their free labor. Additionally, the tensions of the workplace, poor salaries, and dangerous working conditions play havoc with family life.

Because of the privatized family and women's secondary status within it, violence is viewed as an individual act. Women suffer in shameful silence, convinced that no one else is experiencing the horror and that no one wants to know about it. As a result, male domination is restored in the family and in the community. Privatization is dangerous because it allows violence to accelerate while everyone says, "Mind your own business. This is a family problem."

Women occupy different positions in relationship to the wage economy. Women of all classes who do not work for a wage and whose household labor is unpaid find themselves in particularly vulnerable, needy positions when beaten. These women are terrified that they will not survive without their husbands' salary. Acutely aware of the powerlessness that total economic dependence breeds, their husbands say again and again, "She's not going anywhere; she needs me." Men know they can abuse and face few, if any, consequences.

Women who do not work for wages may suffer in another way, as their lack of outside employment provides a rationalization for battering. "She does not work; I work; she should do this for me," is the constant refrain of men who batter. If she is viewed as his bought laborer, then she, in her role as worker, can be chastised. Her work, maintaining a home and caring for children, becomes the terrain for his inspection and potential discipline.

As housewives, women feel the economic crunch most acutely. Women are often in the uncomfortable position of reminding their husbands that they have financial responsibilities to meet. If these men do not want to or cannot afford to meet these obligations, women remain easy scapegoats, reminders of his lack of power.

Women who work for a wage are not necessarily free of their need for a man. Although these women have more resources and are far less dependent on their husbands, lower wages still increase their husbands' power over them. Because on the average a woman earns 59% of what a man earns, she and her children will have a difficult time surviving if she must support them alone.

When women leave violent men, their economic vulnerability often drives them back home. One out of every three female-headed households, as compared to one out of every eighteen male-headed households, is living below the poverty level.[63] Ninety percent of all women who are year-round, full time workers earn less than $15,000 compared to 52% of all men in the same situation. In 1978, the median income for women was 59% of that for men, $9350 vs. $15,730.[64] For fully employed Hispanic women it was $8331, and for black women $9020.[65] Thirty-two out of every 100 women earn less than $7000, and the median income of families headed by women in 1978 was $8537 compared to $19,340 for husband-wife families.[66] Unemployment rates are also consistently higher for women than for men, and women's economic status is declining. Not surprisingly, battered women who return home often comment, "I just couldn't make it on my own; I hated to watch my kids suffer."

It is important to stress that paid work is not necessarily viewed as a liberating option by some women and this influences women's choices to stay in or leave violent relationships. A national survey of women wage-earners found that 55% of them reported having no leisure time; only 14% said that job and family life did not seriously interfere with each other.[67] Although wage work helps many women resist living with brutal men and produces a psychological as well as a material self-confidence, some women experience it as demeaning or barely worth the effort, given the cost and complications of finding decent child care, the expense of transportation and clothing, and the time needed to maintain a home.

Intertwining with sexism and class exploitation, racism places third world women in highly vulnerable positions in several different ways. One half of all minority families headed by women have incomes below the poverty level,[68] and third world women earn lower salaries than any other group of wage workers. Third world battered women also face racist treatment by institutions they turn to for help, such as courts, hospitals, and social service agencies.

It is not only the sexual division of labor, class exploitation, and racism that make women feel powerless and vulnerable under capitalism. Women's bodies are used to sell almost everything, and as one woman described it, "These ads make me furious but they also make me ashamed of myself." The objectification of women's bodies heightens their lack of self-confidence. Similarly, violence against women in the media degrades women, makes them feel insecure, and gives powerful messages to men.

> In many movies and TV dramas, violence against women is glorified and equated with sexual excitation for men. Women are portrayed as helpless, passive, even willing victims....The plot, usually a struggle between the man who is attacker and the man who is rescuer, is heightened by, and sometimes secondary to, the sexual excitement surrounding the graphic rapes and murders.[69]

Whether or not such violent depictions "cause" violent behavior, they reflect dominant fantasies of women as passive and willing victims who are unable to defend themselves. Such images reproduce dominant stereotypes and reveal the depth of women's secondary status and subordination. Their popularity helps recreate this status, just as women's subordination is maintained through actual violence.

As an economic system, capitalism both undermines traditional male authority and bolsters it. Women who are now formally free to work, to divorce, and to leave violent men have made major gains over the last 150 years. However, economic insecurities make that formal freedom somewhat illusive.

> To the extent that it remains at least as difficult as ever to maintain a decent standard of living without "coupling," the overall impact of stagflation, on balance, may be as much to hook most women more tightly into traditional family obligations as to free them.[70]

In this society, battered women face the same contradictions that non-battered women confront when they contemplate leaving their husbands. Most women have been raised to believe that womanhood and marriage are synonymous. Most dream of a good life for themselves and their children, and male income often provides this chance. Yet if a better life also means that violence is unacceptable, battered women must leave. In this case, they may also accept poverty or living at the edge of survival. Child support or alimony are rarely realistic options for maintaining decent living standards. A ten year study of court ordered child support in a Wisconsin metropolitan area showed that within one year of the award, only 38% of the husbands were fully complying and after ten years, only 13% were fully compliant while 70% were paying none of the court ordered child support.[71] Many battered women choose poverty and economic insecurity over violence. Shelters, social supports, job opportunities, and legal reforms over the last century encourage their choice, making the emotional burdens easier to face. However, one wonders about all the women who, because of economic worries, decide to tolerate some level of violence, choosing to leave only when violence seems life threatening to them or dangerous to their children.

In an economy built to supply profits to a few, many women's basic needs are unmet. Women have difficulty gathering adequate financial resources to leave violent men; finding alternatives, like shelters and affordable housing, is another monumental task. Some battered women quite literally save a few cents weekly to buy the bus tickets that are their escape. Women who do not speak English or who are disabled find few, if any, helpful resources. Most shelters still lack space for all the women who want to come. If they are lucky enough to find shelter, women must start over with no clothing, household supplies, or furniture. Many must use welfare assistance for the first time. Day care is available to only a small percentage of women who would like to use it. As an economic system designed for profit, capitalism ignores human need and creates enormous obstacles for women who want to free themselves from brutality.

Female and Male Roles Within the Family

A sexual division of labor and society that defines people's activity, purposes, goals, desires, and dreams according to their biological sex, is at the base of patriarchy and capitalism. It divides men and women into their respective hierarchical sex roles and structures their related duties in the family domain and within the economy.[72]

In our society, the gender division of labor not only allocates domestic duties to women, but also adds a moral dimension to this assignment. Fulfilling household responsibilities represents a sign of love and loyalty to the husband. Women's proper role is to nurture men, and alleviate their emotional burdens. The mythology states that "good" wives, those who cater to their husbands' every need, have a happy family life. The woman alone is responsible for the success or "failure" of the marital relationship.

Child care is not only her full time responsibility, but also connotes a moral obligation since the woman is expected to arrange her life around the children's needs and is held responsible if anything goes wrong. Through this division of labor, men find ample ground to justify their violence, accusing women of being poor wives and mothers. Women often respond to this criticism by feeling guilty and sometimes even say they are responsible for the abuse. And because they are caretakers and nurturers of their children, women who contemplate leaving may be immobilized by the fear of causing their children financial or emotional deprivation.

It is interesting to speculate that women's role as primary or sole caretaker of children might also create conditions leading to abuse. The work of Nancy Chodorow and Dorothy Dinerstein suggests that because of the sexist division of labor, all children are forced to direct their earliest rage at their mothers, their principal source of comfort and deprivation. If fathers are unavailable, the potential anger directed solely toward women increases. Both boys and girls experience this early rage against a woman, and both learn later that women are defined as subordinate to men. This has a special meaning for males, however. In order to differentiate from their mothers and maintain their sense of male superiority, boys must learn to distance themselves from all that is defined as female. Andy McCormack of the Emerge collective explains the results as they are observed later, in the lives of men who batter.

> Boys don't learn to express feelings which makes it difficult to feel comfortable in intimate relationships. In intimate relationships you must be vulnerable. The men who batter say they want to be close to their wives, but it frightens them because in adulthood it evokes homophobic feelings; it is identified as womanly which is so frightening. The men articulate this by saying, "That's for women." At the same time, boys are given proscriptions about role models, being in control outside themselves and inside themselves.[73]

Tracing how childhood dependency on women and anger at them are expressed in adulthood, one activist further explains the behavior of men who batter.

> Men treat their wives like mothers. They are both utterly dependent on them and furious at their own dependency. After he beats her he is nice to her only because he fears that he won't survive without her. Later he is enraged that he displayed his own needs and dependency.[74]

Making the mother primary parent sets up the expectation that women will fulfill men's needs, a clear expectation of men who batter. In many families, men are socialized to be tough, cool, aggressive, and in control. These attributes reflect the dominant position they are supposed to assume in relationship to women and in the work world. Many seem unable to feel or at least are incapable of talking about their feelings. Talking through problems not only requires effort, but also puts the man in a position of taking emotional risks, and therefore feeling vulnerable. Yet it is their pretense of invulnerability that sets men above women. As a result, many men only show their feelings through anger.

While men are taught to be cool and aggressive, women are generally socialized to be warmly nurturing and passive. The dominant middle class norm mandates heterosexuality and marriage for women and men, but while male success and satisfaction are frequently measured through work achievements, female success and satisfaction are to come through marriage. Unmarried women are often considered deviant or inadequate. The resulting pressure to marry, to keep marriages together, and to feel intense personal responsibility when they fail plagues battered and non-battered women alike. These pressures, which help reproduce battering, operate for both working class and middle class women. As one working class battered woman said, "I wanted to do something big in my life, and the biggest thing I could do was to be his wife." Often battered women who are middle class professionals feel the same pressures, as Lenore Walker, author of *The Battered Woman*, explains.

> Most of them sought status in their home lives rather than in their careers. Thus, their self-esteem was dependent on their ability to be good wives and homemakers and was not well integrated with their successful professional activities.[75]

In her sample, Walker found that women felt it was better to be married to a batterer than not to be married at all.

Socialization patterns do vary by class and race. Many third world women, for example, grow up knowing they must work for wages and provide for themselves and their children. Yet their socialization, like that of white women, emphasizes their responsibility for child care and maintaining strong family ties. In addition, many women of color are socialized to fight side by side with men for the survival of their children and extended community networks; racism makes family and community ties even more primary in some ways.

Women raised to believe that their happiness will come through marriage and family will often have trouble dealing with the constant accusations of infidelity and of being poor wives and mothers that men use to rationalize abusive behavior. A battered women's advocate describes the painful process of women overcoming years of sexist socialization.

> Initially all the women blame themselves, saying that the violence is in the man and they bring it out. They say, "if only I could learn not to bring it out."
>
> Many women see intellectually that the violence was not their fault. But it is a struggle; the doubts go on and on. They say, "should I go back and was I responsible."
>
> As time goes on, the women know that the reason he gives for beating them isn't the real reason but it is a back and forth process.[76]

Although women struggle against this sexist socialization, they also have internalized it.

Many battered women express a genuine love for their husbands. Yet sometimes it is difficult for women to sort out exactly what love means in this context, since women are often taught that love and self-esteem lie in self-denial and the capacity to sacrifice for their husbands. "For better or worse" is a constant reminder which serves to reinforce battered women's sense of guilt and responsibility toward their husbands. Women often believe they have the power to reform their husbands, and men play on this, promising to change if only the woman stays.

Women learn that men are to judge female worth: men choose and women wait to be chosen. Male judgments of women's intelligence, bodies, and nurturing abilities are accorded more validity than female evaluations. As a result, women's egos and self-worth are damaged and their self-confidence limited. Women are socialized to seek protection and affirmation from men, and it is easy to understand that when they are battered, they feel as if they have failed in their primary role—keeping a man happy and being protected by him. When women have no political context through which to understand battering, they view it as an isolated struggle between themselves and their husbands. They see the personal failure rather than the unequal power dynamic that allows battering to happen.

The Dynamics of Oppression:
The Logic of Battered Women's Behavior

Sex role socialization, economic dependency, and unsupportive institutions combine to make the task of leaving an abusive relationship particularly difficult. But despite mythology to the contrary, battered women are actively engaged in changing their lives. Many leave their husbands, hoping this will convince him that he must change. Some turn to family networks that, through threats or physical retaliation, pressure him into stopping his violence. Some women leave permanently; we hear little about them because they often do not use battered women's services. There is no research available to tell us how many women leave. In several divorce studies, physical cruelty to the woman is offered as a reason for dissolving one third of the marriages. Marlyn Grossman, a feminist psychologist and activist, found that some women leave immediately upon the first experience of violence, and these women tend to be unmarried and childless. She conjectures that when a woman is in a position to think only of herself, she may leave more quickly.[77] Bowker and MacCallum, two social work researchers, found that as violence continued, women turned increasingly to informal, interpersonal sources of help, like friends, and to formal help. In their study, between the first and last violent incident, the use of lawyers rises from 6% to 50%, while that of social service agencies increases from 8% to 43%.[78] Many women leave and return several times before they make a final break. As one activist explained:

> Whether we have been beaten or not, we all learn to stay and struggle. Battered women recognize the problem and try to cope without necessarily having to change their entire lives. You try to change, change him, hope you can talk things through.[79]

Women want their marriages to work, and sometimes returning is an active attempt to put matters under their control.

Most psychological theories misunderstand that battered women assess their reality continually and make choices based on what they find.

> Battered women learn to be realistic, not helpless. Everyone tells her to go back home. You learn not to ask for help because it's a waste of time. Women say to themselves, "there are no alternatives; I might as well make the best of it."[80]

Unwittingly, psychological theory often denies battered women the control they do maintain. As one activist commented, "women are deciding to stay given how they weigh their alternatives."[81] Women simultaneously make choices and become depressed about the poverty of their options.

Battered women are not passive; rather, they engage in step-like, logical behavior as they attempt to stop the violence or leave. Not all of them are successful because the major variable, the violent man, is outside their realm of control. Staying, especially given the lack of resources and social supports for leaving, should never be read as accepting violence. The more any woman is denied control over her life, especially in violent situations where self-assertion is dangerous, the more difficult change becomes. It is obvious that the women with the fewest resources tend to stay or return. However, when these women find adequate resources, they, too, frequently leave. Some activists and researchers suggest that whether an abused woman leaves depends on a combination of factors, including the existence of a good support network for the woman, and material resources. Here again it is important to underscore women's fears of severe retaliation as a reason for staying.

Third world and ethnic working class women face special emotional complications when they leave. They worry about hostility from their community and from those outside their community. Chris Choy, an Asian American filmmaker and activist, explains that older Chinese women, for example, define battering as their fate, feel intense shame, and would be horrified by community condemnation of the violence.[82] Black battered women often struggle with conflicting emotions. As one writer noted, black women may feel "a grieving for him for never having a chance and for herself, anger for having to perform for both of them and a sense of resentment and guilt for having in some way been a part of his oppression."[83] Resolving these feelings takes time; slowly and at her own pace, each woman must realize for herself that his violence will not cease and then must decide what to do with that knowledge.

To build a theory of violence against women, it is important to analyze male and female socialization and family relationships. It is also essential, however, to recognize those forces outside the family that maintain and perpetuate violence. The institutions of the state and capitalist economic arrangements force women back to violent men. Only by understanding this larger context in which the problem, in all its manifestations, is handed back to the victim to solve alone, does the full logic of battered women's behavior emerge. We must document the ways institutions send women home and thereby maintain the family in order to determine the cause of abuse and to define meaningful strategies to end violence against women in the family.

Questions in Theory Building

Although, as this chapter suggests, we can theorize with some accuracy about many of the factors that cause battering socially and individually, there are also many issues that remain unexplored, vaguely defined, or biased by dominant white, middle class research and writing. For example, we know that the current economic system reproduces battering in multiple ways already considered. We also know, however, that economic and social changes over the last 150 years, including women's movement into the paid work force, have created conditions that challenge male domination. What we do not know is exactly how this challenge operates in relation to battering, how strong it is, and what it means for the future.

Because the battered women's movement is so young, new areas are just now emerging that need to be explored. For example, in recent years some activists in the movement have discovered that women in lesbian relationships are sometimes battered. How does this fit with a theory that has at its center male domination as the cause of battering? One could theorize that models of intimate relationships based on power and domination are so pervasive in this society that they do, in fact, affect the nature of relationships between people of the same sex. However, much more research needs to be done to understand this form of battering. How widespread is it? Is it the case that the battered partner is generally emotionally and/or economically dependent on the abusive partner? Because two women are more likely to be of similar physical strength, are battered lesbians more likely to fight back? How does the reality of being a lesbian—someone not fully accepted by the society—affect how one experiences being abused by one's lover? No one knows the answers to these and related questions, because they are now being raised for the first time. But it is crucial to begin posing them if we are to fully understand the nature of battering. It is also essential to recognize lesbian battering in order to lessen the pain and isolation of those women who are beaten by women.

Right now, lesbians in abusive relationships have special problems finding help. Traditional institutions (police, courts, hospitals) will not recognize the validity of their relationships. Battered lesbians may not feel comfortable turning to feminists in the battered women's movement who have understandably made male violence against women their focus of attention. The battered lesbian may be particularly likely to keep her situation private, convinced she is the only woman battered by another woman.

Although many activists and researchers have recognized the importance of analyzing how class and race factors affect batterers and women who are beaten, the significance of these factors remains unclear. There are few reliable studies and almost no statistics to inform theoretical work or correct distorted assumptions. For example, we know little about class, race, or any other differences between women who are beaten once and women who are beaten repeatedly. We do not know the difference in violence experienced by those women who work outside the home and those who do not. Almost all of the statistics that do exist are shelter statistics. Yet women who use shelters are just one subset of battered women, often those who are most severely beaten and have the fewest resources.

In looking at statistics, one must be aware that they may give a false picture of who is battered. Shelter statistics almost certainly underrepresent middle class violence. Middle class men and women are more likely to avoid data collectors. Middle class women can turn to private doctors and therapists, and much male violence may therefore never appear on police and court records. Perhaps less obviously, statistics may also underrepresent violence against third world women and poor women of all races. Third world women are often reluctant to use shelters, which are frequently staffed by white women and often reflect the racism of the larger society. And because poor people experience so many different kinds of oppression, violence may be responded to as one of many abuses. Poor women, struggling to feed, clothe, and house their families, may not report battering as quickly as women who see it as the biggest problem in their life. In this case male violence is not accepted, but it may be just another part of life that women must endure.

The interconnections between class, gender, and race domination as they influence individual batterers' behavior need to be explored further. It is continually suggested, yet unproven, that the stress created by unemployment and racism, for example, cause individual men to be violent. We need to know if this is true, and if so, why rage and frustration caused by structural forces like unemployment are misdirected toward women.

Some third world women suggest that race and class oppression have a clear impact on the decision to abuse, and that male domination is an inadequate concept to explain the behavior.

Arguing that the dominant definitions of manhood place black men in conflict, I. Nkenge Toure of the D.C. Rape Crisis Center draws the connection between racism and sexism.

> The Black man faces systematic economic exclusion,....In turn his family obligations cannot always be fully met. If the man can provide, he is still politically excluded from participation in determining his own destiny....He has no real power, so numerous adjectives from the larger society's definitions do not apply. Many men seek to compensate for this lack of control by intensifying their identification with the sexual aspects of manhood. Often this means sexual domination, which easily manifests itself in rape, battering and other forms of violence against women.[84]

And Native American women insist that reservation life places serious strains on the family that lead to battering. Native American families have endured constant racism and high male unemployment; alcoholism and violence are two of the results.

Some people feel that all men are socialized to dominate women, to assert male superiority through bonding with other men, and to experience a male culture which often includes displays of violence or aggression. Yet do men of all classes and races strive to be dominant and successful, and do they express their domination of women in the same ways? It is probable that dominant personality structures are created through a variety of complex processes, and we need to examine how this relates to men who batter. It is also clear that all men do not blindly act on what they are taught. Many resist their socialization to be violent or experience conflicts about it which lead them to reject their past. More research is needed to determine why and how this happens.

While poor and working class women have few resources to escape violent men, find new housing, or leave their communities, out of their struggle to survive many have developed more resourcefulness and less fear of being alone than do their middle class counterparts. Poor women more frequently use the courts and welfare and are more prepared to struggle against institutional abuses. For other reasons, however, their vulnerability to violence is increased. Institutional racism and class discrimination make it difficult for women of color and poor women of all races to be taken seriously and find help. These women may also suffer from a different form of guilt than do middle class women. As a result of class and race oppression, they believe that women should stick by their men.

Yet generalizations about class and race must be made cautiously. Although all third world women are affected by their status as women and as members of racially oppressed groups, some, because of their relatively advantaged class position, have more options for escape and self-support. Moreover, different third world peoples have unique historic experiences of oppression that lead them to confront abuse differently. For example, activists note that while some black women will fight back against their abusers, many Latinas will not. Because of religious views and traditional sex role socialization, many Latinas feel they must endure abusive relationships. Third world women raised in the United States often have more tools to stop or resist battering than do recent immigrants. Asian or Mexican women who do not speak English or who may be in the country illegally often remain the virtual prisoners of abusive men. When women have little information about their rights, they are particularly vulnerable to repeated violent attacks. Many remain with abusive men out of a fear of losing their children or of being deported. For these women, the extended family may be the only sustenance. In some cases, these family networks help women escape, while in others, women are made to feel disloyal to the entire family if their "personal" problems are ever made public. They endure abuse in order to maintain the only source of support they have, their family and community.

White middle class women's experiences with violence have much in common with those of women of other races and classes. Yet there are also differences. Many white middle class women have money and therefore options for escape. However, those who do not hold paying jobs may have no access to their husbands' resources. These women are terrified of leaving because of the poverty they will certainly face. They may be further handicapped by sex role socialization; they traditionally have had more opportunities to live out the feminine ideal which calls for dependence on men than have working class and third world women, who have often been forced to earn a living outside the home. As a result, some white middle class women are poorly prepared to survive on their own.

Women of different classes may also experience different kinds of abuse. As Mildred Daley Pagelow writes, "the middle class batterer seems to be more inclined to use psychological battering and forms of 'punishment' which neither destroy the home nor leave obvious marks on a woman's body."[85] She cites a case of a woman locked out of her house with no coat on a bitterly cold night.

Middle class and working class women who are employed outside the home are in some ways freer to leave abusive men than

are unemployed women. However, they may face additional complications. Employed women are often forced to give up their jobs
because of threatened or actual violent harassment at work by their
husbands.[86]

All of the issues raised in this section need to be explored further
as we develop a theoretical framework for understanding battering.
For activists working with abused women and searching for ways to
stop battering, it is essential to examine carefully how race and class
factors, as well as other differences, affect batterers and women who
are abused. In studying violence against women and building
theories, the challenge remains to see violent behavior as individually willed yet socially constructed.

Ending Violence Against Women

It is important to set aside immediate problems and imagine for
a moment conditions under which men would not beat women.
Although only political struggle will create such a possibility, a
vision of the future helps us critically assess the present.

Since male supremacy is the historical source of battering, and
class domination perpetuates male privilege, a long-range plan to end
abuse includes a total restructuring of society that is feminist, anti-
racist, and socialist. While ending capitalism and building socialism
will not stop male domination, they may be necessary steps in the
process. Under capitalism, private ownership creates an economy
based on exploitation and a privatized family, both of which rest on
female subordination. In contrast, social ownership of economic life,
democratic participation in the decisions that affect one's life, and
ending the separation between family and community are the hopes
that a yet unrealized version of socialism offers.

Material preconditions must exist to end violence against
women. These conditions—shelter, adequate jobs, incomes, free
health care, affordable housing, and child care—are essential to
allow women independence from violent men and to enable all people
to live decently. It is questionable whether this is possible under
capitalism. In a privatized, capitalist economy, the social purposes
and value of women's work disappears; women are easily degraded,
subject to the whims of their husbands and isolated from the support
of other women. Resources must be available in the form of goods,
services, and jobs so that power relations between men and women
in the family are equalized.

As part of women's struggle for this material security, the ideological and emotional stigma attached to homosexuality, women raising children alone, and living in non-nuclear families also must be broken. Diverse forms of family life must gain ideological and economic support from the state in the form of services and economic subsidies. A society based on a privatized, nuclear family life, separate from the community, creates unresolvable contradictions in any efforts to end violence against women in the family.

Breaking the private hold entails defining a socialist feminist vision in which male-female equality would be the community norm. Only if men participate equally in domestic tasks and childrearing and if this labor is socialized through mechanisms like community-run child care centers, can we hope to challenge the pervasive re-creation of sexism. Only then would women be psychically and materially freed from total domestic and childrearing responsibilities. If women were neither economically dependent on men nor defined as different and less, then male and female might cease to be rigid, oppositional categories in which men hold more power and are more valued.

In this socialist feminist world, abuse would be defined as a crime against a person. Family life would be open for community scrutiny because the family would be part of and accountable to the community. Community based institutions could hear complaints and dispense justice, and community networks could hold individuals accountable for their behavior and offer protection to women. If a false separation did not exist between the family and the community, women might lose their sense of isolation and gain a sense of entitlement to a violence-free life. The violent man would bear the consequences of his abusive behavior as community censure fell upon him and watchfulness protected her and stopped future violence. If community members were accountable to one another for the well being of all, then male violence would no longer be a woman's individual burden but rather everyone's responsibility to stop.

Over time, children raised in such a context would re-create a different set of social relations than those we know. As we undermine male power and female dependence within and outside of the family, the rationalizations for abuse are removed and the ability to carry it out with impunity ceases.

In a society where social ownership and community control were the norms, women could struggle more effectively to stop the objectification and commodification of their bodies. To eliminate these forms of degradation means to define a human sexuality based on equality, not domination. Only in a different society could women fully reclaim their bodies and assert control over their lives and their sexuality.

RAVEN (Rape and Violence End Now), a St. Louis based male collective, defines the task for men.

> The individual man is not the enemy, nor is he insane. The system which socializes men to deny all emotion other than anger during stress; to seek refuge from the horrors of public life in our homes; and to blame women (and children) for our fears and insecurities, all must be struggled against by all men—in community with women.[87]

Men face the task of working through their networks with other men to declare unacceptable the unequal power dynamics between men and women, challenge institutions, and reshape public consciousness as they refuse the privileges available to them. In the long run, men and women together must work to define and live egalitarian sexual and social relationships in the context of a struggle to end exploitation and oppression.

CHAPTER 10

Services and Politics:
The Need for a Dual Focus

Analyzing the conditions that perpetuate violence against women helps us to understand the need for a battered women's movement and some of the directions that the movement must take. If one accepts the analysis presented, that violence against women is rooted in male domination, then it becomes clear that a battered women's movement cannot succeed if it limits itself to providing services which are seen as separate from a politic. Yet, neither can a movement succeed if it divorces itself from the reality of battered women's lives and minimizes the importance of providing essential services.

Not all women within the movement agree with the analysis of violence in the family put forth here, and from its inception, the battered women's movement has been divided over whether it is primarily service-oriented, whether it is part of a feminist movement, or whether it is both. Ironically, the success of the movement in starting hundreds of services has heightened some of the divisions around this issue. These differing perspectives are made explicit in a 1977 exchange in the *NCN*. One woman writes:

> Dear Friends, I am a volunteer at our Lancaster Shelter. I am doing a survey on abused women....
> I feel coalitions or groups of women working on wife abuse are into the feminist and political side of the problem and not enough down to

> where it's really at: the great need of the abused woman. Please note, this does not refer to every group....[1]

An activist responded in the next *NCN*.

> If feminists have put a lot of energy into the politics of the problem, it is because of our deep belief in this process of individual and collective change, and the conviction that we must fight for what we believe is right. If we don't, no one will, and the problem of battering, along with countless other problems women face every day, will again be obscured and left in the hands of the hostile individuals and institutions who perpetuated and sanctioned the battering in the first place.[2]

Some women in the movement, like those who responded to the Lancaster shelter volunteer, believe that services will stay alive only if a movement does; others, however, fear that the movement endangers funding for services. In addition, tension exists between those who believe in providing more and better services and those who feel that too much service provision is a trap that will limit the movement's fight to end the conditions that breed violence. The need to build a movement for women's liberation is affirmed as primary by many and argued against by others. And still no one has adequately addressed the fact that an exploitative, profit-driven economic system, supported by sexist institutions, makes it impossible for a movement to offer the housing, jobs, child care, adequate welfare benefits, and decent education that women need to free themselves from violence.

The Lessons of Co-optation

The massive pressures upon services over the last several years offer a clue to not only why a movement is needed, but also to why it is so hard to maintain. Subtle and overt signs of co-optation, of a movement diverging from its own purposes and incorporating other goals, have been pointed out throughout this book. Although co-optation may be a moot question as programs are slashed, its historical significance to the battered women's movement is not. Activists report that they have learned, sometimes bitterly and always belatedly, the price of their choices. These lessons suggest that services need to embed themselves in a political vision and practice aimed at stopping violence and politicizing women. This analysis of co-optation does not imply that the battered women's movement is defeated nor that it should reject government funding. And it is not meant to minimize the reality that most shelters and movement organizations engage in a constant struggle with the state for autonomy and control. Rather it is geared toward helping a movement critically consider its past and current alternatives.

According to many women, the goal of sustaining a vision of women's liberation and building a political movement was lost in the struggle to start, fund, manage, legitimate, and maintain programs for battered women. Although services in and of themselves announce a radical and life-saving change in the power relations between the sexes, many activists point to the potential danger when services allow themselves to be shaped by funding agencies. Programs with access to government and foundation funding quickly began specializing and acquiring expertise in areas defined as important by those who were providing funding. As programs expanded and became costly to maintain, it was difficult to critically consider how and why funding was being used.

To help battered women and to survive, shelters had to be credible, respected service organizations, embedded in the community's life, especially in small towns.

> "The Red Cross was just wonderful, they were here by 9 PM after the fire broke out....We are very fortunate, this is a community where all social service agencies work extremely cooperatively together, particularly the police. They have helped us a great deal, even providing guards on our building until we can move back in... We are currently camping out in a large gymnasium, sleeping on Red Cross cots and eating food donated by the community....This is especially difficult because our first shelter was destroyed by Hurricane Frederick last September 12th. During *that* crisis the AHEPHA, an all male, civic Greek organization loaned us their meeting house, and the shelter stayed open...."[3]

Although this drama is atypical, it evokes nods of sympathy from shelters that have faced lice epidemics, men with weapons, or the more mundane problem of no funds with which to purchase food. Community support in the form of money or donated labor has been critical for shelter success. Some activists fear that if shelters place too much emphasis on politics and openly assert that their goals are to increase the collective power of women and change institutions, this support might not be forthcoming. So, while services allowed feminists to mobilize for themselves and other battered women, they also made activists juggle increasingly complicated and sometimes contradictory demands and constituencies.

Women's staggering needs and brutal realities determined the movement's first choice to provide safety and support. This decision is reinforced daily by the dilemmas every shelter faces, both of meeting the immediate needs of shelter residents and of offering assistance to the countless women who must be turned away because there is no shelter space available. The hotline coordinator of Philadelphia's Women Against Abuse estimates that the shelter takes in 1 out of every 20 callers,[4] while in New York City 85 out of every 100 women are denied services because of space shortages. Even though most shelters assist battered women to think of alternatives, the statistics are a devastating indictment; thousands and perhaps hundreds of thousands of battered women still find no help. Shelter workers never forget this reality. Articulating what every shelter worker feels, a former battered woman, actively involved in her local shelter, explains the tasks that need to be done.

> I would like to be instrumental in establishing more shelters, with all of the components needed to be beneficial to a woman and her children. So that any woman who wants to get out of a battering relationship can find a safe place....
>
> I'd like to learn more about the training and follow-up in our police department in regards to cases of Domestic Violence. I'd like to know the how's and why's of our judicial system skirting criminal charges against batterers. And then how I can help prevent this....
>
> I'd like to see hospitals realize the complexity of· what they are dealing with when a woman comes in who has obviously been beaten. If they can give her some sort of immediate counseling and or referrals, they may not have to treat her again for the same causes or worse yet pronounce her or her mate dead on arrival....
>
> I'd like to see counseling agencies trained to help the children better understand. Neither of the two counselors that I took my daughter to could relate to how she must feel....
>
> I'd like to see churches, schools and community organizations encourage programs or activities for single parent families. We should not and our children should not be programmed to feel ashamed because they have only one parent doing the job designed for two.[5]

With so much to be done and so few government and private resources allocated to help, shelter staff and volunteers almost always find themselves overworked and drained. It is often impossible to provide energy for the movement. Keeping the doors open is the central task.

In addition, because few programs have yet developed a personally comfortable and politically clear idea about how to "provide" services, shelters can sometimes undermine the strength of the movement by the way in which they offer help. It is easy to adopt the dominant mental health models and attempt to be the perfect helper, giving residents more and more and taking control away. "Doing good" can be a dangerous motivation that robs battered women of their right to make choices, just as it denies them participation in a movement.

Because traditional institutions treat battered women badly, activists in the movement, protective of battered women, face difficult decisions about whether to attempt to provide more services or to demand that other institutions take on these tasks. As one woman notes:

> When we take on the role of service provider, we allow the system to put responsibility on us. That is the tension between demanding they do it versus our doing it because we don't trust them to do it. We're trying to be job counselors, housing advocates; it's not our responsibility, but if we don't do it, who will. You either demand it, take it on yourself or say there is nothing we can do which is not an acceptable option.[6]

Funding guidelines propelled programs in specific directions, often those based on individualized and professional counseling and advocacy.

> While we all know to fight the obvious...what about the fact that due to government funding, an intake in a shelter may now involve the staff person asking a bunch of questions which are none of her business in order to fill out the forms required. This is cooptive in several ways: it changes the interaction to a less personal, more formalized one, very reminiscent of a woman's experience in any other social service agency she's been to; it gathers irrelevant information which then gets used by who knows whom for what purpose; it takes time away from our real work.[7]

Complaining about how funding transformed her relationship to battered women, another activist offered these insights.

> It's easy to slide into a "client-provider" attitude. What the money does is institutionalize the relationship. It divides people's time differently. It changes how you view people.[8]

Funding can directly affect who gets to stay in a shelter for how long. For example, Title XX reimburses shelters for no more than thirty-day resident stays. Many shelters that began without government funding have refused to follow these guidelines, preferring to lose reimbursements for some women rather than prematurely push them out. Other programs, however, enforce these stipulations, inadvertently acknowledging the primacy of reimbursement rather than of the relationship with battered women.

Affecting staff as well as residents, funding stipulations transform organizational structures even in those programs with the best feminist intentions.

> My board insists on calling me executive director. The outside puts
> that on you. Everyone here does a lot of work. Salaries should be equal.
> We were a collective, but funding sources demanded change. What
> they call you on paper, you end up incorporating.[9]

Framing the issue in terms acceptable to the funder takes its
hold. Within social welfare systems in the United States it is almost
impossible to escape turning political issues into mental health
problems. The tendency to blame the victim, search for the cause of
the problem within individuals, and offer a pat psychological
explanation for a social problem is common. Given these cultural and
funding influences, it is all too easy for shelters to lose sight of a
broader analysis.

Funding possibilities and desperate need send women scurrying
in a thousand directions to keep their doors open.

> They won't give it [the money] for battered women, but will for women
> whose husbands are alcoholic, for instance, or will give money for child
> abuse programs... The funding circuit is such that they're always
> changing what they want to fund, leaving us to choose to go without
> money or take this or that particular direction in order to get continued
> funding. If groups aren't careful, they can end up having absolutely no
> direction at all except that which is dictated by funding priorities.[10]

Given these parameters, it is logical to adopt a mentality of applying
for more and more grants to provide services. Subtly and imperceptibly, solving individual battered women's problems becomes the
overruling concern. Staff must constantly raise money in order to
maintain current levels of service, while their attack on the causes of
violence against women is pushed onto the back burner.

Internally, it is easy for the movement and individual shelters to
develop a standard that the best programs are well staffed and well
funded. Although money is critical and battered women are entitled
to excellent services, the definition of excellence has yet to be
delineated. The politics—the process of creating caring environments that struggle against domination—rather than the external
trappings are the most critical measure. Yet even in many politically
clear programs, the mission of ending violence against women or
organizing women seems too abstract, and the day to day service and
funding crises take priority.

None of these dilemmas suggest easy remedies, especially
because most programs in the battered women's movement are still
inadequately funded. The government channels small grants to

services which are expensive to maintain. Foundations, usually offering one or two years of funding for demonstration projects, are just as problematic and stingy.

> Part I of a three-part study recently published by Women and Foundations/Corporate Philanthropy, Inc... reveals that some of the largest local community foundations in the nation spend only an average of 5.2 percent of their discretionary funds on projects serving women and girls.[11]

No one knows how little foundation support was given to feminists. Even those programs with adequate service staff, a minority, scramble for money to maintain and renovate buildings or hire community educators or organizers, low priorities for foundations and the government alike. Money is a never ending worry, and the search for it drains hours of staff time in writing proposals, lobbying, or meeting with funders. This task was made even more difficult as traditional social service organizations competed for scarce money and offered alternatives to a feminist perspective.

Once funded, organizations face other problems. The staff of the Pennsylvania Coalition Against Domestic Violence estimates that 30%-40% of its time is spent administering grants. And funded programs often face subtle and pernicious pressures to become better agencies of social control. Commenting about her State Welfare Department, one activist writes, "If they had their way, they would hold shelters responsible for the actions and behaviors of every battered woman referred by the shelter."[12] Such pressure weaves its way into the daily concerns of shelter staff, adding to the responsibility already felt by new programs, unsure of themselves or their methods. Producing "model," successful clients, although antithetical to principles of self-determination, is the expectation from the outside. Added to this impossible, undesirable task is the assumption that the shelter will serve everyone. As soon as one small program exists, supposedly battered women's problems are solvable.

When too much emphasis is placed on starting and funding services for victims, then helping individuals and adjusting the "errors" in the criminal justice system can be posed as the only solutions reasonable people might entertain. The government's view that a social movement is irrelevant gains legitimacy as tasks are redefined and conflict disappears. A few funded programs are used to suggest that everyone, even racist and sexist judges or police officers, cares deeply about helping women victims. However, as most battered women's programs note, few major changes are enforced that give control back to battered women unless a move-ment is breathing down an institutions's neck.

When programs gain funding, it is more problematic to express anger at men, sexist institutions, or skimpy government grants. It is difficult to demonstrate against one's funding source on Monday and attend a budget hearing on Friday. If an organizations's reputation is too "radical," battered women or local agencies may stop using it. In the process of toning down the social critique, resistance to bureau-cratic incursions into feminist program guidelines or practices is often simultaneously lessened.

One shelter worker, formerly employed by a small, community based women's center, compares her two jobs.

> Now I have to be more careful about what I say in outreach educationals. I can't be as angry at men as I want to be—I could hurt their funding. I have to speak more to white, middle-class, professional audiences and as a Puerto Rican woman, I feel uncomfortable. I hate their arrogance and their belief that this just happens to Puerto Rican women. I used to knock on doors in my community to reach women, and now I can't do this.[13]

These powerful external pressures work their way into the movement, becoming internal ones. In the most blatant instances, more traditional groups take over funding and call themselves the battered women's movement. Generally, however, the movement starts to accept the definitions or parameters denoted by funding contracts. It is an easy step to lose the perspective that movement and funding agency interests are not the same. While a shelter's stated goals do not change, their daily practice and program directions may. For example, because commitments to empowering women or fighting racism will not receive funding, these goals may quietly disappear. In another case, a shelter may have as a priority building the movement through outreach to battered women. However, money becomes available to train professionals within institutions and the shelter applies for it; organizing battered women is deferred, sometimes permanently. In this way, services are saved, but movements and organizations are not built. It is not surprising that some programs find themselves with paid staff but without large groups of community women committed to the shelter's survival.

The fact that women become paid workers and experts at the same time that they are asked to maintain a political commitment complicates their choices drastically.

When we get paid for the work, we don't want to take a stand against a funding agency which might cost us our money,...When our livelihood becomes completely tied with providing direct services to battered women, it's easy to see why we want to provide and provide and provide services, rather than supporting battered women in doing things for themselves, or encouraging organizing activity rather than services. I also think that there is an inherent tension between the right of women working full time in the movement to a decent living...and the fact that we are about making social change and can't expect that the government or very many private foundations are interested in funding fundamental social changes in women's status in society.[14]

In countries where women are unpaid or poorly paid for shelter work, the tension between careers and movement activity is almost non-existent, and the dichotomy between service and political involvement is not so sharply felt. Once women have a chance to earn a living at this work, complications increase exponentially. A movement needs to sustain its participants and institutions, but often lacks the resources and money to provide that sustenance except through funding channels that mandate service provision and subtly change the focus and direction of the movement. If no alternative movement norms and structures legitimate other skills, like organizing, dangerous precedents are set.

As feminists are caught up in the service spiral, it is easy to forget that solving women's problems extends far beyond our abilities and resources. The vision is lost that reminds staff that the society, not the shelter, must provide what women most need. As the vision disappears, it is easier to isolate the program, internalize anger, and forget about the larger political dynamics at work. The next step is to blame the shelter or the individual battered woman when she returns to her husband. When shelter "success" is judged by the number of women who do not return to their husbands, the shelter has internalized responsibility and forgotten all that battered women face. Unhappy, "burned out" staff end up quitting their jobs, further depriving the movement of the experience that might break this pattern.

It is also common to lose sight of the thousands of women who never go to shelters, who are unaware of the movement's existence or who, because of racism or poverty, refuse to leave their communities in search of help. Although providing shelter services and protecting shelter funding are necessary and vital activities, they have consumed equally important energy needed to make long-range plans for the growth and direction of a movement against sexist violence. Without these plans, little time or effort goes into political analysis or the training of political leadership and organizers. Institutionalizing movement activity within shelters—including maintaining a vision of why the shelter started—disappears in the daily work necessary to ensure battered women a small respite.

In interviews, activists continually reiterated, "we never assessed what the funding would cost us." Funding sharply limits options and subtly determines future directions. When the majority of staff time is devoted to services and fundraising, new staff are hired to meet these current priorities, and activists are replaced by fund raisers and administrators. The important tension between service and organizing often disappears.

Although co-optation is a serious problem for the movement, it is important to remember that it is not "caused" by activists. Many feminists have been politically clever and clear in their organizing efforts, but their resources are limited; too many tasks need to be accomplished, and the forces women fight are stronger than the movement. The movement cannot, for example, fully resolve the dilemma that as it successfully raises issues, it increases the likelihood that others will gain control of new services by offering competing explanations for violence and non-feminist models of help. Nor can the movement totally resolve the fact that, because of a lack of resources, service organizations are put in a position where they must deny help to thousands of women who need it. Understanding the obstacles and contradictions that activists and organizations face, however, only reinforces a sense that the battered women's movement *must* find a way to successfully integrate services and politics.

Services and Their Role in a Political Movement

Some argue that services should not be asked to carry forward a political vision and the weight of a movement. They suggest that while a political vision is important, it could be put forth by other activists and organizations that are not directly involved in providing service. While it is true that feminists who are not working in shelters can provide important energy to a movement to end violence against women, it is essential that services and politics not be separated from each other. Small feminist and grassroots shelters offer not only safety and caring, but also the courage needed by women to rebuild their lives. They actively demonstrate a model of cooperation, a possibility people in this society, especially those of different races and classes, rarely experience together. As institutions, they convey a radically different explanation to battered women and to the society of why women are beaten and what social conditions must be changed to end violence. To minimize this aspect of shelter experience and focus only on providing services is to miss a unique opportunity to build a broad-based feminist movement. Shelters' inseparable role as service organizations and political organizations must be fought for; without these institutions, women's safety networks and agitational bases are lost.

Emphasizing the importance of a movement, one writer notes that when women went to agencies that "served" battered women before the current movement began, they rarely were able to get the help they needed. "Only as women began to speak with one another could their collective voice penetrate the public mythology of domestic violence. It is this collectivity which must be maintained and strengthened, and the shelter movement is the vehicle for this." This writer goes on to say that "the shelter movement represents not simply an escape, but an escape into a community. It offers the possibility of a future."[15]

But without a larger political vision, even the shelter movement is of limited value.

> Unless we can maintain a community-based shelter movement, and one which avoids the pitfalls of institutionalization, we are doomed to setting up universal prisons. We are doomed to replicate treatment programs where a few women are successful and get jobs, a few women join the staff and become professional, semiprofessionals, but the vast majority of women leave the shelter and find their lives very much unchanged.[16]

Unlike social service agencies, a feminist battered women's movement will expose the sexist ideology that justifies abuse by making it look natural and "personal." Only this continued exposure will insure the development of a theoretical model that reveals abuse as a logical extension of unequal power between men and women and of women's general social subordination. Without a movement, individual battered women will be helped, but no challenge is presented to the very ideological framework that men and women incorporate to justify male violence. If shelters operate out of a service mentality only, women will be unable to turn their "individual" fault into a social problem and will be denied outlets through which to express their justified rage. Battered women will see themselves as different, weaker than other women. Staff will separate themselves from residents, while the assumption that violence results from women's social and economic subordination quietly disappears as a fundamental premise of the shelter.

Because shelters use battered women's status as victims to acquire legitimacy and resources, a complicated political problem is created for the battered women's movement. For movement activists, the focus on victimization helps to blur the insight that the struggle for battered women's rights is linked to the more general fight for women's liberation. When activists view battering as victimization, rather than as an aspect of oppression, they have a tendency to see individual problems rather than collective ones. They sever their identification with battered women and forget that they, too, could be targets of male violence. Subtly they disconnect battering from the larger struggle to free women from oppression. As a result, organizing strategies around questions of housing, income and child care are more difficult to delineate and the movement is left somewhat isolated from other political struggles.

Victim is also a label that many shelter residents reject. They do not like viewing themselves solely as battered women. They feel that these words fail to capture their complexity and strength. When women are viewed primarily as victims of male violence, it is more difficult for the movement to hold out the inspiration that attracts women to join in a political struggle. The notion of a sustaining and empowering community of women is lost. And women are left with no collective explanation of why they are abused and how they might organize together to fight back.

Some argue against politicizing within a shelter, noting that such a process is open to abuse. This, however, is also true of any form of psychotherapy. If caring and allowing residents' input remain the framework, abuses can be minimized. As one woman, working in a radical feminist shelter, noted "What is important is caring about each individual woman involved. If it isn't happening, it isn't a good shelter. Caring is what makes people committed to the shelter."[17] Caring, combined with political insight, helps women understand their own feelings and gives them tools to understand their experiences. Battered women are entitled to an explanation for why they were beaten and why they were denied institutional help. This does not mean giving political lectures to residents but rather suggests the need for consciousness raising and group sharing formats. If women leave shelters never exploring these topics, it is highly likely that they will continue to blame themselves for the violence and the "failure" of their relationships.

Only a political vision and participation in a movement help service workers place battered women's lives in a perspective free of victim blaming. Many battered women are plagued constantly by far more than violence, a reason why 30%-50% of them return to their husbands once they leave. One survey of 110 cases summarizes it well.

> Those who returned to their homes had been married the longest. They also had considerably less work experience and were mostly unskilled compared with the "independent" group, which did not return home. The latter group was comprised of women who had professional or skilled work backgrounds.[18]

After her shelter stay, a woman faces her greatest isolation. She may be intensely worried about money, housing, raising children alone, relationships with men, sexuality, and feeling simultaneously loving and hateful towards her husband. Yet battered women's programs generally have no money or staff available to help women after they leave shelters. Only by reiterating publicly that shelters cannot solve these problems does responsibility fall to the community to tackle them and create community based supports for women.

Without a reference point to a movement organizing to change conditions for all women, even self-help, a liberating model for assisting women, can move in dangerously apolitical directions. If empowerment means gaining control over the decisions affecting one's life and finding access to the resources needed to live decently, then self-help within shelters tries valiantly to offer such possibilities to women. Self-help creates the environment in which women demonstrate that society can be changed and that women no longer have to endure abuse, inequality, and powerlessness. Through self-help, grassroots women are able to maintain control of services and lessen the tendency, common in social service agencies, to create hierarchies and professional distance. Yet shelters exist within a society that denies resources to women and undercuts their individual and collective power. Without material resources—housing, jobs, and sufficient incomes—empowerment as a universal goal is unreachable. If women are not aware of this, there is a danger that self-help can turn into self-blame, as women fault themselves for being unable to control their lives.

Self-help is an egalitarian methodology rather than a solution to the conditions that cause violence. Partly because feminist self-help models demand so much time and energy from those involved, women sometimes forget the social critique implied by self-help. At the same time that women maintain self-help, they must also fight

for a society in which their needs are met. If self-help loses its radical
critique and its demands for social change, then there is no direction
for a movement's anger and energy.

Despite the severe pressures exerted upon them, feminist
shelters carry the movement's strength. In many states, feminists
are energized and a vision is sustained through coalitions. This,
however, does not minimize the political significance of shelters; if
coalitions are democratic, they reflect their membership—shelters.
If shelters move in conservative directions, so eventually will
coalitions. Preserving feminist shelters, specifically their commitment to participation and democracy and their analysis of violence,
is a movement necessity.

Only shelters keep activists aware of battered women's current
concerns. Battered women's experiences within their families,
institutions, and the larger society enrage women and motivate
political change. Activists' visions of change come out of the lives of
women; if the maintenance of services becomes so all-consuming
that battered women's participation and involvement are forgotten
issues, then the movement will cease to grow and shelters will lose
their vitality.

> How do we not set up the we-they dichotomy; the caretaker-receiver
> roles. These process questions, if not resolved, will destroy the *spirit* of
> the movement. The movement may survive, but there will be no new
> energy for the struggle.[19]

Dialogue between women who identify primarily as service
workers and those who view themselves as movement organizers is
urgently needed. Many women work within battered women's
services because they sincerely want to help. Their priority is
providing good services, and politics are sometimes foreign and
suspect. Organizers also want to provide services, but they have
other priorities as well, such as organizing battered women or
building alliances with other movements. They are committed to
making demands upon the society—for example, for universal
access to shelter for any woman who needs it—and work for change
on many levels. The role of the service provider and that of the
organizer must both be respected. Incorrectly and unfairly, organizers have sometimes been accused of harming the movement and
detracting from its ability to help battered women.

In a society that fails to adequately provide for the well-being of
its citizens, there are no easy answers to the dilemma of how much
energy to devote to services and how much to building a movement.
Some shelter workers have fantasized giving up particular services

in order to spend their time helping battered women organize themselves. Others imagine leaving services in order to begin direct action or lobbying groups. They have begun to painfully face what it might mean to rearrange priorities. Acknowledging the tension between allocation of resources for services and those for building a movement is difficult, but helps programs reassess their political direction and become aware of the implications of certain choices.

Those individual shelters that have juggled service and political tasks successfully seem to have committed themselves to basing their decisions upon ideological and political clarity. Their self definition simultaneously incorporates being women's political organizations, community organizations, advocacy projects, and caring services.

Within a movement, there is room for diversity, and individuals and groups will resolve the tension between services and politics in distinct ways. It is essential for women with a political vision to continue working within shelters, providing services that are not divorced from an analysis of why women are battered, and helping shelters preserve their feminist or grassroots base. But there is also an important place in the movement for those who choose to leave service work and focus exclusively on political agitation. The movement has monumental tasks ahead. It must maintain alternative institutions that provide needed services; it must also work on the larger struggle to change the conditions that perpetuate violence against women. These awesome goals can only be accomplished by large numbers of women working in varied ways.

When they view themselves as carriers of a vision, service organizations and coalitions are pushed to live their ideals. The sense of belonging to a movement affirms that democratic participation and struggle, as well as personal, organizational, and political growth, are of primary importance. These commitments literally create the energy that keeps women involved, connected to each other, and willing to work hard. Belonging to a movement implies responsibility to each other and to all women which allows frightening issues like racism, homophobia, and competition to eventually be placed on the table for discussion.

CHAPTER 11

An Agenda for the Battered Women's Movement: Internal Issues

I want to remind us that we have won what we now have because we, or others before us, struggled for it. It was not given to us. We had to be responded to because we publicly declared that women could not continue to be beaten. If we lose the political meaning of what we have worked for, the spirit of our work places, and our view of women's oppression, then although we still have won victories and still have protected women, we will have also lost something essential—our part in a struggle for human liberation.[1]

Keeping the larger perspective in mind helps us to confront the difficult issues that are currently simmering within the battered women's movement and in other parts of the women's liberation movement as well. This chapter focuses on four of these issues: the role of men within the battered women's movement; heterosexism and homophobia; race and racism; and the role of battered women within the movement.

Many women are reluctant to deal with differences and are scared by the fantasy—and sometimes the reality—of angry confrontations or accusations. One unfortunate legacy of the women's movement has been ugly "trashing" over sexual and political differences. Some question whether differences should be made explicit in a time of external attack and a growing reactionary movement which demands a strong unified political response. The current atmosphere of cutbacks, anti-feminist backlash, and encroachment into a movement by professional and traditional organizations has understandably led many to focus above all on the need for unity. Although the movement does need to be ideologically clear and politically firm as it deals with the "outside," internally, women must gently and respectfully learn to confront differences and air conflicts. The truth is that unity is frequently gained at the expense of less culturally dominant groups and is therefore false. Rather than suppressing conflicts, women need tools for handling them. If we bury differences for the sake of accomplishing tasks, the movement as a whole moves in a conservative direction.

Far from being monolithic or homogeneous, the battered women's movement incorporates differences among women in ideology, class, race, ethnicity, education, skill and knowledge level, and sexual preference. The fight against battering, like those waged against other forms of male domination, bonds together diverse groups of women. At the same time however, race, class, and sexual orientation differences create unique historical and cultural experiences among us. Just as women can be dominated as a group, some groups of women can exploit others. The battered women's movement cannot escape the reality that gender is not the only oppression many women face. In their eagerness to combat myths and build a movement, many asserted accurately that battering crosses race and class lines; in the process, however, differences among women were glossed over. Because the potential strength of the battered women's movement lies partly in its diversity, it is now at a point where in order to realize this potential, it must acknowledge differences and struggle with them internally.

Men in the Movement

Three emotional, overlapping debates about the role of men in the movement divide women politically: 1. Should men be working within battered women's services?; 2. Who should provide help to men who batter?; 3. Are men to be held accountable for male violence against women?

The earliest question posed in the movement was whether or not men should work in shelters. Those who answer "no" argue that because male domination leads to woman abuse, women need environments in which dependence on men is challenged, not recreated. Feminists fear that because of female socialization and experiences with violence, battered women will defer to male staff, undermining their efforts to achieve autonomy and independence. Because many women are taught to see other women as competitors, a shelter environment should demonstrate that women can support one another and take care of themselves; as residents witness women assuming control over their lives, they learn one crucial aspect of "empowerment." Finally, an all-female environment permits women to talk openly, free of male judgments, intimidation, and retaliation.

Many shelters agree with these arguments, but do not believe they imply that no men can work in shelters. They retain female leadership, but may hire male staff as child care specialists or maintenance men. In a few cases, vehemently disapproved of by feminists, men are employed as women's counselors or shelter directors.

The common arguments for including men emphasize the importance of presenting non-violent role models to children and suggest that men and women must work together to end violence against women. Many third world women develop an additional argument for mandatory inclusion of men on staff and boards: male-female alliances are a necessity for the survival of their communities.

The differences over this issue reflect some fundamental, unresolved differences within the larger feminist movement. Feminists disagree as to whether and to what extent women should organize separately from men and maintain autonomous organizations. For shelters, there is no one correct position here. Based on women's historical and contemporary experience, it is not only valid but often essential for women to form their own organizations which exclude men. Yet it is also legitimate and useful for some feminist organizations to include men and for women's organizations to work cooperatively with community organizations that include men. In the battered women's movement, most shelters that include males use them in limited staff roles or as a minority of board members; women retain primary leadership and control. Labeling all women who exclude men from organizations as anti-male separatists or claiming that all who include men are not true feminists can make divisions appear greater than they are. If neither position is flatly labeled as unacceptable, women will have an important chance to share and struggle with one another while avoiding total divisiveness.

Within shelters, a proper beginning might be to discuss why women want men included or excluded. In this sorting out, the patronizing notion, raised most often by professionals, that battered women can find "corrective" emotional experience through working with male counselors needs to be challenged. It is dangerous to suggest that battered women are inadequate in the way they relate to men or to assume that six weeks of work with a "gentle" male can undo the effects of years of violence.

When women discuss the role of men in the movement, they frequently turn to the question: should the shelter movement help violent men? In community speaking engagements, shelter workers are continuously asked, "so what are you doing to change men? These men will be back on the streets beating the next woman if you don't help them." These challenges, though logical on one level, frustrate and anger many women. The movement's too-limited resources are being used to keep shelter doors open—barely. Women have taken major responsibility, often in the face of hostile opposition, for helping battered women. Now an unsavory burden is suggested that would resubmerge women in the very sexist tradition which they are challenging; women, not men, are being asked to nurture the male perpetrators of violence.

Although most women agree that men need help, their legitimate fear is that limited dollars will be taken from shelters and allocated to assist violent men. Anger has erupted when programs for men received funding without enduring the severe credibility tests women's organizations have faced for years. Fury has increased as professional counseling agencies, new to the issue, tout programs for batterers even though no studies have proven the long-term effectiveness of counseling. Moreover, women remain politically skeptical, concerned that counseling individual men will be viewed as a panacea and serve to discredit a feminist analysis that declares violence a result of male domination, not pathology. Infuriated, some feminists find it impossible to support programs for men.

Sharp disagreements abound in the battered women's movement about the role and efficacy of treatment. One strand of thought argues that battering is a disorder of power that can be therapeutically treated. Men who batter must be helped to stop, or more women will be hurt. Another side argues that although counseling is important, too much energy goes to helping one individual after another and the movement suffers. A final position asserts that any assistance to men who batter is an inappropriate activity for feminists. All sides have had to face the fact that increasing numbers of professional agencies are offering services to men.

One exciting synthesis has developed in male counseling and education collectives that work cooperatively with shelters, rely on women's advice in program planning, and dedicate themselves to the elimination of violence against women. Emerge, the first such program, was founded in Boston in 1977 at the request of women working in area shelters. Emerge describes the problem that mandates its existence.

> ...many of the men who abuse, brought up with a belief in male dominance and inclined to violent activities as a means of proving their own masculinity, do not necessarily see anything wrong with their actions. Rather, such violence is sanctioned among men.[2]

After years of discussion between activists in the battered women's movement and men in the Emerge collective, feminist guidelines for funding programs for batterers were developed jointly. They were presented in November 1980 at a foundation and corporate briefing on "Domestic Violence Prevention: Treatment for Batterers" that was sponsored by the Ms. Foundation for Women.

> 1. No program for men who batter should be funded without the existence of shelters or safe home projects for battered women in the immediate community....(The availability of refuge for battered women when the abuser is in treatment is critical for reasons of safety of the women and children and of the efficacy of treatment for the abuser.)
> 2. Treatment programs for men who abuse must work cooperatively with shelters or safe home projects in their area. Programs for abusers must share the same philosophical understandings of the reasons for violence against women and must work in concert with the shelter movement to end violence against women.
> 3. Where the amount of funding in a community, foundation, or corporation is limited and insufficient to sustain both the shelter and abusers program, the financial resources should be directed to shelter programs until they achieve financial stability.[3]

Feminism, the "men's movement," radical therapy, and previous political experiences were formative influences within Emerge. Paralleling the women's liberation movement, Emerge created an organizational structure that reflects its political analysis.

> At Emerge, our work revolves around issues of power and control. Our clients have learned narrow and destructive concepts of power based on domination of others, particularly women....We cannot offer ourselves as role models, as men who operate from a concept of power based on cooperation and mutuality, if our organizational structure is one which is based in hierarchy and an oligarchic application of power; for these are the very practices which maintain and encourge dominance. We therefore place particular emphasis on cooperative norms, collectivity, and consensus decision making.[4]

Like Emerge, the all-male RAVEN (Rape and Violence End Now) collective in St. Louis, grew by using the support, political theory, and skills of local feminists. In both collectives, male violence, not the male-female relationship, is the counseling focus. RAVEN writes that, "there are no distinctive characteristics which would set the rapist or the woman abuser apart from other men."[5] Yet because male domination is expressed in psychological and interpersonal ways, male collectives have decided that it is their task to offer a counseling model that challenges the male right to beat.

Group counseling is the preferred method in these anti-sexist male collectives and is used to challenge sexist, explosive behaviors and allow men to test honest, non-bullying ones. Abusive men are seen as willful, responsible, and accountable for their behavior; batterers are forced to view women as human just as they are required to find new methods to express feelings and their need to dominate. Emerge's counseling methods have received national attention, and men who have completed the program credit it for major changes in their lives, including the cessation of violence.[6] Some of these men are being trained to lead groups.

The political significance of anti-sexist male collectives extends beyond their group counseling services or their professional training efforts. They challenge the idea that it is women's responsibility, either individually or collectively, to stop men from battering. They place responsibility for stopping violence upon individual men, yet they also look beyond the assignment of personal blame. By linking the psychological to the political, these groups reiterate publicly that without cultural change, men will continue to find their violence socially sanctioned. In counseling and community education presentations, male activists draw attention to how men are socialized to use power and treat women abusively. They challenge centuries-old norms that encourage, tolerate, and justify violence against women. At best, anti-sexist male collectives hold out new norms for male-female relationships based on equality. Their most promising efforts replicate those of feminists who are developing a political analysis of violence against women which is translated into plans for institutional, community, and individual change.

Suggesting that men must organize to stop violence because they perpetrate it has supported the shelter movement and placed it in a less defensive position. No longer are "hostile" women the only ones labeling violence as male domination and challenging it. Just as the anti-sexist male presence alleviates the movement's burden, it also helps individual battered women who find momentary relief from consuming guilt when they hear men are to blame for violence.

Yet only a few programs for batterers articulate a consistent anti-sexist ideology and use it as a basis for psychotherapy and community education. Although seventy counseling programs exist,[7] many base their practice on more traditional therapeutic and political assumptions. For example, the Victim Information Bureau of Suffolk County states that "when a client does not choose to pursue a separation or divorce, the treatment of choice is couple therapy. We believe that battering will not stop unless both partners are involved in counseling."[8] Most feminist counseling programs challenge these assertions, using their work with male clients as evidence. Men and women activists voice strong concern about the kinds of programs that are developing, and the Emerge collective details their critique.

> Common treatment choices among those working with abusive men are family therapy and couples or marital counseling....
> While certainly men who batter are troubled by a variety of problems in their relationships with women and while individual and family or couples counseling is rarely contra-indicated at some stage in the treatment of the problem, until the violence itself is regarded as the primary focus of treatment, and treated as such, family treatment will remain ineffectual at the very least and will often be extremely dangerous for the woman....
> More subtly, a focus on the family system or the marital relationship in treatment gives at least the implicit message that the abuse is an interactional problem. It allows the man to believe that it is not really his problem.[9]

The debate about treatment for batterers is obviously a political as well as a methodological one. Usually, its boundaries are narrowly confined to methodological concerns and the wide ranging political challenge to male domination central to Emerge's and RAVEN's argument is lost. In their worst moments, psychological discussions about batterers solely deplore the ways in which society victimizes men. The truth in this abstract assertion has little to do with why men beat women. It obscures the reality that power and privilege rather than victimization allow men to be violent, negates the fact that men benefit through violence, and muddles attempts at analytic and political clarity.

Most feminists assert that, ideally, men should provide separate counseling services for men and resources should not be diverted from shelters to counseling. If men are counseled by shelters, battered women feel undue pressure to reunite with their partners. Some shelters, however, do offer separate programs for men. A few of these began as feminist attempts to control the type of treatment developed. A debate rages in the movement over whether such services should exist. Those who argue against these services insist that the shelter's primary goal is to help women become independent and that batterers' programs subvert this mission by subtly reinforcing the hope for family reunification.

Many feminists argue cogently that, rather than offer help to men, the movement should force mainstream institutions to provide better services. For example, if courts mandate counseling for abusers, traditional mental health agencies should be taught how to work with this population. Feminist activists believe that there are now enough model programs like Emerge that can teach mental health professionals about working with abusers. The movement's role is to facilitate these learning exchanges or advocate for them. Feminists who see themselves as organizers and activists do not believe that it is the responsibility of the women's movement to divert its resources, in an ongoing way, to men. Nor do they want to see agencies proliferate whose only task is to help violent men.

As a "spouse abuse" and "family pathology" model for explaining violence creeps its way back into public consciousness, it is likely that the battered women's movement will be under greater pressure to start or support programs for men. Traditional social service agencies will initiate more treatment programs and the movement will have to stay organized and vigilant to ensure that psychological explanations for male violence, devoid of an analysis of power, do not replace political ones.

A final debate over men in the movement centers on the issue of how accountable individual men are for violence against women. Some assert that individual men and men as a group are solely responsible. The issue becomes more complex for those who accept the analysis presented here, that there are institutional, historical, and cultural forces that lead and even encourage men to be violent toward women. If these broad forces cause violence, how do we hold individuals accountable yet also go beyond individual assignments of blame?

Although privately, most women in the movement believe men must be accountable for their violence, the politics of this are complex, as are the ways to implement it. In 1977, the Battered Women Action Committee, an organizing group in Boston, offered one approach. After labeling the criminal justice system a dangerous reinforcer of a violent, racist status quo, it went on to say,

> We felt that, ultimately, each individual must grow up with the consciousness that any crime against an individual affects the entire society, and that peer pressure, if used to discourage violent crime... could act as a great deterrent to potential abusers....Accountability by the perpetrators of crime, to the victims in particular and society in general seems to be a vital component to the de-escalation of crime. Also, the quality of rehabilitation must include re-education and in-kind response and apology, as opposed to an emphasis on punishment per se.[10]

When the group formulated ideas to stop men who batter, creative sentencing and public ridicule tied for first place. Public ridicule meant exposing the abuser at his home or workplace, with the permission of the woman involved. Creative sentencing might place restrictions on his movement, appoint the victim, with her consent, as his probation officer, require him to pay a fine to her, confine him to a halfway house with anti-sexist counseling, and legally force him to provide her with financial support.[11]

The Battered Women Action Committee rightly tried to consider how to stop male violence, not only serve victims, yet they too offered problematic solutions; because of the lack of community and institutional sanctions against violence, their solutions also entail holding individuals responsible for abuse in endless and time-consuming ways, while the cause for the violence lies both within and beyond the individual. Without clear direction for its future, the battered women's movement must ask which analysis and methods will most effectively stop male violence and protect battered women and, at the same time, bolster progressive, anti-racist organizing efforts. In a society without democratic, community controlled institutions, solutions are hard to find.

Depending upon how women answer the question—what causes violence against women—a second disagreement erupts over whether anger at men should be muted or allowed full expression. In battered women's shelters and rape crisis centers, activists see daily the results of male brutality in the scarred bodies of women. Men, the perpetrators of abuse, are the target of intense anger that cannot be easily muted. Moreover, anger at men is a necessary part of any battered woman's attempts to psychically heal just as rage at sexist institutions moves shelter activists to politically organize.

On the other hand, for political and practical reasons, most shelters do not want to appear anti-male. Anti-male attitudes scare away potential shelter supporters as well as some battered women. As political activists, many feminists are neither anti-male nor separatists; they are simply and legitimately rageful at men who are violent.

The debate over the legitimacy of anger at men is endlessly complicated by other personal and political issues. Heterosexual women frequently avoid discussing their anger at men with other activists; they have rarely acknowledged that work with beaten women has effects upon their relationships with husbands and lovers. This silence is conspicuous in a movement in which "the personal is political." It suggests that such issues are deeply threatening.

Some heterosexual women blame lesbians for expressing too much anger at men. Frequently, lesbian motivations are grotesquely distorted by heterosexual women. One lesbian notes:

> Lesbianism is how I feel about women, not how I feel about men. Lesbians are considered man haters. Lesbian attitudes about men are, therefore, discounted.
>
> As lesbians we have not been allowed the space to inspect our own motivations and differences. There are enormous differences between separatists and Marxist lesbians but because of our oppression we've not been able to have these discussions.[12]

It is homophobic to assume that anti-male lesbian separatists represent all lesbian opinions about men; on the other hand, some lesbians and heterosexual feminists are vocally anti-male and base their politics solely on a theory in which "men are the enemy." This political choice, with which I disagree, must be distinguished from the legitimate expression of women's anger at men.

Because anger at men divides women within the movement, it is an important discussion topic. It has been avoided too long and labeled erroneously as the sole concern of white radical lesbians. Anger at men is an issue that touches all women within the movement, activists and battered women, heterosexuals and lesbians.

How one deals with anger at men also affects how activists respond to the idea that all men are potential rapists and abusers. Many feminists believe this statement is true to the extent that it implies that because of domination, all men have the potential to abuse women. Yet they also suggest that some men choose not to exercise this power. As the men in RAVEN comment:

> In the context of the permission given for woman abuse by (the) media, advertisement and other educational, judicial and religious institutions, it becomes possible to say that the decision not to abuse, not to rape, can only be an individual moral statement.[13]

If one focuses exclusively on the idea that all men are potential abusers, then all men do become the enemy. If, however, one also faces the facts, demonstrated by practice, that some choose to align with women in anti-sexist work and many men are non-violent, then anger at men may be somewhat muted.

The important issue is what strategy women choose as a result of these insights. Aligning with supportive men makes both political and theoretical sense. If all remain the "enemy," women negate the fact that political movements cause people and institutions to change. The separatist strategy leaves men and women permanently divided. Political solutions to stopping sexist violence become more problematic; withdrawal from men into utopian female communities, while a solution for a few women, fails to meet the needs of millions. A feminist movement must work with men, albeit carefully, even as it preserves its autonomous base from which to challenge sexism and build a women's movement.

Heterosexism and Homophobia

On the eve of the first membership meeting of the National Coalition Against Domestic Violence, one legislator, an active supporter of pending domestic violence legislation, refused to sponsor a congressional reception organized by the National Coalition. He complained that the conference brochure listed a workshop entitled Lesbian Issues in the Movement. Although activists managed to change his mind as a result of quick and plentiful "consciousness raising," his reaction was not unique, nor is it restricted to those "outside" of the movement.

An article by a former shelter worker describes the homophobic process through which she and others were discredited in a battle over the organization's political direction.

> It [was made] known through the informal social service network that the director and her allies had prevented a lesbian (translated 'man-hating') takeover. This was said despite the fact that among the five staff and forty volunteers who left the center perhaps not more than five were lesbian. With this one word—lesbian—no other explanation became necessary.[14]

The few stories of women who have lost their jobs or have been pushed out of leadership positions because they are lesbians worry and dishearten activists across the country. Homophobia has made its ugly way into shelters, forcing lesbians to leave the movement or, more frequently, to remain silent about their identities. Homophobia has divided and will continue to divide the movement unless heterosexual women confront it in themselves and their organizations.

Women often suggest that sexual preference is a personal choice that has no place in movement discussions. This position denies the significance of homophobia—the irrational fear of women emotionally and sexually loving each other—and heterosexism—defining heterosexuality as the only normal sexual expression within our society. Heterosexism and homophobia serve to bind women more tightly into sexual identification with and dependence on men.[15] As an attempt to deny all women the right to define themselves, homophobia attacks the right to self-determination that is the foundation of the battered women's and women's liberation movements.

Sexual identity is an obvious political issue within shelters, where residents face their own ambivalence about living in all-female environments. The homophobia of this culture, which teaches most people to fear and label as sick or evil same-sex love, leads both residents and staff to worry about identifying too closely with other women. To protect themselves, women make derogatory comments about lesbians, thus assuring themselves and others that they are not "deviant."

> A woman might, for the first time, be openly expressing her anger toward men and hearing the same from other women....In the shelter, she will see women taking power in their lives and will probably begin to feel close to some women. These experiences and feelings of fear and confusion might trigger the automatic homophobic responses that we all have been taught....
> Another example is of a battered woman hugging a staffer, then pulling away saying with nervous laughter, "People will think we're a couple of lesbians."[16]

At the beginning of the movement, some shelter staff quickly realized that they had responsibilities to explore their own reactions to lesbianism and respond appropriately to others' so that the shelter environment could remain supportive for all women.

As shelters expanded by adding staff and board members, an attack on lesbians often expressed an underlying power struggle over control of the shelter and the role of feminism within it. Although these attacks have occurred infrequently, their impact is widespread. Because strong, heterosexual feminists also have been lesbian-baited, it is clear that homophobic attacks are meant to discredit strong, *political* women. Hurling epithets undermines specific women, places them in a defensive, weak position, and cuts them off from community support. As activists note repeatedly, "lesbian baiting is a tool to disempower women individually and collectively." Where these attacks have been successful, more traditional staff, often non-feminists, have replaced lesbian and heterosexual women who have been driven from their jobs. On a national level, lesbians, public about their sexual preferences and radical feminist politics, have been attacked for "ruining the movement." Although unsuccessful as a political strategy, these attacks are a painful personal reminder of the brutality of homophobia.

Like all oppressions, homophobia can be internalized, and in one shelter a vicious, public homophobic attack on the lesbian director was initiated by a lesbian staff member. Yet even when used as an ugly weapon by lesbians, homophobia must be defined as a political problem maintained by heterosexism.

As they live in shelters, sorting through their experiences, battered women inevitably raise questions about what it means to be a woman. Heterosexual staff often join with them as they share their personal journeys, but lesbians, some of them former battered women, have been asked to hide their choices. Not only is this painful for lesbian staff, but it means that battered women who want to explore lesbianism as a positive, self-affirming choice are given no support. The heterosexism and homophobia of the larger society are once again reinforced, and it becomes clear that sexual preference remains more than just a "personal choice." Arguing the need for openness about the fact that lesbians work in shelters, the Massachusetts Coalition of Battered Women Service Groups declares:

> We need to be open to dealing with lesbianism as an option for the women who use our services. We must recognize it as a valid choice for women as they redefine their lives. Finally, for many years, lesbian women have been leaders in the women's movement and particularly in the battered women's movement. The fact that we cannot openly acknowledge and appreciate this commitment, is injurious, not only to lesbians and the energy they have to give, but to every woman who hopes to have the power to define her own life.[17]

Others within the movement disagree. Openly acknowledging that they are lesbians places individuals in vulnerable positions and some women advocate only selectively revealing their sexual and lifestyle preferences. Lesbians fear not only for their personal positions, but for that of the shelter in general. Frightened residents and angry communities still accuse shelters of "recruiting" battered

women and their children to lesbian lifestyles. Some women assert
that the battered women's movement will lose public support and
funding if it acknowledges the role of lesbians in the movement. A
portion of these women are opposed to lesbian and gay rights, while
others, both lesbians and heterosexuals, feel their support of or
identity as lesbians must remain private.

Increasingly, lesbians have organized to affirm their identities,
break their enforced silences, and share their anger and fear of
attack. During the last several years at conferences and workshops,
lesbians have supported one another over the dilemma of being "out"
in their programs and have discussed their support for a movement
that sometimes discriminates against them. Particularly for lesbians in rural areas and those who are the only lesbian on their
shelter staff, caucuses and state and regional networks of lesbians
and supportive heterosexual women are vital.

As a result of grassroots organizing and concern, the National
Coalition has begun to raise important questions about sexuality.
How can battered women's organizations facilitate discussions
about lesbian and gay rights and homophobia in safe, nonthreatening
ways? How can rural women's concerns be addressed so that they do
not feel their programs jeopardized? What responsibilities do heterosexual women have in these efforts? How can homophobic crises or
attacks be minimized? The National Coalition Against Domestic
Violence has responded to demands raised at its first membership
meeting by establishing a Lesbian Task Force. NCADV's internal
history is to be rewritten to acknowledge the leadership and
involvement of lesbians, and educational training packets on homophobia are to be drafted. Although such work has yet to materialize,
an active and vocal group continues to push forward concerns that
not only affect lesbians, but are profoundly important to all women.

Sensitizing heterosexual women to lesbian concerns, including
those of battered lesbians, and educating them about their role in
combatting homophobia, have been frequent conference efforts.
More sensitizing workshops and consciousness raising groups are
needed to explore sexuality, homophobia, and heterosexism. As one
activist points out, "We hide lesbians and pretend their issues are
not our movement's because of our fears of being identified as
lesbians." Naming these fears will make everyone stronger. Workshops allow women to find language to gently confront homophobic
comments, stereotypes, and panics within shelters and to label
homophobia, not homosexuality, the problem. As one woman declared, "The power is in the name calling and we have to know

ourselves to break this power."

Women who have dealt with community lesbian baiting attacks suggest asserting the importance, meaning, and quality of shelter work and either ignoring the attack or labeling it as an attempt to discredit women who are helping women. Others have suggested confronting people's worst fears and providing information and consciousness raising about homophobia.[18] In all these efforts, heterosexual women need to be public spokeswomen who declare that women's attempts to be equal to men and reorder power are the provocation for lesbian baiting. Who women choose as emotional and sexual partners cannot be open for public scrutiny. Lesbians should never be forced to quit their jobs; bending to please bigots undermines a program's dignity and ability to fight for all women.

If the battered women's movement, and heterosexual women within it in particular, recognize that lesbian energy galvanized a movement, saved women's lives, and provided creative, sustaining direction to programs and to a national struggle, some of the internal problems and right-wing attacks might dissipate. Women identified women—lesbian and heterosexual—started shelters, and current activists must insure that the movement neither denies its history nor the rights of women within it.

Race and Racism

Speaking of the racism within the battered women's movement, one white woman says:

> Our idea of including women of color was to send out notices. We never came to the business table as equals. Women of color join us on our terms....
>
> Knowing that we grew up in a society permeated with the belief that white values, culture, and lifestyle is superior, we can assume that regardless of our rejection of the concept, we still act out of that socialization. The same anger and frustrations that as women we have in dealing with men whose sexism is subtle, not blatant, is the frustration and anger women of color must feel toward us.[19]

As in the society at large, racism in the battered women's movement operates on many levels. In shelters, it is evident in the selection of food, books, records, and in the standards for child rearing, all of which tend to unselfconsciously reflect a white middle class norm. It is also evident in assumptions that all shelter residents have the same needs. For example, a shelter rule stating that residents cannot call their families for the first seventy-two hours of their stay cuts off black women and Latinas from sustaining contact with extended families and communities.

In most shelters, where staff is predominantly white, workers are often unaware of differences in family patterns and socialization experiences and are not necessarily sensitive to the impact of racism on women's lives. The fact that black women may cope with violence differently from white women, for example, is often ignored.

> [the black woman] has been socialized to live with violence on an everyday basis. She may observe daily in the community one-to-one physical violence inflicted in states of anger, sexual exploitation, and accommodation for goods and services, as well as family violence, and be powerless to intervene. Or, she may find she must defend herself against aggression because she does not have any expectations of anyone coming to her rescue or protecting her from physical and/or emotional harm, even the police. Thusly she learns to not only protect herself or avoid encounters, but to fight back if necessary....
>
> The advocate must be aware of and examine her/his own threshold and attitude towards the tolerance of anger/violence because Black people experience anger and violence differently.[20]

Because of both racism and the reality of being constantly understaffed, shelters often fail to provide the diverse kinds of services that women's different needs demand. One activist explains:

> I spend a lot of my time doing outreach to Puerto Rican women. I'm visiting one woman who had been in the shelter, helping her shop and fix things up. I know she's having a very hard time. Some women call here very confused and I'll meet them in the community to just sit and talk. The shelter doesn't like that I spend so much of my time this way.[21]

If a shelter hires one bilingual staff person for a large Spanish speaking population, it leaves Spanish speaking women isolated much of the day. And hiring one token Spanish speaking woman also assumes that all Spanish speaking women share basic cultural experiences. This misses the point that, for example, women born and reared in Puerto Rico live differently than those raised from an early age in New York City.

Because of the white middle class bias of most battered women's programs, some women of color have been reluctant to use shelters. When they do, they often feel isolated or ostracized. Early in the shelter movement, racism was widespread and blatant. Out of the compelling need to find a way for all women to coexist in the shelter, many programs initiated some form of racism awareness training.

When this was successful, it sometimes led to strictly enforced affirmative action hiring procedures and regularized racism awareness training by white and third world women. But in many places, little changed. And even shelters that recognized racism as a serious problem are not always able to combat it effectively. One black woman offers her perception of the problem of racism within the movement.

> The most common erroneous assumption within the Shelter Movement regarding delivery of service to women of color is the belief in the inherent infallibility/goodness of feminism as a panacea. To assume that recognition of oppression based on gender, particularly female gender, gives the wherewithal to automatically deal with racism is not only an error but is self defeating and exploitive. Until the feminist movement actively and publicly deals with eliminating racism within its own ranks, service to black women and other women of color will be seriously lacking.[22]

Those women of color who work in the movement often complain that they have been thoughtlessly assigned the task of sensitizing white women about racism or providing all shelter services for their particular ethnic or racial group.

> The one Chicana on staff is totally used. She is a translator, advocate, child's advocate and community educator. In general you're supposed to be a 24 hour robot. Everyone in the community calls you at home in the evenings and weekends. We are often exploited in the shelter; you have your own family and then everyone in the community also approaches you.[23]

As third world women from different shelters talked to one another at state coalition meetings or conferences, they shared their dissatisfaction with the lack of outreach to battered women in third world communities and the limited recruiting of third world staff, board members, or volunteers.

Women of color working within the battered women's movement often face hostility from their own communities. One black feminist writer notes that concern about racism allows the black community to ignore sexism.

> They have not been willing to acknowledge that while racism caused white men to make black women targets, it was and is sexism that causes all men to think that they can verbally or physically assault women sexually with impunity.[24]

In Los Angeles, Asian women who started Nalinac, The Center for the Pacific Asian Family, encountered enormous obstacles. They

needed fluency in seventeen languages and also found that the
diverse Asian communities met their efforts to help victims of sexual
assault and battering with marked indifference and a lack of fiscal
support.[25]

Third world women's reactions to women's liberation range
from anti-feminist to a broad spectrum of varying feminisms. Among
women of color, there are major disagreements over whether
violence against them results from sexism or from the racism and
powerlessness third world men experience. More third world women
are now defining themselves as feminists and are considering what
this means for themselves and their communities. An urgent
dialogue is needed among women of color and between them and
white feminists so that activists can learn from one another, clarify
political differences, expand theory, and disregard stereotypes.

One black woman stated emphatically, "if feminism means
women struggling to be strong women, I buy it. If it means white
women separating from white men, I don't."[26] Another black activist
declares:

> You cannot hit black and Hispanic women over the head with
> feminism, meaning men are the enemy, given the history of minority
> communities. For these women, the oppressor is white. There is a
> sense of protection and guilt toward black men because the larger
> society is so hostile. Personally I feel torn in so many directions. I'm
> committed to this movement and to the black community which often
> doesn't even understand why I'm working on this issue. I try to talk
> about strengthening black women, but it's rough on me.[27]

Native American women voice similar concerns.

> Chances are she will use the shelter for protective service and nothing
> else. She has strong ties, not only with her immediate family, but with
> the Tribe (reservation). It is not easy for her to break relationships with
> her husband, lover... For her to go to the law and report or sign a
> complaint against her husband is practically unheard of. She may feel
> she has committed an unforgivable violation against the traditional
> law of having compassion for one another...[28]

Feminists have attacked the nuclear family as the locus of
women's oppression. Marriage has been defined as murderous and
oppressive. Third world and working class women, however, often
see their families as primary support systems in an otherwise hostile
world. That the family is both an oppressive and a supportive
structure for women is part of an extremely complicated but
necessary discussion about the family as it varies by class, race, and
ethnic group. In fact, the "family" which women argue about is not

necessarily the same for all women;[29] for example, an extended family is different from a nuclear one.

Because of the history of racism within the United States, women of color define issues, problems, and priorities differently than do white feminists. Women of color not only need but also want ties to their culturally rich communities. Curdina Hill, the director of Casa Myrna Vazquez shelter, pointed out how this difference in perspective complicated the building of a strong alliance between her shelter's predominantly third world community and the women's movement.

> There's a definite tension: We are part of the shelter movement; however, our analysis of oppression in this society includes and incorporates far more than women. We are dealing with an entire people, including men, who are racially and ethnically oppressed. We can't separate out the inequities against us as women from those due to race and class. For many of us, the ties to our community are stronger than to the women's movement. This doesn't mean we don't also struggle against sexism, but it is a more complex struggle for us. Because it means struggling to become free from violence on all levels—class, race and sex. In carrying out this struggle, we have to gather support on all fronts and align with a range of groups—groups of Third World men and women, poor people's organizations and women's organizations. We need to work on all these fronts all the time.[30]

Women of color often find that their priorities are not respected by white feminists.

> Most third world women identify with their race first. That may be hard to accept by a white woman. My priority is to third world people. This viewpoint may be seen as hostile by white women. Yet, third world women view white women trying to pressure them to be feminist (or just women) as hostile on their part.[31]

Third world feminists sometimes find that their politics are ignored.

> Although Anna identifies herself as a feminist, while Estella does not use this label, both women emphasize their desire to define their feminist beliefs and actions on their own terms. And, as long as Anglo feminists feel we must educate and recruit Chicanas and other Third World women to "our" movement, Third World women, not surprisingly, will feel angry and turned-off...[32]

At state or national coalition levels the problems re-create themselves. Little third world participation at state coalition meetings reflects either a small third world shelter staff or little support for women of color to attend these meetings. The challenge of opening up the movement to third world women has been confronted by some state-wide organizations, with varying degrees of success.

> For our coalition training grant we decided not to hire ourselves but to give opportunities to former battered women and third world women. It was a fine idea but how do you bring in women who didn't start in the same political place as you did and didn't share a vision of where the movement was going. It was a disaster and a set-up for black women. We didn't think enough about the support they would need in "our" organization, and it was "ours." It is perceived by black women as our movement and we have not been willing to break down our issues enough for them to run the movement.[33]

Some coalition activists have introduced the issue of racism by forming state-wide committees like the Racism Committee of the Connecticut Task Force on Abused Women or the Equal Opportunity/Affirmative Action Committee of the Massachusetts Coalition. As a result of these efforts, the stated commitment of coalition member groups often has been changed to include combatting racism through developing training materials, sensitizing staff, hiring third world women, and encouraging third world women to take leadership positions. Results have been mixed and depend largely on the efforts of individuals.

Well aware of racism within the movement, the women of color who attended the first national conference of the National Coalition Against Domestic Violence quickly formed a third world women's caucus to share support and insights. At the national level, women of color felt excluded from the informal networks in which information and power were shared among white women. During caucus reports, third world women raised these issues. Through the efforts of the Women of Color Task Force established after this conference and the National Coalition planning committee, work priorities were re-ordered to respond to the criticisms.

> 1. To bridge the gap between women of color and the battered women's movement [NCADV will form] alliances with other organizations which address issues of primary concern to women of color.
> 2. To increase sensitivity to issues of [importance to] women of color and to facilitate cultural exchange in NCADV, each Steering Committee Meeting will include a cultural historical sensitizing presentation by the host organization in conjunction with the WOC (Women of Color) Task Force.
> 3. To actively promote the leadership of women of color in the steering committee, NCADV will have 25% of the Steering Committee be comprised of women of color and will develop a policy to facilitate that transition of new members onto the Steering Committee.

4a.To insure that the concerns of women of color are integrated into the plan and actions of NCADV, the Steering Committee will establish a task force to act as liaison between the Steering Committee and Third World women caucus.
  b.The task force will represent Hispanic, Pacific/Asian, American Indian, and Black women....
5.To assist the building of domestic violence organizations and services for women of color, NCADV will provide technical assistance in fundraising and organizing....[34]

By December 1981, through the efforts of the Women of Color Task Force, a national network of 100 women of color had been formed.[35] Although these women are in touch with one another, they have not been able to afford a national meeting.

Women of color have also formed networks that go beyond the battered women's movement. On August 21-23, 1980 the First National Conference on Third World Women and Violence, sponsored by the D.C. Rape Crisis Center, convened with approximately 100 women and men of color from around the country. In this historic setting, six panels addressed Feminism and Third World Women; Lesbianism: A Third World Perspective; Criminal Justice; Third World Women and Political Violence. Workshops reflected the needs of isolated third world women and men to define and analyze violence from their own perspectives. The crucial questions, according to one organizer, are, "how are we affected by violence against women? How is it interpreted in our communities; what are its causes; what is our relationship to the experiences of others outside our immediate communities who are working on this issue?..."[36] In analyzing the issues from a third world perspective, some fundamental inadequacies were found in the tools and theories provided by the larger anti-violence against women movement.[37]

Those who attended the conference identified regional contact people and began discussing the need to build a third world women's anti-violence network. The task ahead is large.

> This may require the development of each ethnic group's own ideology within the third world movement or it may result in a single ideology with several ethnic components....
> The greatest points of unity seemed to be an understanding of the vastness of our task as third world women to develop ideology, direction, programs and community support toward the elimination of violence against third world women.[38]

In addition to organizing on a national level, women of color have worked locally and regionally to sensitize activists in the battered women's movement to racism. Many movement conferences have offered racism awareness workshops that focus on the "special needs" of different groups of Asian, Hispanic, black, or Native American women. Many third world women, however, are concerned that not enough white women attend these workshops, that third world women are placed in the impossible position of speaking for differences within and between racial and ethnic groups, and that their issues are ghettoized. Some therefore advocate incorporating cultural diversity into all workshops rather than relegating women of color to "special" sessions.

Another type of conference workshop sensitized women to their own racism.

> Initially, we went around the circle and each woman described why she was attending the workshop. Black women described specific, painful incidents of racism presently confronted in their respective shelters. The white women acknowledged that they were struggling with their own individual racism and attempting to deal with racism in their programs.[39]

At this workshop, Anita Brooks from the University of Minnesota guided a racially mixed group through exercises in which they created racist shelters and racist communities. They then considered how they felt about being women and how they felt about their skin color. They concluded by together designing non-racist shelters and communities.[40] In this kind of workshop, no one leaves unchanged.

> The workshop was a frightening, awesome, trust-building, and women-connecting experience....All of the participants felt that a similar exercise in their home program would be a helpful first step in the struggle to eliminate racism within the shelter movement.[41]

Examining one's own racism is a difficult task for white women. Layers of feelings and experiences need to be gently peeled away and scrutinized.[42] One white activist shares her perceptions.

> We must acknowledge what we think we have to lose by this understanding and find what we have to gain by eliminating our racism. We must believe that racism causes us to be less human and work toward humanizing ourselves.

Her honest reactions are vitally important for white women to face.

> It seems that much of our resistance to change comes from being angry at women of color. There are many times that white women are put in a real bind so that no matter what we do we are accused of being racist. There are times when racism is inappropriately used as an issue when

the disagreements are clearly philosophical. But those, often very legitimate, resentments we have cannot become a justification for perpetuating our racism. The confusion we feel about when and how this movement is racist will not be cleared up until we understand racism as our issue and our responsibility and begin addressing it among ourselves rather than depending totally upon third world women to raise and clarify the issue for us.[43]

A black shelter director urges racism sensitivity training for shelter staff and residents.

Everyone is racist within this society; it's inevitable. We can't help each other by pointing fingers and confronting each other hostilely. We need to create a safe space to talk about our feelings, fears, and attitudes. We must start from, "we all have negative attitudes."[44]

For white women, racism awareness means not only acknowledging anger but also examining what it means to have power, theories, and ownership of organizations challenged and transformed.[45] Many women of color perceive that white women may not be ready for the personal and organizational changes that are inevitable if power, access to information, and leadership are shared.[46]

Even when women undertake personal and organizational efforts to eliminate it, racism continues to permeate people's experiences in the United States. Many white women overpersonalize the problem, and focus on their guilt, making efforts to tackle racism more difficult. Racism is deeply embedded in centuries of institutional practices, and the rage and distrust bred by it are a reality of shelter life.

Women alternately feel hope and despair as they examine the complex tasks ahead. One black woman suggests.

White women are not right now able to hear black women's anger. You have to tell me—"I'm not all white women," but you have to hear my anger.
In terms of feminism, I see a need for strong political analysis and needing a line because of the danger of co-optation. But how do you see these and also allow other people's input. How does my analysis fit in? If my analysis has not been allowed, it makes my buying into your analysis difficult. I feel compromised.[47]

A white woman presents the same dilemma from her perspective.

We are perceived as oppressors and we just can't argue our way out of it. It is crazy making for third world women to hear us say this is a movement for all women. Who creates the truth; who declares reality. We have to let go, step back and not operate out of guilt. We have to let ourselves reexamine theory and practice now.[48]

A real commitment is needed to actually turn racism awareness into anti-racist practice. Some shelters have redefined their purposes and goals to explicitly work toward multi-racial understanding among shelter staff and residents.[49] Many women of color suggest that shelters must engage in more active outreach to third world communities. In the manual *Doing Community Outreach to Third World Women*, Renae Scott proposes steps for analyzing racism, looking at third world communities' perceptions of shelter services, reaching out, bringing in women of color staff and volunteers, and maintaining women of color within organizations.[50] Three Chicanas make the following suggestions.

> We need to deal with schools and chemical dependency programs in our neighborhoods. Shelters need more cultural awareness, bilingual brochures and must turn to resources available in our communities for their training and community education....Shelter staff must experience cultural sensitivity as an ongoing emphasis. Staff must be made to acknowledge the differences in values, importance of family socialization and what it means and to not only acknowledge these differences but to respect them as valid and worthy....Chicanas aren't coming to the shelters but they won't come with conditions like this. Women can't come because it is so foreign to them and then shelters say we can't justify the need for Latina staff.[51]

Some women of color who work within primarily white organizations have begun autonomous organizations like California Women of Color Against Domestic Violence. Through these networks, women of color get needed support and are able to share their experiences. Catlin Fullwood of the Pennsylvania Coalition's Women of Color Task Force is optimistic about the work proceeding in Pennsylvania.

> In Pennsylvania, we as individual women have come together to form our own power base in the form of the Pennsylvania Women of Color Task Force. We have created a forum for the expression of our vision. We believe that we must have this separation so that we may be empowered by one another to go back to our programs to engage in true integration which is among and between equals.
> Our Coalition has made a commitment to increasing the participation and leadership of women of color. We hope that this commitment will grow stronger as we do.[52]

For women of color, self-determination and sharing are crucial. Third world women have thus declared forming relationships and networks among themselves as a priority. This, however, does not mean that white women and women of color are not working for many of the same goals. As one activist says, echoing the sentiments of many, "Let's define our goals in common; this should not be about your joining me or my joining you."[53] Another woman declares:

> ...it is important that white women in the movement understand that it may not be in the best interest of a woman of color to "actively join" a white dominated organization of women, but that this doesn't mean that we are not working actively and effectively toward the same ends. When we make women's issues a priority in our work, we need to define this in the context of our lives as women of color.

This activist believes that the root of the problem of working together is that

> neither white feminists nor people of color see each other's struggles YET as a viable revolutionary position in its own right.[54]

To effectively build a broad based, multi-racial women's movement, activists must understand and respond to the needs of those who face the greatest economic and racial discrimination. This might lead to joint work by white and third world women on such issues as housing, sterilization abuse, child care, welfare rights, and the right to decent jobs. In all their work, activists need to be aware of racism and constantly struggle against it. White women must confront the fact that their lives are impoverished through their failure to know people of different races and cultures. Although much work remains, the battered women's movement has made significant efforts to combat racism. Multi-racial shelters are becoming a reality in more places, third world women are opening more community based services throughout the country, and the National Coalition has increasing representation and leadership from women of color. In the last few years, the battered women's movement, pushed by its participants, has taken many steps forward in the fight against racism.

The Role of Battered Women Within the Movement

The discussions initiated by women of color parallel those that need to take place about battered women's involvement within a movement that is called theirs. Concerns about the lack of participation of battered women have been raised sporadically at national and local levels. Although former battered women, with the assistance of local programs, have organized their own conferences in Minnesota and are planning them in other states, battered women's lack of power has yet to be faced as a major problem.

In most shelters, battered women have received a kind of caring and support offered by few other institutions. Within feminist and grassroots shelters, they have also been encouraged to help determine programmatic and organizational directions; because of the constant turnover and diversity of residents, this sharing of power has been a difficult goal for the movement to achieve. To ease the power disparity between battered women and shelters, many organizations asked former residents to become refuge workers. In a few shelters, ex-residents now even hold the majority of staff positions. This pattern, however, is not typical. Neither are there many former residents who occupy visible local or national leadership roles within the movement. In 1981, scattered reports indicated that in some programs, battered women were losing a portion of the power they once had. And as professionals increasingly provided services, important questions emerged about the class differences between those who live in refuges and those who control them.

Although many middle class women use services of the battered women's movement, the majority who find their way to shelters are working class or poor. Because shelter life is difficult, women who have alternatives often turn to them. On the other hand, the majority of those who determine policy for most shelters are middle class women. Questions of class therefore weave in and out of a multitude of debates concerning battered women's role in the movement.

In shelters, class operates both blatantly and subtly. It emerges on many levels and is evident, for example, in struggles around "lifestyle" and values. Middle class women hold unwavering opinions about how others should care for their children and spend leisure time, and they assume, sometimes unconsciously, that their lifestyles and views of the world are better. Working class women, feeling attacked, fight back, and conflicts flare over how to discipline children, cook, and talk.

Although feminism is a liberating tool which illuminates power relationships between the sexes, in some cases it has blinded women to the power relationships between women of different classes. Testifying before the United States Civil Rights Commission in 1978, one advocate openly and self-consciously shared her insights about the movement's relationship to battered women.

> We have failed in not giving the battered woman and her children a safe place. Too often we have made her feel that we rescued her and that she is forever indebted to us. On too many occasions we have imbued her with the idea that she is not our equal, that she is less than us. Most important, we have failed to honor her social, political, and cultural

ways of being and, thus, we have reenacted the oppression of the larger society.[55]

By misunderstanding women's class differences, at times staff members fail to see residents as important and turn them into objects of service and reform. Intrusive questions become the norm and voluminous case files, closed to the residents, pile up. There is a thin line, easily crossed, between offering respectful advice and reforming. And hiring more professionals only increases these tendencies. In fact, professionalization of services is a dangerous goal for any movement that hopes to organize and liberate women.

Tension mounts when staff members do not trust battered women to make sound choices for their lives or to take responsibility for the shelter. Sometimes underlying this attitude is the belief that staff are different, unlikely targets of male violence, while battered women chose men poorly and irresponsibly. Even though some shelter residents have psychological problems, addictions, or act irresponsibly, the larger question of trust is skirted by focusing on this minority. The lack of trust may reflect a subtle sense of superiority or a fear of women with different life experiences, coping styles, or class backgrounds. More profoundly, it incorrectly suggests that violence is a problem for only some women. This view breaks the identification between victim and helper and severs the bonds of sisterhood.

Tensions exist between shelter staff and battered women for still other reasons. The battered women's movement articulated that violence was a social problem and simultaneously asserted that shelter residents be given responsibility for their lives. Of necessity, shelters urged women to be independent from men and to develop self-confidence and personal autonomy. Yet some residents may not share these goals. Leaving a husband and living alone is not necessarily perceived as a viable option by a woman with few job skills and no money. The issues facing many battered women are so overwhelming—medical problems, loneliness, children with emotional scars, poor housing, and jobs—that they decide to go back to their husbands. Many women want to reunite with their husbands for emotional as well as economic reasons, and they hope the violence will cease. Sometimes shelter goals can feel as oppressive and impossible to meet as those of any other social welfare agency.

The power dynamics between staff and residents are also influenced by staff's need to feel effective. Because the prevailing norm within social service agencies is that staff are helpers to "needy" clients, there is a tendency to push residents to make measurable changes. And the truth is that for staff, it is satisfying to watch a woman concretely change and credit the shelter for her growth. As a result, sometimes residents are pushed too fast to change. As one activist commented, "taking over for the women meets our ego and power needs; it's hard to face this honestly because it contradicts our philosophy."

Several women have suggested that shelter staff develop what look like "class" barriers between themselves and battered women because residents' practical needs and emotional pain are so great that workers cannot function without a self-protective distance. Far from denying their commonality with battered women, they feel it palpably and they act to protect themselves from the daily vulnerable feelings that violence, dislocation, and loneliness evoke.

In a movement striving for sisterhood and unity among women, shelter staff face the uncomfortable task of not only defining what they share with residents, but also acknowledging ways in which they may be different. The staff's feminism and political explanation for violence against women, for example, may contrast sharply with the politics of some battered women. Shelter staff does hold more power than residents, and this is a significant difference between them. And self-help models present few guidelines about conflict resolution and the need to respect differences in situations where one group of people has more power than another. These problems trouble politically conscious activists who only satisfactorily resolve them for brief moments.

Examining the differences between battered women and non-battered staff often leads to the question, "Why don't battered women run the battered women's movement?" In some shelters they do, especially as former residents take their places as staff. Yet hiring former residents does not automatically lead to empowering current ones. In shelters where punitive norms exist toward residents, staff, battered or not, may adopt these norms. Grateful to the shelter for their jobs, some—but not all—former residents find it difficult to be critical toward the program. Moreover, some battered women disagree with feminist ideals of empowering their sisters and encouraging democratic participation. Staff's and residents' needs are not the same, even if both groups are battered women.

There are also problems in the ways in which shelters employ former battered women. Many shelters will hire several battered women, but will not entrust them with leadership positions. These are frequently reserved for professionally trained women who, battered or not, have not lived in shelters. It is often stated that "former residents are not ready yet" or "they are too busy rebuilding their lives." Although this may be true for many women, this retort fails to grapple with the complex class, race, and power questions surrounding the exclusion of former shelter residents. Many shelters have made no concrete plans to carefully work with former residents to build their skills or create transition periods so that former residents work side by side with current staff. In some instances, however, this has happened. One woman describes how an Australian shelter was turned over to ex-residents.

> You cannot tokenize the women. It happened through building an autonomous ex-residents group that was separate from the shelter. We needed an ex-resident *group* to face the power of a feminist collective.
> Sometimes it takes years for ex-residents to work through what happened to them. The women had to be ready on their own terms. As they took over, the shelter changed. For example, now many women in the collective have children and this changes shelter politics because it is not so easy to work endless hours.[56]

As she also notes, feminists have to be prepared to see the shelter they nourished transformed.

Acknowledging that battered women should have more control over shelters or coalitions, however, does not eliminate the nagging questions about the relationship between feminism as a political movement and as a service strategy. Does a local shelter, started by feminists, belong to battered women residents, staff, volunteers, or the women's community? Many shelters attempt to include all these groups as "owners," yet the unsettling question remains—whose priorities will prevail when cutbacks hit or if battered women define their goals differently from the staff or board? The conflicts can be acute. Often, battered women want shelters to provide more services, such as job training programs and second stage housing. Feminists who see themselves as organizers of a movement may feel that expanding in this way saps energy for transforming society on behalf of all women. Or staff defines democratic process, consensus decision making, or participation in a feminist movement as primary, and some residents are angered or bewildered by these norms and choices. Although there are no easy solutions to these conflicts, an open acknowledgment of different interests is imperative.

Because staff work full time in the movement, they become its political leadership, accumulating knowledge, contacts, and power. It is an easy next step for programs to operate for the convenience of staff, not shelter residents. Hiring battered women as staff and involving them in program planning and on boards is one partial way to keep power imbalances under better control. Regular discussions with residents during and after their shelter stay is another. Relying upon resident expertise, criteria could be developed to assess each area of shelter service—the hotline, residence, and follow-up programs—in order to determine if battered women's control and involvement are encouraged or minimized. At the same time, active outreach might be made to former residents to encourage their participation in shelter life or in building a battered women's movement to meet their needs. In this outreach effort it is important to support battered women as single mothers by offering child care and flexible meeting formats and by recognizing that many single parents and working mothers cannot commit themselves full time to the shelter. It is also essential to place more than one battered woman on the board so that "tokens" are not created. Keeping shelters as both formal and informal focal points for battered women who seek support or political involvement remains a central challenge for program staff in their role as service providers and organizers.

Offering staff and institutional resources, shelters might encourage former battered women to start autonomous groups or formal and informal support networks. In several communities, self-help networks have been established, composed only of current or former battered women, that generously provide emotional and practical aid to their members and sometimes engage in political protest. By sharing skills and encouragement with these groups, yet not attempting to control them, shelters and coalitions will help build a real "battered women's movement." As a challenge and support to shelters, organizations of battered women also might evolve into a pressure base from which to influence the movement's political direction and keep their non-battered counterparts on their toes, mindful of their real constituency.[57] Most importantly, battered women's groups offer an urgently needed sense of community for women who are often struggling alone. Without this community, many women find it impossible to endure loneliness and isolation.

Battered women challenge feminist shelters to live their ideals and avoid the rigidity and distance that permeate traditional institutional services. At the same time, through both painful and loving experiences, activists and battered women continue to transform one another.

CHAPTER 12

Organizing in the 80s

In the midst of right-wing attacks and massive cutbacks in human services, it is essential for activists to develop strategies for protecting newly won services. Many programs have already been cut substantially, and are, as one activist declared, "just fighting for survival."[1]

But in the immediate fight for survival, it is crucial not to lose sight of the future. Keeping the long-range goal of ending violence against women in mind, the movement must consider ways in which it can strengthen itself and respond to the concrete problems experienced by millions of women. With creativity and vision, the battered women's movement must confront new political tasks and expand its community bases and links with other progressive struggles. Mobilizing to fight for the survival of individual programs must be accompanied by a commitment to build the movement.

Right-Wing Attacks and Fiscal Cutbacks

A reactionary Republican president and his associated yet distinct New Right and Moral Majority allies have created unprecedented fiscal and ideological assaults upon women, the poor, people of color, lesbians, and gay men. Two backlashes are occurring simultaneously, one against feminism and the other aimed at dismantling the social welfare state.[2]

The economic boom is over; unemployment is high and profits have been decreasing. In response, the Right has declared that poor people are no longer entitled to services from their own government to assure their well being or even survival.

> The program, basically is to respond to a shrinking economic pie by grabbing a larger share of it for the people who are already, by any reasonable standards, well off. The program includes the flat-out exploitation of labor, a growing stratification by race and sex, and the dangerous unleashing of militant nationalism in foreign policy.[3]

The Republican budget plans call for an upward redistribution of income toward corporations and rich individuals; a smaller public sector, resulting from major cuts in taxation and government spending; and a major reduction and reorientation of government regulation, including dismantling efforts on behalf of women and racial minorities, and dramatically increased military spending.[4]

Although the poor are particularly attacked in these reactionary plans, they are not the only ones affected.

> Cuts in Social Security, the public schools, and unemployment benefits will affect greater numbers than less central cuts. But even there it may be shown how attacks on the elderly (who receive more than 50 percent of social welfare benefits) will put increased burdens on middle and working class families who already have been forced to support two wage earners just to meet core family needs. Similarly, the decline of public education may put a real burden on families whose inflation ridden incomes cannot support private education.[5]

Social services, like battered women's shelters, have already faced major cutbacks because of the elimination of federally funded CETA (Comprehensive Employment and Training Act) programs. Almost all shelters have used CETA employees as a source of labor and many shelters in the southeast rely heavily upon CETA staff.[6] Many programs are currently in danger of closing and the future looks grim. Senator Jesse Helms has already suggested that shelters may no longer be eligible for food stamps.

The Family Protection Act, first introduced in September 1979, lays out a comprehensive program for the New Right. It attempts to undermine public education and support racist institutions through tax incentives for private parent-run schools. It sharply limits the activities of Legal Services around abortion, desegregation, divorce, or public advocacy for the poor. The Act includes blatant attacks on the employment rights of lesbians and gay men while it prohibits federal jurisdictional involvement and funding for child abuse and battered women's programs, which could mean the loss of federal Title XX funds for such services. It actually specifies that schools using materials that teach anything other than traditional sex roles would not be eligible for federal funding.

In the plans of the Right, women are again assigned to the "special" sphere of the family, taking care of children and the elderly who will have no government services available to them. By fighting to deny women the right to abortion, the New Right attempts to seal women's fate as childbearers rather than as autonomous human beings. Far from trying to "keep the government out of the family," the New Right wants the government to dictate the kind of family— patriarchal—in which all people must live.

This sexist ideology has economic consequences. Forcing women out of the paid labor force is intended to ease the employment crisis within capitalist states. From England, Lynne Segal quotes a member of the House of Lords who stated that "unemployment could be solved at a stroke, if women went back to the home." Segal analyzes the comment.

> As a way out of the economic crisis, the ruling class is seeking to strengthen the ideology of sexism to justify its attacks on the working class in general, and women in particular, thus revealing more clearly than ever the links between sex oppression and class exploitation.[7]

The existence of shelters challenges the push to enforce women's place in the home and suggests that this subordination, extolled by the New Right, creates violence. Shelters are real and symbolic threats to male control over women because they make possible women's escape from violence. Their existence strengthens all women and builds women's individual and collective power in relationship to men. In order to save the traditional family, reactionaries will advocate mediation and reconciliation rather than shelters. The New Right will juxtapose the "good of the family" to women's "selfish" demand to control their own lives. Of course, it is difficult for the New Right to say that it is in favor of violence; instead, it argues that shelters interfere with the privacy of the family.

On an ideological level, the notion of separate spheres for men and women must be attacked.[8] First, women's subordination in the family creates violence; for at least two million American women who are beaten every year, the family is not a particularly safe place. Secondly, most women do not live in traditional families, and mandating one form of family negates the experiences of millions of women, again denying rights to self-determination. Advocating traditional family forms also ignores the reality that 48% of married women were in the labor force in 1978, most of them needing work, and 58.5% of female heads of households were also in the labor force.[9] Without these jobs, and sometimes with them, more women may join the ranks of what is being called the "feminization of poverty."

> In the 1970's, single women, especially those with young children, became the most predictably impoverished stratum of the American working class. Today, a single woman with children and without professional or managerial skills is virtually condemned to poverty or near-poverty. In 1977, 42% of single mothers had incomes below the Federal poverty line, a rate of poverty more than six and a half times that of husband-wife families.[10]

The New Right would have women suffer. Yet women's incomes frequently mean their families' survival. Public services such as schools and medical care are crucial in keeping millions just out of poverty. The battered women's movement must insist upon women's rights to decent incomes, social security, and welfare benefits so that no woman has to find and stay with a violent man out of fear of starvation.

The battered women's movement may also have to tackle the argument that "selfish" feminists are destroying the family or that feminism is only for middle class women. As Barbara Ehrenreich has noted, the media presented the American public with a view of feminism as a "self-improvement program for the upwardly mobile woman."[11] This image reflected the efforts of that part of the women's movement which focused on women's rights to equality within capitalist society. This notion of equality is an important ideological and political tool, but it is also limited. Many feminists have articulated a broader vision which goes beyond calling for better paying jobs and individual fulfillment, but this has generally been ignored by the media. The battered women's movement must continually talk about women's right to self-determination in a way that speaks to all women. This right includes not only a demand for shelters, but also for decent jobs, housing, child care, educational opportunities, and medical care. For most activists, feminism is not an individualistic philosophy and depends heavily on commitments to other people. The challenge is to convey this sense to a broader range of women.

Just as we propose new ways that people might live together in varied kinds of families free of violence and sexual coercion, the battered women's movement must also offer a vision of a more just, egalitarian, and humane society. Using sophisticated methods, the Right will be able to deplore family violence and blame it on all the disruptive forces, like women's liberation, making conventional male-dominated family arrangements unstable. Unless the battered women's movement conveys a concrete analysis of why women are beaten and a vision of a different society, its message will be watered down as it morally opposes violence but has no plan to end it. We must work for specific reforms that take domination and dependence out of male-female relations in the family and in the economy. The long-range goal of replacing dominance with equality and material security for all needs to be put forward.

As the movement develops new strategies to defeat the Family Protection Act and other reactionary legislation, the influence and power of the Right must be weighed. The Right is not the majority of American people, nor is it internally monolithic. There are major disagreements between the Old Right, the New Right, and religious reactionaries like the Moral Majority. However, these groups are extremely well organized and funded, and play on people's fears about their declining standard of living and changes in the family. Forging an alternative vision and a political program remain urgent tasks in the years ahead, even if the movement temporarily faces the painful reality of losing programs or funding.

Internal Strength

To effectively take on the monumental tasks ahead, the battered women's movement needs to strengthen itself internally. Organizations must develop visions of the future, clarify why they want to move in these directions, and devise concrete plans for getting there. Individual programs will have to devote significant energy to solving organizational problems and clarifying structure and process. And all paid and unpaid workers need to be educated about the organization's history, vision, and purpose.

As programs work in varied ways to make themselves strong, they will have to confront the difficult issue of leadership. Historically, this has been a very touchy subject in the women's movement. In the late 1960s and early 1970s, leadership was defined as "male," and was equated with gaining personal power and notoriety. Such views, a logical reaction to the abuses of power women had previously encountered, led women's organizations to rotate organizational leadership each year. Sometimes this rotation exposed many women to decision making and built their skills and self-confidence; sometimes, however, it cost organizations dearly when old "leaders" were accorded little recognition or respect. Partly because leaders were often trashed, they pretended they did not lead, and thus could not be held accountable.[12] Power existed but women acted as if it did not, and as a result, organizations became chaotic, planning efforts were foiled, and political and intellectual analyses were discredited.

Until recently, few attempts have been made to supply new definitions of leadership. Now, however, feminists are beginning to define leaders as those who work hard, feel accountable to a movement, and help others find their strength. Charlotte Bunch, a feminist activist and theoretician, summarizes these growing insights.

> A number of feminists have begun to develop a new understanding of power seen as the ability to act, to get something done and to see power associated with energy, strength, and effective interaction, rather than with manipulation....
>
> Leaders perform political, spiritual, and intellectual functions as well as managerial and group maintenance tasks. These range from providing vision and strategies for change, to mobilizing a constituency, to facilitating group decisions or creating coalitions.[13]

A feminist anthropologist described leaders as people who keep a view of the whole, work harder, keep connected to others within the group, build involvement, and work toward consensus.[14] It is helpful to conceptualize leadership as neither static nor monolithic. Especially in cooperative groups, different individuals display varying strengths, interests, and abilities. Helping a group break out of an ugly power struggle is as much of a leadership function as being a media spokesperson. Because only the latter is recognized as leadership, many women feel used, unacknowledged, and angry with those who take on the role of public leaders.

In analyzing leadership and power within the battered women's movement, it is important to understand the role that expertise plays. Many experts intimidate others, using their position to acquire privileges or status. Skills come to be used as weapons or as ways to gain power over others. Ideally, feminist leaders, most of whom are experts in certain areas, share their skills and knowledge. A feminist view of expertise acknowledges that information is created by and belongs to a movement. Because the society demands experts on battered women, the movement must respond to the request as it also legitimates a different internal view of the nature and use of expertise.

The notion of trashing must also be explored. Trashing consists of ugly personal or political attacks upon an individual which serve to totally discredit her within a movement or silence her for fear of future attacks. The difficulty in dealing with trashing is that while feminists must deplore this kind of dehumanizing name-calling, they also need to hold leaders accountable when power is abused. Trashing has been damaging to the movement; so, however, have been manipulative leaders who, when criticized for their behavior, have failed to respond to the substance of the criticism and have instead accused their critics of trashing. Leaders often have been incapable of allowing political disagreement and have labeled those who articulate different political views divisive. There is a fine line between trashing and legitimately criticizing individuals for the way in which they exercise leadership. The movement needs to respect the expression of principled conflict and define it as an important vehicle through which women grow politically.

To strengthen organizations, guidelines for direct, respectful confrontation must be developed.[15] Individual programs or coalitions might hold workshops on constructive criticism and handling personal and political conflicts. In a movement where leadership is still in the process of being defined, those who accept leadership positions take certain risks. Activists must be sensitive to these women and make special efforts to support leaders who, though bound to make mistakes, are basically committed to empowering women and being accountable to a movement.

Leadership is also lost to a movement through a phenomena called burnout. Burnout is described as a loss of vision and meaning as well as an inability to gain sustenance from work. Burnout produces a tendency for individuals to withdraw; this isolation then produces further burnout. Those who are burned out describe depression, lack of interest in work, irritability, increased use of drugs or alcohol, a tendency to be highly critical of battered women or co-workers, and an inability to ever escape from work. Burnout depletes the movement as activists leave because of it.

In social work literature, burnout is described as a common experience for human service workers in emotionally draining jobs. It may well be that helping one battered woman after another for fifty hours a week and realizing that violence is extensive and infinite, heightens burnout. Movement activists suggest that there is more to the problem, however. When staff lose a political analysis of why women are beaten, why they return to their husbands, and why a movement is necessary, explanations become personalized. Opportunities to express righteous anger, a good burnout antidote, are lost. As workers feel more and more like failures, their personal connection to other workers and residents—their sustenance—is taken from them.

Another major explanation for burnout is structural. Oppressed by organizations in which no support is offered or in which worker control is minimized, staff become demoralized. Unclear accountability or decision making mechanisms also lead to burnout, as do persistent, unresolved organizational battles.

Burnout is commonly complained about but infrequently analyzed; far more discussion is needed to understand it. Here, suggestions are synthesized from activists who have not burned out. Many claim that a first step in minimizing burnout is an organizational commitment to periodically reexamining goals, structure, and division of labor. In those organizations where workers retain a high level of control and organizational structure and accountability are clear, burnout diminishes. Many shelters allow for task rotation, providing a continual chance for individuals to grow. Shelters also need to acknowledge the pain that comes from working with so much violence and provide ongoing mechanisms through which women can share their fears and vulnerability. In shelters where boards and administrators will not recognize staff's needs, workers may gain strength through employee organizations and unionizing.

Many activists suggest that their antidote to burnout is to combine doing work they believe in with a strong movement support network. For those who see themselves as part of a larger struggle, multiple opportunities exist for an expression of the constant anger experienced working with battered women. Their analysis directs their rage outward, not inward, and allows them to stop assuming responsibility for the problem. Activists believe that burnout happens less when women share the excitement, mastery, and support that results from building a movement.[16]

Organizing to Protect Services

After programs scrutinize their internal strengths and weaknesses, they need to design a plan to face impending cutbacks. Given unique local conditions, only general suggestions can be offered. Programs should gather information about the agency responsible for cutbacks and assess whether there is any possibility of getting cuts restored. If so, they need to consider whether the community will mobilize for this effort. Local groups must determine if there are any other sources of funding available. If so, through what bureaucracy with what rules and at what cost? Local funding sources, for example, can be a conservative influence because they allow a closer monitoring of local efforts. Programs need to carefully examine who their allies and enemies might be.

As long as shelters remain clear about their purposes and autonomy, temporary alliances with social service agencies, church groups, women's political party caucuses, and women's clubs seem essential for fiscal and political protection. Shelters should educate these community groups about battered women's services. In addition to emphasizing the grassroots, life-saving nature of services, it is useful to engage people in discussions about the emotional and political meaning of the work. By suggesting that violence against women is not just between a man and a woman but rather a responsibility of the community to stop, the shelter encourages people to think of ways to get involved. An alliance to save a shelter might eventually offer many new ideas and resources to programs.

Here the distinction between temporary alliances and ongoing coalitions is an essential one. In some localities and states, movement attempts to include everyone and preserve broad-based coalitions have resulted in debilitating and fruitless conflict with groups which are explicitly anti-feminist. Unhappy compromises are made over and over again in order to maintain unity. In such cases, it seems more useful to set clear limits about the purposes of coalescing and adhere to a narrow agenda.

In developing funding strategies, many shelters have suggested the importance of careful outreach before a crisis, to church and elected officials as well as to key bureaucrats. This means that the shelter's services, credibility, and politics need not be tested during an emergency and key individuals will be able to act more quickly on behalf of the shelter. Shelters also need ongoing outreach to people in the media who will portray the issue in sympathetic ways.

If government funding cannot be saved, many groups look toward diversifying their funding base within the community. In fact, many are suggesting the wisdom of diversifying before cutbacks come. Good organizing—using the help and contacts of many—becomes an essential part of these efforts. Some groups have moved toward holding large scale community events and benefits while others are considering launching large direct mail campaigns.

Churches have agreed to co-sign mortgages so that buildings can be bought rather than rented. Shelter board members who work in local corporations have used their contacts to solicit funds, helping shelters build larger fundraising networks. The Western States Shelter Network has developed an excellent book on economic self-sufficiency, *Dollars and Sense: A Community Fundraising Manual for Shelters and Other Non-Profit Organizations,* which explores topics like attitudes toward money, special events fundraising, phone-a-thons, capital fundraising, and small enterprise development.[17]

A 1980 *Aegis* article raised four questions to use in deciding what funding to solicit. 1. How objectionable is the source of funds? (Is it "dirty money"?); 2. What kind of direct or indirect control or influence will the funding agency require or gain if we accept money from it?; 3. What kind of legitimacy will the funding agency use us to gain and will we lose our own credibility?; 4. How critical is the money to our survival?[18] Acknowledging that money is almost always dirty, earned through the exploitation and oppression of segments of this and other societies, they analyze the criteria of control and legitimacy. They suggest that "the most critical thing an organization can do to protect against this [outside control] is to develop clear goals, objectives, policies, and an organizational philosophy *before* seeking or accepting funding from any agency.[19]

Funding diversification raises heated political and moral questions. It is important for groups to consider the varied questions fully. Will diversification mean shifts in board membership with more emphasis on recruiting influential people than battered women? How might this development be minimized? Additionally, will diversified funding efforts build community outreach in working class and poor neighborhoods? If not, how will the shelter be viewed in these communities? A constant search for funds tends to pull organizations in more conservative directions; while awareness of this dynamic is useful, it does not always create more options, especially in the current economic and political climate.

Many have argued that community based funding will not keep shelters functioning at previous staff and service levels. This will mean that programs have to reassess goals and priorities. The Rape and Domestic Violence Information Center in Morganstown, West Virginia, facing a two-thirds reduction in funding, shifted from a staff of seven to three.

> In the shelter, clients now receive about ¼ of the time in counseling as they previously received. Advocacy is emphasized. In retrospect,

RDVIC believes too much time has been spent in counseling, and not enough on advocacy, and so the ¼ figure is not as drastic as it may indicate. Furthermore, it has been found that the women begin more quickly to engage in problem-solving, and to utilize their own resources.[20]

Reconceptualizing ideas about "quality services" and trusting battered women and community volunteers to provide peer support and self-help will be necessary. In Idaho, where shelters have always refused to seek state funding, volunteer efforts have kept shelters open for years. To keep women's institutions alive, even at a reduced level of functioning, is critical over the next several years.

Preparing for and facing cutbacks is painful and depressing. As young organizations, shelters worked endlessly to gain community legitimacy, credibility, and at least symbolic recognition through small funding. Facing cutbacks mandates a mourning process so that individuals do not blame themselves for losses and so that staff, battered women, and supporters can bear the burdens together.

Suggesting that programs diversify funding or reduce services is not meant to support the notion that the government has no responsibility to fund battered women's services. The question is not a movement's right to money nor battered women's right to services; here both are assumed as necessary political demands. Rather, the battered women's movement needs to face the immediate political task of managing with less at the same time that it continually articulates the need for more. If the movement stops talking about women's needs for safety and services, it looks as if the needs have disappeared. Making public demands for services is the only way to place the burden upon those responsible for the institutional and economic discrimination battered women face. Moreover, it is primary that the battered women's movement maintain its own definitions of the issue, its own articulation of battered women's needs, and its own standards of service so that the issues are not defined narrowly and legalistically by bureaucrats.

For those shelters that are particularly vulnerable to losing funding or community support if they engage in political activity, it may be necessary for small groups of women, without formal shelter affiliation, to undertake organizing work. This must be done, however, with the understanding that service providers and battered women participate in planning that activity. A movement is broader than its service organizations, a fact which also means that shelters not discredit diverse forms of political activity.

The organizing battle around funding competes with another

battle already being fought—the right of shelters to control relationships with residents. Building codes and licensing standards vary from locality to locality, as do political realities. In some areas, meeting strict housing codes will put some shelters out of business because they will be unable to afford renovations. Licensing requirements can not only mandate building specifications, but can also set program standards; for example, that only licensed therapists provide counseling to battered women. Some states, like Pennsylvania, are attempting to resist this imposition of program standards by developing their own. Many activists suggest that it is just a matter of time before states will impose standards and the movement should at least have alternatives available. In states with less powerful coalitions, local groups may have to again consider utilizing broad based community support to protest renovation requirements or the undermining of grassroots, self-help service.

Even in a time of fiscal crisis, organizers should continue to assess what kinds of services are most desirable. Many women argue that as shelters grow too large, they destroy personal caring and contact and undermine the vision of a cooperative community linked to a broader movement. Although size is probably not the only variable affecting the quality of relationships, there has been a tendency to create larger shelters with more services offered within them. As an alternative, women have suggested helping new groups start their own small projects. While circumstances often made this option impossible, this direction would allow for the growth of diverse services and would encourage new women to join the movement. More women would have an experience of organizing themselves and defining their own interests together.

In a time of reaction and cutback, it is difficult to imagine any major political activity except protecting existing shelters. However, in most urban areas, more shelter is desperately needed; in many places, no shelter has yet been won, and in still others, feminists no longer control the provision of shelter services. Because of these complexities, no national movement "plan" can be adequately designed. However, coalitions might develop statewide service strategy plans. The Pennsylvania Coalition for example, is trying to place a shelter in each county surrounded by satellite safe homes projects and a statewide hotline to coordinate efforts on behalf of callers. Even when it does not have the strength and resources to develop programs such as these, the battered women's movement must continue to articulate the goals it has not attained. Women, experiencing any level of threat or violence, should have immediate access to safety.

Those shelters funded through statewide mechanisms will need to develop careful strategies in the months and years ahead. If federal Title XX funds become part of state block grants, individual shelters and state coalitions will again have to engage in massive lobbying to insure their survival. Political jockeying will occur constantly among bureaucracies to gain control of new funding. Shelters may be shifted from relatively protective agencies into unknown ones. Building bureaucratic and legislative contacts and supportive "inside" allies, monitoring state agencies, and lobbying are essential. Analyzing budgets and funding distribution mechanisms becomes ongoing work as does sharing information with supportive lobbyists and other social service agencies.

Battered women's coalitions might sponsor skill sharing workshops to train movement fundraisers, lobbyists, and especially community organizers. Utilizing resources from its own and other political movements, coalitions could take a burden off local shelters by offering ongoing educational seminars to increase activists' skills.

When funding is cut, individual shelters lose resources and the movement as a whole also loses. Personal networks, the cement of any movement, are more difficult to maintain; essential information is lost and power is eroded. The concept of mutual aid between and among shelters and services now needs to be expanded.

> Our coalition wants input into how funds are spent. We established criteria for who should be funded. We decided monies would be allocated to shelters whose survival was most at risk.[21]

Although resistance to such ideas is strong, activists need to weigh choices for the movement as a whole rather than only for individual organizations.

To encourage sharing of ideas and skills, coalition staff or individual programs might coordinate meetings, retreats, or one day seminars on a series of major issues: how might budget cuts affect the priorities and politics of member organizations?; how should the limited human and financial resources of shelters and coalitions be expended?; how might shelter staff best use its time?; how can shelters mobilize broad based community support for battered women and their programs?; how do shelters and coalitions best transmit their political vision to a variety of audiences?

In coalition meetings, role playing concrete political dilemmas is one device that can help prepare women to better handle immediate and anticipated problems. At one conference, for example, participants role played two distinct situations. In the first one, the board chairperson announced a $20,000 cutback at a staff meeting. She proposed either equal salary cuts or the elimination of two staff positions and then invited discussion. In this role play, trust immediately broke down, with each staff member trying to protect her own job. In the second role play, the director announced that cutbacks were to happen, but that staff needed to help determine how best to deal with them. In this group, trust stayed much higher and individual attacks on fellow staff were replaced by information gathering and problem solving. At the end of each role play, participants listed the interpersonal processes and feelings that emerged and the political questions that were raised. Variations on this type of exercise, along with planning, will help women through hard times. Those who have been through major fiscal cutbacks and ideological attacks argue that the worst part is often being taken by surprise and watching internal support systems crumble and women turn on one another. In crises, democratic processes can break down, to be replaced by blame and accusation. To avoid this, thoughtful advance planning is needed.

In the rough times ahead, money and programs will be lost. If an internal standard of success labels the meaning and form of accomplishments, such as commitments to a women's movement and democratic process, as important as external gains, then the movement's strength will be reinforced. Coalitions face the task of legitimating and supporting an alternative view of success, keeping the movement organized and united, and increasing the one intangible that will be most difficult to take away, the movement's collective strength.

Progressive Alliances

The battered women's movement must now consider the ways in which it will align with other progressive social change movements. Alliances with community groups, the women's movement, and others working on issues that most affect battered women will help to protect the gains that fiscal cutbacks are undermining. Survival of this and other progressive social change movements depends on alliances which will create the larger power base that we all need. The stronger we are collectively, the easier it is for any one movement to survive.

Not all in the battered women's movement would agree that

alliances should be specifically with progressive movements. Some argue that alliances with any groups are desirable and are willing to join with right-wing as well as progressive groups. This position ignores the reality that even if part of the Right is willing to support some activities of the battered women's movement, these same groups have attacked women's rights to abortion, day care, and adequate welfare grants as well as the right to live openly as a lesbian or gay male. The Right opposes much of what battered women need to survive independently. Right wing alliances internally divide the battered women's movement and also pit parts of the women's movement against each other.

Some would argue that the battered women's movement, especially service organizations, should refrain from overt political involvement, especially in small towns. This argument suggests that shelters identified as too radical could be forced to close. Clearly, alliances and political stands must be discussed strategically; in some cases, shelters might rightly decide that they are unable to engage in certain activities. This position does not advocate unnecessarily jeopardizing shelter services. Rather, it suggests that the movement be clearer about its political choices.

An analysis of violence against women such as the one presented in this book leads to an understanding of some of the changes that need to be made in order to end battering. It helps us identify potential allies of the battered women's movement. Groups working on housing, jobs, union organizing, education, women's issues, rights for the disabled, welfare, and anti-racist struggles are important allies. Political movements have much to learn from each other's histories, and they can share organizing strategies. Dialogues around service and funding issues create a base from which to build trust which may allow groups to develop mutual political strategies and demands. All could agree to support one another if any of their programs, including shelters, are cut or attacked. As suggested earlier, competition over funds will be fierce, and divided political movements will only benefit those already in power.

> If in our efforts to secure more housing and jobs for women, we only secure them for certain women or if our success in obtaining resources for women further divides us from other oppressed groups, then we have problems. What does it mean that you're going to be a priority when the pool of people you are in, say for housing, is already the most disadvantaged. Who is going to get less? We all have a right to services. Coalitions with other oppressed groups are necessary.[22]

Besides uniting to create a defensive or protective strategy, an offensive strategy must also be put forward based on the needs of the majority in this country. Coalitions to demand jobs for all, housing, medical services, and child care facilities, and to attack another major military buildup must be created. Only winning such demands will make women's autonomy actual and will allow women to leave violent men.

Uniting, however, does not mean merging an organization's identity or goals with other organizations'. The autonomy of women's organizations is essential; the women's movement is too young and sexism too old for women to give up their own base of support. Defining mutual goals and strategies, not merging, seems a necessary first step among groups, some of whom are highly suspicious of one another. When feminists work in broad based coalitions, they also need to find ways to articulate, rather than bury, their particular political concerns even if they have no hope of seeing some of their feminist demands incorporated into coalition work.

The battered women's movement also needs to consider building stronger alliances with different parts of the women's liberation movement. Both feminist theory and organizing ability will be strengthened if the various movements for women's liberation share insights, experience, and resources. Broadly conceptualizing the term "violence against women" has been one means of widening the base for discussion and organizing. Advocating that the battered women's movement link sterilization abuse and women's poverty to its own analysis, one activist comments:

> 37.49% of Puerto Rican women of childbearing age have been sterilized under HEW-funded programs. I think we need to educate people about this kind of violence against women.
> I think we need to talk about what it means to deny women access to safe contraceptives, deny them access to abortions, and then in essence force them to forfeit the opportunity to bear children. We must learn to talk about battered women and sterilization abuse. We must find ways to explain to people the contradiction and the violence in the government's budgetary priorities.[23]

As this writer notes, the women's movement needs to explain directly and factually the effects of poverty, racism, and violence upon women's lives and the subsequent needs for resources and services. The damage done to women and their enduring strength must be publicly portrayed.

Not only do women's institutions have much to learn from one another's organizing efforts and histories, but they also can share networks, developing larger bases of protection and support. Without such sharing, important lessons are lost, as this long time anti-rape and battered women's activist painfully noted.

> The battered women's movement could have learned a lot more from the anti-rape movement but didn't. The anti-rape movement was an excellent case example about the relationships with institutions and co-optation. The battered women's movement faced an immediate need to gain legitimacy; the anti-rape movement could have helped critically analyze the political questions of where to put your energy, how much service to provide, planning about long-term funding. Many rape crisis centers, facing the same questions earlier, had moved from providing so much one to one service toward helping women activate their own support network.
>
> We learned that without an economic base, you cannot do what needs to be done. There are too many forces working against us. Given this problem, the purchase of shelters should have been a first priority.
>
> We learned how strings are attached to funding through our fights with LEAA. To make services contingent on reporting when the only outcome is prison is outrageous. Anti-rape work coincided with increased awareness of prisons and prison work. To raise rape as an issue and to have it become a law and order issue divided us from other progressive and anti-racist struggles. We could have learned to evaluate the side effects of money.
>
> The shelter I worked in thought that progressive ideas won't be influenced by grants. They thought they were pulling a fast one on the feds, but this never happens. The rape movement should have taught us that.[24]

Such lessons are too important to be lost but they are, again and again. Local and statewide sharing among women from different issue organizations might be a useful way to accumulate experiences. The personal connections formed among women with common goals might also broaden the sense of commitment from individual service programs to the movement as a whole.

Alliances among women's organizations can also help keep services alive when cutbacks occur. Rape crisis centers, battered women's shelters, and sexual harassment projects may be able to share hotlines and staff resources, and thus continue to provide essential services even when funding is reduced.[25] The concept of a community among women could also be expanded so that organizations of neighborhood women help coordinate child care, obtain insurance together, collect furniture for battered women, provide information about housing, take over a building, or sit-in at a welfare center.

Given the conservatizing tendencies operating upon shelters and the isolation of many feminist refuges, local activists need a reference point to a broader movement in order to maintain their political clarity. As social service agencies respond to this issue, a feminist battered women's movement will have a difficult time surviving without the visible presence of other shelters, state, and national coalitions as well as feminist organizing efforts around abortion, employment, anti-rape, and equal rights struggles. Only well organized and visible feminist and progressive movements will keep any single issue organizing clear and militant. As a broad based feminist movement wins victories, it strengthens the negotiating power of shelters. As its visibility and organization decreases, so does that the battered women's movement. The fates of movements are inextricably connected.

Community Education and Organizing: Redefining Old Tasks

Community outreach efforts were often neglected as shelters expanded and spent more time writing grants, raising money, and operating complex programs. With cutbacks, it is likely that community education will become even less of a priority. This raises serious problems for the movement.

Without outreach and organizing efforts, shelters will be further isolated; battered women will be left unsupported as individuals and as an issue. Even though many shelter workers agree with these statements, they feel burdened by the extra efforts they entail. Yet to suggest that more community people share in this work evokes the legitimate fear that its feminist content might be lost.

Community education and organizing tasks can be divided into two spheres, those that build shelters as institutions and those that offer support to battered women separate from any institutional base. Although these tasks are not mutually exclusive, they will be separated for discussion purposes.

One way to extend support for battered women is to expand the definition of service work and start speaker's bureaus, political action, or community education committees, staffed by battered women and community residents. Such work not only builds service organizations, but also provides more battered women access to information, educates the community, gains public support for shelters, and provides the organization with an ongoing volunteer base. For example, in Brooklyn, after ten weeks of training, the ten women in the Park Slope Safe Homes Project Speaker's Bureau chose to do outreach to community schools, day care centers, PTA's, and tenant groups. Every neighborhood group in this category received information about the project and its services followed by phone calls asking that a Safe Homes Project speaker talk to the group. Every month, each Speaker's Bureau participant specifically solicited three new community groups. Hundreds of neighborhood residents were reached through these efforts, including battered women and new volunteers. Additionally, networks were built with staff or community members in other organizations who then served as supports to battered women and the Safe Homes Project.

Redefining volunteer training as political education, organizations can mitigate fears of losing their feminist content. In the Park Slope Safe Homes Project, most Speaker's Bureau participants had been battered or had worked providing services to battered women. It was assumed that Speaker's Bureau participants had to be as knowledgeable as staff and that political education within the community was their principal task. As a result, their training included discussions like: 1. why we as women work on this issue; 2. why women are beaten; 3. why it is difficult for battered women to leave or find help; 4. why men and the community are responsible for stopping violence against women and; 5. how individuals and groups can help battered women. Myths, facts, and political analyses were torn apart and reconstructed by participants. Within the training group, participants were requested to develop their own presentations; the goal was to clearly and nonrhetorically explain battered women's rights to a better life and to engage the community in efforts to end violence. Although these efforts entail major staff work, they also bring new energy to the movement, politicize more women, and offer women opportunities to grow. Just as services teach volunteers hotline-listening skills, they can also teach public speaking and organizing. To transmit a political vision to more women increases leadership possibilities in a movement that quickly burns out its leaders.

Groups may also want to form political action committees which might establish five-year shelter survival plans. Such groups could analyze budgetary priorities, local forces that could help or hurt the shelter, and alliances necessary to protect the shelter. Or, focusing in a different direction, such groups might form broad based local alliances or ask an outside political action group to publicly document the problems facing battered women. Engaging in a political and moral offensive, urban shelters, through press conferences, public hearings, tribunals, and street theatre, could use their statistics to publicize the unmet shelter, housing, legal, and financial needs of battered women. Political action committees might do public reviews of agencies such as Criminal Court. The community needs to know how cutbacks and institutional problems concretely affect battered women and their children. Lack of services needs to be labeled as brutal and discussed in human, not bureaucratic, terms.

Outreach to the community can also be done through conferences. In the spring of 1981, after months of soliciting interest and ideas, the Park Slope Safe Homes Project sponsored a conference aimed at women's groups and organizations that had expressed interest in establishing community based services for battered women in Brooklyn. Approximately fifty people attended the conference, many of them former battered women. As a result of this organizing effort, several neighborhood women's groups have started services. The dream of a borough-wide women's safety network took one small step forward.

Shelter committees might work with other community groups to develop new sets of norms that condemn violence against women. Outreach to major community institutions like churches, schools, block clubs, or political groups could build support for battered women outside the shelter. For example, in meetings between shelters and local churches, suggestions could be made about forming a neighborhood ecumenical group on violence against women. The shelter might offer several large training sessions, inviting people from each church to learn about battered women and how to help them. In one Brooklyn church, after contact with a local project, the clergyman preached against violence, urged battered women to call their local shelters, and took a strong stand with violent husbands, declaring their behavior wrong and insisting they seek help. He has actively supported women in their efforts to leave abusive husbands and sought information about counseling methods that place responsibility upon the man. Although many religious institutions will not take such stands, individuals within them might. Battered women are enormously relieved to hear a trusted institution publicly articulate that violence against them is wrong and not to be endured. Many women who refuse to call shelters will often turn to a familiar support network, like church peers. Church groups might also provide their own services, like safe homes networks. Shelter input into the politics and content of such services is necessary; while time-consuming, in the long run an important community network could be created, serving as an additional support to the shelter and battered women.

In an educational effort to declare woman abuse wrong, the schools must play an active role. Enlisting teachers to develop a curriculum on child abuse and woman abuse could serve many useful purposes. Many shelters are concerned about gearing educational materials toward adolescents since many young women are already being battered by their boyfriends. Adolescents have questions about differentiating love and affection from jealous possession; in educational presentations, many girls are genuinely frightened of becoming battered women and want to know how to distinguish those men who will batter from those who will not.

Efforts within schools would also provide thousands of children with norms different than those sanctioning violence against women. They would create possibilities for currently abused children or the children of battered women to share their pain, guilt, and fear. Or, self-defense classes for children could teach assertiveness training along with the myths and facts about sexual assault and violence. Young girls need to grow up with the sense that they have a right to control their bodies, rather than feel incapacitated if attacked. Creating new kinds of curricula, especially in these times of shrinking budgets for public schools, is not an easy task. Feminist teachers and parents will have to lobby persistently and persuasively for such changes, working with battered women's organizations that could serve as program consultants. Even if a school agrees to institute new courses, for them to be effective a commitment to teacher education is necessary. Otherwise, the curricula will be depoliticized, and there is always the danger that sexist teachers will reinforce sexist norms. Parent, teacher, or shelter monitoring groups might alleviate some of these worries, yet, like other reforms, the risks, benefits, and time commitments need to be weighed. Some activists are eager to begin work on school projects because developing preventive measures gives them a sense of hope.

Some will choose to work within institutions like hospitals and counseling agencies. Since staff within large bureaucracies reach far more women than shelters, their response is critical. The problem, however, is that training them can consume organizers' energy. It might be more helpful for the movement to identify key supportive personnel within a variety of institutional settings and strengthen their efforts at changing their own agencies. For example, shelters might decide to train several women from each of an area's key hospitals. Training might include not only skill development and political discussion but also strategies for effectively organizing within the hospital to help battered women. Women working at different hospitals could also form their own support network.

Unless a hospital designs a protocol to serve battered women, committing resources to ongoing staff training to carry it out adequately, and unless a social service agency agrees to examine its practices, sensitize staff, and offer advocacy, not just therapy, for battered women, very little actually changes.

On another level, community supports for battered women and new norms opposing violence could be developed through block by block organizing. One activist has suggested finding two women per block who would serve as organizers.[26] After being carefully trained by a shelter or by former battered women, these organizers would approach their neighbors with several concerns; for example, how can people help battered women on the block and how can they stop violence. Dialogues about how battered women and shelters are perceived in the community could provide important feedback to the movement. In these efforts, careful attention must be paid to protecting organizers as well as to discouraging any form of vigilantism or racist solutions. The purpose of these efforts, to extend battered women's support networks and to reeducate the community, would have to be publicly delineated. Within a neighborhood, organizers could become their own support network or could be loosely affiliated with a shelter to avoid isolation or ostracism.

Many battered women do not know shelters exist or will not use them. One examination of 500 case records in 12 LEAA funded family violence projects showed that three-fourths of the victims reported prior abuse or threats, but only 10% reported any prior efforts to seek assistance from domestic violence programs.[27] The movement needs to think about community support for women who do not want to leave their neighborhoods. Community based self-help networks for women who have left their husbands and for those who have not are critical. These groups demonstrate to women that independence from violent men can be combined with community based support. For women who stay with violent men, hope and strength are generated by knowing alternatives are available.

The search for community solutions continues. Safe homes projects may gain greater appeal as more emphasis is placed on neighborhood organizing. Safe homes projects are attractive for two distinct reasons. Because shelters are costly to maintain, some bureaucrats view safe homes, provided by community residents, as a cheap alternative to refuges. In a time of budget cutting, inexpensive programs are appealing. Activists have a different view. For them, safe homes are one possible solution to women's needs for short-term housing and support, especially if a court will order a violent man out of his home within a few days.

Safe homes projects, however, must be linked to shelters so that those women who must flee the area and those who have longer-term housing needs can find refuge. Like shelter volunteers, safe homes providers must be sensitized to battered women's needs and educated about the nature of violence against women. It is important to caution that, like shelters, neighborhood homes can provide safety without empowering battered women or helping them understand why they are beaten. In fact, the problems are potentially greater in safe homes, where women are likely to feel isolated. In these programs, it is therefore essential that battered women are offered sensitive support and advocacy by the safe homes family, project staff, and former battered women.

In Boston, Casa Myrna Vazquez is using community organizers to help battered women who have relocated in new neighborhoods. These organizers help women establish a new network and encourage community institutions to begin services for them. Their efforts connect self-help models to available community resources.[29]

Not all or even most of the community organizing projects described here must be connected to a shelter. Politically, the movement must reiterate that it is a community responsibility to stop violence and help battered women. It is politically dangerous for shelters to make it look as if they solve the problem.

Future organizing work will proceed in numerous directions. Ingenuity and perserverance were the calling cards of the first movement activists and will be needed again. Battered women's services issued a challenge to centuries of male domination and they are now being met with a strong counter-challenge. Even if shelters close, or stay open with few or no staff, the movement faces the task of changing public consciousness and offering battered women support. Whether through woman-controlled shelters, hotlines, community education projects, or direct action groups, women must continue to challenge the male right to batter. Defeats, although numerous, will never negate the historic creation of so many safe spaces for battered women and their children. As long as women stay organized and visible, the soil for the next generation of activists remains fertile.

CHAPTER 13

The Contributions of the Battered Women's Movement: A Premature Assessment

The battered women's movement has given women back their lives and dignity. Because it has labored persistently with care and courage to make this possible, it deserves unqualified praise. A former battered woman justifies this claim.

> My husband beat me, strangled me and told my children and family, who believed him, that I was having an affair with another man.
>
> On May 29th, 1980 I had a business, a husband, brothers and sisters, friends, and two children. On May 31st I woke up and had nothing—no business, husband or family. Everyone disappeared. I lost all material possessions and I lost all my trust in people. I then knew what earthquake victims feel. Everything was gone.
>
> By the time I found the shelter I wasn't sure if I wanted to starve to death, kill myself or someone else. I asked to see a psychiatrist and my advocate went with me to the hospital. The psychiatrist gave me three pills and said, "These pills and a glass of wine will kill you." He gave me permission to kill myself. My advocate won't let me take them. She fought with the doctor for me. All she and I did was talk. That was the turning point. She didn't judge me; we met each other halfway. I found someone to trust.[1]

Thousands of women have changed their lives dramatically as a result of using services or finding support. The women whose stories opened this book are now students, and one is a committed volunteer in a neighborhood women's center. She recently helped to start crisis

services for battered women. Her life and thousands of others
generate the hope and courage that keep activists going, just as the
millions of women who are still abused daily or monthly testify
silently to the need for strong feminist and grassroots movements.

Looking at some of the achievements and problems of the
battered women's movement illuminates both its strengths and
weaknesses. The "laboratory" provided by the movement offers
important insights for the future of feminist theory and practice.

To meet the overwhelming needs of battered women, activists
appealed to the broadest possible audience. This simultaneously
expanded feminism's base and eroded it. Thousands of people's lives
were changed by feminist explanations of violence against women;
in hundreds of towns, many shelter and community residents
became adamant feminists through exposure to services or educational events. Because of the compassionate help and political
explanations they provided, services were a vehicle to convince
many that male domination and brutality had to be stopped. But a
broad based appeal to help battered women had other consequences
as well. It brought into organizations people who either wittingly or
unwittingly undermined the radical insights about violence against
women and cooperative work structures that feminists and grassroots women had created. With no reference point to a larger
women's, progressive, or even self-help movement, it was easier for
many committed people to turn shelters into traditional, professional social service agencies.

The limited power of feminist and grassroots women's organizations showed itself as academics, government bureaucrats, and
professionals jumped upon the issue; for a short, heady moment
battered women became a "relevant" topic in the United States. The
movement faced the paradox, as most small, singularly focused
movements do, that the more it demanded for battered women, the
more individuals and institutions did respond. At least in some
places battered women's needs were recognized and legitimated. Yet
the definition of the problem did not always stay within the
movement's grasp, nor could activists control those drawn to the
issue.

In single issue organizing, it is particularly easy to minimize the
differences that exist within a movement. Today, "battered women's movement" defines what women share, while it also masks
differences created by local conditions, life experiences, and political
views. While there are numerous kinds of divisions, the broadest one
is between those who view violence against women as a political and

social issue and those who see it as an individual problem. The former position leads activists to identify closely with battered women, understanding the vulnerability of all women, while the latter allows individuals to distance themselves from abused women. This is one of the fundamental splits within the movement; these positions get translated into distinct kinds of services and support.

The battered women's movement, like any movement that brings together diverse individuals, struggles for political definition. Generally, winning as much as possible and protecting battered women has been the shared goal. Even this, however, can be problematic, since it tends to downplay the fact that battered women of different races, classes, and geographic areas have different needs. Gaining more for battered women is a logical choice but it also leads to minimizing other forms of oppression, like racism, that equally harm women. If those women with power in the movement hold firmly to the position, "our work is to help battered women and not to confront racism," then it is impossible to build a movement for all women. The experiences of the battered women's movement remind us of the extent of class and race domination within the United States, and underscore the difficulty of building a multi-racial movement at this time, within a single issue framework.

Single issue movements call for constantly shifting alliances. Work occurs simultaneously on many fronts—organizing, lobbying, educating, and maintaining institutions. Only through broad based organizing do women win appropriations, progressive reforms, and the bureaucratic allies necessary for continuing success. The framework—helping battered women—unites these shifting and carefully negotiated efforts. Yet at some point, too much work must be done by too few women to avoid making choices about political direction. As dilemmas heighten, differences threaten to split unity.

If the battered women's movement offers any answers to the problems of organizing among diverse women, they are tentative ones, sometimes inspiring but sometimes limited. State battered women's coalitions serve as one hopeful model for incorporating diversity. Based on women's movement principles of personal caring and sisterhood, many coalitions have insisted on making racism and heterosexism awareness top priorities. In these groups, women have literally learned to hear those with realities different than their own, and they have personally grown and politically changed.

Battered women's coalitions have been highly successful not only because they developed carefully defined and limited goals, but also because they incorporated lessons from the early women's movement: individuals must be respected; all must have an opportunity to speak; trust building is as important as goal setting. Yet the challenge ahead for coalitions is great. They must continue to help women grow from diversity, especially that of race, class, and sexual preference.

At the same time, feminists within broad based coalitions need to clarify and express their own political views. If, in the interest of unity, the feminist battered women's movement ceases to put forward its political visions, the movement will be deprived of one of its primary sources of strength. Feminists defined violence against women as a political problem to be solved with political solutions, and this insight must survive. Without it, battered women will disappear again—their plight reprivatized.

Any analysis of the movement must emphasize that, without feminism, there might have been no battered women's movement. Feminism, especially radical feminism, set the general social and political groundwork for women to label private problems as social ones. Although feminism too quickly lumped all women together in the same mold, women, including battered women, were freed by its sharp focus on gender hierarchies and male domination. As the feminist movement uncovered layers of oppression and provided centers where women could meet and talk, battered women emerged and began to see their experiences as political ones.

Often feminists moved to protect women when no one else would. Even in places where there were no feminists, a local battered women's shelter or rape crisis center owes a debt to its feminist sisters. A feminist political movement, organized and visible, made it possible for all women to demand needed changes and win some of them.

A feminist movement encouraged women to organize on their own behalves; it helped spawn many forms of women's movements and led to the creation of a multitude of reforms and new kinds of services. Although in 1982 many feel that a progressive women's movement is less visible and perhaps dying, the view from the battered women's movement suggests a different assessment. As long as feminist and grassroots women's shelters exist in hundreds of towns across the country, a progressive women's movement with diverse politics is very much alive. Although this movement is difficult to categorize, its fierce commitments to women's self-determination, self-organization, and democratic participation declare it an important bearer of a liberating vision.

When the battered women's movement began, it unleashed a plea for safety and support, long held back in millions of women. It offered an alternative to violence—a safe space—a shelter. As activists continue to demand shelter space, they also realize that refuge is only one step in ending violence against women. Yet this first step was a gigantic one, strengthening women individually and collectively, offering hope, and tipping the power imbalance between the sexes to allow some women to escape and others to stop abuse through their threats of leaving. As a collective effort, the shelter movement not only saves lives, but also inspires women to organize together and help one another. As sisters, not competitors, women learn to find sustenance from one another and their dependence on violent or bullying men is diminished.

Battered women best explain the weighty psychic transformation which occurs in one woman after another.

> I felt dirty, filthy, stupid, ugly, fat. I was 20 pounds underweight. He told me again and again, "You're fat." You hear it for 5 years and you believe it. I began to feel I was stupid. It took me a year to lift my eyes up.[2]

Although women's individual feelings vary, expressing them together creates a liberating impact. Woman after woman declares, "I don't feel so alone; I was wracked with guilt and responsibility before I came; I find strength I did not know was mine." The effects extend into all areas of daily life: "You don't know what it means to be free of terror; I can do what I want with my time; I'm so relieved—this is the first time I've slept in weeks." Emotional support relieves burdens and rebuilds trust.

As private pain is shared, explanations for abuse shift and responsibility is placed squarely in the hands of a violent man.

> It was planned. He would try to get me to argue. It wasn't drugs. He got loaded and said he didn't know what he was doing. Bullshit. He knew what he was doing.[3]

Women reach new understandings about themselves and their lives.

> I've been away from him since last January and I know what I can and cannot do. It feels good that I've got my own apartment and I pay the bills. I have a disability and he thought I'd never be able to take care of the kids.[4]

Battered women's services create the room that allows women to safely reflect and reach their own conclusions. "When I was with him, I wasn't able to feel angry. It's too frightening. When I began to feel angry, I began to heal." She continues, "You develop strengths from years of beating that you did not know you had; you have to have a space to learn about them."[5]

In literally six to eight weeks, shelters not only change women's self-perceptions but also their thoughts about male-female relationships, sex roles, and the meanings behind the violence.

> Do or die I will raise my children with the understanding that no matter how much or what kind of physical abuse man has perpetrated on his subordinates, it is not and cannot be used to make another human being do what you want them to do, nor is it humane to use another person as a punching bag, to take your frustrations out on.[6]

Shelters help women make concrete changes in their lives; women who yearly find apartments or jobs, for example, number in the thousands. Children raised free from terror multiply into the tens of thousands. Other forms of change are more difficult to document but equally potent. The confidence to start over, often with no material possessions or resources, comes not only out of the fear of being killed, but also out of strength. By emphasizing women's ability to act competently for themselves, shelters help women experience their abilities and power. As she traces how external supports become internalized, a former battered woman eloquently captures the transformation from self-blame to self-love.

> I started healing one day when I was full of self-pity and guilt. Then I said, 'you have comforted so many people in your life with a word or a hug. Can you do that for yourself? Can you feel compassion for Tina? Tina has a problem; she hurts; she is in pain. Can Tina give compassion to Tina? Not pity but compassion.'[7]

Shelters politicize women partly through developing a new pride and trust in women as a group.

> ...we include and politicise those women who have been most cut off from the struggles and ideas of women's liberation...and yet these women, through their experience, and through the strength and confidence they gain from the other women in the Women's Aid centre, become politicised and vehement in their struggle for their rights as women, and are not prepared to suffer their oppression as individual isolated women any longer...they are ready to fight and can and must join us in all our struggles as women.[8]

Not only do women develop a new political understanding of why they were beaten, why institutions failed to respond, and why violence is not their fault, but they form this analysis in a supportive environment. In fact, many suggest that a sharing community is the only context in which women can gain the courage necessary to reduce their dependence on men.

Following the lead of the anti-rape movement, battered women's shelters also began to help those children who are sexually and physically assaulted. Even where no direct contact exists between activists providing services to rape victims, battered women, sexual harassment victims, and incest survivors, feminists have gained insights about the exercise of male dominance, power, and violence, inside and outside the family, that are richly cross-fertilizing one another and leading to new theories and counseling methods for women and children victims and their male assaulters.

Collectively the movements to stop violence against women have had an enormous impact on women's consciousness. In the last ten years activists have discovered that violence restricts women's ability to move freely and confidently in the world and therefore hinders their full development. The fear of violence robs women of possibilities, self-confidence, and self-esteem. In this sense, violence is more than a physical assault; it is an attack on women's dignity and freedom.

The battered women's movement has also had an impact on many women who do not use shelters. Though the movement's efforts to effect institutional change were sometimes thwarted, important victories gained at least some battered women more respectful treatment. Challenging years of institutionalized sexism, the movement publicly declared that the courts and police were dangerous to women. In some cases, these institutions responded and improved the ways in which they dealt with battered women.

To challenge or change the institutional treatment of battered women means that women gain more tools to stop violence. Orders of protection or vacate orders can mean the difference between another brutal beating or safety. These orders, however, are more than potential protection; they symbolize that violence is unjust and criminal. They tell women that their pain is taken seriously and they tell men their behavior is wrong, that violence must cease, and that women are the aggrieved party, not the criminals.

According to many activists, the greatest success of the movement has been in changing public consciousness about battered women and thus creating a larger safety net for them. Through continual educational outreach and careful use of the media, the movement has managed, despite opposition, to make battering a social, not a private, problem. While this larger, less specific form of social change is impossible to measure, it can be documented by the countless people who approach activists to talk about how they might help their neighbors or to say that they already did. For many, it is now common sense that violence is caused by men, not pathological or nagging women; people also understand, often in unarticulated ways, that it is the more powerful partner who can invoke violence as a punishing form of social control. The rapidity with which the movement created this new worldview is astounding.

The battered women's movement changed consciousness in another way as well. It challenged the idea that the family is always a safe haven from a brutal world. As violence in the family is documented, many react with anger, guilt, and fear, accusing feminists of hating men and destroying tradition. The family, however, can never be as sacred as it once was, and the seemingly private sphere of the family and the public sphere of social and work life will never be quite so separate again. Although breaking down this distance creates the potential for further abusive state intervention into the family, it also allows women some protection. Male privilege and domination are further eroded as violence is redefined from appropriate chastisement directed toward an inferior to criminal abuse. This radical redefinition signifies how deeply male domination, even within its hidden bastion, is under attack.

The contributions of the battered women's movement involve not only content, but process as well. Its use of feminist self-help as both a service and a political strategy continues a tradition followed within the women's movement and offers important insights for future political activity. Self-help validates non-hierarchical, non-professional service models as the most effective form of helping battered women.

> I never asked an Indian woman who has been beaten how she's feeling. I can see she's feeling miserable. She's scared—I let her know that I know she's scared and let her know that I've been through it and made it. I tell her how I stopped being beaten and got out of it....
> I don't consider her a client because then she'll react like a typical client. I consider her the best friend I ever had and show her she's not alone....[9]

Theoretically, as women experience egalitarian service models, they themselves will start to question hierarchical and authoritarian relations. As more and more women are offered a new vision of how people should treat one another, new political possibilities emerge.

The predominant institutions created by the battered women's movement—shelters, safe homes networks, and coalitions—suggest that women have learned valuable lessons about building organizations based on participation and democracy. In a time when true democracy, people controlling the decisions that affect their lives, is harder and harder to find, such efforts need to be studied closely. Not only have women created a network of institutions that affirm women's rights to control their lives and that validate women as strong, but they have also struggled with major organizational questions. How are democratic models created, maintained, and nurtured? In what ways do different organizational needs or roles subtly work to reinstate hierarchy? Can alternative institutions based on models of cooperation survive in their interactions with government bureaucracies?

The relationship between what a movement politically believes in and how it organizes itself reaches to the center of progressive concerns. If the women's movement sees its goal as creating a new society based on ending all forms of domination, women must practice living these new forms. Given the forces operating against the movement, the task is a difficult one; some might say impossible. However, this attempt not only inspires thousands of women to support the women's movement and to continue struggling, but also generates hope for a new world.

The battered women's movement, like many parts of the feminist movement, affirms the importance of personal relationships. Women shared their skills and experiences, and together, through their networks, legitimated a grassroots view of services which was particularly important as articulate and powerful professionals moved into the field. Perhaps most significant, however, these networks enabled the movement to build a power base and to avoid massive internal divisions and competition. Major differences clearly exist within the movement. However, by emphasizing unity and by refusing to compete with one another, shelters within the same state often stopped bureaucratic maneuvering that might have easily pitted one group against another. By acknowledging the significance of personal ties and connections to other movement organizers and time spent building these relationships, activists formed coalitions centered in norms of non-competition that might well serve as models for other political struggles.

The battered women's movement has brought together women of all classes and races, and in doing so, compels its participants to confront issues of diversity among women. Battered women's shelters were the first facilities in which women of all classes and races lived together for months at a time. The significance of this for the women's movement as a whole cannot be underestimated. Women in shelters were forced to understand the concrete needs of poor and third world women—for housing, welfare, clothing, and food. And women came to see the importance of understanding domination as it operates between women.

In its organizing efforts, the battered women's movement has effectively used models built upon moral persuasion, consciousness raising, and public education. The movement took the facts of women's daily lives, politically reinterpreted them, and insisted on concrete change. The horrors facing battered women, the movement's moral focus on injustice, and its persistence in winning services proved a potent combination. The movement concretized its demands in the form of shelters; it raised a symbol for freeing women from brutality that captured the attention of a far wider network than feminists.

To start 500 shelters, win legal and social service reforms in hundreds of localities, form almost 50 state coalitions, and capture the imagination of a nation in approximately 8 years are extraordinary achievements. Far more critical of itself than outsiders are, the movement must acknowledge the dramatic and powerful changes it has effected for women. Eager to reform the world, radical activists must remember that they have accomplished much while, at the same time, they face the fact that the fight to save shelters and win women's liberation will be a long, hard one, continuing through generations. Activists must remind themselves that battered women's major obstacles continue to be profound sexism, economic discrimination, and a lack of options. While the movement has significantly challenged this reality, it continues pervasively. Hope can easily turn to despair unless women acknowledge all they have done together under difficult conditions in so brief a time.

Most significantly, the battered women's movement has created a vision of a better life for women and an alternative to enduring degrading brutality. But battered women are not the only ones to have benefitted from this movement. In services, coalitions, and organizing work, activists find meaning and mastery as they exercise their skills and share their talents. They, too, feel "empowered," the illusive word that embodies the sense of controlling one's life and circumstances. As women courageously decide to leave violent husbands, sacrificing all they have worked to gain, they are met by those who also sacrifice yet often thrive through their work. Activists grow from the courage battered women display, the strength accumulated through mastering problems and fighting injustice, and the unalienated work and social relationships some experience within movement organizations. For the most part, the match between battered women and activists has been a fortuitous one. Working together, they created the first public spaces in history through which women were offered visible alternatives to violent men. It is not grandiose to suggest that in eight years, the battered women's movement has transformed the world for many. Its vision and hard work, its caring and inspiration, have been sustained through the collective efforts of women.

Appendix

Statement read at the Fifth National Conference on Child Abuse and Neglect, April 1981, Milwaukee, Wisconsin.

With data indicating a considerable correlation of spouse abuse with child abuse and neglect, it would be both cost effective and treatment effective to combine funding and programs for child protection and spouse abuse in a new framework of family violence.

Against Consolidation with Child Abuse Services

by Susan Schechter

Several major problems and dangerous generalizations are presented in this statement that I wish to challenge as a representative of the National Coalition Against Domestic Violence, a grassroots organization of hundreds of battered women's programs. First, we must clarify our terminology, or we will misunderstand completely the important issues raised. Terms like spouse abuse and family violence mislead us and obscure the issues with which we are concerned—systematic violence directed against women and children in the family. Calling the behavior spouse abuse, rather than woman abuse, suggests an equality between men and women that does not exist; probably over 97 percent of serious assaults between adults in the home are directed at women. Secondly, significant data suggest that the majority of men who beat their wives do *not* beat their children. In one analysis of 933 incidents of wife assault, only 62 involved violence directed at a child.[1] Additionally, many men who batter women were not battered children. Although we too are concerned about child abuse, from men or women, the correlation argument is simplistic, grossly exaggerated, and scientifically disputed. That individual men who were beaten as children are more likely to beat their wives still tells us nothing about why women as a group are beaten, or why men who were not beaten as children beat their wives.

We argue against combining services on these and other grounds. Most importantly, battered women exist today as a social category only because former battered women and feminists insisted that safety for women had to be provided as a priority. A political movement, formed through the will and hard work of grassroots

1. R. Emerson Dobash and Russell Dobash, *Violence Against Wives* (New York: The Free Press, 1979), p. 150.

women, created this safety, founding over 500 programs in seven years. The model of service developed was significantly different from that used in child protection. It assumes that battered women are in a situational crisis caused by the repeated violence that this society has allowed men to carry out. Battered women are not disabled; they and their children are facing violence, pain, fear, and major dislocations. Adult women have responded best to small, non-bureaucratic programs in which self-help and self-determination are emphasized. Women regain control over their lives through finding safety, emotional support from other women, and advocacy. Children experience the same support and advocacy within many shelters. These services articulate a vision that sees violence as a result of the unequal power between men and women and sees adult women as competent to control their own lives.

Child abuse and violence against women are different phenomena with different historical roots. A major goal of child protection services is to keep the family united, hopefully free from violence. Our goal is to support a woman in creating a violence-free life for herself and her children in whatever way she chooses. You must provide a form of protection and caretaking that is necessary for children but demeaning and debilitating for adults. Child protection services were organized because children are dependent. Battered women's service provision fundamentally challenges women's dependence, asserting the necessity of independence in order to be free from violence. Two clearly different forms of intervention are required. To use only one means women will be treated as incompetent and denied the very autonomy needed to escape victimization.

Politically, it is in the interest of the Reagan administration and any other state or local government in a time of cutbacks to pit us against one another to fight over the same scarce resources. By pretending to unite us by using the rubric of family violence, the stage has been set for us to compete over a pittance. We will all be the losers. Reactionaries have attacked the rights won by the women's movement; Phyllis Schlafly has called battered women's shelters "luxury hotels." She wants women at home at all costs, even mutilated. In the past we unwittingly made battered women invisible; let us not wittingly make battered women invisible again by hiding them under child abuse services and withdrawing funds, as Reagan recently did. Creating a hierarchy of needs in which abused children are more important than battered women is a gigantic step backward. Such policy creates only one sure result— more women will be beaten and killed in their homes. We cannot forget the real issue—thousands of women and children who need shelter are still turned away due to lack of facilities.

We together need to talk on local, state, and national levels. But first we must define our own interests and more carefully explore the motives of those suggesting we merge. I propose we find ways to support each other's work, on our own terms, respecting our differences and autonomy. Without this mutual respect, we will turn battered women into the problem that social services try to treat. But battered women are not the problem; violence against women is the problem. We cannot end violence by solely helping families one by one. Only a battered women's movement can challenge and stop the violence.

author's note: Special thanks to Barbara Hart, Mary Morrison, Mary Haviland, and Allen Steinberg for their help with this statement.

Notes

Introduction

1. Nancy A. Humphreys, "Foreword" in Albert R. Roberts with the assistance of Beverly J. Roberts, *Sheltering Battered Women: A National Study and Service Guide*, Vol. 3: Focus on Women (New York: Springer Publishing, 1981), p. vii.
2. Francis X. Clines and Bernard Weinraub, "Briefing," citing a column that Jo-Ann Gasper wrote in the *Conservative Digest, New York Times,* 12 January 1982.
3. David Gil, *Violence Against Children* (Cambridge, Mass.: Harvard University Press, 1970), p. 72.

Chapter 1

1. Author's interview with Candice Butcher.
2. Author's interview with Sharon Vaughan.
3. Trude Fisher, with Marion P. Winston, "The Grim Plight of Destitute Mothers Who Need Free Rooms on a Stormy Night," *Los Angeles Times,* 12 March 1973, part II, p. 7, cited in Del Martin, "Overview—Scope of the Problem," U.S. Commission on Civil Rights, *Battered Women: Issues of Public Policy,* a consultation, Washington, D.C., 30-31 January 1978, p. 214.
4. "Shelter Statistics April 20-26, 1981," Family and Adult Services, Human Resources Administration, New York City, undated.
5. Anonymous interview.
6. Mary McGuire, "One Woman's Story—Analysis and Solution," *National Communication Network for the elimination of violence against women* I, Issue 3 (October 1977): 6-7.
7. Murray Straus, "Wife Beating: Causes, Treatment, and Research Needs," in U.S. Commission on Civil Rights, *Battered Women: Issues of Public Policy,* p. 153.
8. J.J. Gayford, "Battered Wives," *Medicine, Science, and the Law, xv,* no. 4: 238.
9. Lenore E. Walker, *The Battered Woman* (New York: Harper Colophon Books, Harper and Row, 1979), Intro. p. xv.
10. R. Emerson Dobash and Russell Dobash, *Violence Against Wives: A Case Against the Patriarchy* (New York: The Free Press, Macmillan, 1979), pp. 23-24.
11. *Ibid.,* p. 122.
12. *Ibid.,* p. 120.
13. Cheri Maples, "Take Back the Night," unpublished speech, Madison, Wisconsin, October 10, 1980, p. 1.
14. J.E. O'Brien, "Violence in Divorce Prone Families," *Journal of Marriage and the Family* 33, no. 4 (1971): 692-698.

15. John E. Snell, Richard J. Rosenwald, and Ames Robey, "The Wifebeater's Wife: A Study of Family Interaction," *Archives of General Psychiatry* II (August 1964): 109.
16. *Ibid.*
17. *Ibid.*
18. *Ibid.*, p.110.
19. *Ibid.*, p. 111.
20. *Ibid.*
21. *Ibid.*
22. M. Faulk, "Men Who Assault Their Wives," in Maria Roy, ed., *Battered Women: A Psychosociological Study Of Domestic Violence* (New York: Van Nostrand Reinhold Co., 1977), pp. 121-122.
23. *Ibid.*, p. 121.
24. *Ibid.*, p. 124.
25. *Ibid.*
26. Snell, Rosenwald and Robey, "The Wifebeater's Wife," p. 112.
27. R. Emerson Dobash, "The Negotiation of Daily Life and the 'Provocation' of Violence: A Patriarchal Concept in Support of the Wife Beater" (Paper presented at the Ninth World Congress of Sociology, August 1978, Uppsala, Sweden), pp. 19-20.
28. Evan Stark, Anne Flitcraft, and William Frazier, "Medicine and Patriarchal Violence: The Social Construction of a 'Private' Event," *International Journal of Health Services* 9, no. 3 (1979): 466.
29. *Ibid.*, p. 467.
30. *Ibid.*, p. 474.
31. Marjory Fields, "Wife Beating: Government Intervention Policies and Practices," in U.S. Commission on Civil Rights, *Battered Women: Issues of Public Policy*, pp. 234-235.
32. Diane Brown, "Out On My Own—Still Being Victimized," unpublished speech, Confronting Woman Abuse: A Working Conference for the Midwest, Chicago, 23-24 April 1979.
33. R. Emerson Dobash and Russell Dobash, *Violence Against Wives*, p. 164.

chapter 2

1. Sara Evans, *Personal Politics* (New York: Alfred A. Knopf, 1979), p. 24.
2. *Ibid.*, p. 170.
3. Jo Freeman, *The Politics of Women's Liberation: A Case Study of an Emerging Social Movement* (New York: David McKay Co., 1975), p. 28.
4. See Nanette Rainone, ed., "Men and Violence," transcript of a taped consciousness-raising session, WBAI Radio, New York, 1970.
5. Beverly Jones, "The Dynamics of Marriage and Motherhood," in Robin Morgan, ed., *Sisterhood Is Powerful: An Anthology of Writings from the Women's Liberation Movement* (New York: Vintage Books, Random House, 1970), p. 47.
6. Kathy McAfee and Myrna Wood, "Bread and Roses," in Leslie B. Tanner, ed., *Voices From Women's Liberation* (New York: Signet, New American Library, 1970), p. 421.

7. Personal communication from Gail Sullivan, based on an interview with Lisa Leghorn and Betsy Warrior.

8. Although other shelters started before Women's Advocates, these programs often began as services for the wives of alcoholics, rather than as projects for battered women.

9. Author's interview with Sharon Vaughan.

10. Author's interview with Rachel Burger; author's interview with Lisa Leghorn.

11. Author's interview with Freada Klein.

12. *Ibid.*

13. Susan Brownmiller, "Introduction" in Florence Rush, *The Best Kept Secret: Sexual Abuse of Children* (New York: McGraw-Hill, 1980), p. viii.

14. Author's interview with Freada Klein.

15. Michelle Wasserman, "Rape: Breaking the Silence," *The Progressive,* November 1973, p. 19.

16. Chicago Women Against Rape, undated brochure.

17. Material distributed by Chicago Women Against Rape, undated.

18. Susan Griffin, "Rape—The All-American Crime," *Ramparts,* September 1971, pp. 26 and 35.

19. Martha Weinman Lear, "The American Way of Rape," *Viva,* November 1974, p. 43.

20. Mary Ann Largen, "Grassroots Centers and National Task Forces: A Herstory of the Anti-Rape Movement," *Aegis: Magazine on Ending Violence Against Women* No. 32 (Autumn 1981): 48.

21. Susan Griffin, "Rape—The All-American Crime," p. 35.

22. I. Nkenge Toure, "An Overview of Third World Women and Violence," report from the First National Conference on Third World Women and Violence, D.C. Rape Crisis Center, 1981, p. 3.

23. Telephone interview with Mary Ann Largen.

24. Elizabethann O'Sullivan, "What Has Happened to Rape Crisis Centers? A Look at Their Structures, Members, and Funding," *Victimology: An International Journal* 3, Nos. 1-2 (1978): 56.

25. Notes from the author's journal.

26. Deb Friedman, "Rape, Racism—and Reality," *FAAR and NCN News* (July-August 1978): 17.

27. *Ibid.,* p. 18, citing Socialist Women's Caucus of Louisville, "The Racist Use of Rape and the Rape Charge."

28. "The Racist Use of Rape and the Rape Charge: A Statement to the Women's Movement from a Group of Socialist Women," Socialist Women's Caucus of Louisville, Kentucky, July 1975, p. 3.

29. Deb Friedman, "Rape, Racism—and Reality," p. 21.

30. Anne Braden, "A Second Open Letter To Southern White Women," *Southern Exposure* 4, No. 4 : 50-51.

31. *Ibid.,* p. 52.

32. Angela Davis, *Women, Race and Class* (New York: Random House, 1981), p. 7.

33. See *Feminist Alliance Against Rape Newsletter* (September-October 1976): 11-12.

34. Freada Klein, "Learning from the Anti-Rape Movement," *National Communication Network for the elimination of violence against women* 1, issue 4 (December 1977): 1-2.
35. Notes from the author's journal.
36. Author's interview with Freada Klein.
37. Author's interview with Freada Klein.
38. Lisa Leghorn, personal communication.
39. Lisa Leghorn, "Social Responses to Battered Women," *Feminist Alliance Against Rape Newsletter* (March-April 1977): 22.
40. Lisa Leghorn, personal communication.
41. Lisa Leghorn, "Social Responses to Battered Women," p. 19.
42. Charlotte Bunch for the Furies Collective, "Lesbians in Revolt," *The Furies*, January 1972, cited in Jo Freeman, *The Politics of Women's Liberation*, pp. 137-138.
43. Anonymous interview.
44. The Combahee River Collective, "A Black Feminist Statement," in Zillah R. Eisenstein, ed., *Capitalist Patriarchy and the Case For Socialist Feminism* (New York: Monthly Review, 1979), pp. 365-366.
45. Marta Segovia Ashley, "Shelters: Short-Term Needs," in U.S. Commission on Civil Rights, *Battered Women: Issues of Public Policy,* a consultation, Washington, D.C., 30-31 January 1978, p. 376.
46. Anonymous personal communication.
47. Special thanks to the women who answered my question after a workshop in Pennsylvania in the winter of 1981.

chapter 3

1. Diane Brown, "Out On My Own—Still Being Victimized," unpublished speech, Confronting Woman Abuse: A Working Conference for the Midwest, Chicago, 23-24 April 1979.
2. Mark A. Schulman, *A Survey of Spousal Violence Against Women in Kentucky*, U.S. Department of Justice, Law Enforcement Assistance Administration, Study No. 792701, July 1979, p. 1.
3. Marjory D. Fields, "Wife Beating: Government Intervention Policies and Practices," U.S. Commission on Civil Rights, *Battered Women: Issues of Public Policy*, a consultation, Washington, D.C., 30-31 January 1978, p. 235.
4. *Ibid.*, p. 249.
5. *Ibid.*, p. 257.
6. Candace Wayne, personal communication.
7. Materials distributed by the Chicago Abused Women's Coalition, undated.
8. Telephone interview with Ruth Slaughter.
9. Women's Center-South, undated leaflet.
10. Suzanne Rini-McClintock, "Pittsburgh's Only Shelter For Women In Crisis May Soon Loose (sic) The Roof Over Its Head," *Pittsburgh New Sun*, 6 May 1976, p. 5.
11. Carol Ford, "Lifeline to Battered Women," *Sojourner*, September 1980.
12. *Ibid.*

13. *Ibid.*
14. Presentation of Marta Segovia-Ashley, read by Shelly Fernández, "Shelters: Short-Term Needs," U.S. Commission on Civil Rights, *Battered Women: Issues of Public Policy*, pp. 101-102.
15. Author's interview with Susan Kelly-Dreiss.
16. Curdina Hill, personal communication.
17. Author's interview with Nydia Díaz.
18. Anonymous, "Living at Harriet Tubman Women's Shelter," *Aegis: Magazine on Ending Violence Against Women*, Summer/Autumn 1980, pp. 18-19.
19. Anonymous interview.
20. Anonymous interview.
21. Curdina Hill and Renae Scott, "Culture in the Kitchen," *Aegis*, November-December 1978, p. 39.
22. Joani Kamman, "Cost Factors in Providing Battered Women's Services in a Rural Community," NELCWIT, 23 January 1980, p. 2.
23. Shirley J. Kuhle, "Foreword" in Bobby Lacy, *Domestic Violence Services in Rural Communities*, Nebraska Task Force on Domestic Violence, undated, p. 3.
24. *Women's Advocates: The Story of a Shelter* (St. Paul: Women's Advocates, 1980), p. 3.
25. *Ibid.*, p. 4.
26. *Ibid.*, pp. 5-6.
27. Sharon Vaughan, personal communication.
28. *Ibid.*
29. *Women's Advocates: The Story of a Shelter*, p. 90.
30. *Ibid.*, p. 58.
31. *Ibid.*, p. 54.
32. Author's interview with Sharon Vaughan.
33. *Women's Advocates: The Story of a Shelter*, p. 75.
34. Author's interview with Sharon Vaughan.
35. See Betsy Warrior and Lisa Leghorn, *The Houseworker's Handbook*, a pamphlet about the social, political, and economic dimensions of women's role as houseworker.
36. Materials from the files of Transition House, undated.
37. Author's interview with Rachel Burger.
38. *Ibid.*
39. Author's interview with Lisa Leghorn.
40. *Ibid.*
41. Carol Ford, "Lifeline to Battered Women," *Sojourner*, September 1980.
42. Author's interview with Lisa Leghorn.
43. Author's interview with Rachel Burger.
44. *Ibid.*
45. *Ibid.*
46. Author's interview with Sharon Vaughan.
47. Materials distributed at Battered Lives: A Conference Sponsored by the Abused Women's Coalition, 9 October 1976.
48. Notes from the author's journal.

49. Diane Brown, "Out On My Own—Still Being Victimized," unpaged.
50. Chicago Abused Women's Coalition *Newsletter*, Vol. 1, no. 1, December 1976.
51. Monica Erler, "Response of Monica Erler," U.S. Commission on Civil Rights, *Battered Women: Issues of Public Policy*, p. 401.
52. Author's interview with Sharon Vaughan.
53. Author's interview with Susan Kelly-Dreiss.
54. Monica Erler, "Response of Monica Erler," p. 404.
55. Del Martin, *Battered Wives* (San Francisco: Glide Publications, 1976), p. 220.
56. Notes from the author's journal.
57. Anonymous interview.
58. Anonymous interview.
59. Author's interview with Sharon Vaughan.
60. Anne Steytler and Ellen Berliner, personal communication.
61. *Women's Advocates: The Story of a Shelter*, p. 1.
62. Author's interview with Lisa Leghorn.
63. Monica Erler, "Response of Monica Erler," p. 407.

chapter 4

1. Colorado Association for Aid to Battered Women, *A Monograph On Services To Battered Women* (DHHS Publication No. (OHDS) 79-05708), p. 19.
2. Minnesota Statewide Research System on Battered Women, summary of 1979 statistics, undated and unpaged.
3. Colorado Association for Aid to Battered Women, *A Monograph On Services To Battered Women*, p. 25.
4. *Ibid.*, p. 23.
5. "White House Meetings on Violence in the Family," Office of Public Liaison, White House, Washington, D.C., undated, p. 11. Originally cited in *Response to intrafamily violence and sexual assault*.
6. Carol Hussa, Director's Report, *Domestic Violence Service Center Annual Report 1979-1980*, Wilkes-Barre, Pennsylvania, unpaged.
7. Barbara J. Hart, testimony before the Senate Subcommittee on Child and Human Development of the Committee of Labor and Human Resources, 6 February 1980. Taken from National Coalition Against Domestic Violence, First National Meeting Handbook, 27 February-1 March 1980, unpaged.
8. Cynthia Dames, testimony before the Subcommittee on Select Education, House Committee on Education and Labor, 10 July 1979. Taken from National Coalition Against Domestic Violence, First National Meeting Handbook, unpaged.
9. These statistics were generously provided by women around the country and by steering committee representatives to the National Coalition Against Domestic Violence in 1980. The complete shelter statistics, from women reporting, were: New Jersey-12; New York-34; Arkansas-4; Maine-5 shelters and 3 safe homes projects; Hawaii-3; Vermont-1; Massachusetts-31; New Hampshire-4 shelters and 5 safe homes projects; Kentucky-11; Minnesota-

17; Kansas-6; Louisiana-5; Illinois-14; Oklahoma-5; Missouri-13; Wyoming-1; North Carolina-9; South Carolina-2; Tennessee-3.

10. Author's interview with Callie Hutchison.

11. Author's interview with Pat Gearity.

12. Author's interview with Carol Hussa.

13. Monica Erler, "Response of Monica Erler," U.S. Commission on Civil Rights, *Battered Women: Issues of Public Policy*, a consultation, Washington, D.C., 30-31 January 1978, pp. 404-405.

14. Presentation of Marta Segovia-Ashley read by Shelly Fernández, "Shelters: Short-Term Needs," U.S. Commission on Civil Rights, *Battered Women: Issues of Public Policy*, p. 104.

15. Monica Erler, "Response of Monica Erler," p. 405.

16. *Women's Advocates: The Story of a Shelter* (St. Paul: Women's Advocates, 1980), p. 91.

17. Marjory Fields, personal communication.

18. Author's interview with Lee Hewitt.

19. Author's interview with Rachel Burger.

20. Marta Segovia-Ashley, "Shelters: Short-Term Needs," p. 385.

21. Author's interview with Lee Hewitt.

22. Dawn Madison, "My Life In A Shelter For Abused Women," unpublished and undated, p. 2.

23. Author's interview with Sharon Vaughan.

24. Susan Williams, "Note From a Sheltered Battered Woman To Staff And Organizers," *National Communications Network for the elimination of violence against women* 1, Issue 4, (February 1978): 12.

25. Author's interview with Renae Scott.

26. Staff of La Casa de las Madres, letter to *FAAR* and *NCN*, July/August 1978, p. 42.

27. Author's interview with Jackie Boyle.

28. "Shelter Security," *Networking*, Massachusetts Coalition of Battered Women Service Groups, no. 3 (July-November 1980), p. 4.

29. Anonymous interview.

30. Anonymous interview.

31. *Women's Advocates: The Story of a Shelter*, p. 93.

32. Ellen Pence, "The NCADV Handbook on Emergency and Long Term Housing" prepared by the National Coalition Against Domestic Violence, for the First National Meeting Handbook, Introduction, unpaged.

33. *Women's Advocates: The Story of a Shelter*, pp. 48-49.

34. Anonymous interview.

35. Kathleen Joan Ferraro, "Battered Women and the Shelter Movement," Ph.D. dissertation, (Arizona State University), 1981, pp. 170 and 186.

36. Author's interview with Rachel Burger.

37. Special thanks to Anne McGlinchey of Project Work in New York City for our discussion on organizational structure.

38. Author's interview with Flora Lea Louden.

39. Anonymous interview.

40. Anonymous interviews.

41. Bobby Lacy, *Domestic Violence Services in Rural Communities: First Steps in Organization*, Nebraska Task Force on Domestic Violence, p. 5.

42. Material taken from the files of Transition House.

43. Bobby Lacy, *Domestic Violence Services in Rural Communities: Direct Services and Funding*, Nebraska Task Force on Domestic Violence, p. 14.

44. See Lois Ahrens, "Battered Women's Refuges: Feminist Cooperatives vs. Social Service Institutions," *Aegis*, Summer/Autumn, 1980, pp. 9-15.

45. Telephone interview with Pat Day Hartwell.

46. *Ibid.*

47. Author's interview with Rachel Burger.

48. Author's interview with Carol Hussa.

49. Del Martin, *Battered Wives* (San Francisco: Glide Publications, 1976) pp. 233-234.

50. Author's interview with Carol Hussa.

51. *Women's Advocates: The Story of a Shelter*, p. 97.

52. See the discussion in Linda Gordon, *Woman's Body, Woman's Right: A Social History of Birth Control in America* (New York: Penguin Books, 1977), p. 299.

chapter 5

1. Author's interview with Susan Kelly-Dreiss.

2. Author's interview with Mary Morrison.

3. Author's interview with Barbara Hart.

4. Author's interview with Carol Hussa.

5. Pennsylvania Coalition Against Domestic Violence, General Standards for Coalition Members, document, unpaged.

6. *Ibid.*

7. Bylaws of Pennsylvania Coalition Against Domestic Violence, Article III, Section 3.02, undated, p. 3.

8. Author's interview with Barbara Hart.

9. Carroll Rhodes, letter to Pennsylvania Coalition Against Domestic Violence newsletter 3, No. 2 (September 1980): unpaged.

10. "Confidentiality," Pennsylvania Coalition Against Domestic Violence newsletter 3, No. 6 (March 1981): unpaged.

11. Author's interview with Barbara Hart.

12. Author's interview with Carol Hussa.

13. Gail Sullivan, "The Movement Against Woman Abuse," in *For Shelter and Beyond: An Educational Manual for Working with Women Who Are Battered*, Massachusetts Coalition of Battered Women's Service Groups, Boston, 1981, p. 19.

14. *For Shelter and Beyond*, The Massachusetts Coalition, pp. 20-21.

15. See *For Shelter and Beyond*.

16. *Ibid.*, p. 20.

17. *Ibid.*, p. 21.

18. Author's interview with Curdina Hill.

19. Author's interview with Margo Smith.

20. Author's interview with Ellen Koteen.

21. New Jersey Coalition for Battered Women, description of the coalition, provided by Ellen Koteen, undated and unpaged.

22. Author's interview with Ellen Koteen.
23. *Women's Advocates: The Story of a Shelter* (St. Paul: Women's Advocates, 1980), p. 79.
24. *SANEnews*, A national newsletter on battered women 1, No. 10 (July 1980): 8.
25. Telephone interview with Ellen Pence.
26. Author's interview with Barbara Hart.
27. Author's interview with Barbara Hart.
28. Telephone interview with Susan Jan Hornstein.
29. Author's interview with Kerry Lobel.
30. Telephone interview with Cheri Maples.
31. "Legal Projects and State Legislation," *Aegis*, November/December 1978, p. 44.
32. Lisa Lerman with the assistance of Leslie Landis and Sharon Goldzweig, "State Legislation on Domestic Violence," *Response to Violence in the Family* 4, No. 7 (September/October 1981):10-11.
33. Julie E. Hamos, *State Domestic Violence Laws and How to Pass Them: A Manual for Lobbyists*, National Coalition Against Domestic Violence. (Rockville, Maryland: National Clearinghouse on Domestic Violence) Monograph series no. 2, June 1980, p. 59.
34. There is no precise data on the variety of local, state, and federal government, foundation, and private allocations to battered women's services. This funding estimate is based on discussions with women around the country, the National Coalition Against Domestic Violence, The Center for Women Policy Studies, and federal government personnel. Frequently federal and state agencies have no detailed breakdown of how local governmental bodies spend funds.
35. Author's interview with Lisa Leghorn.
36. Anonymous interview.
37. Author's interview with Kerry Lobel.
38. Laurie Woods, letter to *National Communication Network for the elimination of violence against women* 1, Issue 1 (April 1977): 14.
39. Donna M. Tapper, "Services for Battered Women in New York City," *Trends and Forecasts, A Report on Human Services in New York City*, Community Council of Greater New York, March 1979, p. 6.
40. Author's interview with Candice Butcher.
41. Author's interview with Kathryn Conroy.
42. Anonymous interview.
43. Anonymous interview.

chapter 6

1. Author's interview with Lisa Leghorn.
2. *Ibid.*
3. Lisa Leghorn, "Newsletter Merger," *National Communication Network for the elimination of violence against women* 1, Issue 1 (April 1977): 12.
4. Susan Flint, "Merger Effected," *National Communication Network* 1, Issue 3 (October 1977): 17.

5. _FAAR and NCN_, July/August 1978, p. 3.

6. Lois Yankowski, "Conference Reports," _Feminist Alliance Against Rape newsletter_, November/December 1976, pp. 15-16.

7. Author's interview with Jan Peterson.

8. Author's interview with Lisa Leghorn.

9. From the files of Valle Jones, undated and unpaged.

10. For a discussion of these issues, see Valle Jones, "Funds for Battered Women—can co-optation be curbed?," _FAAR News_, November/December 1977, pp. 12-16.

11. Telephone interview with Valle Jones.

12. _Ibid._

13. Monica Erler, "Coalitions Growing Strong," _National Communication Network_ I, Issue 4 (February 1978): 2.

14. _National Communication Network_ 1, Issue 4, p. 3.

15. Telephone interview with Valle Jones.

16. "Progress Report—The National Coalition Against Domestic Violence," _Aegis: Magazine on Ending Violence Against Women_, January/February 1979, p. 4.

17. See the Minute Books, the National Coalition Against Domestic Violence Steering Committee, available at the National Coalition Against Domestic Violence office.

18. Author's interview with Lisa Leghorn.

19. _Ibid._

20. "National Coalition Against Domestic Violence News," _Aegis: Magazine on Ending Violence Against Women_, September/October 1978, p. 15.

21. "Federal Legislation Introduced to Aid Battered Women," _Response to intrafamily violence and sexual assault_, Center for Women Policy Studies 1, Issue 5 (October 1977): 1.

22. Virginia Wheaton, "What Happened to the Domestic Violence Act of 1978," quoting Joanne Howes, _The Grantsmanship Center News_, January/February 1979, p. 15.

23. _Ibid._, p. 17.

24. _Ibid._, p. 83.

25. Telephone interview with Valle Jones.

26. Taken from the legislative files of Barbara Hart, legislative chair of the National Coalition Against Domestic Violence during the 96th Congress.

27. Author's interview with Mary Morrison.

28. Taken from the Minute Book, National Coalition Against Domestic Violence Steering Committee, Membership survey as of 10/31/80.

29. General Support Proposal 1980-81, National Coalition Against Domestic Violence, p. 5.

30. Statement presented by the Feminist Socialist Caucus to the National Coalition Against Domestic Violence, First National Meeting, March 1, 1980.

31. Author's interview with Pat Gearity.

32. Barbara Hart, personal communication.

33. Author's interview with Mary Morrison.

34. _Ibid._

35. Senator Gordon Humphrey, _Congressional Record_, 25 August 1980, p. 11477.

36. Phyllis Schlafly, "Domestic Violence Bill to Increase Bureaucracy," New Orleans *Times-Picayune*, 11 February 1980.
37. "Senate to Determine Destiny of Domestic Violence Legislation," *Response to violence in the family* 4, No. 1 (October 1980): 1.
38. Author's interview with Mary Morrison.
39. Telephone interview with June Zeitlin.
40. "NCADV," Pennsylvania Coalition Against Domestic Violence newsletter 3, No. 6 (March 1981): unpaged.
41. Diana E. H. Russell, "Introduction" in Del Martin, *Battered Wives* (San Francisco: Glide Publications, 1976), p. xi.
42. *Ibid.*
43. Jean Rosiello, "Exciting Dialogue Emerges from International Conference on Battered Women," *Aegis*, September/October 1978, p. 18.
44. Hester Watson, personal communication.
45. Mildred Daley Pagelow, "Kitchens, Cultures, and the Feminist Movement," *Aegis*, May/June 1979, p. 7.
46. *Ibid.*, p. 8.
47. Hester Watson, personal communication.
48. Author's interview with Wendy Ayotte.
49. Author's interview with Ludo McFerran.
50. *Ibid.*
51. *Ibid.*
52. *Ibid.*
53. Sue Robertson, "Coordinator's Annual Report," Scottish Women's Aid, September 1979. Thanks to R. Emerson Dobash for supplying this document.
54. Jo Sutton, "The Growth of the British Movement for Battered Women," *Victimology: An International Journal* 2, nos. 3-4 (1977-78): 577.
55. Author's interview with Hester Watson.
56. *Ibid.*
57. Scottish Women's Aid Annual Report 1979-1980, p. 28.
58. Lois Yankowski, "Pizzey Stirs Controversy," article based on information received from the National Women's Aid Federation, *Feminist Alliance Against Rape newsletter*, May/June 1977, p. 26.
59. *Ibid.*
60. Sophie Watson, "Women's Aid Federation Speaks Out," *Aegis*, November/December 1978, p. 38.
61. Author's interview with Hester Watson.
62. *Ibid.*
63. *Ibid.*
64. Jo Sutton, "The Growth of the British Movement for Battered Women," *Victimology*, p. 580.
65. Hester Watson, personal communication.
66. Jo Sutton, "The Growth of the British Movement for Battered Women," *Victimology*, p. 577.

chapter 7

1. Mark A. Schulman, *A Survey of Spousal Violence Against Women in Kentucky,* U.S. Department of Justice, Law Enforcement Assistance Administration, Study No. 792701, July 1979, p. 48.
2. Eisenberg and Micklow, cited in Del Martin, *Battered Wives* (San Francisco: Glide Publications, 1976), p. 93.
3. Breedlove et al., cited in Marjory D. Fields, "Wife Beating: Government Intervention Policies and Practices," U.S. Commission on Civil Rights, *Battered Women: Issues of Public Policy,* a consultation, Washington, D.C., 30-31 January 1978, p. 247.
4. James Bannon, "Law Enforcement Problems with Intra-Family Violence," paper presented to the American Bar Association Convention, 12 August 1975, p. 6.
5. *Ibid.,* p. 5.
6. James Bannon, "Law Enforcement Problems with Intra-Family Violence," Reprinted by American Friends Service Committee, Women's Issues Program, Cambridge, Massachusetts, undated, p. 1.
7. Del Martin, *Battered Wives,* p. 90.
8. Author's interview with Lisa Lerman.
9. Lisa Lerman with the assistance of Leslie Landis and Sharon Goldzweig, "State Legislation on Domestic Violence," *Response to Violence in the family* 4, No. 7 (September/October 1981): 3.
10. See Summary of Developments in Bruno v. Codd sub nom Bruno v. McGuire and Scott v. Hart, National Center on Women and Family Law.
11. Holly Ladd and Esther Mosak, "Bruno v. McGuire: Battered Women Sue Police and Courts," American Friends Service Committee, Women's Issues Program, Cambridge, Massachusetts, unpaged.
12. Ibid.
13. Candace Wayne, "Working on Woman Abuse, Confronting the Present-Future Goals," speech presented at Woman Abuse: A Working Conference for the Midwest, 23-24 April 1979, Chicago, p. 4.
14. Author's interview with Laurie Woods.
15. Author's interview with Barbara Hart.
16. Eisenberg and Micklow cited in Marjory Fields, "Wife Beating: Government Intervention Policies and Practices," p. 233.
17. Julie E. Hamos, National Coalition Against Domestic Violence, *State Domestic Violence Laws and How to Pass Them: A Manual for Lobbyists,* National Clearinghouse on Domestic Violence, No. 2, June 1980, p. 45.
18. Lisa Lerman with the assistance of Mary Bottum and Susan Wiviott, "State Legislation on Domestic Violence," *Response to Violence in the Family* 3, No. 12 (August/September 1980): 1.
19. Lisa Lerman, "State Legislation on Domestic Violence," *Response* 4, No. 7 (September-October 1981): 2.
20. Esther Mosak, "Massachusetts Abuse Prevention Act," American Friends Service Committee, Women's Issues Program, unpaged.
21. *Ibid.*
22. Lisa Lerman, "State Legislation on Domestic Violence," *Response* 4, No. 7, p. 2.

23. Susan Kelly-Dreiss, personal communication.
24. Julie E. Hamos, *State Domestic Violence Laws and How to Pass Them*, p. 34.
25. *Ibid.*, pp. 34-35.
26. *Ibid.*, p. 35.
27. Lisa Lerman, "State Legislation on Domestic Violence," *Response* 3, No. 12, p. 2.
28. Julie E. Hamos, *State Domestic Violence Laws and How to Pass Them*, p. 41.
29. Author's interview with Barbara Hart.
30. Sue Herz, "Update on State Legislation," *Aegis*, May/June 1979, p. 20.
31. Author's interview with Barbara Hart.
32. Author's interview with Laurie Woods.
33. "Do We Have A Right To Self-Defense?" *National Communication Network for the elimination of violence against women* 1, Issue 3 (October 1977): 1-2.
34. *Ibid.*, pp. 2-3.
35. Jean Rosiello, "Legal Projects and State Legislation," *Aegis*, March/April 1979, pp. 42-43.
36. Claudia McCormick cited in "Battered Women—The Last Resort," *National Communication Network* 1, Issue 4 (February 1978): 21.
37. See Reflections on our Movement 1974-1980, issue of *Aegis*, No. 31 (Winter/Spring 1981).
38. Cited in Ann Jones, *Women Who Kill* (New York: Holt, Rinehart and Winston, 1980), p. 286.
39. Ann Jones, *Women Who Kill*, p. 300.
40. *Ibid.*, pp. 318-319.
41. *Ibid.*, p. 313.
42. *Ibid.*, p. 315.
43. Author's interview with Laurie Woods.
44. "Rita Silk-Nauni," Pennsylvania Coalition Against Domestic Violence newsletter, 3, No. 6 (March 1981):unpaged.
45. Ann Jones, *Women Who Kill*, pp. 319-320.
46. Sue Lenaerts, "Killing with Just Cause," *Aegis*, No. 31 (Winter/Spring 1981):69.
47. Telephone interview with Ellen Pence.
48. Anonymous communication.
49. Telephone interview with Ellen Pence.
50. *Ibid.*
51. *Women's Advocates: The Story of a Shelter* (St. Paul: Women's Advocates, 1980):78.
52. Lisa Lerman, "State Legislation on Domestic Violence," *Response* 4, No. 7, p. 3.
53. Notes from the author's journal.
54. Joan Kuriansky, personal communication.
55. Author's interview with Esther Mosak.
56. Charlotte Bunch, "The Reform Tool Kit," *Aegis*, July/August 1979, p. 31.

Chapter 8

1. Mary Ann Largen, "L.E.A.A. Rape Funding Review," *Feminist Alliance Against Rape newsletter,* September/October 1974, p. 10.
2. Data provided by various L.E.A.A. staff through several telephone conversations in 1981.
3. "Funding Alert: LEAA Family Violence Program Grants," *Response to violence and sexual abuse in the family* 2, No. 2 (November/December 1978): 3.
4. Susan Cohen, *Funding Family Violence Programs: Sources and Potential Sources for Federal Monies,* (Washington, D.C.: Resource Center on Family Violence, Center for Women Policy Studies, November 1979) pp. 9-10.
5. *Federally Funded Projects on Domestic Violence,* (Washington, D.C.: Resource Center on Family Violence, Center for Women Policy Studies, September 1980) p. 7.
6. Jeannie Niedermeyer, Federal Agency Panel Discussion, U.S. Commission on Civil Rights, *Battered Women: Issues of Public Policy,* a consultation, Washington D.C., 30-31 January 1978, p. 191.
7. *Federally Funded Projects on Domestic Violence,* Center for Women Policy Studies, p. 14.
8. Grant Project Summary, No. 78DF-AX-0142, in Family Violence Program, Fiscal Year 1978 Local Projects, U.S. Department of Justice, Law Enforcement Assistance Administration, unpaged.
9. Lisa Lerman, "Criminal Prosecution of Wife Beaters," *Response* 4, No. 3 (January/February 1981):19.
10. *Ibid.,* citing interview with Jeanine Pirro, p. 16.
11. Telephone interview with Jan Kirby-Gelles.
12. Family Violence Program Grant Activity 1977-1980, Law Enforcement Assistance Administration, September 10, 1980, unpaged. The grant amounts for each year are: 1977-$132,160; 1978-$249,974; 1979-$334,992; 1980-$334,992.
13. Brochure, The Resource Center on Family Violence, Center for Women Policy Studies, Washington, D.C.
14. Jackie MacMillan, "LEAA Research-East," *Feminist Alliance Against Rape newsletter,* (Fall 1975): 4-5.
15. Betsy Warrior, "National Directory-a rip off?" *National Communication Network for the elimination of violence against women,* I Issue 4 (December 1977): 6-7.
16. Telephone interview with Mary Jane Cronin.
17. "Committee Reviews Federal Domestic Violence Programs," *Response* 3, No.7 (March 1980):4.
18. Anonymous interview.
19. "HEW Opens New Office on Domestic Violence," *Response* 2, No. 6 (April 1979): 2.
20. Telephone interview with June Zeitlin.
21. "ODV Funds Four Projects in 1979," *Response* 3, No. 2 (October 1979): 3.
22. See Renae Scott, *Doing Community Outreach to Third World Women,* Technical Assistance Project of Casa Myrna Vázquez, Boston, 1980.
23. "Project to Coordinate Family Violence Resources," *Response* 3, No. 6 (February 1980): 4.
24. Telephone interview with June Zeitlin.

25. Conference Brochure, Fifth National Conference on Child Abuse and Neglect, April 5-8, 1981, Milwaukee, Wisconsin, p. 5.

26. Author's interview with Mary Morrison.

27. "More Federal Aid for Battered Women," *Response* 4, No. 1 (October 1980): 8.

28. Presentation of Betty Kaufman, Department of Housing and Urban Development, Federal Agency Panel, *Battered Women: Issues of Public Policy*, U.S. Commission on Civil Rights, p. 174.

29. Telephone interview with Helen Helfer.

30. Telephone interview with Ellen Pence.

31. *Ibid.*

32. For example, in St. Louis, the Matrix, a women's organization, rehabilitated single family dwellings which are now used primarily by female-headed households. Cited in Madeleine Golde, "Federal Programs Provide Housing Assistance for Battered Women," *Journal of Housing*, August-September 1980, p. 447.

33. Telephone interview with Mary Ann MacKenzie.

34. *Ibid.*

35. *Ibid.*

36. Telephone interview with Jan Kirby Gelles.

37. *SANEnews, A national newsletter on battered women* 1, No. 12 (July 1981): 4.

38. "Federal Initiatives to End Family Violence Blocked," *Response* 4, No. 4 (March/April 1981): 3.

39. *SANEnews* 1, No. 12, citing *Revenue Sharing: The Second Round*, published by the Brookings Institute, p. 8.

40. *Ibid.*

41. Anonymous interview.

42. Telephone interview with Jan Kirby Gelles.

43. Telephone interview with Mary Jane Cronin.

44. Telephone interview with Mary Ann MacKenzie.

45. Telephone interview with Mary Jane Cronin.

46. "Sources of Funding for Battered Women's Programs," U.S. Department of Labor, Women's Bureau, January 1978, mimeographed, p. 2.

47. Jennifer Baker Fleming, letter to *NCN* 1, Issue 3 (October 1977): 12.

Chapter 9

1. Jo Sutton, "The Growth of the British Movement for Battered Women," *Victimology: An International Journal* 2, Nos. 3-4 (1977-78): 584.

2. For a discussion of these issues see R. Emerson Dobash and Russell Dobash, *Violence Against Wives: A Case Against the Patriarchy* (New York: The Free Press, 1979).

3. Murray Straus, "A Sociological Perspective on the Prevention and Treatment of Wifebeating," in Maria Roy ed., *Battered Women: A Psychosociological Study of Domestic Violence* (New York: Van Nostrand Reinhold, 1977), pp. 194-239.

4. Natalie Shainess, "Psychological Aspects of Wifebattering," in Maria Roy,

ed., *Battered Women*, pp. 114-115.

5. Author's interview with Isidore Penn.

6. Author's interview with Barbara Hart.

7. Murray Straus, Richard Gelles, and Suzanne Steinmetz, *Behind Closed Doors: Violence in the American Family* (Garden City, N.Y.: Anchor Press, 1980), p. 173.

8. Andy McCormack, personal communication.

9. Murray Straus, Richard Gelles, and Suzanne Steinmetz, *Behind Closed Doors*, p. 109.

10. *Ibid.*, p. 121.

11. R. Emerson Dobash and Russell Dobash, *Violence Against Wives*, pp. 154-155.

12. *Ibid.*, p. 155.

13. On page viii of the Foreword to *Behind Closed Doors*, the authors write, "Hopefully our report...is a step forward in understanding the nature of the family and especially why the hallmark of family relationships is both love and violence."

14. "More Refutations of the Battered Husband Myth: Setting the Record Straight," *National Communications Network for the Elimination of Violence Against Women (NCN)* I, Issue 4 (February 1978): 23.

15. R. Emerson Dobash and Russell Dobash, *Violence Against Wives*, p. 20.

16. "Facts: A Focus on 'Battered Husbands'," *Aegis: Magazine on Ending Violence Against Women*, January/February 1979, p. 21.

17. Susan Schechter, Open Letter to Suzanne Steinmetz, undated, p. 1.

18. Straus, Gelles and Steinmetz, *Behind Closed Doors*, p. 44.

19. Author's interview with Joseph Morse and Kenneth Busch.

20. Gloria Joseph, "The Incompatible Menage A Trois: Marxism, Feminism, and Racism," in Lydia Sargent, ed., *Women and Revolution: A Discussion of the Unhappy Marriage of Marxism and Feminism* (Boston: South End Press, 1981), p. 94.

21. Susan Schechter, "Towards An Analysis of the Persistence of Violence Against Women in the Home," *Aegis*, July/August 1979, p. 47.

22. Sheila Rowbotham, *Woman's Consciousness, Man's World* (Middlesex, England: Penguin Books, 1973), p. 117.

23. Dobash and Dobash, *Violence Against Wives*, p. 44.

24. See Dobash and Dobash, *Violence Against Wives*, Chapter 3.

25. Dobash and Dobash, *Violence Against Wives*, p. 33.

26. *Ibid.*, p. 60.

27. *Ibid.*, p. 61.

28. *Ibid.*, p. 56.

29. *Ibid.*, p. 62.

30. *Ibid.*

31. Allen Steinberg, "The Criminal Courts and the Transformation of Criminal Justice in Philadelphia, 1815-1874," Ph.D. dissertation, Columbia University, 1982.

32. Dobash and Dobash, *Violence Against Wives*, p. 63.

33. *Ibid.*

34. Francis Power Cobbe, "Wife Torture in England," cited in Dobash and Dobash, *Violence Against Wives*, p. 72.

35. *Ibid.*, p. 73.

36. Lenore Weitzman, "Legal Regulation of Marriage: Tradition and Change," cited in Del Martin, *Battered Wives* (San Francisco: Glide Publications, 1976), p. 37.

37. Dobash and Dobash, *Violence Against Wives*, p. 22.

38. *Organizing and Implementing Services for Men Who Batter,* a manual, draft copy from Emerge: a men's counseling service on domestic violence, Boston, 1980, pp. 16-17. And interview with Isidore Penn.

39. Anonymous interview.

40. Dobash and Dobash, *Violence Against Wives*, pp. 104-105.

41. R. Emerson Dobash, "The Negotiation of Daily Life and the 'Provocation' of Violence: A Patriarchal Concept in Support of the Wife Beater" (paper presented at the 9th World Congress of Sociology, August, 1978, Uppsala, Sweden), p. 12.

42. *Ibid.*, p. 15.

43. *Ibid.*

44. Anonymous interview.

45. Ianthe Thomas, "A Wife-Beater Tells His Story," *The Village Voice,* New York, 1 August 1977, p. 17.

46. *Ibid.*

47. Author's interview with Joseph Morse.

48. Richard J. Gelles, *The Violent Home: A Study of Physical Aggression Between Husbands and Wives,* Vol. 13 Sage Library of Social Research (Beverly Hills: Sage, 1972), p. 139.

49. Dobash and Dobash, *Violence Against Wives*, p. 102.

50. *Ibid.*, p. 96.

51. *Ibid.*, p. 140.

52. Author's interview with Isidore Penn.

53. Author's interview with Joseph Morse and Kenneth Busch.

54. Dobash and Dobash, *Violence Against Wives*, p. 139.

55. Author's interview with Joseph Morse.

56. Author's interview with Craig Norberg.

57. Anonymous interview.

58. Jalna Hanmer, "Violence and the Social Control of Women," in G. Littlejohn *et al.,* eds., *Power and the State,* (London: Croom Helm, 1978), p. 231.

59. *Ibid.*, pp. 226-227.

60. Zillah Eisenstein, "Developing a Theory of Capitalist Patriarchy and Socialist Feminism," in Zillah Eisenstein, *ed., Capitalist Patriarchy and the Case for Socialist Feminism* (New York: Monthly Review, 1979), pp. 29-30.

61. Dobash and Dobash, *Violence Against Wives*, p. 51.

62. See the discussion in Eli Zaretsky, *Capitalism, The Family, & Personal Life,* (New York: Harper Colophon, 1976).

63. "Women at Work: Barriers to Economic Equality," Women Employed Institute, Chicago, 1980, p. 3.

64. *Ibid.*, p. 5.

65. *Ibid.*, p. 6.

66. *Ibid.*, pp. 3 and 6.

67. Elliott Currie, Robert Dunn, and David Fogarty, "The New Immiseration: Stagflation, Inequality, and the Working Class," *Socialist Review,* No. 54 (November-December 1980):15.

68. "Women at Work: Barriers to Economic Equality," Women Employed, p. 3.

69. Gail Sullivan with Cindy Fascia, "Sexism and Patriarchy" in *For Shelter and Beyond: An Educational Manual for Working with Women Who Are Battered,* Massachusetts Coalition of Battered Women Service Groups, Boston, 1981, p. 16.

70. Currie, Dunn, and Fogarty, "The New Immiseration," p. 15.

71. Cited in Marjory D. Fields, "Wife Beating: Government Intervention Policies and Practices," U.S. Commission on Civil Rights, *Battered Women: Issues of Public Policy,* a consultation, Washington, D.C., 30-31 January 1978, pp. 272-273.

72. Zillah Eisenstein, "Developing a Theory of Capitalist Patriarchy and Socialist Feminism," in Eisenstein, *ed., Capitalist Patriarchy and the Case for Socialist Feminism,* p. 27.

73. Author's interview with Andy McCormack.

74. Author's interview with Barbara Hart.

75. Lenore E. Walker, *The Battered Woman* (New York: Harper Colophon, 1979), p. 23.

76. Author's interview with Jackie Boyle.

77. Marlyn Grossman, "Research into Domestic Violence that Does Violence to Women," paper presented at the meetings of the American Psychological Association, Toronto, August, 1978, p. 4.

78. Lee Bowker and Kristine MacCallum, "Women Who Have Beaten Wife-Beating: A New Perspective on Victims as Victors," University of Wisconsin-Milwaukee, School of Social Welfare, October, 1980, p. 10.

79. Author's interview with Barbara Hart.

80. Author's interview with Betsy Warrior.

81. Author's interview with Barbara Hart.

82. Author's interview with Christine Choy.

83. Anita Bracy Brooks, "The Black Woman Within the Program and Service Delivery Systems for Battered Women: A Cultural Response," *Battered Women: An Effective Response,* Chapter 2, Minnesota Department of Corrections, p. 8.

84. I. Nkenge Toure, "An Overview of Third World Women and Violence," Report from the First National Conference on Third World Women and Violence, Rape Crisis Center, Washington, D.C., August 1980, p. 12.

85. Mildred Daley Pagelow, *Woman-Battering: Victims and Their Experiences,* Vol. 129, Sage Library of Social Research, (Beverly Hills: Sage, 1981), p. 85.

86. *Ibid.,* p. 121.

87. *Raven's Flight* 1, No. 3 (June 1980): 3.

Chapter 10

1. Irene Brubaker, letter to *National Communication Network for the elimination of violence against women (NCN)* I, Issue 3 (October 1977): 22.

2. Lisa Leghorn, letter to *NCN* I, Issue 4 (December 1977): 22.

3. "Penelope House Burns," *National Technical Assistance Center on Family Violence Monthly Memo* II, No. 6 (June 1980): 1.

4. Sheila Oliver, personal communication.

5. Diane Brown, "Two Years Later: Where Am I?", keynote address, Addressing Woman Abuse: Visions and Actions Conference, Lake Geneva, Wisconsin, 12-14 November 1980.

6. Author's interview with Gail Sullivan.

7. Gail Sullivan, "Cooptation in the Battered Women's Movement," draft copy, undated, p. 2.

8. Author's interview with Esther Mosak.

9. Anonymous interview.

10. Gail Sullivan, "Cooptation in the Battered Women's Movement," p. 3.

11. "Foundation Survey Finds Poor Support for Women's Projects," *Response to violence and sexual abuse in the family* 3, No. 2 (October 1979): 6.

12. Gail Sullivan, "Cooptation in the Battered Women's Movement," p. 3.

13. Author's interview with Nydia Diaz.

14. Gail Sullivan, "Cooptation in the Battered Women's Movement," p. 8.

15. "Response of Anne Flitcraft," Anne Flitcraft, U.S. Commission on Civil Rights, *Battered Women: Issues of Public Policy,* a consultation, Washington, D.C., 30-31 January 1978, p. 114.

16. *Ibid.*, pp. 114-115.

17. Author's interview with Rachel Burger.

18. Del Martin, *Battered Wives,* citing a survey by Gale Carsenat, (San Francisco: Glide Publications, 1976), p. 232.

19. Author's interview with Ellen Berliner and Anne Steytler.

Chapter 11

1. Susan Schechter, "The Future of the Battered Women's Movement," keynote address, Addressing Woman Abuse: Visions and Actions Conference, Lake Geneva, Wisconsin, 12-14 November 1980.

2. "A Proposal for Emerge: A Men's Counseling Service on Domestic Violence," undated and unpaged.

3. "Ms.," *Pennsylvania Coalition Against Domestic Violence newsletter* 3, No. 5 (December 1980): 9 and 13.

4. *Organizing and Implementing Services for Men Who Batter,* Emerge: A Men's Counseling Service on Domestic Violence, first draft of a monograph, Boston 1980, pp. 23-24.

5. Cited in Laureen France, "Men Against Violence Against Women," *Aegis: Magazine on Ending Violence Against Women,* Winter/Spring 1980, p. 37.

6. Author's interview with former Emerge client.

7. See "Programs for Men Who Batter: Parts I and II" in *Response to Violence in the Family,* April 1980 and May 1980.

8. Janet A. Geller and James C. Walsh, "A Treatment Model for the Abused Spouse," *Victimology: An International Journal* 2, Nos. 3-4 (1977-78): 630.

9. David Adams and Isidore Penn, "Men in Groups: The Socialization and Resocialization of Men Who Batter," paper presented at the Annual Meeting of the American Orthopsychiatric Association, April, 1981, pp. 4-5.

10. Lisa Leghorn, "Battered Women: Immediate Protection and Long-term Change," *National Communication Network for the elimination of violence against women (NCN)* 1, Issue 4 (December 1977): 8.

11. *Ibid.*
12. Anonymous interview.
13. Cited in Laureen France, "Men Against Violence Against Women," *Aegis,* Winter/Spring 1980, p. 37.
14. Lois Ahrens, "Battered Women's Refuges: Feminist Cooperatives Vs. Social Service Institutions," *Radical America* 14, No. 3 (May-June 1980): 45.
15. See Martha Thompson, letter to *Off Our Backs,* Special Issue on Racism and Sexism ix, No. 10, (November 1979): 30.
16. M. Smith, "Homophobia and Heterosexism," *For Shelter and Beyond: An Educational Manual for Working With Women Who Are Battered,* Massachusetts Coalition of Battered Women Service Groups, 1981, p. 61.
17. *Ibid.,* p. 59.
18. *Ibid.,* p. 62.
19. Ellen Pence, "Racism—a white issue," *Aegis,* March/April 1979, p. 37.
20. Anita Bracy Brooks, "The Black Woman within the Program and Service Delivery Systems for Battered Women: A Cultural Response," *Battered Women: An Effective Response,* Chapter 2, Minnesota Department of Corrections, June 1980, p. 7.
21. Author's interview with Nydia Díaz.
22. Anita Bracy Brooks, "The Black Woman within the Program and Service Delivery Systems for Battered Women," p. 9.
23. Author's interview with Eulalia Reyes de Smith, María Ríos and Frances Zamora.
24. bell hooks, *Ain't I A Woman: Black Women and Feminism* (Boston: South End Press, 1981), pp. 68-69.
25. Author's interview with Kerry Lobel.
26. Author's interview with Renae Scott.
27. Author's interview with Aurie Pennick.
28. Iola Columbus, Sharon Day-Garcia, Bonnie Wallace and Mary Ann Walt, "Battering and the Indian Woman," *Battered Women: An Effective Response,* Chapter 3, p. 9.
29. See Rayna Rapp, "Family and Class in Contemporary America: Notes Toward an Understanding of Ideology," *Science and Society* XLII, No. 3 (Fall 1978):278-300.
30. Author's interview with Curdina Hill.
31. Author's interview with Renae Scott.
32. Bridget Wynne, "Chicanas Speak: about feminism and the women's liberation movement," *Off Our Backs* ix, No. 10 (November 1979):11.
33. Author's interview with Esther Mosak.
34. "Third World Women," *Pennsylvania Coalition Against Domestic Violence newsletter* 3, No. 5 (December 1980):7.
35. Catlin Fullwood, personal communication.
36. I. Nkenge Toure, "Report on the First National Third World Women's Conference on Violence," *Aegis,* Summer/Autumn 1980, p. 71.
37. *Ibid.*
38. *Ibid.,* p. 71-72.
39. "Racism," *Pennsylvania Coalition Against Domestic Violence newsletter* 3, No. 5, (December 1980): 8.
40. Anita Brooks, Racism in the Movement, workshop presented at

Addressing Woman Abuse: Visions and Actions, Lake Geneva, Wisconsin, 12-14 November 1980.
41. "Racism," *Pennsylvania Coalition Against Domestic Violence* newsletter, p. 12.
42. An excellent article on consciousness raising guidelines for racism awareness, originally printed in *Sojourner* and later reprinted in *Off Our Backs* covered three principle areas: 1. Early Memories/Childhood Experiences; 2. Adolescence/Early Adulthood; and 3. Becoming a Feminist/Racism in the Women's movement. The Massachusetts Coalition of Battered Women Service Groups has compiled a series of racism awareness exercises.
43. Ellen Pence, "Racism—a white issue," *Aegis,* March/April 1979, p. 38.
44. Author's interview with Curdina Hill.
45. Author's interview with Renae Scott.
46. Author's interview with Catlin Fullwood.
47. Author's interview with Renae Scott.
48. Author's interview with Esther Mosak.
49. Author's interview with Curdina Hill.
50. See Renae Scott, *Doing Community Outreach to Third World Women,* Domestic Violence Technical Assistance Project, Casa Myrna Vázquez, January 1980.
51. Author's interview with Eulalia Reyes de Smith, María Ríos and Frances Zamora.
52. Author's interview with Catlin Fullwood.
53. Author's interview with Aurie Pennick.
54. Mariana Romo-Carmona, personal communication.
55. Marta Segovia-Ashley, "Shelters: Short-Term Needs," U.S. Commission on Civil Rights, *Battered Women: Issues of Public Policy,* a consultation, Washington, D.C., 30-31 January 1978, p. 399.
56. Author's interview with Ludo McFerran.
57. Michael Merrill, personal communication.

Chapter 12

1. Author's interview with Ellen Koteen.
2. Rosalind Pollack Petchesky, "Antiabortion, Antifeminism and the Rise of the New Right," *Feminist Studies* 7, No. 2 (Summer 1981): 206.
3. Jim O'Brien, "The New Terrain of American Politics," *Radical America* 15, Nos. 1 & 2 (Spring 1981): 8.
4. Jim Campen, "Economic Crisis and Conservative Economic Policies: U.S. Capitalism in the 1980s," *Radical America* 15, Nos. 1 & 2: 43.
5. Ann Withorn, "Retreat from the Social Wage: Human Services in the 1980s," *Radical America* 15, Nos. 1 & 2: 31.
6. Mary Ellen Lipinski, personal communication.
7. Sheila Rowbotham, Lynne Segal, and Hilary Wainwright, *Beyond the Fragments: Feminism and the Making of Socialism* (London: Merlin Press, 1979), p. 203.
8. *Ibid.*, p. 205.
9. Beverly L. Johnson cited in Elliott Currie, Robert Dunn and David

Fogarty, "The New Immiseration: Stagflation, Inequality, and the Working Class," _Socialist Review_, No. 54 (November-December 1980):14.
10. _Ibid._, p. 12.
11. Barbara Ehrenreich, "The Women's Movements: Feminist and Anti-Feminist," _Radical America_ 15, Nos. 1 & 2: 97.
12. See Charlotte Bunch, "Woman Power: The Courage to Lead, the Strength to Follow, and the Sense to Know the Difference," _Ms._, July 1980. Bunch also cites the important contribution of Jo Freeman's, "The Tyranny of Structurelessness."
13. Charlotte Bunch, "Woman Power," pp. 48, 95.
14. Rena Lederman, personal communication.
15. See Kit Evans, "A Feminist Perspective on the Ethics of Communication, Explored in the Context of an On-going Group of Women with Decision making Responsibility," unpublished paper, August 1980.
16. See the excellent article by Barbara Hart, "Burn-out: A Political View," _Aegis: Magazine on Ending Violence Against Women_, Autumn 1981, pp. 35-40.
17. See _Dollars and Sense: A Community Fundraising Manual for Shelters and Other Nonprofit Organizations_, Western States Shelter Network, San Francisco, Ca., 1981.
18. Valle Jones and Deb Friedman, "Hard Cash for Feminists," _Aegis_, Winter/Spring 1980, p. 73.
19. _Ibid._, p. 75.
20. "Retrenchment for Survival," _National Technical Assistance Center on Family Violence Monthly Memo_ III, No. 2 (Spring 1981):1, 2.
21. _Ibid._
22. Author's interview with Esther Mosak.
23. Candace J. Wayne, "Working on Woman Abuse: Confronting The Present-Future Goals," keynote address, Woman Abuse: A Working Conference for the Midwest, Chicago, 23-24 April 1979, p. 9.
24. Author's interview with Freada Klein.
25. _Ibid._
26. Author's interview with Barbara Hart.
27. "URSA Releases Preliminary Data on Family Violence Projects," _Response to violence in the family_ 4, No. 1 (October 1980): 3.

Chapter 13

1. Anonymous interview.
2. From the film, "We Will Not Be Beaten," quoted by permission of Transition House Films.
3. _Ibid._
4. Anonymous interview.
5. _Ibid._
6. Diane Brown, "Two Years Later: Where Am I?", keynote address, Addressing Woman Abuse: Visions and Actions conference, Lake Geneva, Wisconsin, November 12-14, 1980.

7. Anonymous interview.
8. Sophie Watson, "Women's Aid Federation Speaks Out," *Aegis: Magazine on Ending Violence Against Women,* November/December, 1978, p. 37.
9. Jeannie Stephens, "Counseling Battered Indian Women," unpublished paper, pp. 1 and 2.

Selected Bibliography

Ahrens, Lois. "Battered Women's Refuges: Feminist Cooperatives vs. Social Service Institutions." *Radical America* 14, no. 3 (1980): 41-47.

Bannon, James. "Law Enforcement Problems with Intra-Family Violence." Paper read at the American Bar Association Convention, 12 August 1975. Mimeographed.

Barry, Kathleen. *Female Sexual Slavery.* Englewood Cliffs, NJ: Prentice-Hall, 1979.

Boylan, Ann Marie, and Taub, Nadine. *Adult Domestic Violence: Constitutional, Legislative and Equitable Issues.* Washington, D.C.: Legal Services Corporation Research Institute, 1981

Brownmiller, Susan. *Against Our Will: Men, Women and Rape.* New York: Simon and Schuster, 1975.

Boujouen, Norma; Landerman, Donna; and Salisbury, Kathy M. "Evaluation of Outreach to Puerto Rican and Black Women in the Area of Sexual Assault." Conducted for Sexual Assault Crisis Service of Hartford. Hartford, CT: 1981. Mimeographed.

Burgess, Ann Wolbert, and Holmstrom, Lynda Lytle. *Rape: Victims of Crisis.* Bowie, MD: Robert J. Brady. Prentice-Hall, 1974.

Burgess, Ann Wolbert; Groth, Nicholas, A.; and Sgroi, Suzanne M. *Sexual Assault of Children and Adolescents.* Lexington, MA: Lexington Books, D.C. Heath, 1978.

Butler, Sandra. *Conspiracy of Silence: The Trauma of Incest.* San Francisco: New Glide Publications, 1978.

Chodorow, Nancy. *The Reproduction of Mothering: Psychoanalysis and the Sociology of Gender.* Berkeley, CA: University of California Press, 1978.

Clark, Lorenne M.P., and Lewis, Debra J. *Rape: The Price of Coercive Sexuality.* Berkeley, CA: The Women's Press, 1978.

Currie, Elliott; Dunn, Robert; and Fogarty, David. "The New Immiseration: Stagflation, Inequality, and the Working Class." *Socialist Review* 10, no. 6 (1980):7-31.

Davidson, Terry. *Conjugal Crime: Understanding and Changing the Battered Wife Pattern.* New York: Hawthorne Books, 1978.

Davis, Angela Y. *Women, Race and Class.* New York: Random House, 1981.

Delacoste, Frédérique, and Newman, Felice, eds. *Fight Back! Feminist Resistance to Male Violence.* Minneapolis: Cleis Press, 1981.

Dobash, Rebecca E., and Dobash, Russell P. "Wives: The Appropriate Victims of Marital Violence." *Victimology: An International Journal* 2, nos. 3/4 (1977-1978): 426-442.

—————"The Myth of the Wives Who Ask For It: A Response to Pizzey, Gayford and McKeith." *Community Care*, April 1979.

—————"Social Science and Social Action: The Case of Wife-Beating." *Journal of Family Issues*, December 1981.

Dobash, Emerson R., and Dobash, Russell. *Violence Against Wives: A Case Against the Patriarchy.* New York: The Free Press, 1979.

Domestic Abuse Intervention Project. "Research Report." Duluth, MN: 1981. Mimeographed.

Dubois, Ellen; Buhle, Mary Jo; Kaplan, Temma; Lerner, Gerda; and Smith-Rosenberg, Carroll. "Politics and Culture in Women's History: A Symposium." *Feminist Studies* 6, no. 1 (1980): 26-64.

Eisenberg, Sue E., and Micklow, Patricia L. "The Assaulted Wife: 'Catch 22' Revisited." *Women's Rights Law Reporter*, Spring/Summer 1977.

Eisenstein, Zillah. "Antifeminism in the Politics and Election of 1980." *Feminist Studies* 7, no. 2 (1981): 187-205.

————— ed. *Capitalist Patriarchy and the Case for Socialist Feminism.* New York: Monthly Review, 1979.

Evans, Sara. *Personal Politics.* New York: Alfred A. Knopf, 1979.

Firestone, Shulamith. *The Dialectic of Sex: The Case for Feminist Revolution.* New York: Bantam Books, 1971.

Flynn, J.P. "Recent Findings Related to Wife Abuse." *Social Casework*, January 1977, pp. 13-20.

Freeman, Jo. *The Politics of Women's Liberation: A Case Study of an Emerging Social Movement.* New York: David McKay Co., 1975.

Fritz, Leah. *Dreamers and Dealers.* Boston: Beacon Press, 1979.

Ganley, Anne L. *Court Mandated Counseling for Men Who Batter.* American Lake VA Medical Center, Tacoma, WA.

Gelles, Richard J. *The Violent Home: A Study of Physical Aggression Between Husbands and Wives.* Beverly Hills, CA: Sage Publications, 1972.

—————"Abused Wives: Why Do They Stay?" *Journal of Marriage and the Family* 38, no. 4 (1976): 659-668.

Gordon, Linda. *Woman's Body, Woman's Right: A Social History of Birth Control in America.* New York: Penguin Books, 1977.

Griffin, Susan. *Rape: The Power of Consciousness.* New York: Harper and Row, 1979.

Groth, Nicholas A. *Men Who Rape: The Psychology of the Offender.* New York: Plenum Press, 1979.

Hanmer, Jalna. "Community Action, Women's Aid and the Women's Liberation Movement." In *Women in the Community*, edited by Marjorie Mayo. London: Routledge and Kegan Paul, 1977.

Hanmer, Jalna. "Violence and the Social Control of Women," In *Power and the State*, edited by G. Littlejohn et. al. London: Croom Helm, 1978.

Herman, Judith Lewis, with Hirschman, Lisa. *Father-Daughter Incest.* Cambridge, MA: Harvard University Press, 1981.

Hilberman, Elaine. "Overview: The 'Wife-Beater's Wife' Reconsidered." *American Journal of Psychiatry* 137:11 (1980):1336-1347.

hooks, bell. *Ain't I A Woman: Black Women and Feminism.* Boston: South End Press, 1981.

Jones, Ann. *Women Who Kill.* New York: Holt, Rinehart and Winston, 1980.

Joseph, Gloria S., and Lewis, Jill. *Common Differences: Conflicts in Black and White Feminist Perspectives.* Garden City, NY: Anchor Press, Doubleday, 1981.

Katz, Judith H. *White Awareness: Handbook for Anti-Racism Training.* Norman: University of Oklahoma Press, 1978.

Koedt, Anne; Levine, Ellen; and Rapone, Anita. *Radical Feminism.* New York: Quadrangle Books, 1973.

Leghorn, Lisa. "Social Responses to Battered Women." *Feminist Alliance Against Rape.* March/April 1977 and May/June 1977.

Leghorn, Lisa and Parker, Katherine. *Woman's Worth: Sexual Economics and the World of Women.* Boston: Routledge and Kegan Paul, 1981.

Lerman, Lisa. *Prosecution of Spouse Abuse: Innovations in Criminal Justice Response.* Washington, D.C.: Center for Women Policy Studies, 1981.

Lerner, Gerda. ed. *Black Women in White America: A Documentary History.* New York: Random House, Vintage, 1973.

McGrath, Colleen. "The Crisis of Domestic Order," *Socialist Review* 9, no. 2 (1979): 11-30.

McGrath, Patricia E. with Schultz, Phyllis Stine, and Culhane, P. O'Dea, assisted by Franklin, Diana B. *The Development and Implementation of a Hospital Protocol for the Identification and Treatment of Battered Women.* Monograph Series number 5. Rockville, MD: National Clearinghouse on Domestic Violence, November 1980.

Martin, Del. *Battered Wives.* San Francisco: Glide Publications, 1976.

A Monograph on Services to Battered Women. Colorado Association for Aid to Battered Women, DHHS Publication, No. (OHDS) 79-5708, undated.

Moraga, Cherríe, and Anzaldua, Gloria. *This Bridge Called My Back: Writings by Radical Women of Color.* Watertown, MA: Persephone Press, 1981.

Morgan, Robin, ed. *Sisterhood Is Powerful: An Anthology of Writings from the Women's Liberation Movement.* New York: Vintage Books, 1970.

Nichols, Beverly. "The Abused Wife Problem," *Social Casework,* January 1976, pp. 27-32.

Off Our Backs: A Women's News Journal. "Special Issue on Racism and Sexism," 9, no. 10 (1979).

O'Sullivan, Elizabethann. "What Happened to Rape Crisis Centers? A Look at Their Structures, Members, and Funding." *Victimology* 3, nos. 1-2 (1978): 45-62.

Pagelow, Mildred Daley. *Woman Battering: Victims and Their Experiences.* Sage Library of Social Research, vol. 129. Beverly Hills: Sage Publications, 1981.

Petchesky, Rosalind Pollack. "Antiabortion, Antifeminism, and the Rise of the New Right." *Feminist Studies* 7, no. 2 (1981): 206-246.

Pizzey, Erin. *Scream Quietly or the Neighbours Will Hear You.* London: Penguin, 1974.

Pogrebin, Letty Cottin. "Do Women Make Men Violent?" *Ms.,* November 1974.

Rapp, Rayna. "Family and Class in Contemporary America: Notes Toward an Understanding of Ideology." *Science and Society* 42, no. 3 (1978): 278-300.

Reiter, Rayna, ed. *Toward an Anthropology of Women.* New York: Monthly Review, 1976.

Roberts, Albert R.; with the assistance of Roberts, Beverly J. *Sheltering Battered Women: A National Study and Service Guide.* New York: Springer Publishing Co., 1981.

Rowbotham, Sheila. *Woman's Consciousness, Man's World.* Baltimore, MD: Penguin Books, 1973.

Roy, Maria, ed. *Battered Women: A Psychosociological Study of Domestic Violence.* New York: Van Nostrand Reinhold, 1977.

Rush, Florence. *The Best Kept Secret: Sexual Abuse of Children.* New York: McGraw-Hill, 1980.

Russell, Diana. *The Politics of Rape: The Victim's Perspective.* New York: Stein and Day, 1975.

Ryan, William. *Blaming the Victim.* New York: Pantheon, 1971.

Sargent, Lydia, ed. *Women and Revolution: A Discussion of the Unhappy Marriage of Marxism and Feminism.* Boston: South End Press, 1981.

Schulman, Mark A. *A Survey of Spousal Violence Against Women in Kentucky.* U.S. Department of Justice, Law Enforcement Assistance Administration, Study No. 792701, July 1979.

Seifer, Nancy. *Nobody Speaks for Me: Self-Portraits of American Working Class Women.* New York: Simon and Schuster, 1976.

Simon, Barbara Levy. "Social Movements and Institutionalization: Rape as a Case Study." Ph.D. dissertation, Bryn Mawr College, 1981.

Stack, Carol. *All Our Kin: Strategies for Survival in a Black Community.* New York: Harper Colophon, 1974.

Stark, Evan; Flitcraft, Ann; and Frazier, William. "Medicine and Patriarchal Violence: The Social Construction of a 'Private Event.' " *International Journal of Health Services* 9, no. 3 (1979): 461-494.

Steiner, Gilbert, Y. *The Futility of Family Policy.* Washington, D.C.: The Brookings Institution, 1981.

Steinmetz, Suzanne, and Straus, Murray, eds. *Violence in the Family.* New York: Dodd, Mead, 1974.

Straus, Murray A.; Gelles, Richard J.; and Steinmetz, Suzanne K. *Behind Closed Doors: Violence in the American Family.* Garden City, NY: Anchor Press, Doubleday, 1980.

Tanner, Leslie, ed. *Voices from Women's Liberation.* New York: Signet Books, New American Library, 1970.

Tax, Meredith. *The Rising of the Women: Feminist Solidarity and Class Conflict, 1880-1917.* New York: Monthly Review, 1980.

United States Commission on Civil Rights, *Battered Women: Issues of Public Policy,* a consultation. Washington, D.C., 30-31 January 1978.

Walker, Lenore E. *The Battered Woman.* New York: Harper Colophon, Harper & Row Books, 1979.

Warrior, Betsy. *Wifebeating.* Somerville, MA: New England Free Press, 1976.

—————*Working on Wife Abuse.* Cambridge, MA: Seventh Supplemented Edition, 1978.

Women's Advocates: The Story of a Shelter. St. Paul, MN: Women's Advocates, 1980.

Woods, Laurie. "Litigation on Behalf of Battered Women." *Women's Rights Law Reporter,* Fall, 1978.

Zald, Mayer; and Ash, Roberta. "Social Movement Organizations: Growth, Decay and Change." *Social Forces,* March 1966: 327-340.

Zaretsky, Eli. *Capitalism, The Family and Personal Life.* New York: Harper Colophon, 1976.

National Domestic Violence Organizations

**Health Resource Center on
Domestic Violence**
383 Rhode Island Street Suite 304
San Francisco, CA 94103
Office (888) 792-2873
Fax (415) 252-8991

Family Violence Prevention Fund
383 Rhode Island Street Suite 304
San Francisco, CA 94103-5133
Contact: Esta Soler
Office (415) 252-8900
FAX (415) 252-8991

**National Coalition Against
Domestic Violence - Administrative
Office**
PO Box 18749
Denver, CO 80218
Contact: Rita Smith
Office (303) 839-1852
FAX (303) 831-9251

NCADV - Public Policy
119 Constitution Ave. NE
Washington, DC 20002
Office (202) 544-7358
FAX (202) 544-7893

**American Bar Association
Commission on Domestic Violence**
740 15th Street, NW., 9th Floor
Washington, DC 20005-1009
Contact: Roberta Valente
Office (202) 662-1737
FAX (202) 662-1032

**National Network to End Domestic
Violence**
701 Pennsylvania Avenue N.W. Suite
900
Washington, DC 20004
Contact: Donna Edwards
Office (202) 347-9520
FAX (202) 434-7400

**Mending the Sacred Hoop,
National Training Project**
206 West Fourth Street
Duluth, MN 55806
Contact: Liz LaPrairie-Columbus
Office (218) 722-2781
FAX (218) 722-0779

Battered Women's Justice Project
Minnesota Program Development
4032 Chicago Avenue South
Minneapolis, MN 55407
Contact: Denise Gamache
Office (800) 903-0111
FAX (612) 824-8965

**Institute on Domestic Violence in
the African American Community**
University of Minnesota
1985 Buford Ave.
St. Paul, MN 55108-6142
Contact: Oliver Williams Ph.D.
Office (612) 624-8965
FAX (612) 624-9201

**Resource Center on Domestic
Violence: Child Protection and
Custody**
P. O. Box 8970
Reno, NV 89507
Contact: Merry Hofford
Office (800) 527-3223
FAX (702) 784-6160

**Battered Women's Justice Project
c/o PCADV- Legal Office**
6400 Flank Drive Suite 1300
Harrisburg, PA 17112
Contact: Andrea Farney
Office (800) 903-0111
FAX (717) 671-5542

Battered Women's Justice Project
c/o National Clearinghouse for the
Defense of Battered Women

125 South 9th Street - Suite 302
Philadelphia, PA 19107
Contact: Sue Osthoff
Office (215) 351-0010
FAX (215) 351-0779

**National Resource Center on
Domestic Violence**
Pennsylvania Coalition Against
Domestic Violence
6400 Flank Drive, Suite 1300
Harrisburg, PA 17112-2778
Contact: Kathleen Krenek
Office (800) 537-2238
FAX (717) 545-9456

**Sacred Circle/National Resource
Center to Stop Violence Against
Native Women**
722 St. Joseph St

Rapid City, SD 57701
Contact: Brenda Hill
Office (605) 341-2050
FAX (605) 341-2472

National Domestic Violence Hotline
P. O. Box 161810
Austin,TX 78716
Contact: Cyndy Perkins
Office (512) 453-8117
FAX (512) 453-8541

**Center for the Prevention of Sexual
and Domestic Violence**
936 North 34th Street, Suite 200
Seattle, WA 98103
Contact: Rev. Marie Fortune
Office (206) 634-1903
FAX (206) 634-0115

State Domestic Violence Coalitions

**Alaska Network on Domestic
Violence and Sexual Assault**
130 Seward Street, Suite 501
Juneau, AK 99801
Contact: Lauree Hugonin
Office (907) 586-3650
FAX (907) 463-4493

**Alabama Coalition Against
Domestic Violence PO Box 4762**
Montgomery,AL 36101
Contact: Carol Gundlach
Office (334) 832-4842
FAX (334) 832-4803

**Arkansas Coalition Against
Domestic Violence**
#1 Sheriffs Lane, Suite C
North Little Rock, AR 72114
Contact: Sharon Sigmon
Office (501) 812-0571
FAX (501) 812-0578

**Arizona Coalition Against
Domestic Violence**
100 West Camelback Road
Suite 109
Phoenix, AZ 85013
Office (602) 279-2900
FAX (602) 279-2980

**California Alliance Against
Domestic Violence**
926 J St., Suite 1000
Sacramento, CA 95814
Contact: Susan Bazilli
Office (916) 444-7163
FAX (916) 444-7165

**Colorado Coalition Against
Domestic Violence**
PO Box 18902
Denver, CO 80218
Contact: Elaine Gibbes
Office (303) 831-9632
FAX (303) 832-7067

Connecticut Coalition Against Domestic Violence
100 Pitkin St.
East Hartford, CT 06108
Contact: Linda J. Cimino
Office (860) 282-7899
FAX (860) 282-7892

District of Columbia Coalition Against Domestic Violence
513 U Street, NW
Washington, DC 20001
Contact: Sandra Majors
Office (202) 783-5332
FAX (202) 387-5684

Delaware Coalition Against DomesticViolence
P.O. Box 847
Wilmington, DE 19899
Contact: Carol Post
Office (302) 658-2958
FAX (302) 658-5049

Florida Coalition Against Domestic Violence
410 Office Plaza Dr.
Tallahassee, FL 32301
Contact: Lynn Rosenthal
Office (904) 671-3998
FAX (904) 671-2058

Georgia Coalition on Family Violence, Inc.
1827 Powers Ferry Rd., Bldg. 3, Suite 325
Atlanta, GA 30339
Office (770) 984-0085
Fax (770) 984-0068

Hawaii State Coalition Against Domestic Violence
98-939 Moanalua Road
Aiea, HI 96701-5012
Contact: Carol C. Lee
Office (808) 486-5072
FAX (808) 486-5169

Iowa Coalition Against Domestic Violence
2603 Bell Ave. Suite 100
Des Moines, IA 50321
Contact: Laurie Schipper
Office (515) 244-8028
FAX (515) 244-7417

Idaho Coalition Against Sexual & Domestic Vlolence
815 Park Boulevard, Suite 140
Boise, ID 83712
Contact: Sue Fellen
Office (208) 384-0419
FAX (208) 331-0687

Illinois Coalition Against Domestic Violence
730 East Vine Street Suite 109
Springfield, IL 62703
Contact: Vickie Smith
Office (217) 789-2830
Fax (217) 789-1939

Indiana Coalition Against Domestic Violence
2511 E. 46th Street, Suite N-3
Indianapolis, IN 46205-3583
Contact: Laura Berry
Office (317) 543-3908
FAX (317) 377-7050

Kansas Coalition Against Sexual and Domestic Violence
820 S. E. Quincy, Ste. 422
Topeka, KS 66612
Contact: Sandy Barnett
Office (913) 232-9784
FAX (913) 232-9937

Kentucky Domestic Violence Association
PO Box 356
Frankfort, KY 40602
Contact: Sherry Currens
Office (502) 875-4132
FAX (502) 875-4268

**Louisiana Coalition Against
Domestic Violence**
PO Box 77308
Baton Rouge, LA 70879-7308
Contact: Merni Carter
Office (504) 752-1296
FAX (504) 751-8927

**Massachusetts Coalition Against
Sexual Assault & Domestic Violence**
14 Beacon Street, Suite 507
Boston, MA 02108
Contact: Sylvia Guthrie
Office (617) 248-0922 x205
FAX (617) 248-0902

**Maryland Network Against
Domestic Violence**
Whitehall Professional Center
6911 Laurel Bowie Rd., Suite 309
Bowie, MD 20715
Contact: Elaine Hughes
Office (301) 352-4574
FAX (301) 809-0422

**Maine Coalition For Family Crisis
Services**
128 Main Street
Bangor, ME 04401
Contact: Tracy Cooley
Office (207) 941-1194
FAX (207) 941-2327

**Michigan Coalition Against
Domestic and Sexual Violence**
3893 Okemos Rd. Suite B-2
Okemos, MI 48864
Contact: Mary Keefe
Office (517) 347-7000
FAX (517) 347-1377

**Minnesota Coalition for Battered
Women Services**
450 North Sydicate Street, Suite 122
St. Paul, MN 55104
Contact: Mavis Russell
Office (612) 646-6177

FAX (612) 646-1527

**Missouri Coalition Against
Domestic Violence**
415 E. McCarty
Jefferson City, MO 65101
Contact: Colleen Coble
Office (573) 634-4161
FAX (573) 636-3728

**Mississippi Coalition Against
Domestic Violence**
PO Box 4703
Jackson, MS 39296-4703
Contact: Michele Carroll
Office (601) 981-9196
FAX (601) 981-2501

**Montana Coalition Against
Domestic and Sexual Violence**
P.O. Box 633
Helena, MT 59601
Contact: Kathy Sewell
Office (406) 443-7794
FAX (406) 443-7818

**North Carolina Coalition Against
Domestic Violence**
301 W. Main St. Suite 350
Durham, NC 27701
Contact: Karen Luciano
Office (919) 956-9124
FAX (919) 682-1449

**North Dakota Council on Abused
Women's Services**
418 E. Rosser Ave., Suite 320
Bismarck, ND 58501
Contact: Bonnie Palecek
Office (701) 255-6240
FAX (701) 255-1904

**Nebraska Domestic Violence/
Sexual Assault Coalition**
825 M St., Suite 404
Lincoln, NE 68508-2253
Contact: Sarah O'Shea
Office (402) 476-6256

FAX (402) 476-6806

New Hampshire Coalition Against Domestic & Sexual Violence
PO Box 353
Concord, NH 03302-0353
Contact: Grace Mattern
Office (603) 224-8893
FAX (603) 228-6096

New Jersey Coalition for Battered Women
2620 Whitehorse/Hamilton Square Road
Trenton, NJ 08690-2718
Contact: Barbara Price
Office (609) 584-8107
FAX (609) 584-9750

New Mexico Coalition Against Domestic Violence
P.O. Box 25266
Albuquerque, NM 87125-0266
Contact: Mary Ann Copas
Office (505) 246-9240
FAX (505) 246-9434

Nevada Network Against Domestic Violence
100 W. Grove St. Suite 315
Reno, NV 89509
Contact: Susan Meuschke
Office (702) 828-1115
FAX (702) 828-9911

New York State Coalition Against Domestic Violence
Women's Building, 79 Central Ave.
Albany, NY 12206
Contact: Sherry Frohman
Office (518) 432-4864
FAX (518) 463-3155

Ohio Domestic Violence Network
4041 North High Street Suite 101
Columbus, OH 43214
Contact: Nancy Neylon

Office (614) 784-0023
FAX (614) 784-0033

Oklahoma Coalition On Domestic Violence and Sexual Assault
2200 N. Classen Blvd. - Suite 850
Oklahoma City, OK 73106
Contact: Marcia Smith
Office (405) 557-1210
FAX (405) 557-1296

Oregon Coalition Against Domestic And Sexual Violence
520 N.W. Davis, Suite 310
Portland, OR 97209
Contact: Margaret Brown
Office (503) 223-7411
FAX (503) 223-7490

Pennsylvania Coalition Against Domestic Violence
6400 Flank Drive - Suite 1300
Harrisburg, PA 17112
Contact: Susan Kelly-Dreiss
Office (717) 545-6400
FAX (717) 545-9456

Puerto Rico Coalition Against Domestic Violence
P. O. Box 23136
UPR Station
Rio Piedros, PR 00931
Contact: Gloria Rosado Ortiz
Office (787) 767-6843
FAX (787) 767-6843

Rhode Island Coalition Against Domestic Violence
422 Post Road Suite 104
Warwick, RI 02888
Contact: Deborah DeBare
Office (401) 467-9940
FAX (401) 467-9943

South Carolina Coalition On Against Domestic Violence & Sexual Assault
PO Box 7776
Columbia, SC 29202-7776

Contact: Susan L. Higginbotham
Office (803) 750-1222
FAX (803) 750-1246

**South Dakota Coalition Against
Domestic Violence & Sexual Assault**
P.O. Box 141
Pierre, SD 57501
Contact: Verlaine Gullickson
Office (605) 945-0869
FAX (605) 945-0870

**Tennessee Task Force Against
Domestic Violence and Sexual
Assault**
PO Box 120972
Nashville, TN 37212
Contact: Kathy England
Office (615) 386-9406
FAX (615) 383-2967

Texas Council on Family Violence
P. O. Box 161810
Austin, TX 78716
Office (800) 525-1978
FAX (512) 794-1199

**Utah Domestic Violence Advisory
Council**
120 North 200 West, Room 319
Salt Lake City, UT 84103
Contact: Diane Stuart
Office (801) 538-9886
FAX (801) 538-4016

**Virginians Against Domestic
Violence**
2850 Sandy Bay Road - Suite 101
Williamsburg, VA 23185
Contact: Kristi Van Audenhove
Office (757) 221-0990
FAX (757) 229-1553

**Vermont Network Against
Domestic Violence and Sexual
Assault**
PO Box 405
Montpelier, VT 05601
Contact: Judith Joseph
Office (802) 223-1302
FAX (802) 223-6943

**Washington State Coalition
Against Domestic Violence**
8645 Martin Way, Suite 103
Lacey, WA 98516
Contact: Mary Pontarolo
Office (360) 407-0756
FAX (360) 407-0761

**Wisconsin Coalition Against
Domestic Violence**
1400 East Washington Avenue
Suite Z32
Madison, WI 53703
Contact: Mary Lauby
Office (608) 255-0539
FAX (608) 255-3560

**West Virginia Coalition Against
Domestic Violence**
Elk Office Center
4710 Chimney Dr. Suite A
Charleston, WV 25302
Contact: Sue Julian
Office (304) 965-3552
FAX (304) 965-3572

**Wyoming Coalition Against
Domestic Violence & Sexual Assault**
P.O. Box 236
Laramie, WY 82070
Contact: Rosemary Bratton
Office (307) 755-5481
FAX (307) 755-5482

Interviews

The following people were kind enough to grant me interviews, usually
lasting between thirty minutes and three hours.

Wendy Ayotte, September 1980
Louise Bauschard, July 1980
Ellen Berliner, February 1981
Esther Blocker, September
1980
Jackie Boyle, September 1980
Rachel Burger, January 1981
Wayne Burke, January 1981
Kenneth Busch, January 1981
Candice Butcher, December
1980
Christine Choy, December
1981
Kathryn Conroy, December
1980
Mary Jane Cronin, November
1981
Nydia Díaz, September 1980
Christina Fuentes, November
1980
Catlin Fullwood, March 1981
Pat Gearity, November 1980
Marlyn Grossman, April 1981
Barbara Hart, December 1980
Pat Day Hartwell, July 1981
Helen Helfer, September 1981
Lee Hewitt, January 1981
Curdina Hill, January 1981
Susan Jan Hornstein,
November 1980
Carol Hussa, September 1980
Callie Hutchison, November
1980
Valle Jones, May 1981
Joani Kamman, November
1980
Susan Kelly-Dreiss, February
1981
Jan Kirby Gelles, December
1981
Freada Klein, January 1981
Ellen Koteen, January 1981
Mary Ann Largen, June 1981
Lisa Leghorn, October 1980
Lisa Lerman, December 1981

Kerry Ann Lobel, December
1981
Flora Lea Louden, September
1980
Mary Ann MacKenzie, August
1981
Andy McCormack, July 1980
Ludo McFerran, September
1981
Peggy Ann McGarry,
September 1980
Anne McGlinchey, March
1981
Dawn Madison, September
1980
Cheri Maples, April 1981
Joyce Millman, April 1981
Mary Morrison, May 1981
Joseph Morse, January 1981
Esther Mosak, August 1980
Craig Norberg, July 1980
Ellen Pence, April 1982
Isidore Penn, January 1981
Aurie Pennick, September
1980
Anne Pembleton, September
1980
Jan Peterson, September 1981
Eulalia Reyes de Smith,
November 1980
Carol Richards, August 1981
María Ríos, November 1980
Mariana Romo-Carmona,
January 1981
Rosa Salgado, January 1981
Ann Salmirs, March 1980
JoAnn Schulman, November
1981
Renae Scott, July 1980
Barbara Shaw, May 1981
Ruth Slaughter, November
1981
Margo Smith, January 1981
Anne Steytler, February 1981

Gail Sullivan, July 1980
Joan Swan, March 1980
Diane Tabaka, September
    1980
Sharon Vaughan, January
    1981
Mary Ann Walt, November
    1980
Betsy Warrior, January 1981
Hester Watson, January 1981
Barbara Woodmansee,
    September 1980
Laurie Woods, November 1981
Carol Yesalonis, June 1981
Frances Zamora, November
    1980
June Zeitlin, November 1981

Index

Wife-Beating: The Silent Crisis, 214
"Wife Torture in England" (Cobbe), 218
Wisconsin: Coalition Against Woman
    Abuse, 124; Conference on Battered
    Women, 133; Domestic Abuse Prevention
    Council, 124
Women Against Abuse, 56, 244; Legal
    Center, 179
Women in Crisis Can Act, 69
Women in government, 196-200
Women of color, 25, 37, 57, 58, 144, 275; in
    California, 123, 280; task force of NCADV,
    149, 276. *See also* Third world women
Women Who Kill (Jones), 171
Womendez, Chris, 56, 65
Women's Advocates, 68, 79, 111; forma-
    tion of, 33, 62-63; funding for, 64-65, 73,
    82, 86; influence on movement of, 70, 78,
    97; philosophy of, 63; structure of, 64, 99,
    103; *Women's Advocates: The Story of a
    Shelter*, 64
Women's Aid Federation, 151; Chiswick
    Women's Aid, 154; National Women's
    Aid Federation, 153, 154, 155, 156;
    Scottish Women's Aid, 152, 153
Women's Center South (Pittsburgh), 56,
    74, 78
Women's centers, 56
Women's clubs, 73, 85, 295. *See also*
    General Federation of Women's Clubs
Women's Equity Action League, 143, 146
Women's Legal Defense Fund, 137
Women's liberation, 27, 31-34, 45, 57, 79,
    105-106, 242, 243, 252, 257, 261, 268, 274,
    291, 302, 320. *See also* Feminism; Femi-
    nists
Women's Survival Space, 60, 128, 129
Women's Transitional Living Center, 82
Working on Wife Abuse (Warrior), 79, 190

YWCA, 42, 58, 69, 70, 75, 84, 122, 128. *See
    also* Loop Center YWCA

Zeitlin, June, 148

About South End Press

South End Press is a nonprofit, collectively run book publisher with over 150 titles in print. Since our founding in 1977, we have tried to meet the needs of readers who are exploring or are already committed to the politics of radical social change. Our goal is to publish books that encourage critical thinking and constructive action on the key political, cultural, social, economic, and ecological issues shaping life in the United States and in the world. In this way, we hope to give expression to a wide diversity of democratic social movements and to provide an alternative to the products of corporate publishing.

If you would like to receive a free catalog of South End Press books or get information on our membership program—which offers two free books and a 40% discount on all titles—please write us at South End Press, 116 St. Botolph Street, Boston, MA 02115.

Printed in the United States
18609LVS00002B/59